Conviviality at the Crossroads

Oscar Hemer · Maja Povrzanović Frykman ·
Per-Markku Ristilammi
Editors

Conviviality at the Crossroads

The Poetics and Politics of Everyday Encounters

Editors
Oscar Hemer
Faculty of Culture and Society
School of Arts and Communication
Malmö University
Malmö, Sweden

Maja Povrzanović Frykman
Faculty of Culture and Society
Department of Global Political Studies
Malmö University
Malmö, Sweden

Per-Markku Ristilammi
Faculty of Culture and Society
Department of Urban Studies
Malmö University
Malmö, Sweden

ISBN 978-3-030-28978-2   ISBN 978-3-030-28979-9 (eBook)
https://doi.org/10.1007/978-3-030-28979-9

© The Editor(s) (if applicable) and The Author(s) 2020. This book is an open access publication.

Open Access This book is licensed under the terms of the Creative Commons Attribution 4.0 International License (http://creativecommons.org/licenses/by/4.0/), which permits use, sharing, adaptation, distribution and reproduction in any medium or format, as long as you give appropriate credit to the original author(s) and the source, provide a link to the Creative Commons license and indicate if changes were made.

The images or other third party material in this book are included in the book's Creative Commons license, unless indicated otherwise in a credit line to the material. If material is not included in the book's Creative Commons license and your intended use is not permitted by statutory regulation or exceeds the permitted use, you will need to obtain permission directly from the copyright holder.

The use of general descriptive names, registered names, trademarks, service marks, etc. in this publication does not imply, even in the absence of a specific statement, that such names are exempt from the relevant protective laws and regulations and therefore free for general use.

The publisher, the authors and the editors are safe to assume that the advice and information in this book are believed to be true and accurate at the date of publication. Neither the publisher nor the authors or the editors give a warranty, expressed or implied, with respect to the material contained herein or for any errors or omissions that may have been made. The publisher remains neutral with regard to jurisdictional claims in published maps and institutional affiliations.

Cover illustration: Linn Arvidsson/Stockimo/Alamy Stock Photo

This Palgrave Macmillan imprint is published by the registered company Springer Nature Switzerland AG
The registered company address is: Gewerbestrasse 11, 6330 Cham, Switzerland

Preface

This book is a product of the research network *Conviviality at the Crossroads* at Malmö University, Sweden. It grew out of a casual collaboration between Malmö University and Bard College Berlin in response to the large refugee migration from Syria to Europe in the early autumn of 2015. Sweden and Germany were at the time exceptions to the European rule and welcomed refugees. A first seminar in Berlin in November 2015, hosted by Kerry Bystrom and Bard College, was followed by a symposium (*Transit Europe*[1]) in Malmö in September 2016. In less than a year, the situation had dramatically changed; both Sweden and Germany had adopted restrictive migration policies, with border controls disrupting the formerly seamless passage between Denmark and Sweden. In 2016, the EU had moreover been rocked to its foundations by the British Brexit vote and, one year after our first seminar, Donald Trump won the US Presidential election.

At that time Malmö University prepared for becoming a full research university and made an internal call for new trans-disciplinary research networks. *Conviviality at the Crossroads* was one of the selected networks formalised in January 2017. Another research group was created around the notion of "illiberalism" and the resurging threats against (liberal) democracy. Addressing similar questions, this time from slightly different perspectives, the two networks decided to collaborate around a joint symposium on "Conviviality and Illiberalism" in September 2017, eventually joining forces in the application for a research programme, *Rethinking Democracy* (REDEM), with conviviality as one of its four thematic strands. As a result, the research platform REDEM was established at the Faculty of Culture and Society in 2019, and this volume is the first major publication under its aegis.

We are very pleased to publish this book through Open Access, thanks to the generous support provided by different bodies within Malmö University, facilitated by Helena Stjernberg and Carolina Jonsson Malm. We wish to especially thank Rebecka Lettevall, the Dean of the Faculty of Culture and Society, for her support.

Lastly, we thank Mary Al-Sayed and Madison Allums at Palgrave Macmillan for an efficient, smooth and pleasant collaboration, from first contact through book production.

Malmö, Sweden Oscar Hemer
July 2019 Maja Povrzanović Frykman
Per-Markku Ristilammi

Note

1. The Ørecomm Symposium 2016 was a free-standing continuation of the Ørecomm Festivals organised yearly in Malmö, Copenhagen and Roskilde, 2011–2014.

Contents

1 Conviviality Vis-à-Vis Cosmopolitanism
   and Creolisation: Probing the Concepts   1
   Oscar Hemer, Maja Povrzanović Frykman
   and Per-Markku Ristilammi

2 Fantasy of Conviviality: Banalities of Multicultural
   Settings and What We Do (Not) Notice
   When We Look at Them   15
   Magdalena Nowicka

3 Creolisation as a Recipe for Conviviality   43
   Thomas Hylland Eriksen

4 Schleiermacher's *Geselligkeit*, Henriette Herz,
   and the 'Convivial Turn'   65
   Ulrike Wagner

5 Cosmopolitanism as Utopia   89
   Rebecka Lettevall

6	Creolising Conviviality: Thinking Relational Ontology and Decolonial Ethics Through Ivan Illich and Édouard Glissant Encarnación Gutiérrez Rodríguez	105
7	A Convivial Journey: From Diversity in Istanbul to Solidarity with Refugees in Denmark Deniz Neriman Duru	125
8	Bringing Conviviality into Methods in Media and Migration Studies Erin Cory	145
9	Post-2015 *Refugees Welcome* Initiatives in Sweden: Cosmopolitan Underpinnings Maja Povrzanović Frykman and Fanny Mäkelä	165
10	The Bridge: Redux—The Breakdown of Normative Conviviality Per-Markku Ristilammi	189
11	Charting a Convivial Continuum in British Post-war Popular Music 1948–2018 Hugo Boothby	203
12	Footballers and Conductors: Between Reclusiveness and Conviviality Anders Høg Hansen	227
13	Impurity and Danger: Excerpt from *Cape Calypso* Oscar Hemer	247
14	Seeing Johannesburg Anew: Conviviality and Opacity in Khalo Matabane's *Conversations on a Sunday Afternoon* Kerry Bystrom	267

Index   285

List of Contributors

Hugo Boothby Faculty of Culture and Society, Malmö University, Malmö, Sweden

Kerry Bystrom Bard College Berlin, Berlin, Germany

Erin Cory Faculty of Culture and Society, Malmö University, Malmö, Sweden

Deniz Neriman Duru Department of Communication and Media, Lund University, Lund, Sweden

Thomas Hylland Eriksen Department of Social Anthropology, University of Oslo, Oslo, Norway

Encarnación Gutiérrez Rodríguez Justus-Liebig-University Giessen, Giessen, Germany

Anders Høg Hansen Faculty of Culture and Society, Malmö University, Malmö, Sweden

Oscar Hemer Faculty of Culture and Society, Malmö University, Malmö, Sweden

Rebecka Lettevall Faculty of Culture and Society, Malmö University, Malmö, Sweden

Fanny Mäkelä Malmö, Sweden

Magdalena Nowicka DeZIM e.V and Humboldt-Universität zu Berlin, Berlin, Germany

Maja Povrzanović Frykman Faculty of Culture and Society, Malmö University, Malmö, Sweden

Per-Markku Ristilammi Faculty of Culture and Society, Malmö University, Malmö, Sweden

Ulrike Wagner Bard College Berlin, Berlin, Germany

List of Figures

Fig. 12.1 Laurie Cunningham in action for West Bromwich, 1979 Alan Williams/Alamy Stock Photo. This image is not included in the Creative Commons Attribution 4.0 International License   229

Fig. 12.2 Victor conducting. CC BY-SA License/https://commons.wikimedia.org/wiki/File:Cornelins_1.jpg   231

Fig. 12.3 The White Choir 1981. CC BY-SA License/https://commons.wikimedia.org/wiki/File:Cornelins_3.jpg   234

CHAPTER 1

Conviviality Vis-à-Vis Cosmopolitanism and Creolisation: Probing the Concepts

Oscar Hemer, Maja Povrzanović Frykman and Per-Markku Ristilammi

An online search yields the following synonyms for the adjective *convivial*: (1) friendly, agreeable (a convivial atmosphere); (2) fond of feasting, drinking and merry company, jovial; and (3) of or befitting a feast, festive.

Clearly, these are not the primary connotations to the concept that is currently becoming a buzz-word in academia, to the extent that one may even speak of a "convivial turn" within certain fields of the social sciences

---

O. Hemer (✉)
Faculty of Culture and Society, School of Arts and Communication, Malmö University, Malmö, Sweden
e-mail: oscar.hemer@mau.se

M. Povrzanović Frykman
Faculty of Culture and Society, Department of Global Political Studies, Malmö University, Malmö, Sweden
e-mail: maja.frykman@mau.se

P.-M. Ristilammi
Faculty of Culture and Society, Department of Urban Studies, Malmö University, Malmö, Sweden
e-mail: per-markku.ristilammi@mau.se

(Lapina 2016; Neal et al. 2013; Valluvan 2016; Wise and Noble 2016). As Encarnación Gutiérrez Rodríguez shows in her contribution to this book (Chapter 6), the etymology of conviviality as it is used today stems from the Spanish term *convivencia*, which was originally coined to describe the pluri-cultural and pluri-confessional "living together" in medieval Spain (al-Andalus). It was this moral meaning that Ivan Illich transferred to his suggested "tools for conviviality" (Illich 1973). The *convivial society* that Illich envisioned was a post-industrial, localised society of "autonomous individuals and primary groups" (Ibid., 10). The recent debate on conviviality has however almost entirely emanated from Paul Gilroy's refashioning of the concept, 30 years later, against the backdrop of social, racial and religious tensions in post-imperial Britain, "at the point where 'multiculturalism' broke down" (Gilroy 2004: xi). In Gilroy's interpretation, conviviality denoted the acceptance and affirmation of diversity *without* restaging communitarian conceptions of ethnic and racial difference. This understanding has subsequently been refined to provide "an analytical tool to ask and explore in what ways, and under what conditions, people constructively create modes of togetherness" (Nowicka and Vertovec 2014: 2).

When we formed the *Conviviality at the Crossroads* research network at Malmö University, largely inspired by the 2015 refugee migration and its aftermath, we agreed on using "conviviality" as a lens for examining the current challenges to (liberal) democracy, in Europe and beyond. However, we also decided at the outset that conviviality should be applied in conjunction with the inter-related concepts of "cosmopolitanism" and "creolisation", in order to provide both tools for analysis and forms for cross-cutting communication. This book puts forward conceptual discussions of these three concepts, using examples concerning the situation after the 2015 refugee migration in Sweden and Denmark as well as examples with different scopes in both time and space (e.g., the chapters on the German Enlightenment and contemporary South Africa). The book aims to track notions of conviviality, cosmopolitanism and creolisation in terms of the histories of their theoretical treatment as well as the conditions of their emic uses. Such tracking, as suggested by Magdalena Nowicka in Chapter 2, also reveals that different notions have been used to address the very same issue of "living-with-difference", and helps us understand the scholarly struggles with the ambivalences they contain. Moreover, the book is a reminder of how ideas relevant to the field of our concern move and interact across time and scholarly contexts. For example, Ivan Illich's understanding of conviviality as a stance with "the potential of addressing an intrinsic ethical value underlining the interconnectedness and mutual dependency between the human, the planet and the cosmos", discussed by Gutiérrez Rodríguez in Chapter 6, resonates with Rosi Braidotti's radical reconceptualisation of the notion of cosmopolitanism referred to by Nowicka in Chapter 2.

In the case of the first two concepts, the close connection is obvious. For Gilroy conviviality was precisely a substitute for cosmopolitanism, which in his view had been hijacked as a pretext for Western "supposedly benign imperialism" in the aftermath of 9/11 and the war on terror (Gilroy 2004: 66). What he rejected was hence not the cosmopolitan ideal as such, but its interpretations which allegedly did not see a contradiction between this ideal and the categories that confine people to particular, hierarchically located groups. In contrast, the less ideologically burdened concept of conviviality denoted an ability to be *at ease* in contexts of diversity.

Leading scholars in this debate, most notably Magdalena Nowicka, with Steve Vertovec (Nowicka and Vertovec 2014) and Tillman Heil (Nowicka and Heil 2015), follow and elaborate on Gilroy's suggestion that conviviality is a more productive analytical tool than cosmopolitanism. Yet, the latter, with its roots in ancient Greece and its prominent presence in the European history of ideas, has of course not succumbed to this newcomer. The literature on cosmopolitanism veritably exploded in the 1990s, as a key element in the globalisation debate worldwide, and has had new momentum in the last decade, parallel to that of conviviality (Appiah 2006; Beck 2006; Beck and Grande 2007; Beck and Sznaider 2016; Braidotti 2013; Brown and Held 2010; Held 2010; Glick Schiller and Irving 2015; to name just a few).

But, as noted above, rather than replacing one concept with the other, this book seeks to explore the interconnections—commonalities and differences—between them. For example, in recent research within urban studies, conviviality has been used as an antidote for neoliberal commercialisations of urban space resulting in the displacement of unwanted groups (cf. Bates 2018). As is pointed out by Magdalena Nowicka (Chapter 2), the notion of conviviality runs the risk of being reduced to a prescriptive, or even normative, concept whereby physical surroundings could be "tweaked" in order to create social cohesion. We would rather regard it as a *perspectivising* notion by which we can achieve a critical understanding needed for coping with the social tensions that inform life in contemporary cities. Such an approach can also relate to the notions of "vernacular cosmopolitanism" (Bhabha 1996; Appiah 1998) or "cosmopolitanism from below" (Appadurai 2002, 2013).

"Creolisation" may at a first glance appear to be of a different order than the other two concepts. Its articulation was regionally grounded in the New World, especially in the Caribbean, as a means of analysing and expressing processes of cultural intermingling and cross-fertilisation. As a generalised concept, creolisation had its heyday in the late 1980s and early 1990s, when anthropologist Ulf Hannerz and poet–philosopher Édouard Glissant independently of each other proposed it as a denominator for the globalisation of culture—"a world in creolisation" (Hannerz 1987; Glissant 1990).[1] It is worth remembering that the creolisation debate preceded and informed the discussion on "globalisation", which did *not* emerge among economists or political scientists, but in cultural studies.[2]

As cultural aspects of globalisation were overshadowed by economic and political ones, creolisation seemed to lose attraction or be returned to its origin in linguistics and local history. But the generalised use of the concept has experienced a revival in recent years, parallel to the resurgence of cosmopolitanism and conviviality (Cohen 2007; Cohen and Toninato 2010; Monahan 2011; Lionnet and Shih 2011; Gutiérrez Rodríguez 2011; Gutiérrez Rodríguez and Tate 2015). Robin Cohen makes the following comprehensive definition of what he claims to be the key component in cultural globalisation:

> When creolisation occurs, participants select particular elements from incoming or inherited cultures, endow these with meanings different from those they possessed in the original cultures and then creatively merge these to create new varieties that supersede the prior forms. (Cohen 2007)

Although the term "creolisation" has so far seldom been referred to in the conviviality/cosmopolitanism debate, it does appear under the guise of other related terms (e.g., hybridisation and cultural mélange) as an implicit supplement to the other two. For example, Nowicka and Heil (2015) talk of two parallel processes that frame contemporary cosmopolitanism: "border-crossing and hybridization on a world scale, and bordering and consolidation of national, or ethnic, groups". "Hybridization" is here presumably synonymous with "creolisation", and the suggested parallel corresponds well to Glissant's key notions of *Relation* vs *Essence*.[3] Creolisation presupposes a process of inter-mingling without beginning or end, whose outcome is as per definition unpredictable. Moreover, as Thomas

Hylland Eriksen demonstrates in this volume (Chapter 3), there is a common denominator in the discussion on "superdiversity", which could be regarded as a European relative to the Caribbean notion of the "creole".

A popular and persistent perception of cosmopolitanism is that it represents an ideal for an elite of globetrotting academics and executives, far removed from the reality of ordinary people. The tinge of elitism that undoubtedly adheres to the concept is however countered by several articulations of "vernacular cosmopolitanism". Globalisation and the digital revolution have undoubtedly added a new dimension to the contemporary debate, by involving actors who were previously not in a position to become "world citizens". Arjun Appadurai, who coined the notion of "globalisation from below", uses the sister term "cosmopolitanism from below" to describe the situation among the urban poor in Mumbai, India, where he has been carrying out participatory research with Shack/Slumdwellers International[4] (2002, 2013).

The main critique against cosmopolitanism as a concept remains however the one articulated by Gilroy and many postcolonial theorists before and after him; that it is rooted in a Eurocentric worldview. To be truly cosmopolitan it would need to be self-reflective and critically analyse its own roots—thereby also questioning its own analytical sense and value. Rosa Braidotti (2013) sees two possible solutions to this inherent dilemma: either rejection or radical change.

So far, the impulses of global self-reflexion and a radical rethinking of the world have mainly, although not exclusively, been provided by scholars and writers in or from the Global South. Dipesh Chakrabarty attempted "the task of exploring how [European] thought – which is now everybody's heritage and which affects us all – may be renewed from and for the margins" (Chakrabarty 2000: 16). In his case, it was a matter of translating the categories of modern European science to a South Asian context, but the reverse could supposedly be applied to an analysis of the crises in present-day Europe—of the refugee migration, which is not a crisis in Europe but on its borders, and the crises of the European Union (EU) and of liberal democracy, which are indisputably real.

Ulrich Beck's theory of the global risk society (1998, 2009) is an important contribution to the contemporary debate. To Beck, cosmopolitanism is an inescapable feature of globalisation,[5] not a (utopian) vision for the future, but the global reality here and now. The challenge is to acknowledge this cosmopolitan reality—to step out of the still prevailing nation-state perspective and take a cosmopolitan viewpoint. The global risk is an anticipation of catastrophe, but may therefore also be the antidote to disaster, by presenting an opportunity for metamorphosis (*Verwandlung*); that is, new ways of generating and implementing norms. Hiroshima and the Holocaust are examples of watershed events with a "before" and an "after", and, as he suggested in one of his last articles (Beck 2014), climate change may provide a similar moment of metamorphosis.

Urgent global challenges not only require a global (cosmopolitan) perspective; to research contemporary society we moreover need a cosmopolitan method, what Beck defines as *analytical cosmopolitanism*. In response to Beck, Nowicka and Heil (2015: 1) propose the humbler *analytical conviviality*, which focuses on "the everyday processes of how people live together in mundane encounters, of how they (re)translate between their sustained differences and how they (re)negotiate minimal consensuses". Their key question could be formulated as: *How is the minimal sociality possible?* Again, this "non-normative" notion of conviviality clearly speaks to Glissant's concept of *Relation*, as a non-hierarchical and non-reductive system of interconnectedness (see Chapters 12 and 14).

Glissant never used the term conviviality, but he comes very close to what we regard as an exemplary definition. Against the "false transparency" of a world dominated by the West, he posits "the penetrable opacity of a world in which one exists, or agrees to exist, with and among others" (Glissant 1997 [1990]: 114). South African scholar Zimitri Erasmus gives another viable definition without pronouncing the word in her proposal to cultivate *an ethos of contesting inequality and living-together-in-difference* (Erasmus 2017: 23–24). One of the first to put conviviality and creolisation in explicit scholarly dialogue was Encarnación Gutiérrez Rodríguez (2011, 2015; see also Chapter 6), who even proposes the definition of creolisation as *transversal conviviality*.

In 2014 a group of francophone intellectuals, led by sociologist Alain Caillé and including Chantal Mouffe, signed *The Convivialist Manifesto: A Declaration of Interdependence*.[6] It was a plea for a new "art of cohabitation" in the face of the urgent threats to humankind in the early twenty-first century. The manifesto coins the term *convivialism* as a normative "-ism"; a conception of society based on "human cooperation and mutual respect for maximum diversity". Convivialism does not rule out conflict. On the contrary—and this is where Chantal Mouffe's influence may be detected—it accepts and affirms conflict as a necessary and productive feature of life, provided that it is based on the agreement of a shared world. The basic convivialist principle is *mutual aid*, characteristic of voluntary organisations, families and friendship networks—which interestingly, as Nowicka and Heil (2015) point out, resembles Illich's convivial order of "autonomous individuals and primary groups".

This radical activist agenda was in the German debate criticised for neglecting the solidarity and voluntarism "within the neo-liberal regimes" that became manifest in the responses to the refugee migration in 2015, not least in Germany and Sweden (see Chapter 9 by Povrzanović Frykman and Mäkelä). The "Refugees Welcome" and other spontaneous initiatives appear as examples of a more pragmatic form of conviviality (without the -ism) that would be in accordance with Nowicka and Heil's conception.

The urgency of today's global predicament is the recurring argument in the discussion of all three concepts. In the anthology *The Creolization of Theory* (2011), Françoise Lionnet and Shu-mei Shih make an interesting parallel between the dynamics of what they call the dark side of globalisation and of the early process of creolisation, which emerged from violent encounters that were colonial and imperial (Lionnet and Shih 2011: 24):

> In today's world of financial meltdowns and immense power differentials exacerbated by globalisation, people from all areas of the planet are experiencing something akin to the "shock of space and time" of early plantation cultures. (Lionnet and Shih 2011: 30)

While, as Lionnet and Shih underscore, the strength of the concept arises from its historical specificity, the historical connotation to the global slave trade is most probably the reason why creolisation evokes an indefinite uneasiness among (white) Westerners ("Caucasians" in the curious North American racial typology[7]), as opposed to both amiable conviviality and "elitist" cosmopolitanism. Slavery, the fundament of the colonial world system, remains a blind spot to the modern European mind. Even enlightened liberals are reluctant to admit that colonialism is "the underside of Modernity" (Mignolo 2012); that the modern world arguably was born in the plantation economies of the New World. Some of the liberals' militant opponents on the left, in turn, fail to acknowledge that the decolonisation they propose de facto also implies de-modernisation. But the colonial encounter cannot be undone. This is the crucial point. And it is also a principal reason why creolisation is a necessary complement to the other two concepts, or a "recipe for conviviality", as Eriksen puts it (see Chapter 3).

Whereas conviviality may be interpreted as a formula for "living with difference" yet side-by-side and not intermingling—as in common notions of multiculturalism—creolisation is inevitably "messy" and impure. It is in this "messy" crossroads of concepts with political implications that we situate this book. A common denominator is the shared interest of contributing authors in moving beyond the binary thinking that currently prevails (Glick Schiller 2012), in terms of methodologies as well as analytical concepts, and political implementations.

Magdalena Nowicka's contribution (see Chapter 2) has a twofold aim: first, looking back at the last years of the debate with a short overview of the main themes and fields of application of the notion of conviviality, notably concerning migration and diversity. Second, reflecting on conviviality as a mode of thinking of human togetherness. The main question is how the myth of individuality shapes research in this field, and how this research could be different if it introduces the notion of conviviality.

Chapter 3, by *Thomas Hylland Eriksen*, draws on the literature on creolisation as well as on conviviality, but its main thrust is in a description of the Creole identity in the Indian Ocean island states of Mauritius and the Seychelles. Eriksen is comparing the Creole identity to that of bounded, endogamous groups and thereby showing that conviviality in the public sphere is compatible with group boundaries, which Creoledom is not. In this sense, the Creole identity represents an inoculation against divisive identity politics.

Ulrike Wagner's contribution (Chapter 4) looks back and investigates a prominent late 18th-century conception and use of the term conviviality. Inspired by his regular visits to social gatherings organised by Henriette Herz (1764–1847), one of Berlin's most prominent salonières of the time, the German philosopher and theologian Friedrich Daniel Schleiermacher (1768–1834), contributed with *Toward a Theory of Sociable Conduct* (1799) a theory of conviviality that bears interesting and unexplored resemblances to today's conceptions.

Rebecka Lettevall (Chapter 5) explores the utopian aspects of the notion of cosmopolitanism from a starting point of Kant's definition of cosmopolitan right. Since cosmopolitanism is a contested concept without one solid definition, parts of its meaning have, in the present-day, been substituted by the concept of conviviality. Inspired by Ruth Levitas (1990, 2013), Lettevall claims that a better solution would be to see cosmopolitanism as a utopian method in the search for directions for the future.

Informed by the work of Ivan Illich on conviviality and Édouard Glissant on creolisation, *Encarnación Gutiérrez Rodríguez* (Chapter 6) critically probes the conceptual and visionary implications of creolising conviviality. Creolisation as a rhizomatic relational conceptualisation of society departs from the critical understanding of contemporary societies as entrenched in historically produced racialised hierarchies, resulting in economic and social inequalities which impede living together based on equal economic distribution and social justice. Addressing these inequalities requires a decolonial ethics of creolising conviviality.

Deniz Neriman Duru (Chapter 7) considers the meanings of conviviality in the context of different research projects. She uses data from a comparative research project at the EU level to categorise different types of what she sees as convivial solidarity actions in connection to the refugee migration of 2015. She argues that crises can be both an opportunity and a threat for the mobilisation of transnational solidarity support actions.

Erin Cory (Chapter 8) draws on a research project in which conviviality becomes a prism to understand media practices related to migration and refugees and discusses how the concept is best appropriated as a methodological tool in research designs informing current and future activist-based studies. Questions posed are: What can conviviality do, or rather, what can researchers do with it in their efforts to understand the connections between media, mediation and migration? How can researchers across disciplines do conviviality as part of an interventionist research praxis?

Maja Povrzanović Frykman and *Fanny Mäkelä* (Chapter 9) connect the notion of cosmopolitanism to the field of volunteering. Using the aftermath of the *Refugees Welcome* civil initiatives that emerged in Sweden when more than two thirds of some 160,000 asylum seekers entered the country in the last few months of 2015, their chapter explores volunteers' reflections on their work in the years that followed. Without using the notion of cosmopolitanism, these volunteers outline cosmopolitan concerns in the moral and political realm.

In Chapter 10, *Per-Markku Ristilammi* highlights a specific kind of normative state-driven conviviality through the example of the Öresund Bridge that connects Sweden and Denmark. Ristilammi shows how the concept of conviviality can be used in an analysis of the changing roles of the state. Ethnographic examples from border-crossing experiences at the bridge in 2000, in 2015, when border controls were introduced due to refugee arrivals, and in the present-day, show how a breakdown of conviviality opens up for a new form of biopolitical regime at the border.

Hugo Boothby (Chapter 11) explores the tension evident between conviviality and hostility in the experiences of post-war Caribbean migration to Great Britain and how this finds expression in popular music. The music that forms the primary site of analysis for this chapter is that which demonstrates radical intermixture, combining influences from Africa, the Caribbean, the United States and the United Kingdom.

Anders Høg Hansen (Chapter 12) analyses break-away, racialised, migratory and postcolonial experiences through two cases that portray reclusive individuals caught in, and making their way through, a politics of a convivial nature. The discussion evolves around Glissant's notion of *opacity* and the concept of *reclusive openness* that the author proposes in order to capture some of the ambiguities of diasporic experiences.

Oscar Hemer (Chapter 13) assumes as a hypothesis that the underlying structure of nationalism, identity politics and xenophobia, can be explicated by the British anthropologist Mary Douglas' conceptual dichotomy Purity–Impurity (Douglas 1966). Applied to a South African context, the purity–impurity matrix becomes a tool for interrogation of apartheid and its vision of "separate development" as suppressed creolisation. This is done by means of an experimental cross-genre (literary and academic) approach that aspires to be congenial with the subject.

In the chapter concluding the volume (Chapter 14), *Kerry Bystrom* uses the notions of convivial urban encounters and opacity to discuss xenophobic violence against black African immigrants in South Africa. To envision alternatives to this violence the chapter revisits Khalo Matabane's *Conversations on a Sunday Afternoon* (2005), a hybrid fiction–documentary film that traces a South African poet's chance meeting with a Somali refugee in Johannesburg and the encounters with other immigrants it enables. Matabane shows how both conviviality and opacity are necessary to seeing Johannesburg anew and making it a truly hospitable environment.

Finally, let us mention that the subtitle of this book, "The poetics and politics of everyday encounters", is a tribute to one of the most influential books in anthropology of the late twentieth century, *Writing Culture: The Poetics and Politics of Ethnography* (1986), edited by James Clifford and George E. Marcus. We are of course not assuming even a faint resemblance to its importance, but we do wish to state our openness to cross-disciplinary and cross-genre experimentation that aims at being congenial with the subject.

Notes

1. Glissant first used the term *creolisation* in 1981, interestingly in opposition to *Creolité* [creoleness], which originated as an identity-based defence of a homogenised creole language. Against this linguistic militancy, he proposed a definition of *Antillanité* [caribbeanness] for which linguistic formations are but one of many results of the colonial encounter, and in the catalogue of such cultural realities he mentions, almost in passing, "the general cultural phenomenon of creolisation" (Glissant 1989 [1981]: 222, quoted by Chancé 2011 [2005]).
2. The coining of the term "globalisation" is commonly attributed to US American cultural sociologist Roland Robertson, who defined it as "the compression of the world and the intensification of the consciousness of the world as a whole" (Robertson 1992).
3. The choice of one or the other term appears to be a matter of language and scholarly tradition (English vs French, Spanish, Portuguese) or personal preference. Unlike his mentor Stuart Hall, Gilroy rarely refers to creolisation, scholars from the South Asian subaltern studies tradition (Bhabha, Chatterjee, Spivak), generally use the terms hybridity/hybridisation, whereas otherwise Anglo-oriented South African scholars have adopted creolisation (Nuttall, Hofmeyr, Erasmus). To Glissant the terms are however not interchangeable; he clearly distinguishes creolisation from *métissage* (which would be the French equivalent to hybridity/hybridisation):

   > If we posit *métissage* as, generally speaking, the meeting and synthesis of two differences, creolisation seems to be a limitless *métissage*, its elements diffracted and its consequences unforeseeable. (Glissant 1997 [1990]: 34)

4. Shack/Slumdwellers International is a transnational agency network that started through the joint mobilisation of diverse grass-roots organisations in Mumbai in the late 1990s. It has now spread over three continents, with branches in Africa and Latin America, and its head office in Cape Town.
5. Although it may never have occurred to Beck, his depiction of cosmopolitanism as an unpredictable and unmanageable feature of an increasingly complex and interconnected world bears striking resemblance to Glissant's conception of creolisation and what he in more poetical words describes as the emergence of the *Tout-Monde* (1997).
6. Available in full and abridged versions in French and English at the website of "the convivialists", http://www.lesconvivialistes.org.
7. The genealogy of "Caucasian" goes back to the ancient slave trade of predominantly white women in the Caucasus. It was the racialised conception of these (slave) women as the embodiment of beauty that sparked the invention of the "Caucasian race" as white, beautiful and superior (Erasmus 2017: 52).

References

Appadurai, A. 2002. "Deep Democracy, Urban Governmentality and the Horizon of Politics." *Public Culture* 14 (1): 21–47. https://doi.org/10.1215/08992363-14-1-21.

Appadurai, A. 2013. *The Future as Cultural Fact: Essays on the Global Condition*. London: Verso Books.

Appiah, K. A. 1998. "Cosmopolitan Patriots." In *Cosmopolitics: Thinking and Feeling Beyond the Nation*, edited by P. Cheah and B. Robbins, 91–116. Minneapolis, MN: University of Minnesota Press.

Appiah, K. A. 2006. *Cosmopolitanism: Ethics in a World of Strangers*. New York and London: W. W. Norton & Co.

Bates, C. 2018. "Conviviality, Disability and Design in the City." *The Sociological Review* 66 (5): 984–999.

Beck, U. 1998. *World Risk Society*. Cambridge: Polity Press.

Beck, U. 2006. *The Cosmopolitan Vision*. Cambridge: Polity Press.

Beck, U. 2009. *World at Risk*. Cambridge: Polity Press.

Beck, U. 2014. "How Climate Change Might Save the World." *Harvard Design Magazine* 39. Available from: www.harvarddesignmagasine.org/issues/39. Accessed June 15, 2019.

Beck, U., and E. Grande. 2007. *Cosmopolitan Europe*. Cambridge: Polity Press.

Beck, U., and N. Sznaider. 2016. "New Cosmopolitanism in the Social Sciences." *The Routledge International Handbook of Globalisation Studies*, edited by B. S. Turner and R. J. Holton, 572–588. London: Routledge.

Bhabha, H. 1996. "Unsatisfied: Notes on Vernacular Cosmopolitanism." In *Text and Nation*, edited by L. Garcia-Morena and P. C. Pfeifer, 191–207. London: Camden House.

Braidotti, R. 2013. "Becoming-World." In *After Cosmopolitanism*, edited by R. Braidotti, P. Hanafin, and B. Blaagaard, 8–28. Abingdon: Routledge.

Brown, G. W., and D. Held. 2010. *The Cosmopolitanism Reader*. Cambridge and Malden, MA: Polity Press.

Chakrabarty, D. 2000. *Provincializing Europe: Postcolonial Thought and Historical Difference*. Princeton, NJ: Princeton University Press.

Chancé, D. 2011 [2005]. "Creolization. Definition and Critique." In *The Creolization of Theory*, edited by F. Lionnet and S.-m. Shih. Durham, NC: Duke University Press [orig. "Créolisation." In *Vocabulaire des études francophones: Les concepts de base*, edited by M. Beniamino and L. Gauvin. Paris: Pulim].

Clifford, J., and G. E. Marcus, eds. 1986. *Writing Culture: The Poetics and Politics of Ethnography*. Berkeley, Los Angeles, and London: University of California Press.

Cohen, R. 2007. "Creolisation and Cultural Globalisation: The Soft Sounds of Fugitive Power." *Globalizations* 4 (3): 369–384. https://doi.org/10.1080/14747730701532492.

Cohen, R., and P. Toninato. 2010. "The Creolization Debate: Analysing Mixed Identities and Cultures." In *The Creolization Reader*, edited by R. Cohen and P. Toninato, 1–21. London: Routledge.

Douglas, M. 2002 [1966]. *Purity and Danger: An Analysis of Concept of Pollution and Taboo*. London: Routledge.

Erasmus, Z. 2017. *Race Otherwise: Forging a New Humanism for South Africa*. Johannesburg: Wits University Press.

Gilroy, P. 2004. *After Empire: Melancholia or Convivial Culture?* London: Routledge.

Glick Schiller, N. 2012. "Situating Identities: Towards an Identities Studies Without Binaries of Difference." *Identities: Global Studies in Culture and Power* 19 (4): 520–532. https://doi.org/10.1080/1070289x.2012.741525.

Glick Schiller, N., and A. Irving, eds. 2015. *Whose Cosmopolitanism?: Critical Perspectives, Relationalities and Discontents*. New York, NY: Berghahn Books.

Glissant, É. 1990. *Poétique de la Relation. Poétique III*. Paris: Éditions du Seuil.

Glissant, É. 1997. *Poetics of Relation*. Translated by Betsy Wing. Ann Arbor: University of Michigan Press.

Gutiérrez Rodríguez, E. 2011. "Politics of Affects: Transversal Conviviality." *Transversal* 1. http://eipcp.net/transversal/0811/gutierrezrodriguez/en.

Gutiérrez Rodríguez, E. 2015. "Archipelago Europe: On Creolizing Conviviality." In *Creolizing Europe. Legacies and Transformations*, edited by E. Gutiérrez Rodríguez and S. A. Tate, 80–99. Liverpool: Liverpool University Press.

Hannerz, U. 1987. "The World in Creolization." *Africa* 57 (4): 546–559.

Held, D. 2010. *Cosmopolitanism: Ideals and Realities*. Cambridge: Polity Press.

Illich, I. 1973. *Tools for Conviviality*. New York: Perennial Library.

Lapina, L. 2016. "Besides Conviviality: Paradoxes in Being 'At Ease' with Diversity in a Copenhagen District." *NJMR* 6 (1): 33–41.

Levitas, R. 1990. *The Concept of Utopia*. Syracuse, NY: Syracuse University Press.

Levitas, R. 2013. *Utopia as Method: The Imaginary Reconstitution of Society*. Basingstoke: Palgrave Macmillan.

Lionnet, F., and S. Shih, eds. 2011. *The Creolization of Theory*. Durham, NC: Duke University Press.

Mignolo, W. 2012. *Local Histories/Global Designs: Coloniality, Subaltern Knowledges, and Border Thinking*. Princeton: Princeton University Press.

Monahan, M. J. 2011. *The Creolizing Subject: Race, Reason, and the Politics of Purity*, 1st ed. Ashland, OH: Fordham University Press.

Neal, S., K. Bennett, A. Cochrane, and F. Mohan. 2013. "Living Multiculture: Understanding the New Spatial and Social Relations of Ethnicity and Multiculture in England." *Environment and Planning C: Government and Policy* 31 (2): 308–323. https://doi.org/10.1068/c11263r.

Nowicka, M., and S. Vertovec. 2014. "Introduction. Comparing Convivialities: Dreams and Realities of Living-with-Difference." *European Journal of Cultural Studies* 17 (4): 341–356.

Nowicka, M., and T. Heil. 2015. "On the Analytical and Normative Dimensions of Conviviality and Cosmopolitanism." Lecture Held on 25 June 2015 at the Eberhard Karls University Tübingen. Available from: https://www.euroethno.hu-berlin.de/de/forschung/labore/migration/nowicka-heil_on-the-analytical-and-normative-dimensions-of-conviviality.pdf. Accessed June 20, 2019.

Valluvan, S. 2016. "Conviviality and Multiculture: A Post-integration Sociology of Multi-ethnic Interaction." *Young* 24 (3): 204–221.

Wise, A., and G. Noble. 2016. "Convivialities: An Orientation." *Journal of Intercultural Studies* 37 (5): 423–431. https://doi.org/10.1080/07256868.2016.1213786.

Open Access This chapter is licensed under the terms of the Creative Commons Attribution 4.0 International License (http://creativecommons.org/licenses/by/4.0/), which permits use, sharing, adaptation, distribution and reproduction in any medium or format, as long as you give appropriate credit to the original author(s) and the source, provide a link to the Creative Commons license and indicate if changes were made.

The images or other third party material in this chapter are included in the chapter's Creative Commons license, unless indicated otherwise in a credit line to the material. If material is not included in the chapter's Creative Commons license and your intended use is not permitted by statutory regulation or exceeds the permitted use, you will need to obtain permission directly from the copyright holder.

CHAPTER 2

Fantasy of Conviviality: Banalities of Multicultural Settings and What We Do (Not) Notice When We Look at Them

Magdalena Nowicka

INTRODUCTION

Since my first engagement with conviviality in 2011 when preparing the conference I co-organised in Göttingen with Steven Vertovec, Peter van der Veer and Arjun Appadurai, and the year following the conference which I dedicated to the edited volume on comparing convivialities (Nowicka and Vertovec 2014), the term conviviality has gained popularity I/we did not envision. My own motivation for the conference back in 2011/2012 was to move the discussion on diversity beyond cosmopolitanism. At that time, I considered the concept of cosmopolitanism to be too Eurocentric and too normative, as well as too overstrained in the scholarly and public debates to be analytically useful, and I saw two alternatives: to reject it or to radically change it (Braidotti 2013). I thus probed conviviality as a way of reflecting on the shortages of cosmopolitanism and more broadly on how

M. Nowicka (✉)
DeZIM e.V and Humboldt-Universität zu Berlin, Berlin, Germany
e-mail: nowicka@dezim-institut.de

other authors approach the issue of 'living-with-difference'. In particular, it made me re-think 'difference' (Lisiak and Nowicka 2017).

I now look back at the last years of the scholarly debate which followed the proposal (I do not intend to claim that it was earned to our publication) to think of human diversity and inter-personal relations with the help of the notion of 'conviviality'. This review is not only positive: I see a tendency to map places, people and situations as convivial, in opposition to places, people and situations which are less so. I had criticised this kind of tedious exercise in relation to cosmopolitanism, and this critique was one of the reasons I engaged with conviviality. Further, I notice that conviviality becomes particularly popular in the context of studies in settings which are shaped by international migration. While this was also a focus on our first contribution on conviviality (Nowicka and Vertovec 2014), owing to the empirical work we have been doing, I feel this does not meet the expectations I had for this term. I saw its potential rather in how conviviality could help us to reframe the debates on society, not on diversity, as I elaborate in this chapter.

In this chapter I use the term 'fantasy', for it points towards something imaginary, desired but chimerical. In the current and past debates, conviviality emerges as an imaginary of the relationship between me/us and them/others (Gilroy 2004). Alike cosmopolitanism it engages ideas around identity and difference (Moore 2013). The majority of works on conviviality dedicates attention to the myriad of fleeting intersections and interactions between people, leaving the issue of state policies for managing 'diversity' unaddressed. The main challenge for social sciences, it seems, is the chimerical nature of mundane human encounters. On the other hand, many engagements with conviviality convey a fantasy in terms of a desired condition. Thereby, the works which focus the 'factual' are as normative as these works which convey a vision of convivial (future) society, for 'facts' only make sense in a particular normative order (Taylor 2004). Throughout this chapter, thus, I will try to show how the scholarly notion of conviviality is embedded in the Western normative order which relies on the imaginary of an individual as a social being. The potential I see in employing the notion of conviviality relates to a shift in focus on individual towards the sociality. I realise this is not a new postulate (we may think, e.g., of social studies of science and technology which urged us to re-think the notion of individual subject and agency), but I think we have arrived at the point when we could consider the very premise of our scholarly engagement with 'the social' anew.

In order to do so, I engage closer with conviviality as a mode of thinking of human togetherness. My reflections are based on the reading of two books which introduce a historical perspective on norms and ideas around '*con-vivir*'—'living together': Charles Taylor's *Modern Social Imaginaries* (2004) and Almudena Hernando's *The Fantasy of Individuality* (2017). These works serve me as heuristics to make sense of the conviviality debate and to identify its potentials and pitfalls. I do not intend here a comprehensive theory of conviviality through an intense engagement with philosophy or social theory. My ambition is rather small: I look at the field which I know best, which is migration and diversity studies, and develop a proposal for its conceptual renewal along the lines of conviviality. The main question which I follow is how the myth of individuality shapes research in this field and how this research could be different.

I start the contribution with a short summary of the key arguments of Taylor (2004) and Hernando (2017). Out of many possible aspects these authors discuss I selected three which serve me as a lens to look at the conviviality literature: (1) courtesy and civility; (2) collaboration and alliances; and (3) social individuals. As the reader will notice, these aspects are intertwined: courtesy and civility entail collaboration and alliances, and these are possible thanks to and contribute to the sense of an individual as a social being. By analytically distinguishing these aspects I want to emphasise the imaginaries with which the authors writing about conviviality operate. Thereby, my review moves swiftly between the micro- and macro-level of sociality. This is intentional here, but not common in the literature on conviviality which either focuses global challenges or local, ordinary practices. In my review, I am inclined to accept Bourdieu's standpoint that micro-practices are significant for reproduction of macrostructures of societies.

I contrast these practices, ideas and places which are made visible by the literature on conviviality, with what this literature omits when discussing conviviality—family, friendship, relations of care and intimacy, private sphere, power and identity and gender relations. I argue these omissions are to be understood in the context of Western modern social imaginary. This embedding of conviviality in Western modern social imaginary hinders us from developing the full potential of the term 'conviviality'. Thus, I ask how could it be otherwise? What would it mean to reject this heritage and move the discussion beyond it?

(Western Modern) Social Imaginary

The Canadian philosopher Charles Taylor proposed the concept *social imaginary* to describe what he considers builds up the core of Western modernity. *Social imaginary* according to Taylor means ideas, convictions, ideals, understandings, norms and values surrounding living together as humans (Taylor 2004). *Social imaginary* is both factual and normative because the idea of how things should go, and how things usually go, is interwoven: what and how we do things make sense only within this specific *social imaginary*, even if we are not necessarily able to explain our behaviour. *Social imaginary* is thus a largely inarticulate understanding, but some parts of it can be explicated as doctrines or theories of our social world and perpetuated and changed by them. Taylor analyses several elements of what he calls Western modern social imaginary. At the core of it, Taylor argues, is the idea of society of autonomous individuals who come together to form a political entity; these people are understood as rational, sociable agents who have a certain moral obligation towards each other (p. 3). In this modern imaginary, humans are capable of shaping, and thus changing, a social order which appears as having a real, factual existence (p. 11). Further elements of this imaginary include the presumption of equality of humans, value of security as common good, division between private and public space and value of reason and individuality. This modern Western social imaginary manifests in social forms such as the market economy or the state.

Taylor sketches the historical conditions and developments of modernity without aiming at causal explanation of the rise of modern social imaginary (p. 8). He moves between the present day and the early modern times as he discusses the consolidation of the new moral order characterising Western modernity. Occasionally, he draws a comparison with the ancient times to highlight the distinguishing features of Western modernity. In asking how come that we are as we are, we do what we do and we think what we think, Taylor points towards several transformations, but he refrains from assigning power to shape *social imaginary* to any single (nor to several) external factor such as the extension of the markets. Instead, he argues that the unintended and endogenous processes—sets of practices, improvisations—gradually change the meaning people assign to them (p. 30). As Hernando (2017) demonstrates, some aspects of modernity have deeper roots than Taylor's work might suggest. In particular, individuated identity that has developed since the prehistorical times and which is absent in the social order of the present-day *egalitarian societies*[1] made the Western modern moral order possible to emerge.

Hernando (2017) argues that with growing mobility and specialisation of tasks performed to secure survival, humans—primarily men, at first—gradually developed a new type of largely unconscious self-perception (identity) which was based on their belief of own difference from the group they were born into and on the fantasy of own superiority and control vis-à-vis nature (p. 107). She argues that this process was conditioned by the technological advancement which enabled humans to feel in control, and thus safe, in the world (Elias 1991, 1994). Rationality and change are central to this feeling. Both seem to us now natural and universal to the extent that capability of rational thinking and (personal and societal) change as something factual and desirable are considered as intrinsic essence of humanity, despite that they are time and space specific, hence exceptional (Hernando 2017: 60, 63). Rationality has become the main pillar on which Enlightenment thought rests (Honneth 1987; Beiser 1996; Dupré 2004), but Hernando argues that the belief in reason and its power can be traced back to the prehistoric humans and investigated by studying their material culture. Contrary to these authors who associate change as exclusively modern feature (Wagner 2012; Fukuyama 1992; Mouzakitis 2017), she claims that change that humans dare, desire and value as a mode of survival is much older than the modern idea of progress and acceleration (Hernando 2017: 45, 134). Both rationality and change are powerful elements in telling the story of humanity in terms of becoming (better) then we were, embracing risks and imagining the future. It has led to development of (positivist) science and the claim of primacy of scientific expertise. It also ensued in a particular understanding of the world which relies on our reducing of its complexity with the help of simple dichotomies, such as nature–culture, reason–emotion or individual–society (Hernando 2017: 3–4).[2]

The main argument that Hernando develops is that this rational, individuated human (man) can maintain the imaginary of the world and himself only by denying the importance, in fact the necessity, of strong emotional bonds with his or her own group and the indispensability of human interrelatedness and interdependence. Yet to sustain the image of oneself as an individual defined by his or her personal difference from another human (along the lines of gender, skin colour, hair texture, ethnicity, religion, lifestyle, taste, body size, education, class, income, etc.) is possible only if the deepest emotional existential need of humans is fulfilled despite that it is denied. Thus, the myth of individuality requires a complex system of substitution and delegation, and Hernando claims that gender inequality regime is such a mechanism that enables (wo)men to sustain the fantasy of an autonomous and rational individual.[3] Within this regime, women have been in charge of forging bonds, while men have substituted the bonds that had once linked them to their original group for alliances with peers inside and outside their own groups (Hernando 2017). Gender hierarchy is central to this type of emotional relationships maintained by individuated men (Connell and Messerschmidt 2005). Yet Hernando (2017: 111) argues that the fantasy of individuality has long stopped being an exclusive feature of men, and she stresses that both men and women are to various degrees individuated. The coexistence of two modes of identity produces a contradiction, a tension which cannot be escaped easily, and which often disembogues into nostalgia for community and conviviality.

Without judging the historical truth or the correctness of Hernando's or Taylor's arguments, I will apply them as heuristic to engage with the literature on conviviality. I take into account that this approach is necessarily selective and reductionist, but I believe it helps to focus these elements of the conviviality debate which often remain obvious and thus hidden. Also, it opens up a possibility to think of conviviality as an alternative to the current mode of being in the world.

RE-READING THE CONVIVIAL FANTASY WITH HEURISTIC OF (WESTERN MODERN) SOCIAL IMAGINARY

Conviviality as Courtesy

In its everyday meaning, conviviality is related to joyful gatherings, good company and feasting (Dunlap 2009; Freitag 2014; Phull et al. 2015). The growing scholarly interest in meetings involving eating, drinking and conversing seems paradigmatic to the current concern with less formal (comparing to, e.g., community) configurations (Harris 2016). Several themes tend to repeat in the debate. First, various scholars attend to the everyday 'gestures of conviviality' in ephemeral situations in urban spaces. Such gestures express a set of rules that prohibit aggressive or disrespectful conduct and prescribe friendly communication in situations which may not necessarily invite such behaviour (Goffman 1963, 1971; Laurier and Philo 2006; Wise and Velayutham 2014; Georgiou 2017). Second, much scholarly attention is dedicated to a particular social setting in urban spaces saturated by immigrants and by diversity of their languages, practices, products and signage (Amin 2002; Gilroy 2006; Amin 2012b; Noble 2013;

Wessendorf 2014; Wise and Velayutham 2014; Padilla et al. 2015; Wise 2016). In this context, conviviality appears in result of a certain competence people have to navigate this diversity, facilitated by a particular material infrastructure which slows traffic and invites dwelling. Confusingly, this competence was previously labelled intercultural, later cosmopolitan, and now it appears as a basic human feature. Not only is this shift a cause of confusion, for the difference between intercultural, cosmopolitan and convivial is fuzzy; by shifting the focus from cosmopolitan to convivial, it is suggested that the competence to successfully operate in such urban spaces is ordinary and universal.

The heuristic of modern social imaginary helps to address two issues troubling these debates. First, we may argue that the debate of conviviality reveals little new; at least, it misses to declare what is new about such convivial situations it describes. Long before the interest in conviviality, social historians pointed to the fact that all kinds of encounters—from ceremonial and formal to the ephemeral ones in street or coffee houses—are shaped by rituals and conventions (Withington 2007). What now is termed 'gestures of conviviality' is a form of courtesy. Courtesy is a way of acting as though one would be in personal relations with others who are not ones kin. Since Renaissance, courtesy has been the core element of the modern cultural competence (O'Callaghan 2004; Abrams and Ewan 2017). The same kind of skills that enabled people in the early modern Europe to socialise in public across gender and socio-economic status (Curtin 1985; Withington 2007), without questioning it or aiming at its destabilisation—speaking properly (and in foreign language), being friendly, showing respect, displaying tolerance towards other religious beliefs, knowledge of other places and cultures or easiness with and preference for foreign tastes and foods—is now considered central to operate in settings differentiated along the lines of ethnicity, race or religion. But we know that courtesy has been an outcome of (elitist) humanistic education that was not available to all (Taylor 2004). For example, women in Europe (with few exceptions) were long excluded from university studies and were educated for silence rather than for conversation (Gibson 1989). Such 'thin conviviality' indeed operates hand in hand with sexism or racism. By assuming that convivial encounters are a natural instinct of individuals as social beings, and courtesy is a skill we all carry in us to handle such encounters, the scholarship misrecognises the variety of forms of conviviality (Heil 2013).

Sketching the long and complex transformation into modernity, Taylor points to the role of courtesy in development of a new paradigm of sociability (Taylor 2004). In this respect, he follows Norbert Elias who argued the growing importance of conversation and politeness for the civilising process as a mean of regulating living together in the increasingly urbanised world (Elias 1994). Courtesy thus carries a second meaning, as mode of governing of social relations. To look at situations which are now termed 'convivial' through the lens of courtesy helps thus to address a second trouble of the conviviality debate, which is the function of courtesy (and possibly conviviality) for maintaining a particular social order. It is because courtesy in encounters—conversation, talking, pleasing, being tolerant and open—creates a situation of 'quasi-equality' which Taylor (2004) considers characteristic of Western modernity. The systematic treatment of 'others' as if they were equals belonged to the cultural capacity of European elites in the Enlightenment and beyond this period (Gordon 1994; Bryson 1998; Klein 2012). Georg Simmel also attended to how enjoyable gatherings promising egalitarian order are foundational of modern sociability (Simmel and Hughes 1949).

The lens of courtesy brings thus another aspect to light which has so far been largely neglected: the centrality of the normative of equality and how it operates in daily encounters in modern urban spaces to create a set of expectations towards people in such spaces. The (modern) ideal of equality motivates people to suppress the difference (e.g. age, gender, class, religion or ethnicity) and the system which relies on it (Gilroy 2004) and to rest the interaction of the agreement on the commonality (such as friendship, shared interest, ideological conviction, common goals).

Yet bridging differences by mean of courtesy between interacting individuals should not be mistaken for overcoming these differences. Gatherings labelled 'convivial' often remain highly exclusive along the lines of friendship, kin, gender, class or ethnicity and race (Nayak 2017). This kind of simultaneity of conviviality and exclusion due to pertaining hierarchies of power is often addressed as a paradox (Back 2016; Nayak 2017; Tyler 2017; Neal et al. 2018). But if we return to the notion of courtesy, we gain a slightly different angle to look at this coexistence. As Simmel or Taylor emphasised, convivial situations generate nothing more than a mere impression of freedom from material or other axes of inequality between the participants (Simmel and Hughes 1949).

This promise of freedom from structural inequalities is essential and needs further investigation. Such take on conviviality requires us to reconsider the modern Western claims of recognition of individual difference, for example. We also need to dedicate more attention to the workings of equality claims. Paradoxically, the sort of 'convivial cultural competence' resting on the ideal of equality both helps to silence out structural inequalities and produces new lines of exclusion. As Arnold and König (2017) showed for anti-Semitic tendencies in contemporary Berlin, those who do not display convivial conduct in interreligious and interethnic encounters are refused not only having the required cultural competence but more generally civility.

Conviviality as Civility

Civility in Western modernity stands continuedly for a skill that enables cohabitation without rancour, a rational behaviour that requires to abstain from the excesses of antagonism despite differences (Bailey 1996). It is rooted in courtesy, but in the course of the reinforcement of modernity, it starts to denote a mode of governing societies, not only interactions (Bryson 1998). 'Being civil' stands thus not only for behaving properly, but means also being a contributing, active, responsible and conscious member of a group. This aspect of civility is central to these works on conviviality which consider conflict as functional to social order. Partly, this body of work resembles the ideas first formulated by Simmel (1903), but the political theories of agonism seem a stronger source of inspiration. These theories claim that conflict is productive to politics if it is framed by rules (Mouffe 2016). If conflict is practised as conversation ("war with words"), it offers a possibility of convivial interaction despite genuinely different and incompatible identities and ideas people have (Amin 2002; Sandercock 2003; Gilroy 2004: 4; Wood and Landry 2008).

The attractiveness of the agonist approach in urban multicultural setting (Coser 1956; Karner and Parker 2011; Amin 2008, 2012a; Landau 2014; Rishbeth and Rogaly 2018)[4] lies in how it acknowledges the provisional character of identities (Mouffe 2000). This understanding seems to fit the trend in migration and diversity studies to de-centralise and de-stabilise the categories of identities and to demonstrate their hybrid and fluid nature (Bhabha 1994; Hall 1992; Kasinitz et al. 2004; Bradatan et al. 2010). At the same time, political agonism recognises the human need for belonging to a certain social group (Mouffe 2005). Accordingly, urban multicultural spaces can become place for productive engagement with difference if participants adhere to the ethics of agonistic respect and understand ethnic, religious or racial differences as negotiable identifications. Agonism in urban settings can thus enable resolving tensions to produce fresh syntheses and thus result in conviviality (Amin 2002, 2008; Hinchliffe and

Whatmore 2006). Such convivial condition in turn embraces conflict and counters communitarianism which values harmony based on homogeneity (van Leeuwen 2014).

This understanding of conviviality requires a particular kind of public space which is imagined as free from private and economic interests (Peattie 1998; Banerjee 2001) and state influence; instead, it offers the possibility for people to connect to each other through multiple relationships, to access resources and practise empathy (Boyd 2006; Nyamnjoh 2002). Such public space is thus a location of democratic rule and enacting citizenship which goes beyond claiming rights vis-à-vis the state (Robins et al. 2008; Nyamnjoh 2002). Typically, parks (Neal et al. 2015) and communal gardens (Shepard 2009; Aptekar 2015) were investigated so far as places in which people probe a convivial mode of togetherness. Unlike classical civil engagements, convivial civil togetherness is also concerned with the future of humanity as the whole and thus with the condition of the natural environment. Often such (urban) spaces become laboratories for de-growth and green economies and sustainable living in general (Cato 2009; Milbourne 2012).

The everyday civic mode of being in the city can be understood as an element of an emerging community beyond political authority, a bottom-up movement that aims at a new mode of cohabitation on Earth based on human solidarity, also across generations. This aspect is present in Lourdes Arizpe's proposal for conviviability—compatible living together (Arizpe 1998, 2015; Arizpe et al. 2016). Arizpe stresses the centrality of the principle of non-exploitation and cooperation; only if this principle is realised, humans could eliminate problems of poverty, inequality, political persecution and conflict, social exclusion and cultural repression. Arizpe's vision requires more than shifting power to civil society; it also necessitates that this empowered civil society includes groups so far marginalised: minorities, ethnic groups and women.

The recent Convivialist Manifesto (Caillé 2014) makes a similar proposal, inspired by de-growth and other social movements (Adloff 2014). It is critical of how humans subordinated planetary future to the principle of abstract growth. 'Our society' is presented in the text as enslaved by economic measures and consumption. The renewal towards conviviality is the bottom-up task of a civil society, for the politics has proved to be incapable of governing in a sustainable and just manner. The authors of the Manifesto acknowledge the important role of organisations and groups from civil society that so far worked for more justice, women's and minorities' rights, fair trade and sharing economy. And it calls for more solidarity and joint actions among these groups, for a quest for *convivialism*[5] as common guiding principle (Caillé 2014).

Now, let me give a closer look at these two proposals and how they pursue a vision of new, convivial society which is yet restrained within an old idea of liberal civility (Walzer 2002).

Conviviality as Collaboration

The group of Convivialists around Alain Caillé and Lourdes Arizpe both build their proposal around the civil society. It is a liberal civil society in which individuals collaborate across their groups. The aim of such collaboration is clear: more justice and more sustainability to all. Alternative future scenarios enlisted by the Manifesto are ambitious: victory of democracy, end of colonialism, parity and equality of men and women, eradication of hunger and deprivation and autonomy of practice. While it is clear what needs to be done, the Manifesto is more concerned with how to achieve this alternative future, and the answer that it gives is indeed truly modern: convivial society can be achieved through joint effort (solidarity) and exchange (reciprocity) based on the principle of non-exploitation and preservation which remedy for rivalry and violence between humans.

The Manifesto understands collaboration of individuals as interest-free (in economic terms), as taking and giving that includes natural environment and animals. This strongly resembles Arizpe's ideas around sustainable living and inter-generational solidarity. Arizpe's conviviability requires people to re-define their attitudes towards each other as cultural others to achieve a common goal. While Arizpe postulates that individuals change their mental orientation, the Manifesto wants a throughout re-making of the very principles of social life in the spirit of radical universal equality. But alike Arizpe's older proposal, it pictures an individual as naturally aspiring to have its uniqueness recognised. It points to a tension between individual and community if the individual's desire for recognition is not satisfied (Caillé 2014). Prioritising individual's rights and well-being, it seeks a mode of living together which accommodates diversity of both individuals and groups, as well as rivalry between individuals' desires. Individual and society need to be kept in equilibrium. A 'healthy society' depicted in the Manifesto (ibid.: 24) should prevent violence and assure harmony and cooperation (Honneth 1996). The model for future society adopted in the Manifesto is to be based on care and compassion (Caillé 2014: 29). The community is there to serve the individual to develop potentials and capacities. The Manifesto reflects thus the idea of a social order based on autonomy of individuals, which results in their capability for a social contract (Gutmann 2013). The moral obligation is directed from community to the individual: the convivial society is implicated in collaboration of social individuals.

Also, Ivan Illich's much earlier proposal for conviviality relies on the idea of collaborating individuals. To enable such collaboration, people need tools that guarantee their freedom (Illich 1973). In Illich's vision, a convivial society is the one in which ordinary individuals re-gain control over technology to foster sustainable growth and subjective well-being. Illich argues that radical reconfigurations of institutions, in particular the education system, are required to achieve this aim. Illich's convivial society is based on a social economy, on sharing, combining and developing resources and capabilities through new forms of interaction, services and learning methods.

Analysing the work of Illich, Reagan (1980) argued that the collaboration that Illich had in mind is incompatible with the neo-liberal idea of community of autonomous and self-responsible individuals. Instead, the foundations of Illich's proposal for a convivial society are to be found in medieval social thought. The difference is how the relationship between the individual and community is imagined in the liberal social thought that sees the individual freedom in need of protection against the forces of community (Reagan 1980). Illich's imaginary of a community is instead that of an enabling one—an individual gains personal freedom through membership in community. Despite being largely simplistic (Black 1988; Siedentop 2015), Reagan's distinction between the medieval and liberal modern thought is worth attention for it points to the central problem of the conviviality debate: the relationship between individual and community.

Following this trail, we can ask how the relation between individual and community is imagined in these works that focus on fleeting encounters in urban spaces. There is not a single possible answer: some works on conviviality tend to see a community as emerging when individuals choose to collaborate for common good. These are works which focus on semi-public spaces (Peterson 2017), for example co-housing projects (Jarvis 2017). Other works consider the messiness and contextuality of human (and material) encounters, their forms and outcomes (Darling and Wilson 2016). Collaboration—if at all the term is used in this body of work—stands implicitly for an effort of invisible actors who create the infrastructures of convivial encounters: urban planners, managers of public facilities, shop assistants, cleaning staff taking care of parks and streets, etc. At the same time, community—even if in itself ephemeral—is nothing pre-given, but instead, it starts when the individuals give a start to it, by their minimal engagement, personal commitment to respecting others and their individuality and engaging for peace and sustainability.

Alternatively, collaboration stands for 'labour' required from all to create a convivial situation (Lapiņa 2016). Morgan (2009) considers urban fleeting encounters as collaborative activities in which all parties are involved in forms of work. With de Certeau (1984) we could also conceptualise such collaboration as tactics—sizing and using opportunities in encounters, manipulating them and combining elements of culture that are already there in a new way. So is walking in the city, for example tactical: people use shortcuts in spite of a grid of the streets. Tactics as form of everyday resistance can extend to political collaborations of different social groups (Elwood and Mitchell 2013; Mould 2014), sometimes spanning divisions of ethnicity, race, sexuality and religion and giving birth to new collectives. In this sense, their bond is utilitarian, though not necessarily intentional. Often, though, mobilising the marginalised is restricted within the boundaries of an existing group, which makes them no less convivial.

Valentine and Sadgrove (2012) rightly notice that the transformative powers of such fleeting encounters are overestimated, which results in a romantic view of urban public spaces as enabling tolerance and cosmopolitanism. Such celebratory instances of fleeting encounters tend to equalise conviviality to lack of conflicts and tensions. These accounts seem to mistake the mechanism of compassion with others with the scope of this compassion—the definition of boundaries of the relevant 'others' to whom we feel morally obliged, which is not only historically, geographically and culturally specific (Taylor 1989) but also depends on our biographical trajectory, experiences of friendship and suffering, etc. The preoccupation of social sciences with ethnic, racial and religious strangers obscures these aspects of human encounters (Valentine and Sadgrove 2012).

Conviviality Among Social Individuals

Research dedicated to the contact hypothesis proves that encounters are transformative only under certain conditions (Zhou et al. 2018). Thus, we should consider a social meaning of encounters which enable people to feel as a member of a group (Barth 1969) and develop an identity of 'self' which is a social being. Convivial gatherings with friends, eating, drinking, dancing or listening to music reassure our belonging to a particular social group; us sitting on a bench in a park, or strolling along the streets, listening to music, talking with friends—just doing as others do—reassures our identity as sociable selves. There are many ways of performing belonging to a group of peers, for example through similar dressing or consumption (Hernando 2017). A weekly ritual of wearing a fan club's scarf and having a beer while watching a football game is one possible form of performance which gives the pleasure of community (Giulianotti 2005). These are the moments when difference does not produce exclusion, and we can be indeed 'indifferent to difference'. Such moments produce pride, joy and emotional connectivity with temporarily equal strangers (Simmel and Hughes 1949). Hernando (2017) argues that such (symbolic) associations with (unfamiliar) peers substitute relational identity which we marginalised and denied in the course of modernisation. Relational identity relies on the sense of personhood that cannot be imagined outside of relational bonds. Yet instead of imagining the self as non-existent outside of community, an individuated modern person perceives herself or himself as existing in the world. This implies that there is the world, and the others, outside of the 'self' to which the 'self' can have a relationship. Thus, an individuated modern person assigns a great meaning to relationships for they assure her or him of not being alone (Taylor 1995).

Conviviality literature so far focuses almost exclusively relationships between the autonomous and unfamiliar selves. It considers how they are capable of liberating themselves of ties of kin and ethnic group, religious community or racial collective identity and reach beyond them to others in proximity (Wessendorf 2014; Wise and Velayutham 2014) and in distance, being solidary (Gilroy 2004: 90), as though this would be a universal and desired competence. Thereby, this research pushes the participants to reflect upon the nature and reason for their bonds with others and how the encounters with others impact their subjectivity. Werbner (2002) is critical of how, under the postcolonial condition, subjects are compelled to be aware and be concerned about their interdependence and entanglement with significant (cultural) others (see also Du Bois 1903).

The scholarly emphasis on relationships focuses commonalities, it is what makes us work and belong together rather than what separates us, and this implies some sort of non-hierarchical togetherness and sense of equality. But we need to ask: 'equal in what?' (Kelly 2010). In Western modern contexts, the declared and experienced equality is a carefully constructed myth, not only in relations with peers, but in intimate relationships as well (Knudson-Martin and Mahoney 2009). As many people continue to embody traditional gender, ethnic and religious identities, struggles for equality take place mostly in discursive field and are limited to the questions of recognition of difference; they are unsuccessful as long as reason and individuality are considered the only paths to empowerment (Hernando 2017). Thus, those in favour of equality are still capable of sustaining unequal relationships (Hernando 2017).

The supposed division between private and public domains facilitates the fantasy of equality. The dichotomy between private and public has been a main concern of feminist scholarship since more than five decades now (Pateman 1983; Siltanen and Stanworth 1984), but it continues to shape politics, the everyday practices and scholarly debates equally (Armstrong and Squires 2002; Woodward 2015). The conviviality literature is no exception in this respect: it prioritises researching relationships in the public sphere and between strangers, leaving the intimate and kin relationships untouched. This interest corresponds to the devaluation of domesticity and home as irrelevant to politics and social life. Conviviality in private seems given, while in public it needs to be achieved. It has to do with visibility and invisibility of inequality and power and current emphasis on visibility and audibility of ethnic and racial otherness. Exemplarily, migrant women engaged in domestic work continue to be exploited around the globe (Triandafyllidou 2013). While 'conviviality' and 'migrant domestic workers' can be found in one book (Liu-Farrer and Yeoh 2018), these terms cannot be found in one chapter. It seems that global cities inspire conviviality, domestic sphere invites conflict. Both are forms of 'contact zones' between family members and familiar strangers, but they enjoy different kind of scholarly attention.

This tendency goes hand in hand with denying the role of affective and emotional bonds (Hernando 2017). Even if some works trace signs of affectivity and emotions in public spaces, they relate affectivity (fear, hate) rather to distance from others than to bonding with others (Georgiou 2017) or as a quality of spaces rather than people (Anderson 2009). But 'affects' remain largely unspecific in alliances between strangers as in Amin's accounts of urban life (Amin 2012b). Despite that the problem of neglecting affects and emotions is not specific to conviviality literature (for the overview of critique of this tendency in human geography, see [Nayak 2017]), the notion of conviviality sadly does not in fact make any difference to the way social relations are narrated.

Further, conviviality appears as a new label for fleeting encounters in public spaces, as a potential for meaningful and transformative social relationships. Without doubt, these encounters are important for sociality. Yet we ought not to forget that face-to-face interactions, even those most fleeting, are conducted according to conventions, and they are functional. They are personalised—in the sense that they appear to be like between friends—but they serve impersonal functions, such as maintaining of community (Wrightson 2013).

WHAT WE CANNOT SEE AND HOW COULD WE BE OTHERWISE

Through the heuristic of (modern Western) social imaginary, the debate on conviviality appears largely as reflecting classical interest and concerns of modernity, including the concern with global environment risks (Beck 2006, 2007, 2012). It does not surprise that the interest in conviviality intensified now. The accelerated climate change and persistence of violent conflicts around the globe which cause more refugees arriving at the shore of Western countries give a sense of an approaching catastrophe and impotence of an individual vis-à-vis this challenge (Hernando 2017). Similarly, the peak of the post-industrial era and the acceleration of globalisation produced two earlier convivial turns, with key works of Illich (1973) and Arizpe (1998). Conviviality appears thus again in 'time that needs direction' (American Humanist Association 1973).

Focusing the everyday social interactions, the current debate favours urban public and semi-public spaces. It is interested in how people reconcile equality and diversity and establish a friendly environment while assuring the recognition of uniqueness of individuals. A consensual sociality is here contrasted to the oppressive system of racial and gender inequality which operates on the basis of unchosen designations. The debate which operates with the modern liberal civil society framework produces evidence on conviviality as courtesy and as civility.

If the debate would restrain itself to describing people, places or situations as convivial, we could or indeed should be critical of how such exercise might be dull and unproductive. Instead, the notion of conviviality increasingly aspires to be an analytical tool, a new lens to study the social and a new mode of explanation. I think it cannot fulfil this aspiration as long as it is not explicit about its own underpinnings and thus its own contextuality. Without it, conviviality might be just another (temporary) label for situations which have been common anywhere and everywhere. Instead of being productive in understanding such contexts, it might rather reproduce a Western modern model of masculine sociality. By idealising equality and recognition of individual differences, it might obscure injustice and inequality. By idealising the bridging of ethnic difference, it might silent out the emotional bonds which happen within and beyond the kind and which are the very tissue of sociality. By focusing on multicultural urban settings, it might miss to understand sociality beyond intercultural relations and reproduce the difference it wants to tackle. By focusing on courtesy, such conviviality may neglect emotional distance in daily encounters. By stressing civil society, it might obscure the workings of the state as a moral instance which produces selves as belonging to fixed categories. By understanding individuals as 'free choosers' obliged to reciprocity, it is in danger of ignoring the deeper sense of interdependence. By focusing on voluntary encounters, it might reproduce the dichotomy of kin and friendship.

These are multiple dangers to conviviality which the debate should take seriously if conviviality is not to share the fate of cosmopolitanism as a 'blown up notion' (Braidotti 2013). What is indeed needed is a dose of 'epistemic disobedience' (Mignolo 2009). The start for it is, as mentioned above, the transparency about the own roots of the interests driving the conviviality debate. The works of Taylor (2004) or Hernando (2017) could be useful, though there are multiple ways to achieving the same aim. We might not be able to fully reject the social imaginary we are part of, but we can at least assure we are aware of some of the fantasies it includes. We might then try to 'be otherwise'.[6] For me, it means to ask an alternative question as soon as one question is asked. It means destabilising the perspective already taken. Exemplarily, if conviviality focuses civil society, then why not bringing the state into the debate? In many ways, civil society is not external to state power (Corrigan 1981; Walzer 2002). Ignoring the state, we don't see how it produces certain kinds of social identities (foreigner or national, young or old aged, able or disabled, male or female, adult or child, kin or unrelated). Following this trail, we may think of conviviality through the lens of moral regulation and thus address how things which now appear to us as inevitable and natural have become such (Dean 1994; Ruonavaara 1997). But moral regulations are imposed by actors other than the state as well, and so we might ask, for example, how social science makes us see intercultural contact and competence to converse in foreign languages (more or less fluently) more central to sociality than public expression of emotions. To be effective, conviviality needs thus to engage with a sense of the contingency of what appears inevitable.

Second, the debate should look closer at why convivial situations are so precious to us (as ordinary people and as scholars). Probably, we all value such moments for they enable identity to be derived directly from the action being shared. Possibly, many contemporary situations are alike litanies or alternate chanting experiences earlier or in other societies (Taylor 1995). To address this aspect would probably bring us to focusing less on epistemological aspects (describing what people think about themselves and the world around) but more on the phenomenology of being the world. In turn, we would not come around putting emotions and affects in the centre of our scholarly interest. So far, the study of non-Western modern societies provide examples of how collective life is inseparable from all forms of intimate relations and affectivity (Overing and Passes 2000; Whittle 2005; Harris, O. J. T. 2011). These works remind us of an alternative to the take on conviviality which considers social relations separately in public and private domain, or these works which imagine humans and their environment as divided (Given 2018).

Third, if conviviality dares to revise the fantasy of equality, it might be able to embrace inequalities and think of an order which is less exclusive and less oppressive than the one we experience now. The studies in egalitarian societies in Amazonia, for example, could be an incentive to formulate how to achieve complementarity beyond hierarchical relations and value others for what they do and not who they are. Here, interdependence and other-dependence might appear a false dichotomy. Conviviality might help to transform the value of interdependence towards interrelatedness which is beyond the choice of individuals (Boisvert 2010). Such 'convivialist epistemology' based on the irreducible sense of with-ness of existence (Boisvert 2010) would be an alternative to a modern relational view on human-human and human-nature encounters.

Finally, being otherwise, conviviality would also need to abandon its utilitarian approach which relies on the sense of human capacity for achieving change. Moreover, it would require to re-define the value of change or even to draw satisfaction from lack of change. For as long as the conviviality debate has certain ends in view—for example security as mutual benefit of collaboration of individuals or reduction of violence in result of daily encounters across ethnic difference—it resembles communitarianism and misses a significant contribution to re-thinking the social.

Notes

1. These are past and present-day hunter-gatherer societies which have no chief or specialists of any kind; they rely on oral communication and personal relationships to transmit knowledge and have not developed formal logic or the abstract classifications (Hernando 2017; Fried 1976; Flanagan 1989; Ong 2012).
2. Descola (2013) describes this system of knowledge as 'naturalism' and points to alternative systems which could co-exist with it.
3. In this point, Hernando disagrees with Taylor who considers individualism as a modern phenomenon at expense of community (Taylor 2004); for Hernando, individuality happens at expense of gender equality, not community.
4. Thereby, agonist approaches are also present in urban design and urban planning in works that do not link to the conviviality debate (Munthe-Kaas 2015). Some of these works refer to agonism after Laclau instead of Mouffe.
5. The term '*convivialism*' is used by Raymond Boisvert (2010) and the authors of the Manifesto (2014); recently, it gains popularity in context Internet blogs on green living and de-growth initiatives, in particular in France and Germany.
6. I borrow this expression from David Francis, see http://www.carmah.berlin/reflections/auto-draft-12/, accessed on 8 July 2018.

References

Abrams, Lynn, and Elizabeth Ewan, eds. 2017. *Nine Centuries of Man: Manhood and Masculinities in Scottish History*. Edinburgh: Edinburgh University Press.

Adloff, Frank. 2014. "'Wrong Life Can Be Lived Rightly': Convivialism—Background to a Debate." In *Convivialist Manifesto: A Declaration of Interdependence*, edited by Alain Caillé, 5–16. Global Dialogues 3. Duisburg: Käte Hamburger Kolleg.

American Humanist Association. 1973. "Humanist Manifesto II." https://americanhumanist.org/what-is-humanism/manifesto2/.

Amin, Ash. 2002. "Ethnicity and the Multicultural City: Living with Diversity." *Environ Plan A* 34 (6): 959–980. https://doi.org/10.1068/a3537.

Amin, Ash. 2008. "Collective Culture and Urban Public Space." *City* 12 (1): 5–24. https://doi.org/10.1080/13604810801933495.

Amin, Ash. 2012a. *Land of Strangers*. Cambridge: Polity Press. http://site.ebrary.com/lib/alltitles/docDetail.action?docID=10691454.

Amin, Ash. 2012b. *Land of Strangers* 1., Auflage. New York, NY: Wiley.

Anderson, Ben. 2009. "Affective Atmospheres." *Emotion, Space and Society* 2 (2): 77–81. https://doi.org/10.1016/j.emospa.2009.08.005.

Aptekar, Sofya. 2015. "Visions of Public Space: Reproducing and Resisting Social Hierarchies in a Community Garden." *Sociol Forum* 30 (1): 209–227. https://doi.org/10.1111/socf.12152.

Arizpe, Lourdes. 1998. "Conviviability: The Role of Civil Society in Development." In *Civil Society and International Development*, edited by Amanda Bernard, 21–24. Development Centre studies. Paris: OECD, Development Centre.

Arizpe, Lourdes. 2015. "Convivencia: The Goal of Conviviability." In *Culture, Diversity and Heritage: Major Studies*, vol. 12, edited by Lourdes Arizpe, 165–167. SpringerBriefs on Pioneers in Science and Practice 12. Cham: s.l. Springer International Publishing.

Arizpe, Lourdes, Martin Price, and Robert Worcester. 2016. "The First Decade of Initiatives for Research on the Human Dimensions of Global (Environmental) Change." In *Handbook on Sustainability Transition and Sustainable Peace*, edited by Hans G. Brauch, Úrsula Oswald Spring, John Grin, and Jürgen Scheffran, 349–359. Hexagon Series on Human and Environmental Security and Peace 10. Cham: s.l. Springer International Publishing.

Armstrong, Chris, and Judith Squires. 2002. "Beyond the Public/Private Dichotomy: Relational Space and Sexual Inequalities." *Contemporary Political Theory* 1 (3): 261–283. https://doi.org/10.1057/palgrave.cpt.9300059.

Arnold, Sina N., and Jana König. 2017. "Antisemitismus im Kontext von Willkommens- und Ablehnungskultur: Einstellungen Geflüchteter zu Juden, Israel und dem Holocaust." *Jahrbuch für Antisemitismusforschung* 26 (2017): 303–326.

Back, Les. 2016. *Metropolitan Paradoxes: Then and Now*. https://newurbanmulticultures.wordpress.com/2016/05/16/metropolitan-paradoxes-then-and-now/.

Bailey, Frederick G. 1996. *The Civility of Indifference: On Domesticating Ethnicity*. Ithaca: Cornell University Press.

Banerjee, Tridib. 2001. "The Future of Public Space: Beyond Invented Streets and Reinvented Places." *Journal of the American Planning Association* 67 (1): 9–24. https://doi.org/10.1080/01944360108976352.

Barth, Fredrik. 1969. *Ethnic Groups and Boundaries: The Social Organization of Culture Difference*. Oslo: Universitetsforlaget.

Beck, Ulrich. 2006. "Living in the World Risk Society." *Economy and Society* 35 (3): 329–345. https://doi.org/10.1080/03085140600844902.

Beck, Ulrich. 2007. *World Risk Society*. Reprinted. Cambridge: Polity Press.

Beck, Ulrich. 2012. "Global Risk Society." In *The Wiley-Blackwell Encyclopedia of Globalization*, edited by George Ritzer, 273. Wiley-Blackwell Encyclopedias in Social Science. Hoboken, NJ: Wiley.

Beiser, Frederick C. 1996. *The Sovereignty of Reason: The Defense of Rationality in The Early English Enlightenment*. Princeton, NJ: Princeton University Press.

Bhabha, Homi K. 1994. *The Location of Culture*. London: Routledge.

Black, Antony. 1988. "The Individual and Society." In *The Cambridge History of Medieval Political Thought c.350–c.1450*, edited by J. H. Burns, 588–606. The Cambridge History of Political Thought. Cambridge: Cambridge University Press.

Boisvert, Raymond. 2010. "Convivialism: A Philosophical Manifesto." *The Pluralist* 5 (2): 57–68.

Boyd, Richard. 2006. "The Value of Civility?" *Urban Studies* 43 (5–6): 863–878. https://doi.org/10.1080/00420980600676105.

Bradatan, Cristina, Adrian Popan, and Rachel Melton. 2010. "Transnationality as a Fluid Social Identity." *Social Identities* 16 (2): 169–178. https://doi.org/10.1080/13504631003688856.

Braidotti, Rosi. 2013. "Becoming-World." In *After Cosmopolitanism*, ed. Rosi Braidotti, Patrick Hanafin, and Bolette Blaagaard, 8–28. Abingdon and New York: Routledge.

Braidotti, Rosi, Patrick Hanafin, and Bolette Blaagaard, eds. 2013. *After Cosmopolitanism*. Abingdon: Routledge.

Bryson, Anna. 1998. *From Courtesy to Civility: Changing Codes of Conduct in Early Modern England*. Oxford Studies in Social History. Oxford: Clarendon Press.

Caillé, Alain, ed. 2014. *Convivialist Manifesto: A Declaration of Interdependence*. Global Dialogues 3. Duisburg: Käte Hamburger Kolleg.

Cato, Molly S. 2009. *Green Economics: An Introduction to Theory, Policy and Practice*. Reprinted. London: Earthscan.

Connell, R. W., and James W. Messerschmidt. 2005. "Hegemonic Masculinity." *Gender & Society* 19 (6): 829–859. https://doi.org/10.1177/0891243205278639.

Corrigan, Philip. 1981. "On Moral Regulation: Some Preliminary Remarks." *The Sociological Review* 29 (2): 313–337. https://doi.org/10.1111/j.1467-954x.1981.tb00176.x.

Coser, Lewis A. 1956. *The Functions of Social Conflict*. London: Routledge & Kegan Paul.

Curtin, Michael. 1985. "A Question of Manners: Status and Gender in Etiquette and Courtesy." *The Journal of Modern History* 57 (3): 396–423. https://doi.org/10.1086/242859.

Darling, Jonathan, and Helen F. Wilson, eds. 2016. *Encountering the City: Urban Encounters from Accra to New York*. London and New York: Routledge.

de Certeau, Michel. 1984. *The Practice of Everyday Life*, trans. Steven Rendall. Berkeley: University of California Press.

Dean, Mitchell. 1994. "'A Social Structure of Many Souls': Moral Regulation, Government, and Self-Formation." *Canadian Journal of Sociology / Cahiers canadiens de sociologie* 19 (2): 145. https://doi.org/10.2307/3341342.

Descola, Philippe. 2013. *Beyond Nature and Culture*. Chicago: The University of Chicago Press.

Du Bois, William E. B. 1903. *The Souls of Black Folk: Essays and Sketches*. Chicago: Mc Clurg.

Dunlap, Rudy. 2009. "Taking Aunt Kathy to Dinner: Family Dinner as a Focal Practice." *Leisure Sciences* 31 (5): 417–433. https://doi.org/10.1080/01490400902988325.

Dupré, Louis. 2004. *The Enlightenment and the Intellectual Foundations of Modern Culture*. New Haven and London: Yale University Press.

Elias, Norbert. 1991. *The Society of Individuals*. Oxford and Cambridge, MA: Blackwell.

Elias, Norbert. 1994. *The Civilizing Process: The History of Manners and State Formation and Civilization*. Oxford, UK and Cambridge, USA: Blackwell.

Elwood, Sarah, and Katharyne Mitchell. 2013. "Another Politics Is Possible: Neogeographies, Visual Spatial Tactics, and Political Formation." *Cartographica: The International Journal for Geographic Information and Geovisualization* 48 (4): 275–292. https://doi.org/10.3138/carto.48.4.1729.

Flanagan, J. G. 1989. "Hierarchy in Simple 'Egalitarian' Societies." *Annual Review of Anthropology* 18 (1): 245–266. https://doi.org/10.1146/annurev.an.18.100189.001333.

Freitag, Ulrike. 2014. "'Cosmopolitanism' and 'Conviviality'? Some Conceptual Considerations Concerning the Late Ottoman Empire." *European Journal of Cultural Studies* 17 (4): 375–391. https://doi.org/10.1177/1367549413510417.

Fried, Morton H. 1976. *The Evolution of Political Society: An Essay in Political Anthropology*. New York, NY: McGraw-Hill.

Fukuyama, Francis. 1992. *The End of History and the Last Man*. London: Hamilton.

Georgiou, Myria. 2017. "Conviviality Is Not Enough: A Communication Perspective to the City of Difference." *Communication, Culture & Critique* 10 (2): 261–279. https://doi.org/10.1111/cccr.12154.

Gibson, Joan. 1989. "Educating for Silence: Renaissance Women and the Language Arts*." *Hypatia* 4 (1): 9–27. https://doi.org/10.1111/j.1527-2001.1989.tb00865.x.

Gilroy, Paul. 2004. *Postcolonial Melancholia*. Wellek Library Lectures. New York, NY: Columbia University Press.

Gilroy, Paul. 2006. "Multiculture in Times of War." *Critical Quarterly* 48 (4): 27–45.

Giulianotti, Richard. 2005. "The Sociability of Sport." *International Review for the Sociology of Sport* 40 (3): 289–306. https://doi.org/10.1177/1012690205060095.

Given, Michael. 2018. "The Precarious Conviviality of Watermills." *Archaeological Dialogues* 25 (1): 71–94. https://doi.org/10.1017/s1380203818000089.

Goffman, Erving. 1963. *Behavior in Public Places: Notes on the Social Organization of Gatherings*. London: Free Press.

Goffman, Erving. 1971. *Relations in Public: Microstudies of the Public Order.* New York: Basic Books.
Gordon, Daniel. 1994. *Citizens Without Sovereignty: Equality and Sociability in French Thought, 1670–1789.* Princeton: Princeton University Press.
Gutmann, Thomas. 2013. "Theories of Contract and the Concept of Autonomy." Preprints and Working Papers of the Centre for Advanced Study in Bioethics 55. https://www.uni-muenster.de/imperia/md/content/kfg-normenbegruendung/intern/publikationen/gutmann/55_gutmann_-_contract_and_autonomy.pdf.
Hall, Stuart. 1992. "The Question of Cultural Identity." In *Modernity and Its Futures*, edited by Stuart Hall, David Held, and Tony McGrew, 273–316. Understanding Modern Societies 4. Cambridge: Polity Press.
Harris, Anita. 2016. "Rethinking Youth Conviviality: The Possibilities of Intercultural Friendship Beyond Contact and Encounter." *Journal of Intercultural Studies* 37 (5): 501–516. https://doi.org/10.1080/07256868.2016.1211627.
Harris, O. J. T. 2011. "Constituting Childhood. Identity, Conviviality and Community at Windmill Hill." In *(Re)thinking the Little Ancestor: New Perspectives on the Archaeology of Infancy and Childhood*, edited by Mike Lally, 122–132. BAR International Series 2271. Oxford: Archaeopress.
Heil, Tilmann. 2013. "Are Neighbours Alike? Practices of Conviviality in Catalonia and Casamance." *European Journal of Cultural Studies* 17 (4): 452–470. https://doi.org/10.1177/1367549413510420.
Hernando, Almudena. 2017. *The Fantasy of Individuality: On the Sociohistorical Construction of the Modern Subject.* Cham: Springer International Publishing. http://dx.doi.org/10.1007/978-3-319-60720-7.
Hinchliffe, Steve, and Sarah Whatmore. 2006. "Living Cities: Towards a Politics of Conviviality." *Science as Culture* 15 (2): 123–138. https://doi.org/10.1080/09505430600707988.
Honneth, Axel. 1987. "Enlightenment and Rationality." *The Journal of Philosophy* 84 (11): 692–699.
Honneth, Axel. 1996. *The Struggle for Recognition: The Moral Grammar of Social Conflicts*, 1st MIT Press ed., Studies in Contemporary German Social Thought. Cambridge, MA: MIT Press.
Illich, Ivan. 1973. *Tools for Conviviality* 1. Perennial Library ed. Perennial Library 308. New York, NY: Harper & Row.
Jarvis, Helen. 2017. "Sharing, Togetherness and Intentional Degrowth." *Progress in Human Geography*, 0309132517746519. https://doi.org/10.1177/0309132517746519.
Karner, Christian, and David Parker. 2011. "Conviviality and Conflict: Pluralism, Resilience and Hope in Inner-City Birmingham." *Journal of Ethnic and Migration Studies* 37 (3): 355–372. https://doi.org/10.1080/1369183x.2011.526776.

Kasinitz, Philip, John H. Mollenkopf, and Mary C. Waters. 2004. *Becoming New Yorkers: Ethnographies of the New Second Generation*. New York, NY: Russell Sage Foundation. http://www.loc.gov/catdir/enhancements/fy1602/2004046633-b.html.

Kelly, Paul. 2010. "Why Equality? On Justifying Liberal Egalitarianism." *Critical Review of International Social and Political Philosophy* 13 (1): 55–70. https://doi.org/10.1080/13698230903326257.

Klein, Lawrance E. 2012. "Sociability, Politeness, and Aristocratic Self-Formation in the Life and Career of the Second Earl of Shelburne." *The Historical Journal* 55 (3): 653–677. https://doi.org/10.1017/s0018246x12000088.

Knudson-Martin, Carmen, and Anne R. Mahoney. 2009. "The Myth of Equality." In *Couples, Gender, and Power: Creating Change in Intimate Relationships*, edited by Anne R. Mahoney and Carmen Knudson-Martin, 43–62. New York: Springer Publishing Company.

Landau, Loren B. 2014. "Conviviality, Rights, and Conflict in Africa's Urban Estuaries." *Politics & Society* 42 (3): 359–380. https://doi.org/10.1177/0032329214543258.

Lapiņa, Linda. 2016. "Besides Conviviality." *Nordic Journal of Migration Research* 6 (1). https://doi.org/10.1515/njmr-2016-0002.

Laurier, E., and C. Philo. 2006. "Cold Shoulders and Napkins Handed: Gestures of Responsibility." *Transactions of the Institute of British Geographers* 31: 193–207.

Lisiak, Agata, and Magdalena Nowicka. 2017. "Tacit Differences, Ethnicity and Neoliberalism: Polish Migrant Mothers in German Cities." *Gender, Place & Culture* 5 (3): 1–17. https://doi.org/10.1080/0966369x.2017.1334631.

Liu-Farrer, Gracia, and Brenda S. A. Yeoh. 2018. *Routledge Handbook of Asian Migrations*, 1st ed. Florence: Taylor & Francis. https://ebookcentral.proquest.com/lib/gbv/detail.action?docID=5211381.

Mignolo, Walter D. 2009. "Epistemic Disobedience, Independent Thought and Decolonial Freedom." *Theory, Culture & Society* 26 (7–8): 159–181. https://doi.org/10.1177/0263276409349275.

Milbourne, Paul. 2012. "Everyday (In)justices and Ordinary Environmentalisms: Community Gardening in Disadvantaged Urban Neighbourhoods." *Local Environment* 17 (9): 943–957. https://doi.org/10.1080/13549839.2011.607158.

Moore, Henrietta. 2013. "The Fantasies of Cosmopolitanism." In *After Cosmopolitanism*, ed. Rosi Braidotti, Patrick Hanafin, and Bolette Blaagaard, 97–110. New York and London: Routledge.

Morgan, D. H. J. 2009. *Acquaintances: The Space Between Intimates and Strangers*. Sociology and Social Change. Maidenhead: Open University Press. http://site.ebrary.com/lib/academiccompletetitles/home.action.

Mouffe, Chantal. 2000. *The Democratic Paradox*. Phronesis. London: Verso.

Mouffe, Chantal. 2005. *On the Political*. Thinking in Action. London and New York: Routledge. http://site.ebrary.com/lib/alltitles/docDetail.action?docID=10462625.
Mouffe, Chantal. 2016. "Democratic Politics and Conflict: An Agonistic Approach." *Política Común* 9 (20180419). https://doi.org/10.3998/pc.12322227.0009.011.
Mould, Oli. 2014. "Tactical Urbanism: The New Vernacular of the Creative City." *Geography Compass* 8 (8): 529–539. https://doi.org/10.1111/gec3.12146.
Mouzakitis, Angelos. 2017. "Modernity and the Idea of Progress." *Frontiers Sociology* 2: 177. https://doi.org/10.3389/fsoc.2017.00003.
Munthe-Kaas, Peter. 2015. "Agonism and Co-Design of Urban Spaces." *Urban Research & Practice* 26 (1): 1–20. https://doi.org/10.1080/17535069.2015.1050207.
Nayak, Anoop. 2017. "Purging the Nation: Race, Conviviality and Embodied Encounters in the Lives of British Bangladeshi Muslim Young Women." *Transactions of the Institute of British Geographers* 42 (2): 289–302. https://doi.org/10.1111/tran.12168.
Neal, Sarah, Katy Bennett, Allan Cochrane, and Giles Mohan. 2018. *Lived Experiences of Multiculture: The New Social and Spatial Relations of Diversity*. Routledge Research in Race and Ethnicity 23. London: Routledge, Taylor & Francis Group.
Neal, Sarah, Katy Bennett, Hannah Jones, Allan Cochrane, and Giles Mohan. 2015. "Multiculture and Public Parks: Researching Super-Diversity and Attachment in Public Green Space." *Population Space Place* 21 (5): 463–475. https://doi.org/10.1002/psp.1910.
Noble, Greg. 2013. "Cosmopolitan Habits: The Capacities and Habitats of Intercultural Conviviality." *Body and Society* 19 (23): 162–185.
Nowicka, Magdalena, and Steven Vertovec. 2014. "Comparing Convivialities: Dreams and Realities of Living-with-Difference." *European Journal of Cultural Studies* 17 (4): 341–356. https://doi.org/10.1177/1367549413510414.
Nyamnjoh, Francis. 2002. "'A Child Is One Person's Only in the Womb': Domestication, Agency, and Subjectivity in the Cameroonian Grassfields." In *Postcolonial Subjectivities in Africa*, edited by Richard P. Werbner. 1. publ. Postcolonial Encounters. London [u.a.]: Zed Books.
O'Callaghan, Michelle. 2004. "Tavern Societies, the Inns of Court, and the Culture of Conviviality in Early Seventeenth-Century London." In *A Pleasing Sinne: Drink and Conviviality in Seventeenth-Century England*, edited by Adam Smyth, 37–51. Studies in Renaissance Literature 14. Cambridge: Brewer.
Ong, Walter J. 2012. *Orality and Literacy: The Technologizing of the Word*. With the assistance of J. Hartley, 30th anniversary edition. New Accents. London and New York: Routledge.

Overing, Joanna, and Alan Passes, eds. 2000. *The Anthropology of Love and Anger: The Aesthetics of Conviviality in Native Amazonia*. London and New York: Routledge.

Padilla, Beatriz, Joana Azevedo, and Antonia Olmos-Alcaraz. 2015. "Superdiversity and Conviviality: Exploring Frameworks for Doing Ethnography in Southern European Intercultural Cities." *Ethnic and Racial Studies* 38 (4): 621–635. https://doi.org/10.1080/01419870.2015.980294.

Pateman, Carole. 1983. "Feminist Critiques of the Public/Private Dichotomy." In *Public and Private in Social Life*, edited by Stanley I. Benn and Gerald F. Gaus, 281–303. London: Croom Helm.

Peattie, Lisa. 1998. "Convivial Cities." In *Cities for Citizens: Planning and the Rise of Civil Society in a Global Age*, edited by Clyde M. Douglass and John Friedmann, 247–253. Chichester: Wiley.

Peterson, Melike. 2017. "Living with Difference in Hyper-Diverse Areas: How Important Are Encounters in Semi-Public Spaces?" *Social & Cultural Geography* 18 (8): 1067–1085. https://doi.org/10.1080/14649365.2016.1210667.

Phull, Surinder, Wendy Wills, and Angela Dickinson. 2015. "Is It a Pleasure to Eat Together? Theoretical Reflections on Conviviality and the Mediterranean Diet." *Sociology Compass* 9 (11): 977–986. https://doi.org/10.1111/soc4.12307.

Reagan, Timothy. 1980. "The Foundations of Ivan Illich's Social Thought." *Educational Theory* 30 (4): 293–306.

Rishbeth, Clare, and Ben Rogaly. 2018. "Sitting Outside: Conviviality, Self-Care and the Design of Benches in Urban Public Space." *Transactions of the Institute of British Geographers* 43 (2): 284–298. https://doi.org/10.1111/tran.12212.

Robins, Steven, Andrea Cornwall, and Bettina von Lieres. 2008. "Rethinking 'Citizenship' in the Postcolony." *Third World Quarterly* 29 (6): 1069–1086. https://doi.org/10.1080/01436590802201048.

Ruonavaara, Hannu. 1997. "Moral Regulation: A Reformulation." *Sociological Theory* 15 (3): 277–293.

Sandercock, Leonie. 2003. *Cosmopolis II: Mongrel Cities of the 21st Century*. London: Continuum.

Shepard, Benjamin. 2009. "Community Gardens, Convivial Spaces, and the Seeds of a Radical Democratic Counterpublic." In *Democracy, States, and the Struggle for Global Justice*, edited by Heather Gautney, 273–296. New York: Routledge.

Siedentop, Larry. 2015. *Inventing the Individual: The Origins of Western Liberalism*. London: Penguin Books.

Siltanen, Janet, and Michelle Stanworth. 1984. "The Politics of Private Woman and Public Man." *Theory and Society* 13 (1): 91–118. https://doi.org/10.1007/bf00159258.

Simmel, Georg. 1903. "Die Grosstädte und das Geistesleben." In *Die Grossstadt. Vorträge und Aufsätze zur Städteausstellung: Jahrbuch der Gehe-Stiftung Dresden*, edited by Theodor Petermann, 185–206. Dresden: Zahn & Jaensch.

Simmel, Georg, and Everett C. Hughes. 1949. "The Sociology of Sociability." *American Journal of Sociology* 55 (3): 254–261. https://doi.org/10.1086/220534.

Taylor, Charles. 1989. *Sources of the Self: The Making of the Modern Identity*. Cambridge, MA: Harvard University Press.

Taylor, Charles. 1995. "The Dialogical Self." In *Rethinking Knowledge: Reflections Across the Disciplines*, edited by Robert F. Goodman and Walter R. Fisher, 57–67. SUNY Series in the Philosophy of the Social Sciences. Albany: State University of New York Press.

Taylor, Charles. 2004. *Modern Social Imaginaries*. Durham and London: Duke University Press.

Triandafyllidou, Anna, ed. 2013. *Irregular Migrant Domestic Workers in Europe: Who Cares?* Farnham, Surrey: Ashgate.

Tyler, Katharine. 2017. "The Suburban Paradox of Conviviality and Racism in Postcolonial Britain." *Journal of Ethnic and Migration Studies* 43 (11): 1890–1906. https://doi.org/10.1080/1369183x.2016.1245607.

Valentine, Gill, and Joanna Sadgrove. 2012. "Lived Difference: A Narrative Account of Spatiotemporal Processes of Social Differentiation." *Environment and Planning A: Economy and Space* 44 (9): 2049–2063. https://doi.org/10.1068/a44491.

van Leeuwen, Bart. 2014. "Absorbing the Agony of Agonism? The Limits of Cultural Questioning and Alternative Variations of Intercultural Civility." *Urban Studies* 52 (4): 793–808. https://doi.org/10.1177/0042098014528548.

Wagner, Peter. 2012. *Modernity: Understanding the Present*. Cambridge: Polity Press.

Walzer, Michael. 2002. "Equality and Civil Society." In *Alternative Conceptions of Civil Society*, edited by Simone Chambers and Will Kymlicka, 34–49. Princeton, NJ: Princeton University Press.

Werbner, Richard P. 2002. "Postcolonial Subjectivities: The Personal, the Political and the Moral." In *Postcolonial Subjectivities in Africa*, edited by Richard P. Werbner. 1. publ. Postcolonial Encounters, 1–22. London [u.a.]: Zed Books.

Wessendorf, Susanne. 2014. "'Being Open, but Sometimes Closed'. Conviviality in a Super-Diverse London Neighbourhood." *European Journal of Cultural Studies* 17 (4): 392–405. https://doi.org/10.1177/1367549413510415.

Whittle, A. 2005. "Lived Experience in the Early Neolithic of the Great Hungarian Plain." In *(Un)settling the Neolithic*, edited by Douglass W. Bailey, 64–70. Oxford: Oxbow Books.

Wise, Amanda. 2016. "Becoming Cosmopolitan: Encountering Difference in a City of Mobile Labour." *Journal of Ethnic and Migration Studies* 42 (14): 2289–2308. https://doi.org/10.1080/1369183x.2016.1205807.

Wise, Amanda, and Selvaraj Velayutham. 2014. "Conviviality in Everyday Multiculturalism: Some Brief Comparisons Between Singapore and Sydney." *European Journal of Cultural Studies* 17 (4): 406–430. https://doi.org/10.1177/1367549413510419.

Withington, Phil. 2007. "Company and Sociability in Early Modern England." *Social History* 32 (3): 291–307. https://doi.org/10.1080/03071020701425338.

Wood, Phil, and Charles Landry. 2008. *The Intercultural City: Planning for Diversity Advantage*. Reprinted. London: Earthscan.

Woodward, Kath. 2015. "Public and Private Spaces and Relationships." In *The Politics of In/Visibility: Being There*, edited by Kath Woodward, 80–95. Genders and Sexualities in the Social Sciences. London: Palgrave Macmillan UK; Imprint; Palgrave Macmillan.

Wrightson, Keith. 2013. *English Society 1580–1680*, 2nd ed. Hoboken: Taylor & Francis. http://gbv.eblib.com/patron/FullRecord.aspx?p=1223029.

Zhou, Shelly, Elizabeth Page-Gould, Arthur Aron, Anne Moyer, and Miles Hewstone. 2018. "The Extended Contact Hypothesis: A Meta-Analysis on 20 Years of Research." *Personality and Social Psychology Review* 20:108886831876264. https://doi.org/10.1177/1088868318762647.

Open Access This chapter is licensed under the terms of the Creative Commons Attribution 4.0 International License (http://creativecommons.org/licenses/by/4.0/), which permits use, sharing, adaptation, distribution and reproduction in any medium or format, as long as you give appropriate credit to the original author(s) and the source, provide a link to the Creative Commons license and indicate if changes were made.

The images or other third party material in this chapter are included in the chapter's Creative Commons license, unless indicated otherwise in a credit line to the material. If material is not included in the chapter's Creative Commons license and your intended use is not permitted by statutory regulation or exceeds the permitted use, you will need to obtain permission directly from the copyright holder.

CHAPTER 3

Creolisation as a Recipe for Conviviality

Thomas Hylland Eriksen

What on earth is happening to the world's cultural variation in this overheated era? It already seems an eternity ago that Joseph Conrad's Kurtz found his dark and unfathomable Africa following a dangerous and strenuous journey across sea and land, and it feels about as long ago that Hemingway demonstrated his true machismo by going on a safari to East Africa. Today, housewives from Clapham go on safari to East Africa, and the great-grandchildren of Conrad's Africans fly Ethiopian to New York to present their economic problems to the United Nations. At least some of them do.

Superficially, it may seem as though most of the significant cultural differences my generation grew up with are all but gone; that we all become increasingly similar as indigenous peoples and former tribal peoples worldwide are drawn into formal schooling and wage work, are forced to obtain identity papers and spend their small surplus on phonecards and sneakers. A profound *Entzäuberung*, to use Max Weber's expression, seems to permeate the world, which no longer conceals dark and fascinating secrets. The white spots on the map are gone. *Tristes tropiques*: the formerly pure and

T. H. Eriksen (✉)
Department of Social Anthropology, University of Oslo, Oslo, Norway
e-mail: t.h.eriksen@sai.uio.no

© The Author(s) 2020
O. Hemer et al. (eds.), *Conviviality at the Crossroads*,
https://doi.org/10.1007/978-3-030-28979-9_3

uncontaminated *Naturvölken*, semi-naked savages, have lost their innocence and swapped the bamboo flute for a smartphone, and the tropics have become a dilapidated backyard of the rich world.

According to this interpretation of our time, which is by no means uncommon, 'exotic places' no longer exist; there are no longer peoples who are untouched by the white man, capitalism and mass consumption. Ostensibly exotic travel destinations are industrial products whose exotic character is carefully manufactured, where the cultural attractions are people who are paid by the tour operators to dress in old-fashioned clothes and perform traditional dances. One of cultural relativism's brave defenders, Clifford Geertz, expresses it thus in an essay from the mid-1980s: cultural differences 'will doubtless remain - the French will never eat salted butter. But the good old days of widow burning and cannibalism are gone forever' (Geertz 1986: 105).

Celebrating Impurity

A different interpretation of the cultural processes characteristic of the world today, would, rather than emphasising or even parodying commercialisation and homogenisation, instead look towards the many new cultural forms emerging at this time, brought about by the encounters, mixing, flows and paradoxes engendered by increased mobility, the spread of consumerism and, not least, instantaneous electronic communication. These processes create frictions, but also serve to forge new ties of mutual understanding and solidarity. Yet in order to overcome the fear of the other, she/he must be reconceptualised as a member of a shared humanity. A social ontology whereby difference is not a threat needs to replace ontologies assuming that sameness is a prerequisite for sharing. I therefore turn to elucidating such an alternative, taking my point of departure in the mainly Caribbean notion of the creole and eventually its European relative, superdiversity.

In academia, the preoccupation with cultural flows and mixing was to a great extent a fin-de-siècle trend, peaking in the 1990s with Homi Bhabha and third cultures, Arjun Appadurai's ethno- and technoscapes, Ulf Hannerz' encompassing concept of cultural creolisation, James Clifford's predicaments of culture, Stuart Hall and the voluminous cultural studies literature on hybridity (Bhabha 1994; Appadurai 1996; Hannerz 1987; Clifford 1988; Hall 1992). The early 1990s saw the destabilisation of geographic and spatial boundaries through large-scale political changes and technological innovations—the end of the Cold War and of apartheid, neoliberal deregulation, the spread of mobile phones and the Internet—and at the time, the creole societies of the New World were seen as important sites for the exploration of social and cultural dynamics in an era of accelerated transnational traffic in signs, things and people. It was also in this period that one of the most important books in the tradition of British Cultural Studies, namely Paul Gilroy's *The Black Atlantic* (Gilroy 1993), was published, a book that may be read retrospectively as a bittersweet celebration of creolisation.

The mixed cultures *par excellence* are those of the Caribbean and their cousins in the Indian Ocean. For years, they were held in low esteem by anthropologists—they were created by miscegenation and contamination, they had evolved under the bright floodlights of modernity, and were deemed mundane and unexciting under the strongly, if understated, exoticising gaze of anthropology. At the height of the double wave of postcolonial and postmodern sensibilities, from the publication of *Orientalism* (Said 1978) until the dust began to settle after the reflexive and deconstructive tour-de-force *Writing Culture* (Clifford and Marcus 1986), the Caribbean was briefly accorded a place in the sun, offering, as it did, a kind of cultural configuration that seemed to suit the new sensibilities well. But the Caribbean was also a key site for the development of a global, historical anthropology, given its enormously important role in the growth of the modern world. To mention but one prominent example, the late Sidney Mintz's research in three of the major language areas—the Spanish, the English and the French—is well known (Mintz 2010), not least for Mintz's insistence that what defined Creoledom was not cultural mixing as such, but the fundamental changes in social organisation resulting from uprootedness and displacement from subsistence communities to plantation societies (Mintz 1998). Mintz's book with Richard Price, *The Birth of Afro-American Culture* (Mintz and Price 1992 [1976]), argued against the previously common view, defended by the influential American cultural anthropologist Melville Herskovits (1941), that African retentions, or perhaps 'survivals', delineated and to no small extent defined Caribbean culture. Mintz and Price emphasised invention and creativity, resulting from the admittedly enforced confluence of diverse sources, highlighting the newness of creole culture and society (see also Eriksen 2003, 2019a, on which this section is partly based). Building on the comparative historical anthropology from Eric Wolf and Mintz, but enriching it with critical discourse analysis and a postcolonial approach, Michel-Rolph Trouillot

(1995) soon added new layers to the already vibrant discourse on power, cultural creativity and mixing with the Caribbean as a focal point. And there were others.[1] From having been a poor man's alternative to fieldwork in a truly exotic location, the region was suddenly fashionable. Ulf Hannerz himself did a stint of fieldwork in the Caribbean, publishing his findings in *Caymanian Politics* (Hannerz 1974). There was something about the Caribbean that seemed, towards the end of the twentieth century, to encapsulate, condense and highlight central features of a globalising world, providing productive templates for thinking about flows, boundaries, power, individualism and cultural creativity elsewhere—and I would add, from a normative perspective, forms of life where a shared identity was not based on similarity, but on complementarity and the basic implications of living in the same place.

The Caribbean and creole societies in general have more recently faded away from the attention of mainstream anthropology. Yet, it can and should be argued that at this particular juncture in history, it may be worthwhile to revisit the creole societies. Apart from its intrinsic intellectual interest, there are strong moral and political reasons for reviving interest in the creole world. At a time when nativism and divisive identity politics threaten people's autonomy and well-being across the planet, from autochthonism in Africa to militant Islamism in the Middle East and xenophobic ethnonationalism in Europe, an ontology of social being which does not privilege boundaries and origins over connectedness and impurity is deserving of sustained and systematic attention, as was recently argued in Cohen and Sheringham's (2016) anthropological travelogue about creolisation as a way of living together.

Cultural creolisation is a concept based on an analogy from linguistics. This discipline in turn took the term from a particular aspect of colonialism, namely the uprooting and displacement of large numbers of people in the plantation economies of certain colonies, such as Louisiana, Jamaica, Trinidad, Réunion and Mauritius. Both in the Caribbean basin and in the Indian Ocean, certain (or all) groups who contributed to this economy during slavery were described as creoles. Originally, a *criollo* meant a European (normally a Spaniard) born in the New World (as opposed to *peninsulares*); today, a similar usage is current in La Réunion, where everybody born in the island, regardless of skin colour, is seen as *créole*, as opposed to the *zoréoles* who were born in metropolitan France. In Trinidad, the term creole is sometimes used to designate all Trinidadians except those of Asian origin. In Suriname, a creole is a person of African origin, while in neighbouring French Guyana a creole is someone who has adopted a European way of life. In spite of the differences, there are resemblances between the various conceptualisations of the creole. Creoles are uprooted, they belong to the New World, and are contrasted with that which is old, deep and rooted.

What Is and What Isn't Creole

A question often raised by people unfamiliar with the varying uses of the term is: 'What is *really* a creole?' They may have encountered the term in connection with food or architecture from Louisiana, languages in the Caribbean or people in the Indian Ocean. The standard response is that whereas vernacular uses of the term creole vary, there exist definitions of creole languages in linguistics and of cultural creolisation in anthropology. There are nevertheless similarities, although there is no one-to-one relationship, between the ethnic groups described locally (emically) as creoles in particular societies, and the phenomena classified as creole or creolised in the academic literature.

A wider usage of the term creolisation, using it as a comparative concept rather than a localised and historically delineated one, was proposed by Ulf Hannerz in his seminal 1987 article 'The world in creolisation'. Uninterested in unadulterated authenticity, Hannerz was attracted to 'the cultures on display in market places, shanty towns, beer halls, night clubs, missionary book stores, railway waiting rooms, boarding schools, newspapers and television stations' (Hannerz 1987: 546). The use of the creolisation analogy in anthropology nevertheless leads to some conceptual difficulties that it shares with creole linguistics, as well as raising even trickier issues regarding the possibility to describe cultural worlds as enduring entities. If culture is never stable or homogeneous, this counter argument goes, then everything creolises, and the concept is worthless. To this view, one may retort that not everything flows, mixes and leads to innovation, and certainly not at the same speed or with the same consequences. In any case, cultural creolisation must be seen as a matter of degree if it is to be used as a comparative concept, as advocated by Hannerz.

With creole *societies*, similar issues may arise. Just as the social category of the creole has porous and negotiable boundaries, the category of the creole society eschews an unequivocal delineation, confirming Nietzsche's maxim to the effect that only concepts with no history could be defined accurately.

Perhaps we can do no better than invoke Wittgenstein's notion of family resemblances. Moreover, as noted by Virginia Dominguez in her historical study of creole society in Louisiana (Dominguez 1993), the term creole 'acquired diverse meanings' over the years—as it did elsewhere. However, there is a case for retaining a concept along the lines of the Black Atlantic as envisioned by Paul Gilroy—and I would add the smaller universe of the Black Indian Ocean.

Notwithstanding the extension of the term to include ethnically complex cities in Indonesia (Knörr 2014), Pacific islands (Willis 2002), contemporary cities in Western Europe (Cohen and Sheringham 2016; Eriksen 2019c) and urban culture in the Solomon Islands (Jourdan 2018), the semantic core of the concept of the creole society is arguably to be found in post-slavery societies from Louisiana to Brazil, from Curaçao to the Seychelles. Nigel Bolland (1998) states simply that 'the term "Creole", referring to people and cultures, means something or somebody derived from the Old World but developed in the New' (Bolland 1998: 1), but it needs to be narrowed further to be genuinely useful. A crucial aspect is the loss of original political and social organisation and the need to reinvent even some of the most basic social relations owing to enforced displacement, brutal oppression and social fragmentation. By this token, ironically, the first peoples designated as creoles, or *criollos*, fail to meet the requirements, namely Europeans born in Nueva España, about whom the term was used as early as the mid-sixteenth century. As noted by Stephan Palmié (2007: 68), *criollo* does not today denote mixing or displacement, but local identity, as in *comida criolla*, local style cooking. And as pointed out by Charles Stewart (2007: 5), echoing Nietzsche's insight, 'the term "creole" has itself creolised, which is what happens to all productive words with long histories'.

A creole society, in my understanding, is based wholly or partly on the mass displacement of people who were, often involuntarily, uprooted from their original home, shedding the main features of their social and political organisations on the way, brought into sustained contact with people from other linguistic and cultural areas and obliged to develop, in creative and improvisational ways, new social and cultural forms in the new land, drawing simultaneously on traditions from their respective places of origin and on impulses resulting from the encounter. It can be argued that this delineation of the creole society fits well with some of the super-diverse cities in contemporary Europe, which I will pay a visit later.

The quintessential creole societies share important historical features; syncretic religion was often developed, as well as creole languages, genealogies tend to be cognatic and shallow, and—most importantly—society had to be reconstructed from scratch upon arrival. The descendants of Indian indentured labourers in such societies as Trinidad and Mauritius were not creoles according to these criteria, and significantly did not develop creole languages, but instead became bilingual in Bhojpuri and the local French- or English-based creole. Although uprooted and displaced, Indian migrants could arrive as couples or even families and were able to reconstruct Indian villages in their new land, reproducing their systems of kinship and inheritance, religious practices and value systems—far from unchanged, yet representing a continuity that was unavailable to the slaves and their descendants. The latter were thrust into modernity before virtually anyone else, beginning just after the conquest and soon developing into a large-scale business in the next centuries, producing newness not by choice but by necessity, becoming individuals, in the Dumontian sense (Dumont 1992), on the proto-factory that was the plantation.

Key concepts for any examination of creole society are, accordingly, *displacement* and *invention*. Indeed, the word *crioulo* signified newness right from the beginning, referring as it did to a Portuguese born in the Cape Verde Islands (Lobban 1998), incidentally the first major hub for the transatlantic slave trade, later extended to include any European born in the New World and thus liberated, or alienated, from the thick webs of kinship and tradition. The miracle of creolisation, to use Trouillot's (1998) expression, consists in the extraordinary cultural creativity, ranging from music and language to religion and food, which almost inexplicably grew out of a centuries-long history of unspeakable suffering and oppression. Every creole society has its culinary specialties with multiple origins, often European, African and Asian at once; every creole society has its version of the blues, a musical style giving a poetic form to longing and deprivation; and every creole society has its local discourse over identity, the past versus the future, openness versus closure.

The creole social identity is typically flexible. In Mauritius, the census category of 'General Population' was in its time defined as including 'every person who does not appear, from his way of life, to belong to one or other of those three communities', referring to the Hindus, the Muslim and the Chinese. Apart from the small white, Franco-Mauritian minority, they are by popular consent considered creoles. While in Trinidad, anyone who does not identify as Indian can be considered a Creole, Mauritians with mixed

Indian origin may, 'depending on their way of life', see themselves and be seen by others as being Creoles (see also Eriksen 2007).

The creole identity does not sit easily with the concept of boundaries which has been a staple in anthropological studies of social identity since Barth (1969, see also Eriksen 2019b), until it began to be unravelled through the increasing use of concepts such as creolisation and hybridity, which helped making the instability, negotiations and destabilisation of boundaries legible. It is an open identity, a residual category, difficult to fit into models of plural societies consisting of a finite number of named ethnic or religious groups, although this has been tried by governments and scholars alike, with limited success, in places like Mauritius.

Creoledom is sprawling and internally diverse, but owing to the shared history and, in most cases, shared contemporary situation of political and economic vulnerability due to small scale, some broad societal themes recur and reverberate throughout the Creole world. One is the relationship to Africa and the African heritage. Just as the question of the 'African substratum' has been vigorously discussed among linguists writing about creole languages—which have been described as idioms with 'a European vocabulary and an African grammar' (Chaudenson 2010)—so is the question of African roots an issue which is persistently being addressed by Creole intellectuals, with a bearing on both inequality and difference.

Celebrated by that uniquely Creole religious movement, Rastafarianism, and romanticised by an earlier generation of Francophone Creole intellectuals, the founders of the *négritude* movement, Africanness is almost obliterated in the more recent *créolité* movement with its point of gravity in Martinique, originating in Édouard Glissant's work and developed further by Jean Bernabé, Raphaël Confiant and Patrick Chamoiseau in their programmatic *Éloge de la créolité* (Glissant 1981; Bernabé et al. 1989, see also Hemer forthcoming). Whereas the older *négritude* movement led by Léopold Sedar Senghor, Aimé Césaire and others invoked radical cultural difference—*L'émotion est nègre, comme la raison est hellène*, as Senghor phrased it (1939: 295), and while Marcus Garvey advocated a return to Africa and Rastamen mythologised Ethiopia while dismissing white culture as the epicentre of Babylon, the authors of *Éloge de la créolité* emphasised the present, not the past; enrichment rather than oppression, creativity instead of dependency. If *négritude* is an ideology of cultural difference and Rastafarianism a movement celebrating uniqueness while condemning historical oppression, *créolité* is surprisingly free of the hierarchies of colour and class, instead emphasising newness, mixing and openness as universal human virtues. In the eyes of its critics, this makes it politically toothless—a cultural product 'along the lines of the United Colors of Benetton' (Price and Price 1997: 27)—while its defenders would argue that créolité is a way forward beyond postcolonial inferiority complexes, victimhood and mental colonisation.

The créolité movement, with its emphasis on newness and creation, has a cheerful and worriless air about it which stands in stark contrast to the postcolonial dilemmas to which it must be related, not least with reference to the legacy of Fanon, later developed in Paul Gilroy's empirical work, developing the dilemma of 'double consciousness' (Gilroy 1993), a concept originally coined by W. E. B. DuBois, later writing about conviviality in ways that have inspired the present volume in a decisive way (Gilroy 2004); but it also represents a rupture with the past, a presentism and a post-racial egalitarianism which was bound to resonate with cosmopolitan sensibilities elsewhere. There seemed to be no identity politics based on boundary-maintenance, no missionary religion of conversion and blind adherence, no single recipe for living in the world of the créolistes. Mixing, diversity and cultural openness were the order of the day.

As I write these lines, the Hindu nationalist Narendra Modi has just been re-elected as prime minister of India; Jair Bolsonaro has opened up new parts of the Amazon for logging and livestock raising, at the detriment not only of the ecosystem, but also of traditional livelihoods and indigenous people; a die-hard Brexiteer has recently become the new prime minister of the UK, and a jihadist bomb wounds a dozen random bypassers in Lyon. Conviviality and the accompanying relaxed attitude towards diversity seem to be losing. At the same time, creole sensibilities, attitudes and forms of life are thriving in many parts of the world, not least in the very societies mentioned. India has always been a subcontinent based on difference rather than similarity, a region where diversity is seen as a resource rather than a shortcoming, where difference denotes complementarity rather than an insurmountable gulf. Britain, a mongrel, hybrid creature from the beginning, has for centuries been a crossroads happily absorbing outside influences, often re-exporting them after reshaping them. France has, since the 1789 revolution, represented republican values and citizenship as opposed to rooted ethnic identities, while Brazil was the cradle of the perhaps first theoretical analysis of cultural hybridity as an asset rather than an aberration, in Gilberto Freyre's celebration of cultural impurity (Freyre 1933). The cultural resources on which a creole social ontology depend are, in other words, abundantly available, even in some of the societies where the winds currently seem to be blowing from the opposite direction. And I still haven't even mentioned the United States.

Excursus on Super-Diversity as Creolisation's Offspring

Pondering the implications of increased international migration into many of the cities of the world, the anthropologist Steven Vertovec coined the term *super-diversity* some years ago (Vertovec 2007). He describes the current situation as a *diversification of diversity*. Whereas, in the post-war decades, diversity in many cities could credibly be described by using conventional classifying devices, it had by now exploded and bifurcated in so many directions as to turn contemporary cities into statisticians' nightmares and anthropologists' wet dreams. The term designates a new social pattern, where migrant mobility and cultural streams have accelerated and changed in character. Whereas people formerly came from a few places and went to a few places, Vertovec says, they now come from many places and go to many places. More than 300 languages are currently spoken in London, Vertovec points out, but as he has stressed time and again (e.g. Vertovec 2017), super-diversity is not merely about the proliferation of ethnic and cultural minorities. It also denotes the diversification of all kinds of identification. The people who live in a city like London might be refugees, EU labour migrants, the children of migrants from the colonies (such as the Windrush generation), or the beneficiaries of family reunification; they may also be students who stayed on after graduating, tourists who somehow forgot to leave after their visa expired, au-pairs from the Philippines or adventure-seekers from Denmark.

The 'diversification of diversity' described by Vertovec, Jan Blommaert (2013) and others suggests a situation where it cannot be taken for granted how people identify and on what grounds they define their social identity.

Gerd Baumann's (1996) study of Southall in south-west London was an early expression of the perspective later developed into the study of super-diversity. Notwithstanding the fascinating ethnographic details on everything from drinking habits to marriage practices, the main theoretical contribution of Baumann's *Contesting Culture* is his identification of two kinds of discourses about social identities: the *dominant* discourse and the *demotic* (popular) discourse. The dominant discourse, reproduced chiefly through the media and in the public sector, tends to equate ethnicity (often vaguely defined) with community and culture; one ethnic group comprises a community with a shared culture. Since dominant notions of 'communities' can be based on either language, religion or origin, any individual can belong to several communities, for example, a Gujerati one uniting Hindus and Muslims, a Muslim one uniting people of any linguistic or regional origin, and a subcontinental one uniting Indians and Pakistanis. Be this as it may, Baumann's ethnography shows that the demotic discourse is more flexible and complex, that it recognises the situational and multi-faceted character of individual identification and contests some of the terms in which the dominant discourse is framed: alternative identifications such as blackness (which may or may not include Asians), feminism, socialism, interfaith networks and multiculturalist ideologies of tolerance contribute to softening the ethnic boundaries, creating 'frontier zones' instead.

In spite of the lack of fit between the dominant discourse and popular representations, which is confirmed in the lack of a simple fit between class and ethnicity, many Southallians continue to reproduce the dominant discourse in certain situations. This could be seen as a simple effect of elite influence, but it is probably more accurate to say that since resources flow through ethnic or religious channels as defined by the authorities, people have no choice but to present their claims in ethnic or religious terms: 'The dominant discourse represents the hegemonic language within which Southallians must explain themselves and legitimate their claims' (Baumann 1996: 192). What Baumann shows is that the classificatory system characteristic of the modern, liberal state encourages the social construction of ostensibly stable, reified, ethnic or religious *communities* (he himself italicises this word throughout the book, as if it were a problematic and untranslatable 'native concept'). It is by virtue of their ethnic identity that minorities are discriminated against, but it is also chiefly through that identity that they can claim rights. They have no option other than classifying themselves as members of bounded groups, even if the facts on the ground indicate that they belong to lots of partly overlapping groups.

In a later study from Hackney in London by Susanne Wessendorf (2014), the super-diversity of this area often entails the creation of shifting public arenas and foci of group identification which are based not on ethnic or religious origins but on shared interests or activities. Whether this kind of fluid identification is sufficient to create a sense of belonging is an empirical question, of relevance not only to researchers but also to policymakers, civil servants and—primarily—the residents of these complex, often fluid residential areas. Issues typically taken up by politicians concern conditions for the integration of diverse populations into a shared urban fabric, while residents are concerned with the challenges of everyday life. The contrast between Wessendorf's Hackney and Baumann's Southall, divided not only by most of London but also by twenty years, shows a transition from complex diversity to super-diversity. Hackney contains far more nationalities than Southall—among other things, EU labour migrants live there—and a broader range of identity constructions. Group membership is less important in Wessendorf's analysis, and many of the residents have such mixed origins that their allegiance to the place is more significant than their provenance, which resembles rhizomes more than roots.

Wessendorf's Hackney comes across as a thoroughly creolised place, and interestingly, Paul Gilroy often mentions certain parts of London as exemplars in his depiction of conviviality as a mode of interaction following the loss of empire and formerly hegemonic assumptions about cultural and ethnic hierarchies. At the same time, one striking commonality between Southall in the early 1990s and Hackney in the early 2010s is the continued importance of the public/private boundary. Conviviality across ethnic and cultural differences is the norm in the public sphere, whereas informal social networks continue to follow these lines; less so in Hackney than in Southall, but religion, language and ethnicity continue to function as organising principles at the micro-level of social organisation.

There are echoes of the classic models of the plural society, described by Furnivall (1948) for south-east Asia and Smith (1965) for the West Indies, in this configuration: the discrete groups meet in the market place, but remain separate in other domains. There are nevertheless important differences. Notably, there is no ethnic division of labour, there are many institutions apart from the market where people intermingle, from schools to civil society associations, and in the case of Hackney, intermarriage is widespread. Public life in Hackney thus comes across as an instance of what Josephides and Hall (2014) speak of as everyday cosmopolitanism, fuelled by conviviality and founded in shared interests that are based on place rather than kinship. It satisfies the main criteria of creoledom I have suggested earlier, notably those of displacement, mixing and the need to create a society for which there is no pre-existing template.

In a remarkable forthcoming book *Contaminations & Ethnographic Fictions: Southern Crossings* (with chapter titles like 'Bengaluru boogie'), Oscar Hemer (forthcoming; see also Chapter 13 in this book) discusses creolisation and other forms of identity contamination from the perspectives I have outlined, but he adds a feature which may be disturbing to some readers, but which pushes the creolisation paradigm a step further. The book has an unnamed protagonist who resembles the author most of the time, but who changes his or her (or 'hir') gender en route, preferring the pronoun 'ze' as a way of denoting something indeterminate. Although he does not engage with the super-diversity literature, Hemer thereby adds a hitherto untheorised dimension to it. In Mauritius, a country proud of its tolerance for cultural diversity, anti-gay tendencies have recently surfaced, leading to public controversy and debate over the nature and scope of diversity. As many of my Mauritian friends and I agree, openness to diversity is not necessarily about multiculturalism or ethnic variation, but a set of values, or—as I would put it—a social ontology. Living with difference presupposes a convivial attitude towards not only Hindus, Jews, Christians, Muslims, New Age spiritualists and atheists, but also towards other aspects of personhood.

After this long excursus into urban Europe, super-diversity and the destabilisation of *all* aspects of human identity, we shall return to the creole worlds of the Indian Ocean, exploring briefly some of the implications of creoleness for social theory and the art of living with difference.

Creole Lessons from the Indian Ocean

The openness of creole cultural worlds, famously characterised by borrowing, mixing and a general disdain for purity and roots, has often been commented upon. As early as 1963, V. S. Naipaul wrote about the way in which men in Port of Spain, Trinidad, upon leaving the cinema after watching *Casablanca*, walked exactly like Humphrey Bogart. Soon afterwards, Naipaul would write, in a less humorous mode, about the mimic men of the Caribbean (Naipaul 1963, 1967).

My own entry into the creole world took place in 1986, as I was carrying out fieldwork in Mauritius (see Eriksen 2019b, on which this section is based, for a full account). I was immediately struck by the discrepancy between social categorisations and cultural flows: in this multi-ethnic island-state, cultural meaning travelled easily, zigzagging from ethnic group to ethnic group, while social boundaries remained relatively fixed (Eriksen 1988). I had half expected to encounter a series of postmodern, reflexive and ironic identities in this place where four major religions meet, more than fifteen ancestral languages are revered and the inhabitants have origins in all three continents of the Old World. Instead, what met me was a concern bordering on an obsession with social classification and subclassification, where Mauritians consistently read and interpreted social life and politics through an ethnic lens. At the same time, cultural meaning, practices and values flowed and mixed, and whether they were Hindu or Creole, Franco-Mauritian or Sino-Mauritian, people were integrated into the same educational, occupational and media worlds. Only later would I obtain a vocabulary for talking about this discrepancy whereby group boundaries appeared to be fixed and crisp, while symbolic meaning was fluid—groups were discontinuous, while meaning was continuous, groups were bounded in a digital way whereas meaning was distributed in an analogue way. Fredrik Barth's brash admonition to neglect 'the cultural stuff' while studying ethnic relations (Barth 1969) did not help. Only later did it occur to me that my work in Mauritius had all been about boundaries and non-boundaries. I had studied networks, interethnic relations, attempts to lift identification from the communal to the republican level, stereotypes, genealogies and marriage patterns, and it was all about the reproduction, subversion, relativity, destabilisation and reinforcement of boundaries aimed to create order. Perhaps more than anything else, the material from Mauritius was about the relationship between the Creole and the non-Creole. Creoles, in the Mauritian context, are of African and Malagasy origin, while the non-Creoles are mainly of South Asian origin. The Creoles, somehow, didn't fit in; they did not come across as corporate groups with clear criteria for membership and crisp boundaries.

Mauritius, an island-state in the Indian Ocean with no indigenous population, is one of the most self-consciously multiculturalist societies in the world (Eriksen 1998). Its population came from various parts of India, continental Africa and Madagascar, China and France, and the official ideology unanimously presents ethnic and cultural diversity as a positive quality of Mauritian society. 'We are the tomato of the Indian Ocean', a publicity stunt once had it; 'we go with everything'. At major public ceremonies, it is the rule rather than the exception that several cultural traditions are presented through song and dance numbers, recitals of poetry or similar. Hindu, Catholic, Muslim and Buddhist religious holidays are acknowledged, and Mauritians sometimes talk of their society as *une société arc-en-ciel*, a rainbow society.

In spite of the admirable spirit of compromise and mutual recognition pervading Mauritian society, it easily lends itself to exemplifying three contradictions, or paradoxes, that I would like to call attention to, all of which have a bearing on boundaries through the relationship between the symbolic and the social, and show how the Creole identity sits uneasily with the 'ethnic groups and boundaries' paradigm.

First, multiculturalism in the public sphere, which I here take to mean the active encouragement of expressions of cultural diversity, does not necessarily encourage mixing and impurity. The celebration of cultural diversity often conflicts with individual liberties, notably the freedom not to belong to an ethnic community or to mix influences from different cultural streams. The Mauritian ideology can thus, slightly facetiously, be described as apartheid with a friendly face. Of course, there are other voices or alternative scripts, which challenge the rainbow society by mixing the colours. A much-loved popular musical group called *Grup Latanier* was formed by the Indo-Mauritian brothers Ram Joganah and Nitish Joganah in the heady time of cultural radicalism around 1980 and has been active since then. The group mostly play séga songs, a genre associated with the Creoles, but often incorporate Indian instruments such as tablas, performing engaged songs based on a class analysis rather than a perspective of Mauritian society as being mainly ethnically diverse.

There are, moreover, many Mauritians who deny the validity of ethnic categorisations. They see culture as a shared resource, something belonging to humanity and not to be monopolised by communities or interest groups. Indeed, an old friend of the Joganah brothers, namely, the linguist, playwright and poet Dev Virahsawmy (b. 1942), in his youth argued in favour of mixing (or creolising) the religious practices in Mauritius in order to strengthen the sense of community and unity (Eriksen 1988). This did not go down well in the wider public. Years later, commenting on another, related matter, the then Archbishop of the Mascareignes, Mgr Jean Margéot, pronounced that 'we should keep the colours of the rainbow distinct for it to remain beautiful', signalling support for multicultural coexistence but not for its transformation into generalised creolité.

The metaphor of the fruit salad is also sometimes used in describing Mauritius in positive terms. In practice, this entails that intermarriage is not encouraged in public or by politicians. While cultural mixing is often uncontroversial—even if what is usually celebrated is the purity of ethnic cultural expressions—intermarriage, which threatens to break up the very structure of the multi-ethnic society, is not. Few parents are particularly enthusiastic about the prospect of their son or daughter marrying someone from another community (Creoles often are an exception here). Intermarriage does take place not infrequently in Mauritius, and it can naturally work well for all parties, including the in-laws, but it is not part of the Mauritian social contract, where your community membership to no small extent defines who you are. Interestingly, the children of mixed marriages are often categorised as Creoles, even if neither of their parents identified as one. For example, the daughter of a Hindu father and a Chinese mother might be considered by others, and consider themselves, as Creole.

The creole social identity is typically flexible, and Creoles are not an ethnic group like the others. In Mauritius, the census category of 'General Population' was in its time defined as including 'every person who does not appear, from his way of life, to belong to one or other of those three communities'—the Hindu, Muslim and Chinese. Apart from the small white, Franco-Mauritian minority, they are often considered creoles. While in Trinidad, anyone who does not identify as Indian can be considered a Creole, Mauritians with mixed Indian origin may, 'depending on their way of life', see themselves and be seen by others as being Creoles (see also Eriksen 2007).

Creole identities do not sit easily with the concept of boundaries which has been a staple in anthropological studies of social identity since Barth (1969), until it began to be unravelled through the increasing use of concepts such as creolisation and hybridity, which helped making the instability, negotiations and destabilisation of boundaries legible. It is an open identity, a residual category, difficult to fit into models of plural societies and bounded ethnic groups, although this has been tried by governments and scholars alike, with limited success, in places like Mauritius.

Identity politics, including nationalism, communalism, populism and Islamism, can be a reaction to creolisation and the blurring of boundaries, or it can mirror another group's identity politics. The identity politics of the state is frequently one of control and cohesion, while that of minorities is often a reaction against perceived exclusion. The rise of militant Islamism and right-wing nativism must at least partly be understood against this backdrop: both are ideologies of the disgruntled, the marginalised, the ostensible losers of globalisation. In order to come to terms with the rise of virulent identity politics in Europe and elsewhere, therefore, it is necessary to understand not only their cultural and political expressions, but its social roots in inequality and disenfranchisement. Creolisation offers a minimal recipe for living together in a diverse, shifting, unpredictable world, and it is a viable template for conviviality. Yet it does not solve the problems of inequality, perceived or real, giving rise to militant identity politics.

In other words, creolisation can be a solution to many of the practical boundary problems arising in a world with increased mobility, mixing both through cultural flows and procreation, and more intensive intergroup encounters, but it does not solve every problem. An attitude based on creolisation as an ideal strives to make origins irrelevant and rejects intergroup boundaries, but understates, or diverts attention from, class and existing ethnic or racial hierarchies. This, among other things, is why widespread cultural mixing is rejected by so many people in the world today; it dilutes their corporate symbolic capital, just as clan exogamy might in kinship-based societies. But there is another reason as well, namely that continuity with the past is often existentially important to human well-being, and it can only be achieved by tracing your lifeworld back in time. In this overheated world of mobility, withdrawals, frictions and cultural symbiosis, therefore, concerns with roots and traditions are the powerful (and sometimes dangerous) dialectical negation of precisely these processes. A normative version of this argument, trying to keep the politics out of identity, as it were, is made by Claudio Magris (1989) in his evocative and appropriately meandering essay on the cultural and political history of the Danube, where he points out that a fascist is not someone who has intimate friends, who loves his *Heimat*, the local folk music, his country's nineteenth-century romantic poets and so on, but someone who is incapable of seeing others, who love *their* home village, folk music and so on, as equals. In this way, we may see the entire cultural production of humanity as a common good, but not one which is available to everyone at any time. Cultural meaning tends to be caught up by, and entangled with, social processes involving power, boundaries, hierarchies and indeed existential issues to do with personal identity. This is why Creoles often are faced with no pragmatically feasible alternative to reinventing themselves as an ethnic group. Social identity always has a political dimension and an existential or affective one. The alternative to portraying oneself as an ethnic group is to insist that human beings have boots and not roots or to show that the rootedness of people in the past tends to take a rhizomatic form, just as the case is with those uprooted, mixed, hybrid peoples typically spoken of as creoles. In this world, we are all creoles, and embracing the rhizomatic contaminations of our past and present may serve as an antidote to divisive politics of identity. In any case, there is little doubt that the major ideological divide in today's world can be drawn between rootedness and mobility, purity and mixing—or, indeed, ethnic identity and creole identity.

Note

1. See Stewart (2007) and Cohen and Toninato (2009) for overviews of approaches to social and cultural creolisation, Knörr and Trajano Filho (2018) for a comparison between linguistic and cultural creolisation.

References

Appadurai, A. 1996. *Modernity at Large*. Minneapolis, MN: University of Minnesota Press.
Barth, F. 1969. "Introduction." In *Ethnic Groups and Boundaries: The Social Organization of Culture Difference*, edited by F. Barth, 9–37. Oslo: Universitetsforlaget.
Baumann, G. 1996. *Contesting Culture: Discourses of Identity in Multi-ethnic London*. Cambridge: Cambridge University Press.
Bernabé, J., P. Chamoiseau, and R. Confiant. 1989. *Éloge de la créolité*. Paris: Gallimard.
Bhabha, H. 1994. *The Location of Culture*. London: Routledge.
Blommaert, J. 2013. *Ethnography, Superdiversity and Linguistic Landscapes: Chronicles of Complexity*. Bristol: Multilingual Matters.
Bolland, O. N. 1998. "Creolisation and Creole Societies: A Cultural Nationalist View of Caribbean Social History." *Caribbean Quarterly* 44 (1/2): 1–32.
Chaudenson, R. 2010. *La genèse des créoles de l'océan Indien*. Paris: L'Harmattan.
Clifford, J. 1988. *The Predicament of Culture: Twentieth-Century Ethnography, Literature, and Art*. Boston, MA: Harvard University Press.
Clifford, J., and G. Marcus, eds. 1986. *Writing Culture: The Poetics and Politics of Ethnography*. Berkeley: University of California Press.
Cohen, R., and O. Sheringham. 2016. *Encountering Difference*. Cambridge: Polity Press.
Cohen, R., and P. Toninato, eds. 2009. *The Creolization Reader*. Abington, PA: Routledge.
Dominguez, V. 1993. *White by Definition: Social Classification in Creole Louisiana*. New Brunswick, NJ: Rutgers University Press.
Dumont, L. 1992. *Essays on Individualism*. Chicago: University of Chicago Press.
Eriksen, T. H. 1988. Communicating Cultural Identity and Difference: Ethnicity and Nationalism in Mauritius. Occasional Papers No. 16. Oslo: Department of Social Anthropology.
Eriksen, T. H. 1998. Common Denominators: Ethnicity and the Politics of Compromise in Mauritius. Oxford: Berg.
Eriksen, T. H. 2003. "Creolisation and Creativity." *Global Networks* 3 (3): 223–237.

Eriksen, T. H. 2007. "Creolization in Anthropological Theory and in Mauritius." In *Creolization: History, Ethnography, Theory*, edited by C. Stewart, 153–177. Walnut Creek, CA: Left Coast Press.
Eriksen, T. H. 2019a. "Between Inequality and Difference: The Creole World in the Twenty-First Century." *Global Networks* 19 (1): 3–20.
Eriksen, T. H. 2019b. "Beyond a Boundary: Flows and Mixing in the Creole World." In *Ethnic Groups and Boundaries Today: A Legacy of Fifty Years*, edited by T. H. Eriksen and M. Jakoubek, 133–151. London: Routledge.
Eriksen, T. H. 2019c. "The Tragedy of the Cultural Commons: Cultural Crossroads and the Paradoxes of Identity." In *The Handbook of Diasporas, Media, and Culture*, edited by J. Retis and R. Tsagarousianou, 49–61. New York: Wiley.
Freyre, G. 1946 [1933]. *The Masters and the Slaves: A Study in the Development of Brazilian Civilization* (Casa Grande & Senzala). New York: Knopf.
Furnivall, J. S. 1948. *Colonial Policy and Practice: A Comparative Study of Burma and Netherlands India*. Cambridge: Cambridge University Press.
Geertz, C. 1986. "The Uses of Diversity." *Michigan Quarterly Review* 25 (1): 105–123.
Gilroy, P. 1993. *The Black Atlantic: Modernity and Double Consciousness*. Cambridge, MA: Harvard University Press.
Gilroy, P. 2004. *After Empire: Melancholia or Convivial Culture?* London: Routledge.
Glissant, E. 1981. *Le discours antillais*. Paris: Seuil.
Hall, S. 1992. "The Question of Cultural Identity." In *Modernity and Its Futures*, edited by S. Hall, D. Held, and A. McGrew, 274–316. Cambridge: Polity Press.
Hannerz, U. 1974. *Caymanian Politics: Structure and Style in a Changing Island Society*. Stockholm Studies in Social Anthropology, 1. Stockholm: Department of Social Anthropology.
Hannerz, U. 1987. "The World in Creolization." *Africa* 57 (4): 546–559.
Hemer, O. Forthcoming. *Contaminations & Ethnographic Fictions: Southern Crossings*. Houndmills and Basingstoke: Palgrave Macmillan.
Herskovits, M. 1941. *The Myth of the Negro Past*. Boston, MA: Beacon Press.
Josephides, L., and A. Hall, eds. 2014. *We the Cosmopolitans: Moral and Existential Conditions of Being Human*. Oxford: Berghahn.
Jourdan, C. 2018. "The Shades of Legitimacy of Solomon Islands Pijin." In *Creolization and Pidginization in Contexts of Postcolonial Diversity*, edited by J. Knörr and W. Trajano Filho, 78–95. Leiden: Brill.
Knörr, J. 2014. *Creole Identity in Postcolonial Indonesia*. Oxford: Berghahn.
Knörr, J., and W. Trajano Filho, eds. 2018. *Creolization and Pidginization in Contexts of Postcolonial Diversity*. Leiden: Brill.
Lobban, R. A. 1998. *Cape Verde: Crioulo Colony to Independent Nation*. Boulder, CO: Westview.
Magris, C. 1989. *Danube*. New York: Farrar, Strauss and Giroux.

Mintz, S. W. 1998. "The Localization of Antropological Practice: From Area Studies to Transnationalism." *Critique of Anthropology* 18 (2): 117–133.
Mintz, S. W. 2010. *Three Ancient Colonies: Themes and Variations*. Cambridge, MA: Harvard University Press.
Mintz, S. W., and R. Price. 1992 [1976]. *The Birth of African-American Culture*. Boston, MA: Beacon Press.
Naipaul, V. S. 1963. *The Middle Passage*. London: Andre Deutsch.
Naipaul, V. S. 1967. *The Mimic Men*. London: Andre Deutsch.
Palmié, S. 2007. "The 'C-Word' Again: From Colonial to Postcolonial Semantics." In *Creolization: History, Ethnography, Theory*, edited by C. Stewart, 66–83. Walnut Creek, CA: Left Coast Press.
Price, R., and S. Price. 1997. "Shadowboxing in the Mangrove." *Cultural Anthropology* 12 (1): 3–36.
Said, E. 1978. *Orientalism*. New York: Pantheon.
Senghor, L. S. 1939. "Ce que l'homme noir apporte." In *L'homme de couleur*, edited by S.E le Cardinal Verdier et al., 291–313. Paris: Plon.
Smith, M. G. 1965. *The Plural Society of the British West Indies*. London: Sangster's.
Stewart, C., ed. 2007. *Creolization: History, Ethnography, Theory*. Walnut Creek, CA: Left Coast Press.
Trouillot, M.-R. 1995. *Silencing the Past: Power and the Production of History*. Boston, MA: Beacon Press.
Trouillot, M.-R. 1998. "Culture on the Edges: Creolization in the Plantation Context." *Plantation Society in the Americas* 5 (1): 8–28.
Vertovec, S. 2007. "Super-Diversity and Its Implications." *Ethnic and Racial Studies* 30 (6): 1024–1054.
Vertovec, S. 2017. "Talking Around Super-Diversity." *Ethnic and Racial Studies* 42 (1): 125–139. https://doi.org/10.1080/01419870.2017.1406128.
Wessendorf, S. 2014. *Commonplace Diversity: Social Relations in a Super-Diverse Context*. London: Palgrave.
Willis, D., ed. 2002. *The Age of Creolization in the Pacific: In Search of Emerging Cultures and Shared Values in the Japan-America Borderlands*. Hiroshima: Keisuisha.

Open Access This chapter is licensed under the terms of the Creative Commons Attribution 4.0 International License (http://creativecommons.org/licenses/by/4.0/), which permits use, sharing, adaptation, distribution and reproduction in any medium or format, as long as you give appropriate credit to the original author(s) and the source, provide a link to the Creative Commons license and indicate if changes were made.

The images or other third party material in this chapter are included in the chapter's Creative Commons license, unless indicated otherwise in a credit line to the material. If material is not included in the chapter's Creative Commons license and your intended use is not permitted by statutory regulation or exceeds the permitted use, you will need to obtain permission directly from the copyright holder.

CHAPTER 4

Schleiermacher's *Geselligkeit*, Henriette Herz, and the 'Convivial Turn'

Ulrike Wagner

Across disciplines and particularly in the field of migration studies, it has become quite popular in recent years to examine constellations of human togetherness and cohabitation through the prism of conviviality. The "convivial turn" grew out of the shortcomings critics identified in conceptualisations of terms such as cosmopolitism, multiculturalism or diversity, and many begun to regard the semantics of conviviality and its theoretical capaciousness as a productive complement or alternative to the normative and essentialist categories associated with concepts like cosmopolitanism.[1] While the primary focus of the contributions collected in this volume is centered on the role of conviviality with regard to contemporary themes and questions, I take a look back and investigate a prominent late eighteenth-century conception and use of the term. Inspired by his regular visits to social gatherings organised by Henriette Herz (1764–1847), one of Berlin's most prominent salonière at that time, the German philosopher and theologian Friedrich Daniel Schleiermacher (1768–1834) contributed

U. Wagner (✉)
Bard College Berlin, Berlin, Germany
e-mail: u.wagner@berlin.bard.edu

with his "Versuch einer Theorie des geselligen Betragens" ["Toward a Theory of Sociable Conduct"] (1799) a principal theory of conviviality that bears interesting and unexplored resemblances to today's conceptions.[2]

I bring Schleiermacher's essay into dialogue with Magdalena Nowicka's and Tilmann Heil's "On the analytic and normative dimensions of conviviality and cosmopolitanism", and by working out common concerns of an eighteenth- and a twenty-first-century theorisation of conviviality, I seek to bring into view a shared historical and cross-disciplinary aspect of this term that has sparked such contested critical debates.[3] Both texts, I argue, develop a non-teleological understanding of conviviality that is productive not only for research in contemporary migration studies but also for developing a more nuanced perspective on a unique historical moment in late eighteenth-century Berlin when gatherings at Jewish homes instigated crossings of religious boundaries, social hierarchies and gender roles.

More specifically, I suggest that this dual theoretical focus on the past and present helps unlock facets of Henriette Herz' writings that otherwise would be overlooked or blended into overarching narratives of acculturation and conversion. Looked at through the lens of Schleiermacher's definition of conviviality as underwritten by "Zwecklosigkeit" [lack of purpose] and Nowicka's "analytic conviviality", Herz' social engagements appear as brief sparks, sometimes full of potential to unsettle social relations or as moments of shock and surprise that open unexpected possibilities or inspire her to think what had seemed unthinkable.

This brief period when women like Henriette Herz opened their houses to highly diverse groups of people would have been unthinkable without the rise of the Haskalah (from the Hebrew *sekhel*, "reason", or "intellect")[4] or Jewish Enlightenment. With the philosopher Moses Mendelssohn (1729–1786) at the center, this time witnessed a broad range of new encounters between Jewish and German culture, and Berlin was the place where the Maskilim, as enlightened Jews referred to each other, instigated a new period in the history of Judaism. Inspired by the tenets of the Enlightenment, and its propagation of reason and religious tolerance, orthodox positions and the rabbinical elite's monopoly on the exegesis of the Torah came under attack. Publications such as Mendelssohn's translation of the Pentateuch "brought the scared language of the synagogue out into the open air of an enlightened public sphere", propagating that being observant and committed to the Jewish faith may coexist with being a secular citizen of the state.[5] Mendelssohn and his generation used the contemporary language of reason, humanism, and tolerance to fight discrimination and exclusion of Berlin's Jewish community from public life and reinterpreted the foundations of their faith through the lens of the enlightened discourse they found themselves inhabiting and engaging. Gotthold Ephraim Lessing (1729–1781), famously, created with his drama *Nathan der Weise* [Nathan the Wise] (1779) a lasting memorial for Mendelssohn's commitment to the fostering of a trans-confessional dialogue and the overcoming of religious differences.

Besides journals and book publications, venues of sociability such as bookshops, reading societies, private homes, and various clubs powered the dissemination of these intellectuals' revolutionary take on the theme of Jewish emancipation and religious renewal, and the convivial activities organised by Jewish women played thereby a key role: Rahel Levin Varnhagen (1771–1833), Dorothea Mendelssohn Veit Schlegel (1764–1839), Sarah Itzig (1761–1854), and Henriette Herz, many of them the wives, sisters, and daughters of the Maskilim, opened their houses for formal and informal social gatherings, bringing together people from various social and cultural backgrounds and creating sites crucial for the exchange and proliferation of enlightened ideas: "Men and women, Jews and Christians, noblemen and commoners, professors, poets, scientists and merchants mingled in private houses to discuss art, politics, literature and the sciences, but also to cultivate friendships and love affairs. Jewish women were central to the creation of this new milieu (…)".[6] Clark's acknowledgement of these private social gatherings as important vehicles for the Haskalah's formation and direction stands out as an exception in the scholarly literature focused on enlightened Judaism.

In *The Jewish Enlightenment*, Feiner turns to Rahel Varnhagen as an example of the group of alienated "young Jews, who aspired to be accepted by the high bourgeois society and break all ties to their Jewish origins".[7] He introduces the private get-togethers at Henriette Herz' and Dorothea Mendelssohn's homes as social hubs for Berlin's Romantic scene with Schleiermacher and the brothers August and Friedrich Schlegel at the centre but not as nodal points of the Haskalah.[8] In Moshe's *Haskalah and Beyond: The Reception of Hebrew Enlightenment and the Emergence of Haskalah Judaism* these women are not mentioned at all.[9] As Schulte has pointed out, women are not recognised as enlightened Jewesses, as Maskila or, in the plural, as Maskilot whose private investment in conviviality is considered as an articulation of and contribution to the Haskalah movement. To date, most of the research on the writings and social activities of Jewish women happens in the field of *Germanistik* and in studies of Romanticism.[10]

While the reasons for this lack of recognition of the Haskalah's female members are complex, the above quote from Feiner's study points to the main cause: Whatever networks and influences Henriette Herz, Rahel Varnhagen, and other Jewish women with backgrounds and interests similar to theirs might have had at the time, in retrospect their activities are interpreted as having paved a gradual road towards assimilation, culminating in baptism and conversion.[11] In "A Dream of Living Together: Jewish Women in Berlin Around 1800", Hahn similarly resumes:

> Sooner or later, all the women we will be considering here took the same course, with the exception of the Itzig daughters. It is readily apparent under which pressure Jewish upper-middle class society stood, not merely to acculturate but also to leave behind their distinctive history, culture, and faith. The opening of Jewish houses as an attempt at a common life between Christians and Jews, the rich social life that these women developed, remains—in retrospect—an episode.[12]

To be sure, there is no dispute regarding the turns many of these women's lives took, following this brief yet vibrant period of trans-confessional sociality. But rather than considering their contributions to the Haskalah teleologically, meaning always with an eye towards subsequent conversions or even, as some critics have it, as early indications of an always already malformed relationship between German and Jewish culture, foreshadowing the terrors of the mid-twentieth century, I suggest analysing the experiences they record in letters, billets, and autobiographical writings on their own terms and as expressions of enlightenment thinking in practice.[13]

In the critical literature on Berlin's Jewish salons, the Herz couple's home occupies a distinct status because both partners organised social gatherings for different circles of people in adjacent rooms of the house, and because their so-called "Doppelsalon" is considered the period's original one.[14] Like her father Benjamin de Lemos (1711–1789), her husband Marcus Herz (1747–1803) was a maskil and a doctor. He was Moses Mendelssohn's student and friend and studied with Immanuel Kant in Königsberg before coming to Berlin. By the time his significantly younger wife Henriette joined him in his social activities, his home was already a reputable address for researchers and intellectuals interested in hearing the host lecture on physics and medicine. Friedrich Wilhelms University had not yet been founded, and meetings such as those at Marcus Herz' home were important venues for the proliferation and exchange over research proceedings. This cursory glance at the format of these meetings and the topics covered should suffice for calling into question the adequacy of labelling the gatherings at the Herz house "salon" or even "Doppelsalon" ["double salon"].

The term raises high-flown associations yet is misleading when considering the concrete historical situation of Berlin's Jewish community and of women especially. Their areas of interaction and spheres of influence were by no means comparable to those of, say, French aristocratic women or upper middle-class English women.[15] Moreover, the hosts never actually used the term themselves to refer to their activities. Reviewing letters, billets, private correspondences, and biographical memories, Lund finds around five different names the two hosts and their guests used to refer to social events and "salon" is not one of them.[16] In the light of such findings, the contributors to the recently published volume *Die Kommunikations-, Wissens- und Handlungsräume der Henriette Herz (1764–1847)* suggest replacing the term by more descriptive ones such as "convivial formations".[17]

This emphasis the latest criticism places on the openness and informal nature of the social events the Herzens hosted or attended resonates with the experiences Henriette's close friend Schleiermacher had during his visits at her house. His essay "Toward a Theory of Sociable Conduct" grew out of his regular visits between 1797 and 1802.[18] The fragment was published anonymously in the February issue of the *Berlinisches Archiv der Zeit und ihres Geschmacks* in 1799, and he had planned to complete and publish his text in a future issue yet that never happened. The fragment we have today theorises conviviality or sociability—I use both terms here as synonymous translations of the German "Geselligkeit"—from two vantage points. While the essay's first section develops a set of general assumptions of "freie Geselligkeit" ["free sociability"], the second and longer part details formats and laws for free social interaction in "wirkliche[n] Gesellschaften" (260) ["specific and actual societies", 25]. The rules and regulations for convivial interaction articulated here provide interesting insights into the dynamics of the social world of his time in Berlin, yet for the purpose of unlocking moments of fresh and unconventional thinking in Henriette Herz' writing and for drawing out points of connection between Schleiermacher and contemporary debates on conviviality, the essay's first part is a more productive point of reference.

The essay's opening paragraphs untether conviviality from any purposes:

> One of the first and noblest needs insisted upon by all cultured persons is a free sociability that is neither tied to nor determined by any external purpose. Whoever is merely tossed to and fro between the cares of domestic life and the affairs of public life approaches the higher aim of human existence even more slowly the more faithfully one repeats this path. A profession banishes the activity of the mind to a narrow sphere; no matter how noble and praiseworthy it may be, its effect and outlook on the world will always be tied to a single point of view. The highest and most complex of professions, therefore, like the simplest and lowest, produce one-sidedness and limitation. Domestic life places us in contact with only a few individuals and always with the same ones. (20)[19]

According to Schleiermacher, the liberating potential of conviviality can unfold only when individuals detach themselves mentally from their professional and domestic responsibilities and objectives. Such acts of distancing oneself are crucial because regardless of how reputable and intellectually stimulating one's engagements might seem, they are per definition specialised and thereby constrict and limit the workings of the mind. Even activities such as dancing inhibit rather than nurture conviviality in Schleiermacher's eyes because a dancer's attention is primarily focused on one person rather than the group (see 259). Similarly, lectures or theatre performances do not actually promote free conviviality but rather various forms of "gebundene Geselligkeit" (258) ["constrained sociality"]. Because such events are underwritten by pedagogical, moral or other objectives and are directed at forming and addressing the audience in one way or another, they countermand free conviviality and fail setting in motion a "frei[es] Spiel" (254) ["free play", 21] of their mental powers. It is this idea of creating a convivial space conducive to setting in motion a free play of the participants' trains of thinking that constitutes one of the most forward-looking and productive aspects of Schleiermacher's theory.

Why, however, one might ask, is a detachment of conviviality from any confines and normative restrictions of such importance to Schleiermacher? A quick glance at his major work *Über die Religion. Reden an die Gebildeten unter ihren Verächtern* [On Religion. Speeches to Its Cultured Despisers] (1799) illustrates that his vision of creating a free space of convivial interaction grows out of his understanding of how humans generate and proliferate social norms and hierarchies. He was working on *Über die Religion* while writing the conviviality essay, and both texts suggest that our religious, cultural, and political norms and values are formed through social contact and communication.[20] It is therefore logical for him to assume that humans are most likely to try and feel themselves into and comprehend someone else's modes of thinking in a non-constrictive environment. We know from many of his other publications that the experiences he had during his frequent visits to Jewish homes shaped this belief in the transformative power of conviviality.[21] Most important in this context were his regular conversations with Henriette Herz who also read and discussed his work with him. Hopfner terms her activities a "geistige Undercover-Tätigkeit" ["intellectual undercover job"] common to women of her age.[22] The thoughts she shared with him were foundational to his understanding that conviviality should be geared towards unsettling familiar categories formed by one's professional or domestic obligations, and by creating a

> (…) condition (…) where the sphere of an individual is present in such a way that it is intersected by the spheres of others as diversely as possible and where one's own outer limits affords one the view into a different and alien world. In this manner, one can come to know all the appearances of humanity little by little, and even the most alien persons and relations can grow familiar and become, as it were, neighbors. This task is accomplished through the free association of rational and mutually-cultivating persons. (20–21)[23]

A condition free of pedagogy, prescribed themes and moral ends, Schleiermacher suggests, builds an atmosphere conducive to forming and being formed and reformed by others in a free-flowing exchange of ideas. He refers to the purpose of such processes of reciprocal formation as a moral one: "Dies ist der sittliche Zweck der freien Geselligkeit" (254) ["This is the moral end of free sociability", 21]. It is interesting, however, how he further determines the characteristics of this moral purpose, resulting from a situation of "Wechselwirkung" (259) ["reciprocal action", 25]: What one might expect here is a humanist vision of harmonious understanding, a situation where members of diverse cultural and societal backgrounds not only tolerate their differences but feel emotionally and intellectually connected, viewing themselves as equal members of a global community. But instead of formulating such a pluralistic ideal of sociality, he shifts the focus to the *activity* of conviviality as such:

> If we now look at the purpose that is to be attained under this form of thoroughgoing reciprocity, we notice that the predicate of freedom implies that there should be no mention of a single and determinate purpose in free sociality since this conditions and limits the activity in conformity to material and objective rules. There should be no particular action executed communally, no product brought about jointly, nor any judgment methodically acquired. The purpose of society is not at all to be conceived as lying outside it. The action of each individual should be aimed at the activity of the others, and the activity of individuals should be their influence on the others. However, nothing else can be affected in a free being except that it is thereby stimulated to its own activity and that the activity is given an object. By virtue of what was said above, this object in turn can be nothing other than the activity of one invited to participate in society. It can, therefore, be conceived as nothing other than the free play of thoughts and feelings whereby all members mutually stimulate and enliven each other. The reciprocal action accordingly is self-constrained and complete. The form as well as the purpose of sociable activity is contained in the concept of reciprocal action and this action constitutes the entire essence of society. (24–25)[24]

Any further determination of the purpose of convivial interaction would imply corseting social activities into a set of rules, geared towards prescribed outcomes, and the objective of the participants' socialising would lie in gaining insights jointly and in steering their energies towards communally executed projects. According to Schleiermacher, however, conviviality is free only when it is based on a structure of "Wechselwirkung", of reciprocity. All members ought to stimulate and energise one another, and this constellation of active moments of "Wechselwirkung" is the *form* as well as the *purpose* of conviviality. His untethering of the term from normative constraints and his emphasis on reciprocal action as the format and objective of social interaction provides contact points for current theorisations of conviviality as well as a productive lens for assessing Henriette Herz' writings.

In their lecture "On the analytic and normative dimensions of conviviality and cosmopolitanism", Nowicka and Heil define conviviality as an "analytic term", and their definition bears conceptual resemblances to Schleiermacher's theory. With his claim that the gearing of social behaviour towards a "particular action" or "product" that ought to be "executed communally" (24) disrupts the freedom of sociability, he highlights a discrepancy between convivial situations and the normative criteria they are measured up against; this divergence also takes centre stage in the essay by Nowicka and Heil.[25] Reviewing critical research on conviviality such as Paul Gilroy's *After Empire: Melancholia or Convivial Culture?*, the two authors draw attention to the term's ties to associations such as "ethnic plurality" that contain "a normative and often idealistic aspiration for peaceful togetherness".[26] The predicament of assessing conviviality within such vertical frameworks is that investigations are always focused on tensions between concrete practices of sociability on the one hand and the question to what degree they approximate overarching criteria of togetherness and communication on the other. Nowicka and Heil, by contrast, advocate for an analysis of conviviality premised on the assumption that "the normative is the empirical". Rather than asking to what extent social interactions approximate ideals of ethnic pluralism or further a cosmopolitan mindset, they ask how "minimal sociality [is] possible". "Even within the framework of conflict", they suggest "there are plenty of situations in which people live and/or work together peacefully, obviously beyond their identities, attitudes, solidarities, belongings to different communities and despite their differential positions in social structures".[27]

With their emphasis on the value of fleeting moments of mutual understanding, Nowicka and Heil conceptualise conviviality as a fragile condition that embraces ongoing tensions and conflicts between people of different sociocultural backgrounds and interests as well as situations where "ad hoc and temporary communalities and similarities and consensus over issues of interest or concern in this moment of time" may develop.[28] Over two centuries lie between this analytic and situation-focused notion of conviviality by Nowicka/Heil and Schleiermacher's theory. To be sure, each approach grew out of specific historical, cultural and disciplinary constellations that should by no means be conflated; yet despite their differences, the three authors articulate a strong interest in scrutinising moments of convivial interaction as such, and it is because of this non-judgmental, situation-centred focus that their theories provide a productive lens for identifying and assessing Henriette Herz' practices of sociability.

Like all social events, the gatherings she held or attended were centered on oral communication and thus per definition ephemeral and fleeting. Therefore, all critical attempts to reconstruct the contents and social dynamic of such events always involve a high degree of speculation. In the case of Herz, however, critics deal with an additional layer of complexity having to do with the transmission of her writings. We have letters and her *Jugenderinnerungen* ["Recollections of her Youth"], autobiographical recollections of her youth and first years of marriage, yet the manuscript breaks off in 1780/1781 and does not cover the period commonly viewed as the high point of her social activities. Her self-proclaimed biographer J. Fürst provides insights into her life and multiple social engagements after this early phase but the reliability and trustworthiness of *Henriette Herz. Ihr Leben und ihre Erinnerungen* from 1850 has always been contested in the critical literature.[29] Despite its ambivalent status, however, Fürst's autobiographical text is still a major source for subsequent editions such as Janetzki's edited collection *Henriette Herz. Berliner Salon. Erinnerungen und Portraits*; the texts Janetzki selected and the commentary he provides concentrate specifically on her role as a socialite. To date there is not critical edition of her work and correspondences providing researchers with a reliable text foundation and corrective to Fürst's version.[30]

In this essay, I refer to her *Jugenderinnerungen*, and I also draw on Fürst's accounts of her life as well as the latest critical research, assessing her social activities. To be sure, these sources cannot compensate for the lack of a critical edition; taken together, however, they provide a good starting point for reexamining socially destabilising and thereby empowering moments in her convivial activities. The accounts of her social life exhibit different instances of what Schleiermacher and Nowicka/Heil describe as unexpected and fleeting moments of a shifting power dynamic: her social engagements of sorts unsettle linguistic power relations, ideas of love and marriage, and debates over literary canon formations.

Herz grew up in an open house with regular visits from family, friends and her father's students. After marrying and moving in with Marcus Herz, the couple continued their families' tradition of hosting—"Alle junge Leute die mein väterliches Haus besuchten und die meistens Studenten waren kamen nun auch zu mir (…)" ["All the young people who came to visit my father's house and who were mostly students also came to visit me"]—and of attending social events.[31] During their frequent visits to family friends, Henriette met Ewart, a young English officer who became smitten with her and a regular guest at the Herz house. Ewart and Henriette read together, socialised with the Mendelssohn family, and through their conversations and shared readings, Henriette's English improved significantly to the point of surpassing her husband's.[32] Because of her linguistic superiority, she then was the one who translated to her husband the love letter sent to her by Ewart, putting her in a position where she decided how and what to translate.[33]

Henriette's socialising with Ewart could easily be overlooked, but against the backdrop of the discussed theories of conviviality their encounter is significant: crucially, their interactions empowered her not only linguistically, but also fundamentally broadened her view of love and marriage with far-reaching effects. She talked over her experiences with Moses Mendelssohn's daughter Dorothea Veit, and through analysing what happened between her and Ewart whom she insisted she never had any true feelings for while feeling flattered by his attention, her perspective on relationships underwent a transformation. It occurred to her for the first time that a married woman could love and be loved by somebody who was not her husband:

> Before my acquaintance with E. it had not occurred to me that a married woman could be loved by another man or love someone other than her husband. As in a dream, a veil was gradually lifted from me, and behind it I saw and felt a large new world – I often said that to Dorothea whom I saw once a week; the reading circle at her house gave me the option.[34]

Dorothea Veit was unhappily married to the merchant and banker Simon Veit, and her interactions with Henriette at the reading circles hosted at her family's house were an important stepping stone towards her decision to get out of her arranged and unfulfilled marriage. Later when Henriette begun hosting her own readings, Dorothea would be a frequent visitor, and the shared readings and conversations had a life-changing effect on her. She fell in love with Friedrich Schlegel, and it was Henriette who talked to her husband and helped arranging her divorce so that she could remarry.

As Schulte points out, most critics consider instances where Jewish women broke with conventions in the context of their future baptism and cultural assimilation, a development that could not have been foreseen by the hosts and visitors of Berlin's reading circles and other social events around the turn of the century. In light of such assessments, their actions' emancipatory potential fades into the background and what moves into the centre of attention instead is their failure to be Jewish and German at the same time.[35] Schleiermacher and Nowicka/Heil, by contrast, suggest evaluating and valuing such moments of convivial interaction when subjects break away from something in and of themselves. So rather than placing those conflict-ridden instances when conventional perspectives get sort of reshuffled within broader historical narratives or normative frameworks, they focus on the convivial activity as such. In following this direction, I closely examine the convivial settings that fostered such turning points, resulting in alternative life paths or options for women to participate in and contribute to public conversations.

When Marcus Herz married Henriette De Lemos in 1779, his house, where he had been giving lectures on Kant and physics for four years, was already a well-known centre of enlightenment thinking. Very aware of her wit and beauty, Henriette saw her chance to gather her own circle:

> [almost] every known intellectual foreigner (…) visited [our house] - Herz attracted people because of his intellect and fame as a doctor, and I because of my beauty and my sense for all intellectual endeavors; there was hardly an intellectual field of inquiry that I did not feel pretty much at home in, and some I pursued seriously – such as physics and later several languages.[36]

Seventeen years younger than her husband, she attracted a younger and socially more diverse group of men and women, Jews and Germans, writers, aristocrats, and visitors to Berlin interested in reading and socialising together. The events organised by her husband were targeted at men interested in scientific research and philosophy such as the young Humboldt brothers. Soon, however, Wilhelm and Alexander von Humboldt became more interested in his wife and her circle than his lectures[37]:

> Early on the Humboldt brothers distinguished themselves by intellect and knowledge; they were lively, funny, well-behaved and very endearing – and I often saw them at our house – and definitely one evening every week in a reading society that had been arranged and that consisted of the smartest and most distinguished people of the time. Dohm, Engel, Klein, H. Zöllner and us women - – K. u. and H.s [Kunth and the Humboldts] were there too. During the summer we would be in the Bauers' garden, and during the winter at the castle – We young people played all kinds of games outside, and sometime the older ones would join us. We also read shorter and longer essays as well as theater pieces together every time. And we women read as well, and because I was beautiful people found that I also read beautifully. In the winter we danced after dinner and Alexander von Humbldt taught me how to dance a Minuet a la Reine. We lived very happily that way for a year, and everyone gained intellectually from this. I took note of the impression I had left on W. [Wilhelm von Humboldt], and we also wrote to each other.[38]

These convivial events where intellectual debates went hand in hand with flirtation and amorous friendships like the one between Henriette and Wilhelm opened new perspectives for all participants, and especially for women.

Weissberg emphasises that their shared readings of texts such as Rousseau's *Nouvelle Héloïse* or Goethe's *Werther* inspired women to envision life as a path of self-development, centred on Bildung and its notion of the subject's continuous unfolding—an effect that certainly was not intended let alone approved by all.[39]

While shaking the foundations of commonly held views of love, marriage and female role models, these social gatherings also influenced the directions of the public literary discourse. Henriette and her guests read and critically discussed modern literature, and the hostess was well aware that these readings, celebrating subjective feelings and sentiments, marked a "Wendepunkt in der schönen Literatur" ["turning point in classical literature"], and she remarks on her husband's critical attitude towards the arrival of Romanticism:

> My husband, who was older than I and friends with Lessing (…), rejected everything even in classical literature that had not been written with the clarity and transparency he knew from Lessing's writings (…). With the beginnings of the Romantic school my aesthetic suffering increased. Everything here was false and incomprehensible for Herz.[40]

While Marcus, surrounded by enlightened men, would stick to the lecture format, Henriette's diverse group would engage in open discussions over literary texts, artworks and theatre plays, promoting an aesthetics of feeling. Surely, social hierarchies did not become irrelevant here but certainly more permeable and less restrictive by virtue of this new mode of horizontal interaction.[41] Moreover, new options for participating in and shaping the directions of the reception of literary works opened up:

> People sought to comprehensively familiarize themselves with German literature, and by good fortune its first flourishing began right back then. The master works of German literature matured with us. It is something special to witness the emergence of a great literary epoch; you develop an interest and an understanding of the works, and you contribute to forming first judgements about them in ways different from someone who encounters these same works of literature as completed ones, finalized judgements about them included.[42]

Henriette gestures at the role her social group had in forming the literary canon and cultural historical discourse, and the authority of their critical judgments was also well known among her contemporaries. Wilhelm von

Humboldt, for instance, came to meetings to find out about the reception of Friedrich Schiller's work. He viewed the discussions taking place at her house as representative for what the reading public thought of his friend's works.[43]

This cursory glance at convivial gatherings that took place at the Herz couple's home and beyond gives a first impression of how important these get-togethers were for temporarily destabilising social hierarchies and power relations, and for giving women a voice in intellectual debates of their time. Taking my cue from what I find to be a shared transhistorical and cross-disciplinary concern in debates over the significance of conviviality, I argued that we need to assess the social interactions among members of the Herz circle non-teleologically, meaning not always habitually with an eye towards subsequent tensions and failures of relations between Jews and Germans but as momentary situations, testifying to the unpredictable and unintended power of forms of conviviality to unravel and remap traditional constellations and gender divisions in the domains of marriage, love, language, and literature. It was the vibrant social life that set in motion what Schleiermacher describes as free interactions centred on stimulations untethered from existing forms that had significant feedback effects on individuals.

To be sure, I sidelined some of the twists and turns in the second part of Schleiermacher's fragment that would have complicated the comparison with Nowicka's and Heil's theory and would have called for a more in-depth analysis. A comprehensive examination, including a historical survey of Schleiermacher's work on the topic of conviviality, however, was not my goal. My goal was to zero in on a crucial argumentative aspect that connects a past and present theory of conviviality; this intellectual historical perspective highlights the term's usefulness as a theoretical lens across different cultures and historical contexts. Both texts refrain from corseting conviviality into normative and essentialising frames. Instead, they propagate a situation-focused approach, a delving into the messiness of human social interaction full of volatile tensions, social cohesion and dissent. Living together and interacting might now, later or not at all contribute to a better live where the members of a community or shared space agree that more equality, mutual respect and support are beneficial for all.

Notes

1. For overviews of how conviviality has been theorised and used to replace, refine or complement other prominent terms like cosmopolitanism, multiculturalism or diversity, see Magdalena Nowicka and Steven Vertovec, "Comparing Convivialities: Dreams and Realities of Living-with-Difference," *European Journal of Cultural Studies* 17, no. 4 (2014): 341–356; Linda Lapina, "Besides Conviviality: Paradoxes in Being 'At Ease' with Diversity in a Copenhagen District," *Nordic Journal of Migration Research* 6, no. 1 (2016): 33–41. On the shift from a normative debate centred on cosmopolitanism to the "quotidian practices of everyday interactions" associated with conviviality, see Ulrike Freitag, "'Cosmopolitanism' and 'Conviviality'? Some Conceptual Considerations Concerning the Late Ottoman Empire," *European Journal of Cultural Studies* 17, no. 4 (2014): 375–391.
2. Friedrich Schleiermacher, "Versuch einer Theorie des geselligen Betragens," in *Studien, Materialien, Register*, ed. Konrad Feilchenfeldt, Uwe Schweikert, and Rahel E. Steine (München: Matthes & Steitz, 1983), 253–279. Translations are cited from "Toward a Theory of Sociable Conduct," in *Friedrich Schleiermacher's 'Toward a Theory of Sociable Conduct' and Essays on Its Intellectual-Cultural Context*, ed. Ruth Drucilla Richardson, transl. Jeffrey Hoover (Lewiston: E. Mellen Press, 1995), 20–39.
3. In a multi-step argument and through engaging with how cosmopolitanism has been defined and employed by critics such as Paul Gilroy, Magdalena Nowicka and Tilmann Heil discuss in their lecture "On the Analytical and Normative Dimensions of Conviviality and Cosmopolitanism," why conviviality is a more productive term. The lecture also provides an overview of recent scholarly contributions to theories of conviviality. "On the Analytical and Normative Dimensions of Conviviality and Cosmopolitanism," Humboldt University, June 25, 2015, 1–20, accessed May 10, 2019, https://www.euroethno.hu-berlin.de/de/forschung/labore/migration/nowicka-heil_on-the-analytical-and-normative-dimensions-of-conviviality.pdf.
4. "Hascala: Judaic Movement," *Encyclopaedia Britannica*, accessed May 10, 2019, https://www.britannica.com/topic/Haskala.
5. Christopher Clark, *Iron Kingdom: The Rise and Downfall of Prussia, 1600–1947* (Cambridge, MA: Belknap Press of Harvard University Press, 2006), 261.
6. Clark, *Iron Kingdom*, 264.
7. Shmul Feiner, *The Jewish Enlightenment* (Philadelphia: University of Pennsylvania Press, 2004), 260.
8. Feiner, *The Jewish Enlightenment*, 303.
9. Moshe Pelli, *Haskalah and Beyond: The Reception of the Hebrew Enlightenment and the Emergence of Haskalah Judaism* (Lanham, MD: University Press of America, 2010).

10. Christoph Schulte, "Die Töchter der Haskala – Die jüdischen Salonièren aus der Perspektive der jüdischen Aufklärung," in *Die Kommunikations-, Wissens- und Handlungsräume der Henriette Herz (1764–1847)*, ed. Hannah Lotte Lund, Ulrike Schneider, and Ulrike Wels (Göttingen: V&R unipress), 57–70.
11. For an overview, see Schulte, "Die Töchter der Haskala," 58–60.
12. Barbara Hahn, "A Dream of Living Together: Jewish Women in Berlin Around 1800," in *Jewish Women and Their Salons: The Power of Conversation*, ed. Emily D. Bilski and Emily Braun (New York: Jewish Museum Under the Auspices of the Jewish Theological Seminary of America; New Haven: Yale University Press, 2005), 149–150.
13. While discussing a number of reasons for why scholars of the Haskalah have not attributed a central role to the social activities of Jewish women, Schulte also advocates for a non-teleological approach for assessing their contribution to the formation and development of the Haskalah movement in "Töchter der Haskala": "Es stellt sich also die Frage, warum die jüdischen Salons zwischen 1780 und 1806 nicht einmal völlig unteleologisch, also ohne Projektion auf spätere Taufen und vermeintliche Assimiliation, welche ja 1782 oder 1799 noch nicht vorherzusehen war und nur mit dem nachträglichen Wissen der Historiker in die Historiographie jener Jahre eingetragen wurde, untersucht werden. Warum also sind die jüdischen Salons auch von der Haskala-Forschung nicht als ein Resultat, ein Symptom, eine Instanz oder eine Begleiterscheinung der Haskala, mitten in und mitten aus dem maskilischen Milieu, betrachtet und analysiert worden?" (60). On the German *Sonderweg*, or special path, debate that some have seen leading up to the gates of Auschwitz, see Clark's introduction to *Iron Kingdom* where he points to the discussion as a construction based on hindsight, and as a kind of falsifying historical projection that distorts the complexities of German-Jewish relations (xii–xviiix).
14. Hannah Lotte Lund, "'ich habe so viele sonderbare Menschen hier' – Vergesellschaftungsformen im Hause Herz der 1790er Jahre," in *Die Kommunikations-, Wissens- und Handlungsräume der Henriette Herz*, 29.
15. See preface to *Die Kommunikations-, Wissens- und Handlungsräume der Henriette Herz*, 14.
16. "(…) mehrere Quellen deuten darauf hin, dass es im Hause Herz in den frühen 1790er Jahren vier bis fünf ineinander übergehende Geselligkeitsformen gegeben haben könnte. Neben den in den Erinnerungen erwähnten 'Collegia' gab es nachmittäglichen Tee und Abendessen (…). Als Beispiel für den fließenden Übergang zwischen verschiedenen Geselligkeitsformen in diesen Häusern muss viertens ein 'Damentee' erwähnt werden, auch 'Kränzchen' genannt, da sich Anfang der 1790er Jahre regelmäßig und *unter anderem* bei Henriette Herz traf," Lund, "Vergesellschaftungsformen im Hause Herz," 39–40.

17. The volume editors of *Die Kommunikations-, Wissens- und Handlungsräume der Henriette Herz* point out that the term "Jüdischer Salon" is misleading in a two-fold way: "Nach bisherigem Forschungsstand weist er erstens einer zahlenmäßig sehr kleinen Gruppe von neun bis zwölf Frauen den Status einer Institution zu, den sie zu Lebzeiten so nicht besaßen. Zweitens sagt er, nicht nur angesichts der Konversionen und Identitätsüberschneidungen, nichts über das Selbstverständnis der beteiligten Frauen und Männer aus. Wir plädieren daher dafür, den Begriff des ‚Salons' in der Forschung längerfristig abzulösen und z.b. durch ‚gesellige Formationen', Kommunikations-, Wissens- oder Handlungsräume zu ersetzen, weil diese Bezeichnungen die unterschiedlichen Formen, in denen solche Geselligkeit gelebt wurde, offener abbilden," 12–13.
18. Friedrich Schleiermacher, "Versuch einer Theorie des geselligen Betragens," in *Studien, Materialien, Register*, ed. Konrad Feilchenfeldt, Uwe Schweikert, and Rahel E. Steine (München: Matthes & Steitz, 1983), 253–279. Translations are cited from "Toward a Theory of Sociable Conduct," in *Friedrich Schleiermacher's 'Toward a Theory of Sociable Conduct' and Essays on Its Intellectual-Cultural Context*, ed. Ruth Drucilla Richardson, transl. Jeffrey Hoover (Lewiston: E. Mellen Press, 1995), 20–39.
19. Freie, durch keinen äußeren Zweck gebundene und bestimmte Geselligkeit wird von allen gebildeten Menschen als eins ihrer ersten und edelsten Bedürfnisse laut gefordert. Wer nur zwischen den Sorgen des häuslichen Lebens hin und her geworfen wird, nähert sich, je treuer er diesen Weg wiederholt, nur um desto langsamer dem höheren Ziel des menschlichen Daseins. Der Beruf bannt die Thätigkeit des Geistes in einen engen Kreis: wie edel und achtungswerth er auch sey, immer hält er Wirkung auf die Welt und Beschauung der Welt auf einem Standpunkt fest, und so bringt der einfachste und niedrigste, Einseitigkeit und Beschränkung hervor. Das häusliche Leben setzt uns nur mit Wenigen, und immer mit denselben in Berührung (253).
20. The key text addressing the interdependence of religion and the social is the fourth speech "Über das Gesellige in der Religion oder über Kirche und Priesterthum" of Schleiermacher's "Über die Religion. Reden an die Gebildeten unter ihren Verächtern," *Kritische Gesamtausgabe*, vol. 12, ed. Günter Meckenstock (Berlin and New York: de Gruyter, 1995). Referring to a letter by Schleiermacher to Henriette Herz, Hoover points out in the introduction to his translation that it was because of his work on "Über die Religion" that Schleiermacher's conviviality essay remained a fragment: "Schleiermacher had intended to offer a continuation of this essay in future issues, but he never returned to the project once it was interrupted by his work on *Über die Religion* (…) Schleiermacher gives evidence of this interruption in a letter to Henriette Herz (…)," Hoover, 9–10.

21. See Deborah Hertz, "Henriette Herz as Jew, Henriette Herz as Christian—Relationships, Conversion, Antisemitism," in *Die Kommunikations-, Wissens- und Handlungsräume der Henriette Herz*, 123.
22. "Fragt man nun aber konkret nach dem Einfluss, den Henriette Herz auf Schleiermachers wissenschaftliches Denken und speziell auf seine Pädagogik hatte, so stößt man auf ein Phänomen, das man als geistige 'Undercover-Tätigkeit' von Frauen in der bzw. für die Wissenschaft bezeichnen könnte. Denn oft wirken Frauen im Verborgenen, regen Gedanken an und bringen ihre Ideen in Gespräche ein, motivieren explizit oder implizit zu wissenschaftlichen Werken, beurteilen die produzierten Texte kritisch oder lesen – in Anführungszeichen – ‚nur' Korrektur. (…) Die Beziehung zwischen Henriette Herz und Friedrich Schleiermacher ist geradezu exemplarisch für das theoriegeschichtliche Phänomen solcher Frauen, die im Schatten männlicher Gelehrter oder großer Pädagogen stehen oder – auch das gilt es zu bedenken – sich ganz bewusst in deren Schatten stellen," Johanna Hopfer, "Zwischen Kanzel und Salon. Friedrich Schleiermacher und Henriette Herz. Ein Beispiel für den weiblichen Einfluss auf die Pädagogik," *Vierteljahresschrift für die wissenschaftliche Pädagogik* 76, no. 4 (2000): 533, cited in Ulrike Wels, "Überschreitungen *in nuance* – Überlegungen zum religiösen Selbstverständnis der Henriette Herz," in *Die Kommunikations-, Wissens- und Handlungsräume der Henriette Herz*, 194.
23. (…) Zustand (…) der die Sphären eines Individui in die Lage bringt, daß sie von den Sphären Anderer so mannigfaltig als möglich durchschnitten werde, und jeder seiner eignen Grenzpunkte ihm die Aussicht in eine andere und fremde Welt gewähre, so daß alle Erscheinungen der Menschheit ihm nach und nach bekannt, und auch die fremdesten Gemüther und Verhältnisse ihm befreundet und gleichsam nachbarlich werden können. Diese Aufgabe wird durch den freien Umgang vernünftiger sich unter einander bildender Menschen gelöst (253–254).
24. Sehen wir nun auf den Zweck, der unter dieser Form der durchgängigen Wechselwirkung erreicht werden soll, so fällt in die Augen, denn es liegt in dem Prädikat der Freiheit, daß hier von einem einzelnen und bestimmten Zweck gar nicht die Rede seyn soll; denn dieser bestimmt und beschränkt auch die Thätigkeit nach materiellen und objektiven Regeln. Es soll keine bestimmte Handlung gemeinschaftlich verrichtet, kein Werk vereinigt zu Stande gebracht, keine Einsicht methodisch erworben werden. Der Zweck der Gesellschaft wird gar nicht außer ihr liegend gedacht; die Wirkung eines Jeden soll gehen auf die Thätigkeit der übrigen, und die Thätigkeit eines Jeden soll seyn seine Einwirkung auf die andern. Nun aber kann auf ein freies Wesen nicht anders eingewirkt werden, als dadurch, daß es zur eigenen Tätigkeit aufgeregt, und ihr ein Objekt dargeboten wird; und dieses Objekt kann wiederum zufolge des obigen nichts anderes seyn, als die Thätigkeit

des Auffordernden; es kann also auf nichts anders abgesehen seyn, als auf ein freies Spiel der Gedanken und Empfindungen, wodurch alle Mitglieder einander gegenseitig aufregen und beleben. Die Wechselwirkung ist sonach in sich selbst zurückgehend und vollendet; in dem Begriff derselben ist sowohl die Form als der Zweck der geselligen Thätigkeit enthalten, und sie macht das ganze Wesen der Gesellschaft aus (259–260).
25. Magdalena Nowicka and Tilmann Heil, "On the Analytical and Normative Dimensions of Conviviality and Cosmopolitanism," Humboldt University, June 25, 2015, 1–20, accessed May 10, 2019, https://www.euroethno.hu-berlin.de/de/forschung/labore/migration/nowicka-heil_on-the-analytical-and-normative-dimensions-of-conviviality.pdf.
26. Nowicka and Heil, "On the Analytical and Normative Dimensions of Conviviality and Cosmopolitanism," 6; Paul Gilroy, *After Empire: Melancholia or Convivial Culture?* (New York: Routledge, 2004).
27. Nowicka and Heil, "On the Analytical and Normative Dimensions of Conviviality and Cosmopolitanism," 7, 12.
28. Nowicka and Heil, "On the Analytical and Normative Dimensions of Conviviality and Cosmopolitanism," 12.
29. Henriette Herz, *Jugenderinnerungen von Henriette Herz*, in *Mittheilungen aus dem Litterturarchive in Berlin* 5 (1896): 141–184, accessed March 27, 2018, http://sophie.byu.edu/texts/henriette-herz-ihr-leben-und-ihre-erinnerungen-autobiography-1850; J. Fürst, *Henriette Herz. Ihr Leben und ihre Erinnerungen* (Berlin: 1850), available from: http://sophie.byu.edu/texts/henriette-herz-ihr-leben-und-ihre-erinnerungen-autobiography-1850, accessed March 27, 2018. For an overview and review of the different editions of Herz' writings and the philological challenges they pose, see Lund, Schneider, and Wels, "Einleitung: Zehn Thesen – für Henriette Herz – gegen den 'Salon'", in *Die Kommunikations-, Wissens- und Handlungsräume der Henriette Herz*, 9–11.
30. Ulrich Janetzki, ed., *Henriette Herz. Berliner Salon. Erinnerungen und Portraits* (Frankfurt am Main: Ullstein Verlag, 1984).
31. Herz, *Jugenderinnerungen*, 164–165. Unless otherwise indicated, all English translations are my own.
32. Compare Herz, *Jugenderinnerungen*, 175.
33. "Der Umgang mit E. hatte mir eine ziemliche Fertigkeit im Verstehen des Englischen gegeben, wir lasen viel mit einander u. daher ist es kein Wunder dass ich mehr wusste als H. ich musste ihm daher den Brief wörtlich übersetzen (…)," Herz, *Jugenderinnerungen*, 176.
34. Vor meiner Bekanntschaft mit E. hatte ich nie die Möglichkeit gedacht dass eine verheiratete Frau von einem anderen als von ihrem Manne geliebt werden, oder einen anderen lieben als ihn lieben könne. Wie durch einen allmähligen Zauber ward mir langsam ein Vorhang weggezogen hinter welchem ich eine neue grosse Welt erblickte u. fühlte – oft sagte ich das zu

D-a Dorothea die ich jede Woche Ein Mal sah, wozu eine in ihrem Hause eingerichtete Lesegesellschaft Gelegenheit gab. Herz, *Jugenderinnerungen*, 177.
35. Schulte, "Die Töchter der Haskala," 60.
36. [fast] jeder an Geist bedeutende Fremde (…) besuchte unser Haus - Herz zog durch seinen Geist u. als berühmter Arzt die Leute an sich, ich durch meine Schönheit u. durch den Sinn den ich für alles Wissenschaftliche hatte, denn es gab kaum eine in der ich mich nicht einigermassen umgesehn hätte u. einige trieb ich ernstlich – so Physic u. später mehrere Sprachen. Herz, *Jugenderinnerungen*, 183.
37. On Herz' lectures on experimental philosophy and his guests, see *Jugenderinnerungen von Henriette Herz*, in *Mittheilungen aus dem Litterturarchive in Berlin* 5 (1896): 181–182, accessed March 27, 2018, http://sophie.byu.edu/texts/henriette-herz-ihr-leben-und-ihre-erinnerungen-autobiography-1850. To prepare Wilhelm and Alexander von Humboldt for their studies at the Prussian University in Frankfurt/Oder, their private tutor Johann Christian Kunth introduced them to Marcus Herz.
38. Schon sehr früh zeichneten sie sich the Humboldt brothers durch Geist u. Kenntnisse aus, sie waren lebendig, witzig, artig u. sehr liebenswürdig – u. ich sah sie sehr oft bei uns – u. gewiss in jeder Woche einen Abend in einer Lesegesellschaft die eingerichtet ward u. die aus den damals gescheidesten, ausgezeichnetsten Leuten bestand. Dohm, Engel, Klein, H. Zöllner u. wir dazu gehörigen Frauen – K. u. die H.s Kunth and the Humboldts waren auch dabei. Im Sommer waren wir im Bauerschen Garten, im Winter auf dem Schloss – Wir jüngeren Leute spielten allerlei Spiele im Freien, zu denen sich indess auch oft die Älteren gesellten, doch aber ward auch jedesmal gelesen, kleinere und grössere Aufsätze, theatralische Sachen u.s.w. auch wir Frauen lasen u. weil ich schön war fand man auch dass ich schön las. Im Winter tanzten wir nach dem Abendessen u. Alex. H. lehrte mich die Menuet a la Reine. So lebten wir ein ganzes Jahr auf hoch vergnügliche Weise mit einander, von manchem geistigen Nutzen für alle. Der Eindruck den ich auf W. Wilhelm von Humboldt gemacht entging mir nicht, auch schrieben wir einander. Herz, *Jugenderinnerungen*, 182.
39. Liliane Weissberg, "Lehrjahre des Gefühls – Wilhelm von Humboldt befreundet sich mit Henriette Herz," in *Die Kommunikations-, Wissens- und Handlungsräume der Henriette Herz*, 147.
40. Mein Mann, älter, mit Lessing persönlich befreundet (…) wies selbst in der schönen Literatur alles zurück, was nicht mit Lessingscher Klarheit und Durchsichtigkeit geschrieben war (…). Mit dem Auftauchen der romantischen Schule steigerten sich nun vollends meine ästhetischen Leiden. Hier war für Herz alles unwahr oder unverständlich. Ulrich Janetzki, ed., *Henriette Herz. Berliner Salon: Erinnerungen und Portraits* (Frankfurt am Main: Ullstein, 1984), 39–40.

41. Anne Baillot, "Das Netzwerk als Kunstwerk," *Die Kommunikations-, Wissens- und Handlungsräume der Henriette Herz*, 47.
42. Man suchte sich mit der deutschen schönen Literatur in ihrem ganzen Umfange bekanntzumachen, und eine besondere Gunst des Geschickes wollte, dass die Blütezeit derselben eben damals begann. Ihre Meisterwerke wurden mit uns, und es ist etwas anderes, eine große Literaturepoche zu erleben, schon was das Interesse an ihren Erzeugnissen und das Verständnis derselben betrifft, und an dem ersten Urteil über die letzteren mitzuarbeiten, als wenn sie als ein Abgeschlossenes nebst den fertigen Urteilen über sie und ihre Werke überkommen. Henriette Herz, *Berliner Salon*, 47.
43. Hannah Lotte Lund, "'ich habe so viele sonderbare Menschen hier' - Vergesellschaftungsformen im Hause Herz der 1790er Jahre," in *Die Kommunikations-, Wissens- und Handlungsräume der Henriette Herz*, 37.

References

Clark, C. 2006. *Iron Kingdom: The Rise and Downfall of Prussia, 1600–1947*. Cambridge, MA: Belknap Press of Harvard University Press.

Feiner, S. 2004. *The Jewish Enlightenment*. Philadelphia: University of Pennsylvania Press.

Freitag, U. 2014. "'Cosmopolitanism' and 'Conviviality'? Some Conceptual Considerations Concerning the Late Ottoman Empire." *European Journal of Cultural Studies* 17 (49): 375–391.

Fürst, J. 1850. *Henriette Herz. Ihr Leben und ihre Erinnerungen*. Berlin. Available from: http://sophie.byu.edu/texts/henriette-herz-ihr-leben-und-ihre-erinnerungen-autobiography-1850. Accessed March 27, 2018.

Gilroy, P. 2004. *After Empire: Melancholia or Convivial Culture?* New York: Routledge.

Hahn, B. 2005. "A Dream of Living Together: Jewish Women in Berlin Around 1800." In *Jewish Women and Their Salons: The Power of Conversation*, edited by E. D. Bilski and E. Braun, 149–157. New York: Jewish Museum Under the Auspices of the Jewish Theological Seminary of America; New Haven: Yale University Press.

Hertz, D. 2017. Henriette Herz as Jew, Henriette Herz as Christian—Relationships, Conversion, Antisemitism. In *Die Kommunikations-, Wissens- und Handlungsräume der Henriette Herz (1764–1847)*, edited by H. L. Lund, U. Schneider, and U. Wels, 117–139. Göttingen: V&R unipress.

Herz, H. 1896. *Jugenderinnerungen von Henriette Herz*. In *Mittheilungen aus dem Litterturarchive in Berlin* 5: 141–184. Available from: http://sophie.byu.edu/texts/henriette-herz-ihr-leben-und-ihre-erinnerungen-autobiography-1850. Accessed March 27, 2018.

Hopfer, J. 2000. "Zwischen Kanzel und Salon. Friedrich Schleiermacher und Henriette Herz. Ein Beispiel für den weiblichen Einfluss auf die Pädagogik." *Vierteljahresschrift für die wissenschaftliche Pädagogik* 76 (4): 532–544.
Janetzki, U., ed. 1984. *Henriette Herz. Berliner Salon. Erinnerungen und Portraits.* Frankfurt am Main: Ullstein Verlag.
Lapina, L. 2016. "Besides Conviviality: Paradoxes in Being 'At Ease' with Diversity in a Copenhagen District." *Nordic Journal of Migration Research* 6 (1): 33–41.
Lund, H. L. 2017. "'Ich habe so viele sonderbare Menschen hier' – Vergesellschaftungsformen im Hause Herz der 1790er Jahre." In *Die Kommunikations-, Wissens- und Handlungsräume der Henriette Herz (1764–1847)*, edited by H. L. Lund, U. Schneider, and U. Wels, 23–44. Göttingen: V&R unipress.
Nowicka, M., and S. Vertovec 2014. "Comparing Convivialities: Dreams and Realities of Living-with-Difference." *European Journal of Cultural Studies* 17, no. 4: 341–356.
Nowicka, M., and T. Heil 2015. "On the Analytical and Normative Dimensions of Conviviality and Cosmopolitanism." Humboldt University, June 25, 2015, 1–20. Available from: https://www.euroethno.hu-berlin.de/de/forschung/labore/migration/nowicka-heil_on-the-analytical-and-normative-dimensions-of-conviviality.pdf. Accessed May 10, 2019.
Pelli, M. 2010. *Haskalah and Beyond: The Reception of the Hebrew Enlightenment and the Emergence of Haskalah Judaism.* Lanham, MD: University Press of America.
Schulte, C. 2017. "Die Töchter der Haskala – Die jüdischen Salonièren aus der Perspektive der jüdischen Aufklärung." In *Die Kommunikations-, Wissens- und Handlungsräume der Henriette Herz (1764–1847)*, edited by H. L. Lund, U. Schneider, and U. Wels, 57–70. Göttingen: V&R unipress.
Schleiermacher, F. 1983. "Versuch einer Theorie des geselligen Betragens." In *Studien, Materialien, Register*, edited by K. Feilchenfeldt, U. Schweikert, and R. E. Steine, 253–279. München: Matthes & Steitz.
Schleiermacher, F. 1995a. "Über die Religion. Reden an die Gebildeten unter ihren Verächtern." In *Kritische Gesamtausgabe*, vol. 12, edited by Günter Meckenstock. Berlin and New York: de Gruyter.
Schleiermacher, F. 1995b. "Toward a Theory of Sociable Conduct." In *Friedrich Schleiermacher's 'Toward a Theory of Sociable Conduct' and Essays on Its Intellectual-Cultural Context*, edited by R. D. Richardson and translated by J. Hoover, 20–39. Lewiston: E. Mellen Press.
Weissberg, L. 2017. "Lehrjahre des Gefühls – Wilhelm von Humboldt befreundet sich mit Henriette Herz." In *Die Kommunikations-, Wissens- und Handlungsräume der Henriette Herz (1764–1847)*, edited by H. L. Lund, U. Schneider, and U. Wels, 141–157. Göttingen: V&R unipress.
Wels, U. 2017. "Überschreitungen in nuance – Überlegungen zum religiösen Selbstverständnis der Henriette Herz." In *Die Kommunikations-, Wissens- und*

Handlungsräume der Henriette Herz (1764–1847), edited by H. L. Lund, U. Schneider, and U. Wels, 187–218. Göttingen: V&R unipress.

Open Access This chapter is licensed under the terms of the Creative Commons Attribution 4.0 International License (http://creativecommons.org/licenses/by/4.0/), which permits use, sharing, adaptation, distribution and reproduction in any medium or format, as long as you give appropriate credit to the original author(s) and the source, provide a link to the Creative Commons license and indicate if changes were made.

The images or other third party material in this chapter are included in the chapter's Creative Commons license, unless indicated otherwise in a credit line to the material. If material is not included in the chapter's Creative Commons license and your intended use is not permitted by statutory regulation or exceeds the permitted use, you will need to obtain permission directly from the copyright holder.

CHAPTER 5

Cosmopolitanism as Utopia

Rebecka Lettevall

Since the end of the Cold War, cosmopolitanism has undeniably experienced a renaissance. It re-emerged in the humanities and social sciences as well as among political theorists, until it was criticised for being overstrained with content, and alternative concepts were suggested to cover parts of its meaning. One of the most influential points of reference in the discussions of cosmopolitanism is the Enlightenment philosopher Immanuel Kant (1724–1804). In the context of the recent refugee arrivals in Europe, the Kantian definition of cosmopolitan right as hospitality made cosmopolitanism less attractive as it demonstrated a gap between theory and practice that had changed over time. The restricted Kantian definition of hospitality as the right to visit, not to be treated hostile, and for the host, the right to reject the visitor as long as there was no risk for life, was formulated in a time of colonialism, perhaps to save parts of the world from colonisers. As the situation was quite different in the recent refugee situation, Kant's cosmopolitan right was turned upside down. However, Kant's cosmopolitanism is not just a cosmopolitan right.

R. Lettevall (✉)
Faculty of Culture and Society, Malmö University, Malmö, Sweden
e-mail: Rebecka.Lettevall@mau.se

The purpose of this chapter is to highlight the complexity of cosmopolitanism as theory, with its long history, as well as its use in different intellectual and cultural spaces, and to demonstrate what might be lost if it is rejected. I suggest cosmopolitanism to be read as a utopian idea. After an opening section on cosmopolitanism and its critics, I present utopia as a method. Then, I discuss utopia in Kant's work and lift forward other aspects of his cosmopolitanism in order to understand it as an important part of an implicit utopia, before ending up with concluding reflections on cosmopolitanism as utopia.

Cosmopolitanism and Its Critics

With a background in ancient Greek and Roman thinking, the notion of cosmopolitanism has a rich tradition within especially the Western world (Cheneval 2002). With such a long history, it is not surprising that it has been loaded with different content over the centuries. Among the elements that construct its core are those of universalism and human dignity, elements that take different shapes depending on spatial and temporal situations and contexts. The complexity of the concept, its wide range of connotations and meanings today encourages the introduction of other concepts to partially replace it.

Cosmopolitanism was one of the ideas that were enthusiastically re-explored around the latest turn of century. Scholars within a wide range of disciplines in the humanities and social sciences considered it as a necessary stance for creating a better world through jointly finding solutions to problems that do not correspond to national borders, such as environmental and climate threats, and making efforts towards ending historically embedded globe-spanning injustices. This re-exploration has contributed to what sociologist Gerard Delanty (2019b) refers to as cosmopolitanism studies, an academic field characterised by a mixture of normative analyses and empirical applications, whose diversities were recently demonstrated in a revised an enlarged collection edited by him (first edition 2012), *Routledge International Handbook of Cosmopolitanism Studies* (Delanty 2019a). Cosmopolitanism has been criticised for its Eurocentric, exclusive, and idealistic tendencies, and for ignoring controversies and clashes (Bernasconi 2001, 2011; Gilroy 2015). Paul Gilroy's critique of cosmopolitanism for being born out of colonialism and European expansion (2004) led him, as well as many other authors, to prefer the concept of "conviviality". It is an indisputable fact that the concept of cosmopolitanism is overstrained, as Magdalena Nowicka puts forward in Chapter 2 in this volume. She also prefers "conviviality", as it reframes the discussions on human togetherness, society, and the state and opens for focus on sociality rather than diversity.

It is tempting to understand cosmopolitanism as a coherent theory or at least as a well-defined concept because of its literal form as an "ism". Besides, when a word has been in use for a long time, as cosmopolitanism has, it may be considered as something of a catchword and hence be applied as a rhetorical tool (Kurunmäki and Marjanen 2018: 246). Today, cosmopolitanism refers to a very wide range of theories and practices including universal embracement of humanity, political systems, ethics, migration politics, education, attitudes, multiculturalism, the vernacular, and elite cultures as well as everyday cultures (see Delanty 2019a). This is not the first or only time that its referential frame has been so vast. In the late eighteenth century, the concept had several diverse meanings, for example in Germany, where these connotations pertained to moral cosmopolitanism, international federal cosmopolitanism, cosmopolitan law, cultural cosmopolitanism, market cosmopolitanism and romantic cosmopolitanism (Kleingeld 1999). Being cosmopolitan could then also be used as an invective (Lettevall 2008). Today, it is more common to identify three main varieties of cosmopolitanism: cultural, moral and political (Etinson 2010) while yet another definition speaks of societal cosmopolitanism (Pendenza 2017).

One of the main questions of cosmopolitanism concerns the multiplicity of realms of cosmopolitanism as theory and cosmopolitanism as practice. Cosmopolitanism as theory has been criticised for being too distant from practical experience and, as has already been mentioned, for its alleged Eurocentric as well as elitist perspective. However, cosmopolitanism as theory could mean the ability to see what unites rather than the differences and particularities. This has been illuminatively explored through the application of the "cosmopolitan lens" to the empirical case of a neighbourhood in Sweden, characterised by a working-class past and a diverse presence with cosmopolitanisation from within at a particular time and space (Povrzanović Frykman 2016). Cosmopolitanism as practice—i.e. research on cosmopolitan practices—often refers to forms of living together. One way to practise cosmopolitanism is to develop the idea of world citizenship. The inter-war period's attempt to issue a certain kind of identity cards— the so-called Nansen passports—for refugees who had lost their citizenship through the First World War can be understood as such a cosmopolitan practice, even though the project was not very successful (Lettevall 2012). The former US bomber pilot Garry Davis' initiative after the Second World

War to reject his US citizenship in order to create a world citizenship could also be conceived as part of such a movement (Gustafsson 2019, forthcoming).

In some debates, the neologism cosmopolitics has been introduced in the attempt to bridge between theory and practice (Cheah and Robbins 1998). It refers to politics within and beyond the nation where the perspective of global social justice and equality is included, as well as more concrete attempts to deal with the global challenges without the abstract universalism of cosmopolitanism (ibid.: 13). Defined like this, cosmopolitics could be a tool for a cosmopolitan utopia.

It has been argued that cosmopolitanism as practice depends on an idea of openness towards others (Skrbiš and Woodward 2013: 27). The openness that characterises cosmopolitanism is not universal, but rather depending on situation and context, which means that there is a performative dimension to the openness. Skrbiš and Woodward suggest that when researchers study expressions of cosmopolitan identities as practice, they must search for performances and manifestations (ibid.: 28). Besides the idea of openness as a crucial principle of cosmopolitanism in practice, Skrbiš and Woodward lift forward the idea of an applied ethics of inclusiveness (ibid.: 40).

As mentioned above, the openness that characterises cosmopolitanism as practice is dependent on time and space, while interpretations of cosmopolitanism as theory do not always pay attention to this. However, it can be argued that the historicity of a concept is an important part of the production of its meaning. From Gadamer's perspective of *Wirkungsgeschichte*, often translated as "effective history", but sometimes as "reception history", a concept is always dependent on its history, as its interpretations over time also become part of the concept and thus interpretations cannot be separated from the concept itself (Gadamer 1960). Earlier interpretations influence the meaning the concept is attributed today—thus the need for being aware of its history.

General criticism of cosmopolitanism often targets its universalism. Abstract universalism cannot solve specific problems in the world. One example of this is the relation between, on the one hand, abstract and general human rights and, on the other hand, the possibilities of implementing them in particular situations. Ever since Hannah Arendt's (2000 [1949]) sharp criticism of universal human rights as a failure unless there are citizen rights to protect them through a government, the question has been whether cosmopolitanism with its implicit universalism can include some kind of citizenship. Both international law and nation states have failed to guarantee rights for the many victims of war that have lost either their citizenship or their possibility to stay in their countries. This was true in the inter-war period, after the Second World War and not least today. The recent refugee situation in Europe has brought into light the rights of strangers, and it has been argued whether Kant's concept of hospitality as a cosmopolitan right implies a right to asylum or not (Brown 2019: 18). Is it possible to combine national citizenship with world citizenship? Being a crucial question when discussing cosmopolitanism, this is where the Kantian understanding of hospitality becomes relevant.

The definition of Kant's cosmopolitanism as cosmopolitan right springs from a rather narrow understanding of cosmopolitanism, where it is understood as hospitality in a restricted form that only grants the right of a stranger to visit a place when there is a risk for her life. If we approach cosmopolitanism through such a narrow reading, large parts of the historicity of the concept tend to be ignored. When cosmopolitanism is dismissed because of the narrow understanding of Kant's definition of cosmopolitan right, many other parts of cosmopolitanism are also dismissed. While hospitality without doubt plays an important role concerning mobility and migration, cosmopolitanism can easily refer to several other issues.

The long tradition of discussions on cosmopolitanism contains many perspectives that stretch over time and space and should thus be understood with a sensibility to temporality. Since Diogenes, who is attributed to having introduced the concept, and over the different meanings developed during the Enlightenment and onwards to our time, cosmopolitanism has contained a utopian dimension. I propose to look at its potential to be used as a tool in a utopian method.

Utopia as a Critical Method

The function of utopias has been described both as offering a dreamy escape from the real world and as stimulating societal changes. Sociologist Ruth Levitas (2013) argues that utopia is a reflexive method for conceiving alternative—better—futures in a time and space suffering from different crises, whether ecological, social, economic, political or existential. Utopia offers an integrated way to think about these different areas.

> The core of utopia is the desire of being otherwise, individually and collectively, subjectively and objectively. Its expressions explore and bring to

debate the potential contents and contexts of human flourishing. It is thus better understood as a method than a goal – a method elaborated here as the Imaginary Reconstitution of Society, or IROS. (Levitas 2013: xi)

For Levitas, utopia is understood as the expression of a hope and desire for a better way of being or living and of the conviction that the present society could be different from what it is now. Utopia is existential as well as relational. Levitas argues that her definition of utopia is analytic rather than descriptive and that it generates a method which is primarily hermeneutic but oscillates between the social and structural and the existential-aesthetical. For Levitas, "utopia has at least three potential functions: compensation, critique and change" (ibid.: 107). The three functions are intertwined. While compensation primarily refers to the (individual's) imagination of living in a better world, critique refers, rather, to the group or a more general societal perspective on the private experience such as identifying the dissatisfaction as depending on something systemic. Change is the most important function of utopia. According to Levitas, the importance of utopia consists of its capacity to embody hope rather than desire and to stimulate fantasies about a transformation to a better world. She observes that contemporary public discourse and political culture are anti-utopian, partly because of the fear of the totalitarian political consequences a "perfect society" would imply (ibid.: 7).

The utopian method comprises three modes: the archaeological, the ontological and the architectural (ibid.: 153). These modes are not isolated from one another but rather overlap. The archaeological mode combines "the images of the good society that are embedded in political programmes and social and economic policies" (Levitas 2013: 153). Further, the archaeological mode enables the imagination and reconstitution of a whole society from fragments. The ontological mode tries to answer the question about the kind of people a certain society develops and encourages—or "the historical and social determination of human nature" (ibid.: 153). The architectural mode, finally, imagines potential alternative future scenarios, including the descriptions and imaginations of a new world and its social institutions, as well as the imagination about and consequences for the people that might inhabit them. Levitas argues that the core of good society is equality (ibid.: 215), and that utopia is a fertile method to help us think differently about the present and the future and imagine ways of reaching equality. This threefold holistic utopian method is not limited by technological determinism but founded on imagination (Goode and Godhe 2017).

Ever since Thomas More's *Utopia* (1516), the mode to describe an ideal society placed in another time and space has been a practice for criticising the present society or some of its components. Utopia has been a method for describing future goals, whether political, social or religious. In fact, that tradition prevailed even long before Thomas More's work. It seems to have been an important idea of many religions as well as in ancient Greece (Manuel and Manuel 1979). Because of the liberty of the projection into time and space, utopias tend to contain descriptions of societies without change and movement, where there are no dynamics between different expressions of ideas and thus no further development. These are the characteristics of the visions of utopian societies from the paradise to the future golden age. In their major work *Utopian thought in the Western world*, Manuel and Manuel summarise that

> [u]topians of the past have dealt with war and peace, the many facets of live, the antinomy of need and desire, the opposition of calm felicity and dynamic change, the alternatives of hierarchy or equality, the search for a powerful unifying bond to hold mankind together, whether universal love or a common identification of a transcendent being. (Manuel and Manuel 1979: 802)

Manuel and Manuel conclude that utopia might be an imagined dream world. It could, however, also have realistic characteristics. From around the First World War and onwards, the genre of dystopia developed within literature and film, in which future societies were portrayed as being horrifying. Utopias and utopianism have been criticised for being unrealistic and fluffy constructions of dreams suitable for the most committed idealists. Still, with the support from Levitas, it is clear that they could be useful for exploring the directions for the future. In the following, I will use cosmopolitanism to explore the idea of expression of a hope and desire for a better future. Here, I define cosmopolitanism as a utopia, which means that it is not understood as a concrete plan or model for change, but as a hope for the better through imagination that supports a new view of the present and the future. It is hardly possible to construct an ideal world theoretically, but it is possible to outline utopias. Kant's political and historical philosophy is implicitly utopian, and cosmopolitanism is an important part of that utopia.

Kant's Implicit Utopia and Cosmopolitanism

One of the interesting peculiarities of Kant's work is that, even though he put such an effort into defining the boundaries of human knowledge, he concentrates perhaps most of his intellectual work on what seems to lie beyond those borders, on what is not really a part of that which can be conceived as knowledge. Kant's philosophical system is often referred to as an architecture, also by himself, and within it we can find an implicit utopia. This is developed mainly in his smaller works on history and politics but has a foundation in his large critical works, the *Critique of Judgement* (1790) in particular. Besides *Towards Perpetual Peace* (1795), also *What Is Enlightenment?* (1784), *Conjectural Beginning of Human History* (1786), *Idea for a Universal History from a Cosmopolitan Perspective* (1784) and the *Anthropology* (1798, 1800) belong to the works that sometimes are referred to as the historic-political writings.

Kant's implicit utopia concerns humanity in general, and the human being's development towards fulfilment of her capacities, especially reason. The human being, according to Kant, is part of the world of necessity and nature on the one hand and the world of freedom on the other. His famous definition of Enlightenment as "the human being's emancipation from its self-incurred immaturity", where immaturity is the "lack of resolve and courage to make use of one's intellect without the direction of another" indicates a part of that development (Kant 2006 [1784]: 17). Within his main works on the critical philosophy, it is particularly in the third critique that Kant describes the teleological development of mankind. In short, Kant's implicit utopia is described as if nature had a purpose, a teleological purpose directed towards the final goal, which is the fulfilment of the capacities of the faculties of the human being and especially the development of reason. It is as if nature helps the human being to reach the development of all her capacities.

One part of Kant's implicit utopia is thus the supposed teleology, the "as if" philosophy, to act as if or conceive the world as if there was a final end. In some of his later writings, he sketches the history of mankind assuming its way towards a perpetual peace, thereby connecting to the tradition of millenarianism. He seeks empirical evidence that humanity as a whole is making progress towards a better world. Still, it is not the past but rather the future that he is interested in. One of his observations is that human beings are characterised by unsocial sociability, "ungesellige Geselligkeit", a feature that makes them neither satisfied with others, nor satisfied with being alone.

Cosmopolitanism is thus one of the important components of Kant's implicit utopia. The central question is the telos in the historical world, and that the human being is the final goal, not just concerning the faculties she has in common with non-human creatures, but her unique rational capacity to construct an ideal society governed by human reason—and where no laws are needed, as human actions are guided by a moral law. According to Kant's thought experiment, human history began when the human species left a peaceful Arcadia and then began to develop their reason. As the destiny of a person cannot be fulfilled in a lifetime, the alternative is that it be fulfilled through history. Human beings are characterised by an antagonism between nature and freedom and by unsocial sociability. Through conflicts, humans are spread all over the globe, but because of its spherical form, they cannot spread forever. At some point, they need a developed rational capacity in order to advance towards an ideal world where peace of mind as well as peace between states prevails.

Cosmopolitanism is central to this development, since Kant considers it as being a part in the development of the rationality of the human being. One important part of the fulfilment of the human capacities is the development of a moral law, leading to a utopia where there is no contradiction or conflict between moral law, political law and the inclination of the will and desire.

According to Kant, human nature is not peaceful, and humans will occasionally break out in quarrels, hostilities and war. For this reason, a system of law is needed, founded on a constitution that guarantees the freedom of each individual in coexistence with the freedom of others. The ideal constitutional form is what he describes as republican, and the free republics should then unite in a federation founded on federal right (Kant 2006 [1795]: 74f.). Kant's system of right regulates the law between citizens (republicanism) and the law between states (international right) and adds the third cosmopolitan right, between states and the individual who is not a citizen and where hospitality is a central concept (ibid.: 82).

In *Towards Perpetual Peace* Kant formulates, in the shape of a peace treaty, one of his theses as follows: "Cosmopolitan right shall be limited to the conditions of universal hospitality" with the limitation that the stranger can be turned away if it can be done without causing his death (ibid.: 82). If Kant's cosmopolitan right is understood as his cosmopolitanism, this is a very narrow definition. Nevertheless, as mentioned above, this definition has been strongly in focus in recent years, with the refugee situation becoming an urgent global topic. However, cosmopolitanism is, from Kant's point of view, much larger than the concept of hospitality. Rather, it should be recognised as a part of an implicit utopia.

In the thesis from *Perpetual Peace*, mentioned above, Kant concludes:

> The growing prevalence of a (narrower or wider) community among the peoples of the earth has now reached a point where the violation of right at any *one* place on the earth is felt in *all* places. For this reason the idea of cosmopolitan right is no fantastic or exaggerated conception of right. Rather it is a necessary supplement to the unwritten code of constitutional and international right, for public human right in general, and hence for perpetual peace. Only under this condition can one flatter oneself to be continually progressing toward perpetual peace. (Kant 2006 [1795]: 84f.)

In this passage, the strictly defined cosmopolitan right opens up for a "community among all the peoples of the earth" which is attached to an idea of development towards fulfilment of the final goal, or of the full development of human capacity. As noted above, Kant's cosmopolitanism is an important part of the implicit utopia that is sketched within his philosophical system. This utopia has been analysed in different ways in different periods. For example, in times when Kant was interpreted as an analytic philosopher, as in the Anglo-Saxon tradition in the twentieth century, it is dismissed as a minor speculation. Manuel and Manuel's (1979) description of Kant's "Idea for a World History from a Cosmopolitan Point of View" [1784] provides an example of such a reading:

> The argument has none of the rigor of his thinking in other fields of philosophy. It is not at all formidable, this polite essay on the purpose and meaning of history as an introduction to euchronia, and it has an emotional quality that the professional bachelor of Königsberg hardly ever allowed to intrude into his writings. (Manuel and Manuel 1979: 519)

Nonetheless, only about a decade later, this part of Kant's philosophy was judged differently. After the fall of the Berlin wall and the collapse of the Soviet Union (1989/1991), Kant's *Towards Perpetual Peace* once again gained a position at the core of the academic debate. His ideas of a world peace and the way he suggested it to develop became a source for inspiration in the imagined new political landscape. That the work reached its bicentennial in 1995 did not decrease its popularity, and several conferences as well as publications were launched to celebrate his ideas.

However, even if Kant's *Perpetual Peace* is difficult to understand in full, it is not hard to see the relevance of Arendt's critique that Kant's late writings on history and politics do not compare in quality and depth with Kant's other writings and that a fourth critique was never written (Arendt 1992 [1970]: 7). The way in which Kant proposes states' internal organisation or his perception of the federation or the possible "state of peoples" (Kant 2006 [1795]: 81) has been in focus for long debates among philosophers (Cavallar 1999; Kleingeld 2011). Allen Wood (1998) argues, quite opposite to Arendt's position, that it is possible to consider the issues of *Perpetual Peace* as central in Kant's architectonic philosophical system, if we read the whole critical philosophy with a historical sensibility and as something that addresses a specific situation within the development of human history. With a sophisticated argumentation, Wood describes what I suggest is cosmopolitanism as utopia. He exemplifies how previous ideas that seemed utopian has been unexpectedly realised. One such idea is the peace project of Abbé de Saint-Pierre, a peace negotiator (1713), he called by him the European Union, which actually was realised a couple of centuries later. Wood suggests that some further utopian projects based on Kantian philosophy might be realised in the future, even though that does not seem feasible in our lifetime (Wood 1998: 73).

Cosmopolitanism as Utopia?

What do we talk about when we talk about cosmopolitanism? There are countless definitions, and the concept has been given dozens of attributes only over the past decades (Delanty ; Skrbiš and Woodward 2013: 4–5). As cosmopolitanism has the rhetoric form of an ism, this contributes to the false assumption that it more or less always refers to the same set of ideas. There have appeared several classifications of cosmopolitanisms at least since the end of the eighteenth century, some of which have been mentioned here. From other standpoints, the concept has been considered not useful for theorising on social and political challenges. Still, cosmopolitanism seems to maintain its attraction and keeps re-emerging, even though its effective history is so rich and contributes to several challenges for our understanding.

By the end of the Cold War, it was argued that this historical situation was the end of history as such (Fukuyama 1992). Of course, history cannot have an end; neither should utopia be conceived as a final end, but rather as a method for imagining a future whose central principle is expected to be equality and that is in dialogue with each particular time and space.

Levitas' theory of utopia as a reflexive method for imagining a better future seems appropriate for cosmopolitanism and its future. Kant's hope for a free human being in a peaceful world has been food for imagination for a long time. This implicit utopia, and not least its cosmopolitanism, consists of several embedded fragments that could serve as ideas for reconstruction according to the archaeological mode suggested by Levitas. Concerning the ontological mode in Levitas' method, it would problematise the view of the human being and show how the ideals are situated in time and space. As suggested in this chapter, the whole idea of cosmopolitanism does not need to be dismissed on the ground of racism or dismissal of women as citizens as has been done in some of the previous works referred to (Bernasconi 2001, 2011). It would include that cosmopolitanism does not have to be elitist and excluding. Such a reinvented cosmopolitanism could perhaps be a utopia in Levitas' sense and constitute a crucial tool in the making of the future (Levitas 2013: 220). Other theorists argue in a similar way and suggest that cosmopolitanism could serve as a toolkit which helps us to labour on the cosmopolitan project (Skrbiš and Woodward 2013: 52).

Utopia as a reflexive method for better futures might contain too much of nothing but reflection and formulation of ideals without roots in lived life. The social imagination and hopes for a potential future are part of each specific situation. It is worth considering the performances and practices as suggested by Skrbiš and Woodward, as well as cosmopolitics. In this respect, the utopian method would be in dialogue with its own time and space, which also implies that it must be reconsidered depending on the situation. If we consider cosmopolitanism just as a value in itself we neglect the personal, social and political relations within a society, which demonstrates the necessity of anchoring of cosmopolitanism in a practical idea of the human being (Pendenza 2017: 13).

I have suggested that cosmopolitanism is far wider than hospitality or the rights of refugees—it could be elaborated into a utopia of a better world for everyone, a utopia formulated in a specific time and space, which could then serve as an inspiration for action and organisation, just as Kant (2006 [1795]: 84) writes that a "violation of right at any *one* place on earth is felt in *all* places". A utopia has the potential to lead to a will for change and thereby also action and mobilisation. According to Levitas, utopia must be continually reinvented as one of the tools of making the future. To consider cosmopolitanism as utopia is an invitation for imagination for a better future, even if it may not be a solution in itself.

References

Arendt, H. 1992 [1970]. *Lectures on Kant's Political Philosophy*, edited by R. Beiner. Chicago: University of Chicago Press.

Arendt, H. 2000 [1949]. "The Perplexities of the Rights of Man". In *The Portable Hannah Arendt*, edited by P. Baehr, 31–46. New York: Penguin Books.

Bernasconi, R. 2001. "Who Invented the Concept of Race? Kant's Role in the Enlightenment Construction of Race". In *Race*, edited by R. Bernasconi, 11–36. Oxford: Blackwell.

Bernasconi, R. 2011. "Kant's Third Thoughts on Race". In *Reading Kant's Geography*, edited by E. Stuart and E. Mendiata, 291–318. Albany: State University of New York System Press.

Brown, G. W. 2019. "Kant and Cosmopolitan Legacies". In *Routledge International Handbook of Cosmopolitanism Studies*, edited by G. Delanty, 2nd ed., 11–20. London and New York: Routledge.

Cavallar, G. 1999. *Kant and the Theory and Practice of International Right*. Cardiff: University of Wales Press.

Cheah, P., and B. Robbins. 1998. *Cosmopolitics: Thinking and Feeling Beyond the Nation*. Minneapolis: University of Minnesota Press.

Cheneval, F. 2002. *Philosophie in weltbürgerlicher Bedeutung: Über die Entstehung und die philosophischen Grundlagen des supranationalen und kosmopolitischen Denkens der Moderne*. Basel: Schwabe & Co.

Delanty, G. 2019a. "Introduction: The field of Cosmopolitanism Studies." In *Routledge International Handbook of Cosmopolitanism Studies*, edited by G. Delanty, 2nd ed., 1–8. London and New York: Routledge.

Delanty, G. (ed.). 2019b. *Routledge International Handbook of Cosmopolitanism Studies*, 2nd ed., London and New York: Routledge.

Etinson, A. 2010. "Cosmopolitanism: Cultural, Moral, and Political." In *Sovereign Justice: Global Justice in a World of Nations*, edited by D. P. Aurelio, G. De Angelis and R. Queiroz, 25–46. Berlin and New York: Walter de Gruyter. https://doi.org/10.1515/9783110245745.1.25.

Fukuyama, F. 1992. *The End of History and the Last Man*. New York: Avon Books.

Gadamer, H.-G. 1960. *Wahrheit und Methode. Grundzüge einer philosophischen Hermeneutik*. Tübingen: Mohr.

Gilroy, P. 2004. *After Empire: Melancholia or Convivial Culture?* New York: Routledge.

Gilroy, P. 2015. "Cosmopolitanism and Conviviality in an Age of Perpetual War." In *Whose Cosmopolitanism? Critical Perspectives, Relationalities and Discontents*, edited by N. Glick Schiller and A. Irving, 232–244. New York and Oxford: Berghahn.

Glick Schiller, N., and A. Irving, eds. 2015. *Whose Cosmopolitanism? Critical Perspectives, Relationalities and Discontents*. New York and Oxford: Berghahn.
Goode, Luke and Michael Godhe. 2017. "Beyond Capitalist Realism—Why We Need Critical Future Studies". *Culture Unbound: Journal of Current Cultural Research* 9 (1): 109–129.
Gustafsson, J. 2019, forthcoming. "Värnpliktsvägran för världens skull: Världsmedborgarrörelsen och visionen om medborgarskap för fred." In *Det lyckliga femtiotalet: Sexualitet, politik och motstånd*, edited by A. Burman and B. Holmqvist. Stockholm/Höör: Symposion.
Kant, I. 2006 [1784]. "An Answer to the Question: What Is Enlightenment?" In *Toward Perpetual Peace and Other Writings on Politics Peace, and History*, edited by P. Kleingeld, 17–23. New Haven and London: Yale University Press.
Kant, I. 2006 [1784–1798]. *Toward Perpetual Peace and Other Writings on Politics Peace, and History*, edited by P. Kleingeld. New Haven and London: Yale University Press.
Kant, I. 2006 [1795]. "Toward Perpetual Peace." In *Toward Perpetual Peace and Other Writings on Politics Peace, and History*, edited by P. Kleingeld, 67–109. New Haven and London: Yale University Press.
Kleingeld, P. 1999. "Six Kinds of Cosmopolitanism in Late Eighteenth-Century Germany". *Journal of the History of Ideas* 60: 505–524.
Kleingeld, P. 2011. *Kant and Cosmopolitanism: The Philosophical Ideal of World Citizenship*. Cambridge: Cambridge University Press.
Kurunmäki, J., and J. Marjanen. 2018. "A Rhetorical View of Isms: An Introduction." *Journal of Political Ideologies* 23: 241–255. https://doi.org/10.1080/13569317.2018.1502939.
Lettevall, R. 2008. "The Idea of Kosmopolis: Two Kinds of Cosmopolitanism." In *The Idea of Kosmopolis: History, Philosophy and Politics of World Citizenship*, edited by R. Lettevall and M. K. Linder, 13–30. Stockholm: Södertörn Academic Studies.
Lettevall, R. 2012. *Neutrality in Twentieth-Century Europe: Intersections of Science, Culture, and Politics After the First World War*. New York: Routledge.
Levitas, R. 2013. *Utopia as Method: The Imaginary Reconstitution of Society*. Basingstoke and Hampshire: Palgrave Macmillan.
Manuel, F., and F. Manuel. 1979. *Utopian Thought in the Western World*. Oxford: Basil Blackwell.
Pendenza, M. 2017. "Societal Cosmopolitanism: The Drift from Universalism Towards Particularism." *Distinktion: Journal of Social Theory* 18 (1): 3–17. https://doi.org/10.1080/1600910x.2017.1290668.
Povrzanović Frykman, M. 2016. "Cosmopolitanism in Situ: Conjoining Local and Universal Concerns in a Malmö Neighbourhood." *Identities: Global Studies in Culture and Power* 23 (1): 35–50. https://doi.org/10.1080/1070289X.2015.1016525.
Skrbiš, Z., and I. Woodward. 2013. *Cosmopolitanism: Use of the Idea*. Los Angeles: Sage.

Wood, A. 1998. "Kant's Project for Perpetual Peace." In *Cosmopolitics: Thinking and Feeling Beyond the Nation*, edited by P. Cheah and B. Robbins, 59–76. Minneapolis: University of Minnesota Press.

Open Access This chapter is licensed under the terms of the Creative Commons Attribution 4.0 International License (http://creativecommons.org/licenses/by/4.0/), which permits use, sharing, adaptation, distribution and reproduction in any medium or format, as long as you give appropriate credit to the original author(s) and the source, provide a link to the Creative Commons license and indicate if changes were made.

The images or other third party material in this chapter are included in the chapter's Creative Commons license, unless indicated otherwise in a credit line to the material. If material is not included in the chapter's Creative Commons license and your intended use is not permitted by statutory regulation or exceeds the permitted use, you will need to obtain permission directly from the copyright holder.

CHAPTER 6

Creolising Conviviality: Thinking Relational Ontology and Decolonial Ethics Through Ivan Illich and Édouard Glissant

Encarnación Gutiérrez Rodríguez

Introduction

In *Tools for Conviviality*, Ivan Illich (1973) questions how the tools of industrial and technological advancement can serve a common good. He discusses conviviality by focusing on the relationship between technological tools and their communal use. Édouard Glissant, in *Le Discours Antillais* (1981) and in *Poétique de la Relation* (1990, 1997b), writes about the twofold character of creolisation as on the one hand deriving from colonial racial rule and on the other prescribing a future of communal living to come. Taking the analyses of these two authors on conviviality and creolisation, this chapter asks, (a) how we can think conviviality in relation to creolisation, and (b) how we can conceptualise creolising conviviality. These questions are addressed by setting Illich's discussion of convivial tools in dialogue with Glissant's concept of creolisation. The chapter engages with

E. Gutiérrez Rodríguez (✉)
Justus-Liebig-University Giessen, Giessen, Germany
e-mail: E.Gutierrez-Rodriguez@sowi.uni-giessen.de

the historical analyses underpinning these concepts, their relational ontological assumptions and their decolonial ethical implications.

Illich and Glissant work with concepts that engage with the relational and ethical potential of living together with a commitment to social justice. However, while the industrial society and its technological endeavours, which pay very little attention to the pursuit of a common good, are at the centre of Illich's analysis, Glissant's perspective on creolisation outlines a decolonial critique of the racialised hierarchisation and compartmentalisation of modern society that impedes living together on equal ethical terms. The chapter is structured as follows. First, we will engage with the concept of conviviality by tracing it back to the Spanish etymology "convivencia", living together. From here, we will continue our discussion by engaging with lllich's notion of "convivial tools", followed by a brief discussion of Paul Gilroy's observations about "convivial culture". From there, we will trace some of the debates in social and cultural anthropology, sociology and human geography on the anthropology of encounters and the "conviviality turn". What this perspective entails for the conceptualisation of "transversal conviviality" will then be examined by drawing on my own study on migration, domestic work and affect. It is from that perspective that we will draw on Glissant's concept of creolisation and set it in relation with Illich's conviviality.

Conviviality: On Relational Ontology

In 1973 Illich published his essay, "Tools for conviviality", in Harper & Row's World Perspectives series. He wrote in the foreword that the idea had evolved during a series of events that took place at Centro Intercultural de Documentación (CIDOC) in Cuernavaca, Mexico, in 1972. CIDOC was created in 1966 and replaced the Centre of Intercultural Formation (CIC), founded at the Jesuit University of Fordham, where Illich had held a professorship in sociology in the late 1950s. CIDOC was a civil association recognised by Mexican law, hosting a language school, a conference centre, a library and an independent publisher. Illich was the director, and during its ten years of existence renowned intellectuals such as Erich Fromm, Paulo Freire, Andre Gorz and others worked within this intellectually and politically engaged centre (Grünig Iribarren 2013). While working at CIDOC, Illich developed a critique of modernisation driven by industrialisation resulting in the commodification and monetarisation of life, increasing the gap between rich and poor. Silvia Grünig Iribarren, drawing on Kalle Dietrich, explains how Illich summarised his analysis of industrialisation by discussing the phenomenon of "modernised poverty" (Grünig Iribarren 2013: 50). The divide between rich and poor is established along the lines of industrial development and its capital growth. Based on this analysis, Illich pointed to the disastrous consequences this development has for humanity and the planet. At the centre of monetary and financial gains stands the maxim of capital profit. Humanity and the planet figure only in these financial calculations as assets for capital growth. Confronting and contesting this logic of social development, Illich proposed the convivial use of technological tools to bring wellbeing and economic justice to all. Conviviality, for him, has the potential to address an intrinsic ethical value underlining the interconnectedness and mutual dependency between human beings, the planet and the cosmos. Conviviality in Illich's sense goes beyond the living together of people and embraces a planetary cosmological thinking which realises that one's individual life depends on the wellbeing of the planet. Illich's concept entails a critique of capitalism and formulates a proposal for a radical humanism. He traces this argument by drawing on the Spanish debate on "convivencia", which was rooted in Spanish counter-narratives to the colonial and imperial monocultural and monolingual project of fascist Spain.

Countering Spanish Fascism: "Convivencia"

The term "convivial" in Illich's work refers etymologically to the Latin verb "convivere" and its development in the Spanish language to "convivencia". The Romance genealogy is thus relevant, as the English translation "convivial" emphasises "joyful coming together" rather than the idea of a moral living together that the Spanish "convivencia" carries. Concretely, it means "to live in the company of others, living in the same habitat". While it is a consequence of cohabitation (in Spanish *coexistencia*), "convivencia" goes a step further than just describing the inhabiting of a commonplace. It also has moral implications as it emphasises a communal being in the world, one that is tied to a respectful and caring living together. Illich was inspired in his use of this term by the Spanish discourse on "convivencia" of the twentieth century. This discourse was initiated by the work of the cultural historian and philologist Américo Castro y Quesada. In his 1948 account of Spanish intellectual history, *España en su historia*, Castro argues for a transcultural genealogy of artistic and intellectual practice and thought in Spain.

While for historians of the Iberian Medieval Age, this approach might not be entirely accurate and might fail to capture the complexity of these times (Manzano Moreno 2013; Soifer 2009; Szpiech 2013), from a political standpoint Castro's proposal represents, within the parameters of his time, a vision of a progressive, democratic and transcultural society (Glick 1992; Shamsie 2016; Wolf 2009). As Miriam Bodian notes in her essay "Américo Castro's Conversos and the Question of Subjectivity" (2017), this account is not without racial stereotypes, as in Castro's use of "caste" which, he argues, refers to lineage and not to biological race. Nonetheless, as Bodian observes, this distinction is not always neatly presented in his work. However, Castro does attempt to challenge the discourse on national identity of the nineteenth century. Taking up the preoccupation of the intellectual generation of 1898, a generation of Spanish intellectuals who failed to come to terms with anti-colonial struggles and the end of the Spanish Empire, Castro raises the question of "who the Spaniards are, how they are made up, and their ultimate worth as a nation" (Castro 1971: 583). Yet, while the critique of the Spanish colonial project does not figure in his analysis either, he challenges the dominant view of Spanish history at this time. The generation of 1898 was engaging with a conservative nationalist project that sought to construct an "eternal Gothic Castilean" Spain, referring to the Spanish Medieval Golden Age as a point of departure. Taking 711 as a starting point from which to think the intellectual and aesthetic coming into being of the Spanish nation, Castro traces the interfaith dialogue and cultural encounters during the Umayyad Caliphate of Cordoba between 929 and 1031, where Jews, Christians and Muslims built intellectual circles to exchange and translate ideas in the Mediterranean region (Glick 1979/2005; Menocal 2002). Further, he engages with notions of cultural mixing by focusing on the intellectual figure of the *converso*.

Drawing on the analysis of the fifteenth-century writings of Fernando de la Torre, an aristocratic *converso* from Castile, Castro formulates the observation that Spain's cultural identity crisis is rooted in the denial of the multi-faith history of the Early Medieval Iberian Peninsula. By doing this, Castro places exchange and mixing between the Jewish, Muslim and Christian cultures at the heart of the historiography of the Iberian Peninsula. Further, again reflecting debates on national identity in the Spain of the late nineteenth and early twentieth centuries, he develops an account of the way of being—the spirit of life of the inhabitants of Spanish territory— by focusing on what Bodian (2017: 6) calls "Spain's morada vital". Castro saw the articulation of this specific spirit (Geist) in the literary expression of sixteenth- and seventeenth-century works written by *conversos*. As Bodian (2017: 4) writes, it "was in this romantic vein that he developed his twin ideas of the *morada vital* of a people—that cluster of characteristics that makes up the unique "nosotros" of a people—and the accompanying concept of *vividura*, or the consciousness of a people of being part of that collective existence." The Spanish conservative state and in particular the Francoist regime, with their respective traditional intellectuals, as Castro argues, have failed to acknowledge and capture the hybrid spirit shaping the cultural expressions of Spanish territory.

For Castro, this process of historical oblivion was carried out through the expulsion of the Muslims and Jews from Spain in the fifteenth and sixteenth centuries.[1] Drawing on his teacher Menéndez y Pelayo, who developed the concept of "convivencia" through his analysis of linguistic variances in Spain, Castro reconnects to the attempt to produce a national historiography. However, his project represents an attempt to create a hegemonic historiography in Antonio Gramsci's sense, engaging with a project for inclusive democracy embracing social justice. Thus, while his teacher belonged to the group of traditional intellectuals who promoted a conservative understanding of Spanish historiography, Castro's approach is based on attempting to create a progressive, inclusive, democratic account as opposed to the Francoist project of *Hispanidad* in which Spain is configured as a white, Catholic, colonising and imperial nation. Written from his exile in the United States, his historical account *España en su historia* represents a counter-historiography nourished by a political vision of a democratic transcultural nation. The project does connect to European historiographies engaging with the building of the modern nation state in the nineteenth century. Yet, Castro's national project embracing "convivencia" as a counter-discourse to fascist Spain, imagined a transcultural nation with multiple religious believes, languages and cultures.

This project, imagining European nation-states in multi-faith, multilingual and transcultural terms, still remains a point of struggle in contemporary political debates in Europe (Sakrani 2016), for example, in relation to the rise of extreme right-wing political forces proclaiming a Christian, white, ethnically monocultural Europe detached from its history of colonialism, the transatlantic slave trade, imperialism and European settler colonialism-migration. Right up to this day in Europe, the myth of the nation as rooted in one and the same ethnic, racial, religious, linguistic and cultural origin haunts and circulates in the media and in political speeches on national belonging and the formation of the nation-state.

While Illich does not make any explicit reference to Castro's work, as we will see in the following his reference to "convivencia" was based on a dynamic process of encounters and the creative and intellectual potential of living together. However, the social inequalities pre-empting the potential of living together complicate and limit the possibility of conviviality, as the material analysis of the convivial potential of technological tools in Illich's work shows.

Tools for Conviviality: Material Underpinnings and the Common Good

Illich introduces his approach to conviviality by discussing the technological transformation of society as a process of alienation. Arguing that the "technical development of consumer society needs to serve people's common needs" (1973: 18), he draws attention to the role of tools serving the goals of an industrialisation that addresses the needs of capital accumulation. Countering this use of tools, he suggests that we conceive of tools as a way of promoting social justice, providing a communal good living for all. Technological tools used with the sole goal of capital gain disregard the fact that a sustainable society cannot be reproduced on these terms. It is in this sense that Illich discusses the convivial dimension of tools serving the needs of all and the planet. As he notes, we need to

> consider conviviality to be individual freedom realised in personal interdependence and, as such, an intrinsic ethical value. I believe that, in any society, as conviviality is reduced below a certain level, no amount of industrial productivity can effectively satisfy the needs it creates among society's members. Present institutional purposes, which hallow industrial productivity at the expense of convivial effectiveness, are a major factor in the amorphousness and meaninglessness that plague contemporary society. (Illich 1973: 17)

Industrial productivity is carried by the logic of capital accumulation, leading to the individual benefit of a few, while the larger part of the population experiences a deterioration in their living conditions. The use of technological tools within the project of capital growth is related to labour exploitation, land grabbing, extractivism, the expropriation of communal land, the privatisation of the provision of food and basic needs such as education, health and care, just to mention a few factors. Within the context of the industrial-prison-complex and migration and asylum control policies, technological tools are also related to incarceration, camps technologies, holding parts of the population in dehumanising conditions. Thus, as Illich notes referring to the aim of producing docile bodies attending to consumer and capital production needs, the use of technological tools attends to socio-political and economic circumstances. Countering this development, Illich discusses conviviality as a counter-project addressing the potential of human practices and knowledge in creating conditions for a living together driven by a common good. For Illich:

> People need not only to obtain things, they need above all the freedom to make things among which they can live, to give shape to them according to their own tastes, and to put them to use in caring for and about others. (Illich 1973: 17)

This observation brings us to what I call *Being-In-Relation,* addressing communal practices of care and responsibility. In Illich's sense, conviviality subscribes to a project that takes the relational and interdependent character of social Being and Becoming as its starting point. Evoking the function of institutions in providing and securing the realisation of communal life, Illich proposes the establishment of a convivial use of tools serving social justice and economic distribution, drawing on

> a new consciousness about the nature of tools and on majority action for their control. If tools are not controlled politically, they will be managed in a belated technocratic response to disaster. Freedom and dignity will continue to dissolve into an unprecedented enslavement of man to his tools. As an alternative to technocratic disaster, I propose the vision of a convivial society. A convivial society would be the result of social arrangements that guarantee for each member the most ample and free access to the tools of the community and limit this freedom only in favour of another member's equal freedom. (Illich 1973: 17–18)

Illich's vocabulary is quite revealing of a period in which Marxist utopianism was commonplace in Western academia. Other scholars writing at this time such as Adorno, Herbert Marcuse and Paulo Freire were formulating similar diagnoses of society and emphasising the role of the senses, libido and desire in producing common awareness and counter-strategies to the appropriation and alienation tendencies produced by the logic of production and accumulation of capital.

In a period when the gap between rich and poor is rapidly increasing, precariousness and the cheapening of the workforce have become the rule for people in employment, families are evicted from their homes and their access to public health care and education is further restricted, human beings are held in refugee camps or in a limbo of human and citizenship rights, the need for a vocabulary that can be used in understanding practices of conviviality is pertinent. In this context, conviviality represents an intrinsic ethical value based on the moral principle of the common good. It is this spirit that Paul Gilroy (2004) captured thirty years later in his work on the melancholia of Empire in British society.

Convivial Culture: Practices of a Living Together

In *After Empire*, Gilroy briefly refers to "convivial cultures" when he observes everyday life in the streets of London. Gilroy describes these as ordinary features of multicultural societies. He defines convivial culture as the "process[es] of cohabitation and interaction that have made multiculture an ordinary feature of social life in Britain's urban areas and in postcolonial cities elsewhere …" (2004: xi). By using this term, Gilroy shifts the perspective on identities to local communal practices, addressing people's everyday life. This perspective has sparked and inspired research in anthropology, sociology and geography invested in the understanding of people's practices and encounters as well as in the building of local support networks.

Research on diasporic pathways and aspiring cosmopolitan cities has mobilised Gilroy's concept of convivial culture in order to understand the dynamics and relationality in which living together takes place (Glick Schiller et al. 2006; Gutiérrez Rodríguez 2011, 2015). Further, research on super-diversity and conviviality (Nowicka and Vertovec 2014; Heil 2015; Padilla et al. 2015) and the limits of conviviality (Lapina 2016) have engaged with empirical questions concerning the potential and limits of conviviality.[2] In addition, ethnographic research on conviviality has been conducted in the field of migration studies and the anthropology of encounters (for the South African context, see Vigneswaran 2014; Brudvig 2014; for south-east Asian contexts, see Gandhi and Hoek 2012; Wise and Velayutham 2013). On another level, studies on the dynamics of support of refugees by German civil society have addressed the question of communal support (Foroutan et al. 2017; Karakayali and Kleist 2016; Schiffauer et al. 2017) and solidarity (Glick Schiller and Caglar 2010; Glick Schiller 2016; Kymlicka 2016; Nowicka 2019). These studies discuss the transcultural fabric of society and investigate the potential of forging common ground between the recently migrated populations, which are placed through asylum and migration policies within categories such as "refugee", "EU migrant", "third country migrant", and the seemingly established population. Looking at education, work, housing and health, these studies show how an infrastructure of support can be established in order to create inclusive public support. In sum, the perspective on conviviality in these studies disrupts the pattern of thinking in "divided communities", stressing instead the universal claim to sustainable common lives. This conceptual perspective adjusts the methodological and theoretical lens by questioning the "ethnic lens" and conceptions of homogeneous communities with shared cultural boundaries found in much scholarship on ethnic, racial, and religious minorities and in research on transnational migration (Wimmer and Glick Schiller 2002).

Connecting with Gilroy's observation, empirical research operating within the parameters of convivial cultures and conviviality is complicating discourses on "fragmented" and "parallel" societies by showing how everyday culture relates to practices operating through connections and producing connections beyond ethnic and racial divides. This research resonates with Gilroy's observation of convivial cultures shaping everyday encounters in British society. As he notes in his analysis of postcolonial Britain, the transcultural fabric of British society has not only been shaped by the (post)colonial diasporic and migratory movements in the second half of the twentieth century, but also by a long-standing history of colonialism and imperialism dating back to the seventeenth century. The phenomenon of "convivial culture" is thus an outcome of historical global entanglements, which are also reflected in Glissant's concept of creolisation.

Creolising Conviviality

The term "creolisation" stands at the heart of French Caribbean Radical Thought (Nesbitt 2013; Gutiérrez Rodríguez and Tate 2015). It refers to a cultural transformation of society based on the experience of displacement and diasporic movements brought about through European colonialism, the Atlantic slave trade, and imperial trade and expansion policies. Focusing on the Caribbean as a territory marked and constituted through this history, the Martinique intellectual Édouard Glissant (1981) introduces the concept of creolisation, drawing on Caribbean ontologies and material historical conditions. For Glissant, creolisation engages with a new perspective on understanding the world in relational and interconnected ways, and as such he considered it a universal proposal directed to everyone ('Tout-Monde') (Glissant 1997a, b; see also Mercier 2012; interview with Schwieger Hiepko 1998). He argues that "creolisation" cannot be conflated with the notion of *métissage*, meaning the organisation of the social through compartmentalised racial coding. Colonial governance took place by producing ethnic and racial entities and relating them to each other in a hierarchical order, creating instances of superiority and inferiority along the colour line. Opposing this ideology of cultural mixing, thinking cultures as standing side by side and reproducing themselves always by reproducing the pattern of racial social divides, he says: "One can mix without being touched at all—mixing can be mechanical—white peas and black peas. As long as the idea that the coloniser and its culture are superior persists, mixing can't be other than mechanical" (transl. by the author).[3]

Countering this notion of cultural mixing as reproducing the racialised hierarchical social order, "creolisation" describes the potential of creating something new, a rhizomatic transformation of culture, not producing old patterns of thinking but attending to the "unforeseeable" ('*l'inattendue*') (1996). As Glissant says in *Odyssées immigrées* (2010), creolisation announces "*le différance que se mette au contact et que produise l'imprévisible*" [the difference that makes contact and produces the unforeseeable].[4]

As the Jamaican writer and philosopher Sylvia Wynter (1989) notes with regard to the concept of *Antilleanity*, the concept of creolisation can be considered a "forceful episteme" through which the world can be thought. This Caribbean episteme thus introduces an ontological and historical understanding of the world that takes the process of the racial codification of social hierarchies based on the scientific classification of populations and territories in European modernity as a point of departure. The late Peruvian sociologist Aníbal Quijano's epistemic and material matrix of the "coloniality of power" (2000, 2008), organised around the axis of "race", configures the modern European perception of the world since the advent of European colonialism in the fifteenth century. Since then racialisation, the organisation of social inequalities, capital extraction and labour exploitation along the colour line, has structured modern societies (cf. Gutiérrez Rodríguez 2019). While creolisation emerges within this context of modern racial classification, it implies a vision of surpassing this pattern of categorisation by relying on "multiple, rather than singular, roots and foundations that, when taken as a whole, aim at the dual objectives of liberation and of setting foundations for freedom beyond the trappings of the dialectics of asymmetrical recognition" (Gordon and Roberts 2009: 6).

For Glissant, creolisation counters the remnants of European colonial thinking. As Shirley Anne Tate and I argue in our edited volume *Creolizing Europe: Legacies and Transformations* (2015), creolisation denotes a project of decolonising the kind of thinking that reproduces racial and ethnic hierarchies. In times of growing nationalism, when the media representation of refugees and migrants as well as right-wing political speeches on the "failure of multiculturalism" either imply or state a need for further restrictions and severe control mechanisms on migration and the deportation or internment of refugees and asylum seekers, a change in the understanding of our contemporary societies is pertinent. Creolisation offers us a new way of comprehending social development. It offers a counter-strategy that stresses the variation of cultural mixing, not always prescribed by an officially recognised nomenclature, going beyond the existing patterns of classification and categorisation. As such, creolisation announces what is to come, a future to embrace the multiplicity deriving from processes in motion, constantly transforming as it goes, appearing at the juncture of what we know and what is unknown.

Attempts at organising a living together evolve within processes of creolisation. On the one hand, we live in societies where racial coding still organises society. Although they are not always explicitly spelt out, racial hierarchies as such dominate our society. At the same time, processes of disrupting and creating new ways of being within and beyond the colonial patterns of racial classification are taking place aesthetically (see Tate 2009), intellectually, organisationally and quotidianly. Besides the rules of racist colonisation and racial capitalism, new forms of being and becoming in the world are happening, countering these systems of oppression. Creolisation is one enunciation of this process. Yet, creolisation is not fulfilled if the coloniality of power remains in place. Creolisation and decolonisation are two sides of the same project of anti-colonial struggle. Thus, creolisation engages with practices and notions of liberation at the same time as it is situated within a cognitive script of colonial domination.

In a similar vein Illich's conviviality, rather than describing a *fait accompli*, relates to everyday practices forging a living together. Both concepts, creolisation and conviviality, engage with social processes and practices of transformation in everyday culture. Further, they foresee possible futures of a living together.

Transversal Conviviality in the Private Household

As I have shown in my study on migration, domestic work and affect in private households (Gutiérrez Rodríguez 2010), conviviality is shaped by a transversal moment within a context of a creolised society. Drawing on Félix Guattari's notion of "transversality", which he developed during his work as a psychiatrist in the psychiatric clinic La Borde, I consider private households employing migrant domestic workers as translocal sites, where the sphere of the rational is permeated by less tangible moments and experiences (Gutiérrez Rodríguez 2011). As such the private household does not only reflect the societal context—existing social inequalities, the forms of governing and the hegemonic social order—in which it is embedded. It is also a point of encounter, where desires are articulated, feelings circulate and emotions are impressed and expressed. As such households are affective sites, places permeated by the circulation and transmission of feelings of joy, happiness and love, but also of sadness, contempt and disdain. The private household is a site where the members might be affectively animated when they encounter feelings of appreciation, but also disanimated when they experience feelings of degradation. It is within this context that I have reflected on the (dis-)affective (dis-)encounters between domestic workers and their employers. However, the term "encounter" needs to be contextualised. As Enrique Dussel (1995) argues in regard to the description of European colonialism as a site of cultural encounters, encounters do not always happen on a voluntary basis. People meet, as Mary Louise Pratt (1992) points out in her discussion of "contact zones", under political and social conditions of coercion and dependence. Members of different classes might meet at a restaurant, at a shop or at their children's school. Yet their encounter does not dissolve the relationship of inequality within which they are located. Thus, in the restaurant a person might wash the dishes, one might cut the vegetables, one might cook, one might serve and one might be sitting at a table with friends. This encounter is prescribed by the relationship between provider and user of services and employment relationships. The relationship between the restaurant client and the employees serving or working in the restaurant kitchen is one of interdependency. Client satisfaction depends on the gastronomic skills and the service, and the cook and the waitress depend on satisfaction for their salary. This is the relationship of interdependency and social divides in which everyday encounters between different social groups occur. Within this context, conviviality is a desiderate, something we might long for, but it is not always realised due to the social inequalities that structure our common lives.

When we look at the relationship between domestic workers and their employers in private households, the paradox of proximity and distance inscribed in their encounter becomes evident. The private household is commonly idealised in society as a site of intimacy. In fact, the private household is a space ruled by subjective aspirations, desires, fears, expectations and habits. The domestic worker is plunged into a workplace marked by a sensorial network and affective fabric configuring the household and the relationship of its members to it, to themselves and the outer world. The domestic worker faces this inner world of the household members, following their physical, existential and emotional traces, arranging them, sorting them. She not only makes the beds, prepares the meal, cleans the floor, she is the person in charge of the wellbeing of the household members through the physical and emotional labour she invests in recreating an agreeable habitat. She is thus responsible for the social reproduction of the household on two levels: on the generative level, making sure the basic needs for reproduction on the individual level are met, and second, by creating an agreeable and liveable environment. The domestic worker enables the forging of a living together. This living together, however, does not embrace Illich's intrinsic ethical value of conviviality as it is founded on unequal terms.

When an (un)documented migrant woman is employed in a private household, the immediate *effects* of migration and border regimes become tangible. The dividing line between "citizen" and "non-citizen" marks the encounter between these two women. Through the outsourcing of domestic work to another woman, two social groups that usually live in segregated spaces meet in the private household. We could say that due to the need for a cleaner or a carer, private, middle-class professional households become open to a social group to which they do not have any form of attachment. In this space, the employers and the domestic workers meet as two women living in divided spaces ruled by different timescales and professional demands. In this encounter, these two women articulate and negotiate their desires, needs and moments of identification and disidentification. They share some aspects related to the social construction and assignation of "femininity" in the households. However, this common experience, which might create a proximity between these women, is challenged by the structural distance between them imposed by migration control policies (among others). The divide between "citizen" and "migrant" positions them on different societal scales. For example, as my study on undocumented migrant domestic workers (2010) shows, they might not only lose their job if they assert their right to decent pay, they also risk deportation. Under these conditions, these two women experience an intimate encounter, a "living together" entrenched in structural divisions sustaining a "living apart". They usually do not live in the same neighbourhoods. Very often the domestic worker needs to travel a long distance to reach their employer's household, which is likely to be located in a predominantly racially and nationally homogenous area. Their children usually do not attend the same schools and their friendship circles do not overlap, but in the privacy of the households these two women meet and share moments of unprecedented intimacy (Gutiérrez Rodríguez 2007).

Thus, the encounter between the domestic worker and the employer is one based on a (dis-)encounter, due to the unevenness underlying their meeting, marked by the social invisibility of this labour, the lack of social recognition and the degradation of the person performing this work. The encounter between these two sides, employer and domestic worker, takes place on the grounds of a system of social (re-)production shaped by social inequalities. It is the domestic worker that provides the foundations for liveability and the possibility of a living together. However, the lack of cultural, social and economic recognition of her work and the employment relationship her labour is based on complicate the potential of conviviality. This example demonstrates that the discussion on conviviality needs to consider the material conditions in which moments of a living together are forged.

Considering the spontaneous and relational character of our lives, and also our emotional and material dependencies on others, makes us realise that we constantly transgress the imagined boundaries set by monocultural and monolingual societal prescriptions. Affiliations are guided by needs, feelings, affects and desires that bring us together in unexpected ways. It is in this regard that our relationships unfold in transversal ways, converging and diverging at different points. The project of creolising conviviality is informed by transversal vital forces moving us in different directions and embracing the principles of interconnectedness and interdependence.[5] Attending to the rhizomatic movement of our lives, the concept of creolisation proposes an ethic of a "living together" driven by the unexpected and resulting from our multiple encounters and connections (Glissant 2002).

In the European context, creolisation not only signals "the underside of European modernity"[6] but also brings to mind the transformation of European societies through the impact of postcolonial migration and diaspora. It frames a space in which a rhetoric of identity and community is contested. In this sense, Glissant describes Europe as inevitably inscribed in the project of creolisation. Creolisation, thus, delineates a different understanding of conviviality. Engaging with an ethic of relationality and transversality, it resonates with cosmological visions of a better world.

Creolisation speaks about an affective being in the world—the sensibility that nourishes the potential for conviviality. This is seen in Glissant's observation and question:

> Creolisation is the movement of the world – why would you like to go against the movement of the world? The movement of the world is first to create a kind of being and collective – which are not based on affiliation, legitimation and the unique root – sure, the whole movement is a liberation movement and not a movement of oppression.[7]

In this sense, creolisation stands at the heart of a political and ethical project of conviviality.

Conclusion: Decolonial Ethics of Conviviality

Going back to Illich, conviviality as a societal model of "living together" cannot be realised under unequal economic and legal conditions. Yet, as a model of solidarity, conviviality can be envisioned through practices of support. As Illich contends, conviviality might be understood as an intrinsic ethical value that, as argued here, needs to be related to the material conditions of our lives.

Illich's approach to conviviality has a twofold character. It engages with the material grounds, practices and use of technological tools on the one hand, and on the other hand, it deals with the ontological and ethical proposal of a living together. In this sense, conviviality does not describe an empirical reality, but a potential one. It is what Glissant calls a future to come when he introduces his concept of "creolisation" as a new way of understanding the world in relational and interconnected ways.

Framing conviviality from the perspective of creolisation entails working with a cosmological perspective focusing on the interconnectedness and relationality of Being. Hence, attempts to create a living together derive from survival strategies emanating from the "contact zone" configured by different modes of production, through which various social groups are forced to live together, but through which human ability and creativity in connecting and forging common lives are triggered.

Creolising conviviality establishes the basis on which claims for a critical humanism can be formulated. This is a humanism that presupposes the universal recognition of all human beings, fundamental respect and the right to a dignified life. This is only possible if the logic of exploitation and the epistemological premises of an autonomous subject, detached from its environment, its social and affective Being, are dismantled. Humanity does not have its end in the individual recognition of the subject. Humanity is realised when we embrace a decolonial cosmology, involving the recognition of the interconnectedness and interdependency of the whole of humanity.

Notes

1. In 1492, the Alhambra Decree, issued by the Catholic Monarchs Isabella I of Castile and Ferdinand II of Aragon, instituted the expulsion of practicing Jews from the Kingdom of Castille and Aragon. This Decree targeted mainly *conversos*. Between 1609 and 1614 further royal orders expelling the Muslim population, known as *moriscos* were passed.
2. See also a recently initiated project at Lund University entitled "Beyond Racism. Ethnographies of Antiracism and Conviviality": https://portal.research.lu.se/portal/en/projects/beyond-racism-ethnographies-of-antiracism-and-conviviality(d74d2684-0da4-42c1-b4ee-2c68f5c1cc1b).html (retrieved February 20, 2019).
3. The quotation is from a radio programme on pathways, territory and history in the French radio station Aligre FM broadcast in 2010: www.edouardglissant.fr/mediatheque.html (see also Gutiérrez Rodríguez 2015).
4. English translation by the author.
5. See further discussion in Glissant, *Introduction à une poétique du divers* and *Poetique of Relation* [?? Is this intended to be the French title or the title of the English translation ?].
6. Dussel (1995).
7. Comment made by Glissant in an interview with Sophie Haluk for the radio programme Aligre FM, "Odyssées immigrées: Créolisation et Décolonisation", broadcast on the 16 July 2010. See http://www.edouardglissant.fr/audio.html, accessed September 12, 2012. Translation by the author. The original quote is: Créolisation c'est le mouvement même du monde—pourquoi voulait vous que nous allions à l'encontre du mouvement du monde? Le mouvement du monde c'est de créer premièrement un sort d'être

et de collectivité—ils ne sont plus basée sur l'affiliation, la légitimité et la racine unique—sur le mouvement entière c'est un mouvement libérateur et ce n'est pas un mouvement oppresseur.

References

Bodian, M. 2017. "Américo Castro's Conversos and the Question of Subjectivity." *Culture & History Digital Journal* 6 (2). http://dx.doi.org/10.3989/chdj.2017.018.

Brudvig, I. 2014. *Conviviality in Bellville: An Ethnography of Space, Place, Mobility and Being in Urban South Africa*. Mankon, Bamenda: Langaa RPCIG.

Castro, A. 1948. *España en su historia: cristianos, moros y judíos, 1885–1972*. Buenos Aires: Editorial Losada.

Castro, A. 1971. *The Spaniards—An Introduction to Their History*. Berkeley, Los Angeles, and London: University of California Press.

Dussel, E. 1995. *The Invention of the Americas: Eclipse of 'the Other' and the Myth of Modernity*. Translated by M. D. Barber. New York: Continuum.

Foroutan, N., U. Hamann, N. El-Kayed, and S. Jorek. 2017. *Zwischen Lager und Mietvertrag—Wohnunterbringung von geflüchteten Frauen in Berlin und Dresden*. Berlin: Berliner Institut für empirische Integrations—und Migrationsforschung.

Gandhi, A. and L. Hoek. 2012. "Introduction to Crowds and Conviviality: Ethnographies of the South Asian City." *Ethnography* 13 (1): 3–11.

Gilroy, P. 2004. *After Empire: Melancholia or Convivial Culture?* New York and London: Routledge.

Glick Schiller, N. 2016. "The Question of Solidarity and Society: Comment on Will Kymlicka's Article—'Solidarity in Diverse Societies'." *Comparative Migration Studies* 4 (1): 1–9. https://doi.org/10.1186/s40878-016-0027-x.

Glick Schiller, N. and A. Çaglar. 2010. *Locating Migration: Rescaling Cities and Migrants*. Ithaca: Cornell University Press.

Glick Schiller, N., A. Çaglar, and T. C. Guldbrandsen. 2006. "Beyond the Ethnic Lens: Locality, Globality, and Born-Again Incorporation." *American Ethnologist* 33 (4): 612–633. https://doi.org/10.1525/ae.2006.33.4.612.

Glick, T. F. 1992. "Convivencia: An Introductory Note." In *Convivencia: Jews Muslims and Christians in Medieval Spain*, edited by V. B. Mann, T. F. Glick and J. D. Dodds, 1–10, New York: Braziller.

Glick, T. F. 2005 [1979]. *Islamic and Christian Spain in the Early Middle Ages*. Leiden: Brill.

Glissant, É. 1981. *Le discours antillais*. Paris: Gallimard.

Glissant, É. 1990. *Poétique de la Relation. Poétique III*. Paris: Gallimard.

Glissant, É. 1997a. *Poetics of Relation*. Translated by B. Wing. Ann Arbor: University of Michigan Press.

Glissant, É. 1997b. *Traité du Tout-Monde. Poétique IV.* Paris: Gallimard.
Glissant, É. 2002. "The Unforeseeable Diversity of the World." In *Beyond Dichotomies: Histories, Identities, Cultures, and the Challenge of Globalization*, edited by E. Mudimbe-Boyl, 287–296. Albany: SUNY Press.
Gordon, J. A. and N. Roberts. 2009. "Introduction: The Project of Creolizing Rousseau." *CLR James Journal* 15 (1): 2–16.
Grünig Iribarren, S. 2013. *Ivan Illich (1926–2002): The Convivial City.* Environnement et Société. Français: Université Paris-Est.
Gutiérrez Rodríguez, E. 2007. "The 'Hidden Side' of the New Economy: On Transnational Migration, Domestic Work, and Unprecedented Intimacy." *Frontiers: A Journal of Women Studies* 28 (3): 60–83.
Gutiérrez Rodríguez, E. 2010. *Migration, Domestic Work and Affect—A Decolonial Perspective on Value and the Feminization of Labour.* New York and London: Routledge.
Gutiérrez Rodríguez, E. 2011. "Politics of Affect. Transversal Conviviality." *Transversal: Multilingual Webjournal.* Available from: http://eipcp.net/transversal/0811/gutierrezrodriguez/en. Accessed March 1, 2019.
Gutiérrez Rodríguez, E. 2015. "Archipelago Europe: On Creolizing Conviviality." In *Creolizing Europe: Legacies and Transformations*, edited by E. Gutiérrez Rodríguez and S. A. Tate, 80–99. Liverpool: Liverpool University Press.
Gutiérrez Rodríguez, E. 2019. "Political Subjectivity, Transversal Mourning and a Caring Common: Responding to Deaths in the Mediterranean." *Critical African Studies* 10 (3): 345–360.
Heil, T. 2015. "Conviviality: (Re-)negotiating Minimal Consensus." In *Routledge International Handbook of Diversity Studies*, edited by S. Vertovec, 317–324. New York and London: Routledge.
Illich, I. 1973. *Tools for Conviviality.* New York: Harper & Row; London: Calder & Boyars.
Karakayali, S. and J. O. Kleist. 2016. *EFA-Studie 2: Strukturen und Motive der ehrenamtlichen Flüchtlingsarbeit in Deutschland, Forschungsbericht—Ergebnisse einer explorativen Umfrage vom November/Dezember 2015.* Berlin: BIM, Humboldt-Universität zu Berlin.
Kymlicka, W. 2016. "Solidarity in Diverse Societies. Beyond Neoliberal Multiculturalism and Welfare Chauvinism". *Comparative Migration Studies* 3 (1), S. 1–19. https://doi.org/10.1186/s40878-015-0017-4.
Lapiņa, L. 2016. "Besides Conviviality: Paradoxes in Being 'at EASE' with Diversity in a Copenhagen District." *Nordic Journal of Migration Research* 6 (1): 33–41. https://doi.org/10.1515/njmr-2016-0002.
Manzano Moreno, E. 2013. "Qurtuba: algunas reflexiones críticas sobre el Califato de Córdoba y el mito de la convivencia." *Awraq: Estudios sobre el mundo árabe e islámico contemporáneo* 7: 225–246.

Menocal, M. R. 2002. *The Ornament of the World: How Muslims, Jews, and Christians Created a Culture of Tolerance in Medieval Spain*. Boston: Little Brown.

Mercier, J. B. 2012. Édouard Glissant: Du Tout-Monde au Traité du Tout-Monde. Intertextualité, Identité et espace: Pour une étude comparative. PhD thesis submitted to the Department of French and Italian, University of Kansas.

Nesbitt, N. 2013. *Caribbean Critique: Antillean Critical Theory from Toussaint to Glissant*. Liverpool: Liverpool University Press.

Nowicka, M. and S. Vertovec. 2014. "Introduction: Comparing Convivialities: Dreams and Realities of Living-with-Difference". *European Journal of Cultural Studies* 17 (4): 341–356. https://doi.org/10.1177/1367549413510414.

Nowicka, M., Ł. Krzyżowski, and D. Ohm. 2019. "Transnational Solidarity, the Refugees and Open Societies in Europe." *Current Sociology* 67 (3): 383–400. https://doi.org/10.1177/0011392117737817.

Padilla, B., J. Azevedo, and A. Olmos-Alcaraz. 2015. "Superdiversity and Conviviality: Exploring Frameworks for Doing Ethnography in Southern European Intercultural Cities." *Ethnic and Racial Studies* 38 (4): 621–635.

Pratt, M. L. 1992. *Imperial Eyes: Travel Writing and Transculturation*. London and New York: Routldege.

Quijano, A. 2000. "Coloniality of Power, Eurocentrism, and Latin America." *Nepantla: Views from the South* 1: 533–580.

Quijano, A. 2008. "Coloniality of Power, Eurocentrism, and Social Classification." In *Coloniality at Large: Latin America and the Postcolonial Debate*, edited by M. Moraña, E. D. Dussel, and C. A. Jáuregui, 181–224. Durham, NC: Duke University Press.

Sakrani, R. 2016. "Convivencia: Reflections About Its 'Kulturbedeutung' and Rereading the Normative Histories of Living Together." Research Paper Series, Max-Planck-Instiut für Europäishce Rechtsgeschichte; Max Planck Institute for European Legal History.

Schiffauer, W., A. Eilert, and M. Rudloff. 2017. *So schaffen wir das—eine Zivilgesellschaft im Aufbruch. 90 wegweisende Projekte mit Geflüchteten*. Bielefeld: Transcript.

Schwieger Hiepko, A. 1998. "L'Europe et les Antilles: Une interview d'Edouard Glissant." Mots Pluriels, 8. Available from: http://www.arts.uwa.edu.au/MotsPluriels/MP898ash.html. Accessed June 2, 2018.

Shamsie, M. 2016. "Introduction: The Enduring Legacy of Al-Andalus." *Journal of Postcolonial Writing* 52 (2): 127–135. https://doi.org/10.1080/17449855.2016.1164969.

Soifer, M.I. 2009. "Beyond *Convivencia*: Critical Reflections on the Historiography of Interfaith Relations in Christian Spain." *Journal of Medieval Iberian Studies* 1 (1): 19–35. https://doi.org/10.1080/17546550802700335.

Szpiech, R. 2013. "The Convivencia Wars: Decoding Historiography's Polemic with Philology." In *A Sea of Languages: Rethinking the Arabic Role in Medieval*

Literary History, edited by S. Akbari and K. Mallette, 135–161. Toronto: University of Toronto Press.

Tate, S. A. 2009. *Black Beauty: Aesthetics, Stylization, Politics. London*. New York: Routledge.

Vigneswaran, D. 2014. "Protection and Conviviality: Community Policing in Johannesburg." *European Cultural Studies*, 17 (4): 471–486.

Wimmer, A. and N. Glick Schiller. 2002. "Methodological Nationalism and Beyond: Nation–State Building, Migration and the Social Sciences." *Global Networks* 2 (4): 301–334.

Wise, A. and S. Velayntham. 2013. "Convivialities in Everyday Multiculturalism: Australia and Singapore Compared." *European Journal of Cultural Studies* 17 (4): 406–430.

Wolf, K. B. 2009. "Convivencia in Medieval Spain: A Brief History of an Idea." *Religion Compass* 3 (1): 72–85. https://doi.org/10.1111/j.1749-8171.2008.00119.x.

Wynter, S. 1989. "Beyond the Word of Man: Glissant and the New Discourse of the Antilles." *World Literature Today: A Literary Quarterly of the University of Oklahoma* 63 (4): 637–647.

Open Access This chapter is licensed under the terms of the Creative Commons Attribution 4.0 International License (http://creativecommons.org/licenses/by/4.0/), which permits use, sharing, adaptation, distribution and reproduction in any medium or format, as long as you give appropriate credit to the original author(s) and the source, provide a link to the Creative Commons license and indicate if changes were made.

The images or other third party material in this chapter are included in the chapter's Creative Commons license, unless indicated otherwise in a credit line to the material. If material is not included in the chapter's Creative Commons license and your intended use is not permitted by statutory regulation or exceeds the permitted use, you will need to obtain permission directly from the copyright holder.

CHAPTER 7

A Convivial Journey: From Diversity in Istanbul to Solidarity with Refugees in Denmark

Deniz Neriman Duru

Introduction

This chapter probes the concept of convivial solidarity by narrating my analytical journey from ethnographic research on conviviality and diversity in Istanbul, to research on solidarity with the migrants and refugees living in Denmark. In the first part, I briefly describe how I engaged with the concepts of multiculturalism and coexistence before I went to conduct fieldwork in Istanbul, and explain how I came to use the concept of conviviality while analysing my ethnographic data (Duru ,2015, 2016). In the second part of the chapter, I present the EU Horizon 2020 project on transnational solidarity with migrants and refugees, 'Transnational Solidarity in times of crisis' (Duru et al. 2016), which employed altruistic and mutual solidarity as concepts without using the concept of convivial solidarity in the deductive design of mapping solidarity initiatives of civil society organisations. Nonetheless, after conducting the interviews with

D. N. Duru (✉)
Department of Communication and Media, Lund University, Lund, Sweden
e-mail: deniz.duru@kom.lu.se

the representatives from the civil society, in the inductive analysis stage of the material I realised that the interviewees referred to what I conceptualised as *convivial solidarity*, which is a new concept that I have developed (which appeared first in Duru et al. 2016). In this chapter, I tentatively use this concept to open a discussion about how convivial solidarity explains what cannot be described by the concepts of mutual and altruistic solidarity nor by conviviality.

Part 1: Diversity in Istanbul

Pre-fieldwork Literature Review

When starting my doctoral studies in Social Anthropology at the University of Sussex in 2008, I wanted to understand how people of different backgrounds (including but not limited to ethnicity, religion, and social class) live together in diverse societies. While the Balkans and Turkey have long been pathologised as places of ethnic turmoil (Todorova 1997) and un-mixing of people (Hirschon 2003), I investigated Burgaz, one of the Princes' Islands of Istanbul, where people of different ethnic, religious and socio-economic backgrounds have been living for centuries. Peace there did not break down despite pogroms in 1955 (where violence took place in other Princes' Islands and parts of Istanbul (see Güven 2006; Kuyucu 2005), Turkification policies, the worsening relations between Turkey and Greece over Cyprus, and the Turkish invasion of Cyprus (Akgönül 2007; Güven 2006). How do, and how did people from different backgrounds live together? What do they do to manage tensions? What makes people bond to each other? How can we describe, explain and conceptualise this?

In the academic literature I had read prior to my fieldwork (before 2009), multiculturalism, coexistence, cosmopolitanism and super-diversity were used as theoretical frameworks to describe diverse societies and living with difference. Multiculturalism and coexistence theories had a tendency to divide societies into ethnic and/or religious compartments. In my non-communitarian approach in researching diversity, I built on Cowan (2006), who criticised the communitarianism of Joppke and Lukes' (1999) "mosaic" multiculturalism. Also, theories on post-conflict coexistence (Phillips 1996; Gidron et al. 2002; Dayton and Kriesberg 2009) postulated the existence of ethnic and religious groups as given and generally saw conflicts as triggered by ethnic and religious differences. In a post-Yugoslav context, coexistence approach assumes that the differences and identities of e.g.

Serbs and Bosnians have always existed as such, disregarding/forgetting the realm of everyday life, and common ways of living shared in the same neighbourhoods over centuries. A person is not only a Bosnian or a Serb but a *komšija* (from *komşu*—neighbour in Turkish), a friend, a hairdresser, a grumpy woman or a chatterbox man. Both multiculturalism and coexistence theories focus on culture as difference and undermine what people share in common. The culture as difference, or "culture as mosaic" approach (criticised in Eriksen 2001) posits boundaries between groups as it homogenises and essentialises 'their culture'.

The concept of cosmopolitanism as I encountered it in the literature I read before 2009 referred to the individual practice of engagement of the 'self' with an 'Other' (Hannerz 1990), and hence did not help me theorise the sense of collectivity or unity I encountered in the field.[1] Finally, the theory of super-diversity (Vertovec 2007) recognised that differences are diversified, that we should go beyond the categories of ethnicity and religion, and explore and understand the complexity of diversity. Nonetheless, for me it was more helpful as a way of asking critical questions driven by my ethnographic material, rather than for conceptualising how it is to live in diversity.

I conducted fieldwork on Burgaz for 14 months in 2009–2010. As an anthropologist, I believed that ethnography was the valid methodology to understand what occurs on the ground (Cowan 2006), and what people actually do. I focused on the 'multicultural' as an adjective to describe plurality on the ground—in opposition to multiculturalism as a political project, i.e. as top-down approaches (characteristic for policies, politicians, political theorists) that focused on how people should live together and what policies or laws should be used in order to manage diversity. Thus, an in-depth, ethnographic exploration of everyday practices of living together in diversity was my response to Grillo's call (2007) for anthropologists to go beyond the normative analysis of multiculturalism and to move away from the philosophical reflections at an abstract or institutional level.

Post-fieldwork Analysis: Conceptualising Conviviality

My fieldwork revealed that people from different backgrounds form relations based on common interests, lifestyles, tastes, and also in order to fight for a common cause (Duru 2013). While the lens of coexistence and toleration search for cohesion and conflict based on ethnic and religious differences and implies 'living with difference', in Burgaz, I could see what people have in common: shared ways of living and acts of solidarity. I paid attention to the everyday living and to how the islanders represented/articulated their pluralism by the words and metaphors/allegories they used. The islanders' conceptualisation of their diversity challenged Taylor's (1992) and Kymlicka's (1995) approaches to recognition of differences as a basis to secure equality and rights, and Joppke and Luke's (1999) description of society in the form of mosaic. As stated by the islanders, the diversity in Burgaz was not about the identity of different groups. People's ethnicity and religion were recognised but what was important was the bonding, conviviality, intimacy and solidarity between individuals, and their collective sense of belonging in Burgaz. Similar to Valluvan (2016: 218), the islanders were able 'to invoke difference, whilst avoiding communitarian, groupist precepts'. The Burgaz islanders described their diversity as 'marbling' (*ebru* in Turkish) in opposition to 'mosaic' where the patterns have distinct borders and are hence more vulnerable to destruction. In *ebru*, even though patterns still keep their distinctiveness, their boundaries fuse into each other and form a more solid picture as a whole (Duru 2015).

I wanted to look for concepts that could explain cohesion, solidarity, tension, and conflict, but were not based on established views of coexistence/toleration. Rather, I wanted to find concepts to explain these phenomena *which reflected the 'marbling' view of diversity that I experienced in Burgaz*. I came across Overing and Passes' (2000) work of conviviality in Amazonia, where they had developed conviviality, from the Spanish word 'convivencia', that refers to joint/shared life. These authors argued that conviviality does not only comprise peaceful moments but also tensions, management of conflicts that are grounded in the sharing of daily life. In my thesis (Duru 2013) and further publications (Duru 2015, 2016), I used conviviality as a framework to overcome the pitfalls of multiculturalism and coexistence. Building on Chau's (2008) sensorial production of the social, and Ring's (2006) and Overing and Passes' (2000) management of everyday tensions, I described conviviality as an embodiment of diversities and diverse senses (Duru 2016). Islanders attend each other's religious places, feasts, parties, and funerals; experience the island with their senses, while swimming and fishing in the sea, smelling and touching the mimosas, eating the berries and the green bitter plums of the trees, watching the sunset and the sunrise; they also fight with each other about who gossiped from behind whom, or who beats the carpet and lets the dust fall on the neighbour below. All of these pleasures, conflicts, and tensions make the islanders feel that it is *their* island, creating a sense of unity and a strong sense of belonging to the island that overrides ethnic, class, and religious identities of individuals at times of crisis and despite political tension in Turkey. At times of crisis and hardship, survival of the community of Burgaz islanders takes priority over individual or group differences. Conviviality as I saw it in Burgaz was neither about fleeting encounters or courtesy (see Nowicka, Chapter 2 in this volume), nor only about collaboration; the communal bonding led to the survival of the community at critical times.

After completing the dissertation, I moved on to post-doc projects on cross-border practices, the physical and virtual mobility of Turkish migrants in Europe, and—most recently—to the project on civil society actors' solidarity with refugees and migrants. My interest in conviviality was set aside. However, when I collected the qualitative empirical material, conducting interviews with civil societies that support migrants and refugees in Denmark, their perceptions on solidarity made me rethink what I knew about conviviality. In the project I present in more detail below, convivial solidarity emerged as a concept I found suitable for describing civil society organisations' solidarity initiatives and actions with refugees in Denmark in 2016.

Part 2: Convivial Solidarity with Refugees in Denmark

Research Design and Methods

In 2014–2015, I was a part of a consortium made of researchers from eight European countries[2] in a Horizon 2020 project on Transnational Solidarity, where we aimed to explore solidarity initiatives towards vulnerable groups (migrants and refugees,[3] disabled people and unemployed people) during the recession that followed the 2008 financial crisis. The project was designed prior to the peak of asylum seeker arrivals in 2015, while the data collection took place mostly in 2016 and collided with the emergence of many 'Refugee Welcome' initiatives in different parts of Europe. These initiatives were referred to by Glick Schiller (2016) as 'convivial practices' that ranged from demonstrations at train stations, to welcoming and providing temporary shelters, food and support, all with the aim of countering the anti-refugee discourses and restrictive migration policies. The project investigated legal and constitutional solidarity (Duru et al. 2018), grassroots, and small civil society organisations' solidarity activities and initiatives (Duru et al. 2016), and public perceptions on solidarity. A quantitative survey was employed to explore individual responses and perceptions on solidarity and mediated representations in one part of the project, and responses of solidarity in the news media and social media in the other. Each national partner had a leading role in a work package or an event. For some work packages such as the ones on civil society and on the media, all national teams had to collect and analyse the national data as designed by the leading team. The data I refer to in this section comes from the work package on civil society initiatives.

Implementing a mixed-methods design, this work package first mapped the existing practices regarding what kinds of solidarity actions were provided by civil society as presented on their online websites, through a hub search on the internet. We identified hubs/subhubs through keyword searches (refugee, migrant, asylum combined with organisation, association, network, initiative), which contained a large number of links (total of 267) connecting to the websites of civil society organisations supporting migrants and refugees. These hubs/subhubs were retrieved and exported to excel in the form of links to civil society organisations' websites by search engine experts. We then randomly selected 100 organisations and social movements that had at least one transnational solidarity characteristic such as support, activity and beneficiaries beyond national borders, or international partners. A codebook was prepared by the team responsible for mapping the transnational civil society initiatives, and deductive coding was applied in the eight countries listed above. Coders' training and inter-coder reliability tests were done in the beginning, middle, and towards the end of the data collection process.

From those hundred coded transnational solidarity organisations (TSOs), we sampled/selected ten small NGOs, charity organisations, grassroots movements, and protest groups within the field of migration and refugee support. Each national team interviewed one representative from each of the ten sampled TSOs in each partner country. They were asked about their role and experience in the TSO, their views on how the crises affected the solidarity actions, the challenges faced, and their reflections on solidarity actions. I conducted ten interviews in Copenhagen between August and October of 2016. Even though I aimed for a gender balance, the sample of interviewees was dominated by women (8 women and 2 men). Nonetheless, there was a diversity of age: 3 young, 4 middle-aged, and 3 informants in their late 70s. Many of the informants only started to work in their specific organisations within the last couple of years. Some were involved as volunteers, others had a higher degree of involvement such as management committee members, chairpersons, or founders. I did inductive coding during the qualitative analysis in order to explore approaches to and types of solidarity from the perspectives of our informants. Before I explore the empirical material, in the next section I will establish the sociopolitical context in Denmark in regard to incoming refugees and the situation of migrants in the country.

Danish Context: In Between Civic Initiatives of Solidarity and Hostility Towards the Refugees

Following the economic recession of 2008 and the increasing number of refugees arriving in Europe in 2015, European solidarity has been challenged with respect to the shared responsibilities of accommodating refugees and providing humanitarian support to other parts of the world (Federico and Lahusen 2018: 11). When state support was insufficient or cut down in some countries, the need for more support triggered many civil society actions both in the form of civic responses at the grassroots level, as well as increased formalised and organised support.

Even though Denmark has been relatively little affected by the financial crisis, the civil society sector experienced financial cuts and retrenchment. The building blocks of Danish society are its strong welfare state, popular trust in state institutions, and solidarity among its citizens, who see work and volunteering as an important part of the Danish identity (Henrik et al. 2013; Jöhncke 2011). In addition to the private donors and volunteers, the Danish state also supports civil society organisations through tax exemption. However, as an outcome of the financial crisis, the government at the time of the research and its predecessor both restricted benefits and support for migrants and refugees, and decreased the funding and resources of the civil society organisations. According to Gammeltoft-Hansen (2017), Denmark used policies of deterrence to discourage asylum seekers from applying in Denmark. The government at that time was supported by the Danish People's Party, which amassed the second largest number of votes in the 2015 elections and held an anti-immigrant agenda. Social benefits in the form of financial support for the refugees was cut in half, and it has gotten harder and harder to get refugee status and to obtain Danish citizenship. This situation created a twofold change in the Danish society. On the one hand, migrants and refugees were threatened by anti-immigrant discourses in the mass media, social media and in daily life. For instance, my interviewees who worked with Muslim beneficiaries pointed out that it had never been easy to be a Muslim living in Denmark and that the populist and anti-immigrant tone of the politicians and the dominant negative stereotyping of refugees in the media brought more threats to the Muslim population. One interviewee who offered physical and health education to Muslim women who suffered from some disability and/or health problems narrated in the interview[4]:

> In the first place, it started many years ago. We (Danes) wanted people to come and do bad work in Denmark and they came with their families (…) We should have said (to them): "you don't live (here) as in Pakistan or Turkey, you must learn about Danish society, because you live in Denmark"(…) Many who came at that time, did great work here and still do. Then we hear about people who make problems, and just get money from the social system. And now the rules are that it is very difficult to get any money. It is not as easy to live in Denmark as it was 30 years ago. The laws are very tightened up. (…) There have been many politicians who said: "They misused Denmark!", there have been many parties, Dansk Folkeparti, has been very good since the nineties (in saying) "We have to stop this (migration) because they are eating all our bread. They are taking our country. They have to go out. They are stealing from Denmark!" Uuuf. There are many people here who have done a lot of work for Denmark. This we forget. (Mette)

On the other hand, this harsh situation made more and more people volunteer and join civil society organisations in order to counter the harsh anti-immigrant tone and to fight the restrictions and hardship that refugees and migrants face. As stated by Stig:

> The 'refugee crisis', or what you want to call it, has impacted that there has been more people and more volunteers, because I myself, would not have been a volunteer, you know, without hearing about these things and how we treat (immigrants), I have always been opposed to the way we treat immigrants but I have not known how to do anything or I have not been wired up enough to go out and seek to do anything. (Stig)

The incoming asylum seekers had thus rather been choosing to apply in neighbouring Sweden, which offers better conditions for accommodating them. Denmark also encouraged this by not controlling its borders, and letting the refugees pass through and reach Sweden where they were registered. Nonetheless, when Sweden implemented border controls between itself and Denmark in November 2015, many refugees had to remain in Denmark and hence their numbers increased from around 5000 in 2010 to around 20,000 in 2016.[5] It was in this sociopolitical context that I conducted interviews with transnational civil society organisations' representatives in the summer of 2016.

Convivial Solidarity as a Concept

In the design of the quantitative part of the research, we built on the notions of mutual and altruistic solidarity, which are not mutually exclusive concepts. Altruism includes both the intent and behaviour that ranges from philanthropy, generosity, and volunteering with the aim to benefit others (Jeffries 2014). Solidarity refers to intergroup interaction, when people bond together and unite over common goals (Jeffries 2014). Solidarity thus can be in the form of in-group cooperation and can be mutual, where there is a self-interested reciprocal exchange among the people who engage with it (Bruni 2008). In our sample, those we identify to promote mutual solidarity are those who offer group empowerment/support, such as a Muslim youth organisation that helps Muslim youth. Weiss and Peres (2014) would describe this kind of mutual solidarity as 'soft altruism', which implies mutual care and reciprocity (the solidarity actions will benefit the self/ego), in opposition to 'hard altruism' (which they find impossible to apply to real life), when the self/ego has to be destroyed/annihilated in order to help others. Weiss and Peres (2014) are critical of the dichotomy between 'hard altruism' and 'soft altruism', and hence criticise political theorists and philosophers who conceptualised altruism and ego/egoism as mutually exclusive by arguing that there is egoism in altruism and vice versa. Nonetheless, in both mutual and altruistic solidarity, there is always a self in relation to another. Altruistic solidarity stresses the difference between the helper and the one that is helped and implies that the helper/volunteer is separated/different from the ones that are helped, such as when a non-disabled person is helping a disabled one.

Convivial solidarity differs from mutual and altruistic solidarity by ontologically not separating the self from the other. Convivial solidarity is a collective work in order to fight for a common aim and to find solutions for a common concern in a non-communitarian way without separating/classifying people by ethnicity, religion, citizenship, or nationality.

Hence, in the situation of solidarity enactment there is no separation or hierarchy between the refugees, asylum seekers, and people who engage in solidarity activities. Convivial solidarity is my construct, referring to practices which include, (1) face-to-face social interaction, (2) a sense of common humanity (Glick Schiller 2016) emphasised by those who engage with it, and (3) a normative drive towards fighting for equal rights, (such as aiming to change asylum and migration policies). While conviviality refers to day by day living together, convivial solidarity inspires the people involved in possible future convivial living. When there is a situation of tension or crisis (e.g. concerning the high number of incoming refugees), convivial solidarity aims to 'solve' the situation and show support by the means of convivial practices. Crisis situations catalyse people's engagement in convivial solidarity, which is performed by civil society organisations and citizens, with a normative aim for convivial living.

I coded the websites of Danish civil society organisations in order to get information on what types of solidarity activities are performed, their aims/goals, and the route chosen by the civil society sector to achieve these aims. The quantitative results signalled to me that the majority of the solidarity actions were aiming to create a more inclusive society, trying to promote better communication and understanding for everyone. These solidarity actions largely chose direct contact in the form of face-to-face interactions, which made me think about the convivial tendency of civic actions that aim to create a sense of collectivity. The quantitative results showed that of the organisations surveyed, most disseminate information because they would like to raise awareness (86%), on the difficulties refugees and migrants face and the conditions at the asylum centres. Most (85%) of the organisations promote social exchange, direct contact, and integration in the society. 83% fight discrimination and promote equal participation in society, and 81% aim to increase tolerance and mutual understanding. They do so by doing face-to-face direct actions and solidarity activities (84%), which include providing basic/urgent needs (79%), and organising social and cultural activities (50%).

In terms of direct actions/solidarity activities, they volunteer in the asylum and detention centres and spend their time with refugees and asylum applicants, teaching them Danish, gathering the paperwork they need, and engaging in creative activities (painting, drawing) to communicate and to relieve their stress. Basic/urgent needs comprise food, accommodation, clothing, medical and psychological help and support, human rights, legal advice, and language lessons. A smaller number of the selected organisations have a clearly stated political agenda on their website, with the aim of changing the system (31%), policy reform (30%), lobbying (24%), collective protest action (14%), and changing the government (9%) or taking the legal route (21%) (e.g. challenging Danish asylum policy through the courts, providing legal assistance to migrants). Nonetheless, in the interviews I conducted I came across a wide spectrum of political engagement, ranging from raising awareness, dissemination of information regarding the situation and conditions of asylum in order to fight the anti-immigrant rhetoric and attitudes, to protesting and lobbying for policy change (Duru et al. 2016: 131). This also made me think that convivial solidarity can include a wide range of political engagement.

I came to conceptualise convivial solidarity while I was analysing the semi-structured interviews conducted with the representatives of ten TSOs (which were sampled from the quantitative coding), particularly their statements about the solidarity activities and initiatives that their organisations were engaged in. I asked the representatives about their involvement with the organisation as well as what solidarity actions they did in their organisation, whether they took new initiatives, which other organisations they collaborated with, what they did differently compared to other organisations, and how they reflected on particular solidarity actions. In the following, I illustrate what I see as convivial solidarity, with the quotes taken from the interviews. Many interviewees mentioned that their organisations engage in face-to-face activities such as giving one-to-one Danish lessons and offer social activities ranging from dance and health classes, social hangouts, painting and drawing activities, to having coffee and tea together. Stig—a male volunteer in his late twenties who had just finished his Masters' degree in digital communication and IT and volunteered in a TSO which did creative activities at one of the asylum centres[6] in Denmark, spoke about the purpose of his organisation and the activities they do.

> The main purpose is that we generate some value in the daily life of the inhabitants of the camp. Our focus is creative things, to paint, draw, cut something in cardboard. Last week, one of the guys (asylum seeker) started an event, (…) a piece of wood, with some faces painted on, and the inhabitants could take spray and spray on it and they will be put on the fence of (the asylum centre) to create some life. Different things… But mostly creative. We don't force anyone to do anything, sometimes people just come in, sit and talk and have some coffee.

That's fine as well, but the focus is on generating some value with creative things (...). (Stig)

As asylum seekers are 'locked in' the asylum centres and are separated from the Danish society, some of the organisations (like the one where Stig volunteers) show convivial solidarity with the asylum seekers to help them organise a daily life. Here, creativity is the realm of non-hierarchical relations. Social activities, ranging from having coffee to drawing, playing football, and sewing workshops are seen as providing daily life content that has value and meaning. These activities are not 'practices of conviviality' because the asylum seekers are separated from the Danish society and hence do not live together day by day, but they are 'convivial practices' that aim to generate meaning and a daily life together with the volunteers and the asylum seekers in a limited time and space. The following quote explains how the stress of waiting for a decision or receiving a rejection detaches the asylum seekers from an agreeable daily life:

> Some days the tensions are really high at (name of the asylum centre) and lately because a lot of people got a notice, on the same day, that they were rejected, and stuff like that changes the interaction, some days there are a lot of interviews (as a part of their application), some days it is really hard and people don't want to do anything, people had a bad day or the food was bad, and many things can change the interaction (between volunteers and the asylum seekers). (Stig)

Throughout the interview, Stig stressed that many of the asylum seekers are in a limbo: they cannot start a life as they are waiting for a decision. The waiting time to process the asylum application can take years, and asylum seekers can also be moved from one centre to another. It seems that daily life is taken away from them, as the waiting time is marked by waiting, tension, and anxiety. The volunteers at the asylum centre thus aimed to create a context where both volunteers and asylum seekers interact through convivial practices, such as playing football, drawing, or having a cup of coffee.

Disseminating information and raising awareness for better communication in the society in order to enhance mutual understanding and tolerance brings in the non-communitarian aspect of convivial solidarity. The quote below is from Christina, who is running two different solidarity initiatives: one of them is legal assistance, the other one is an online archive about issues relating to refugees. She explains below the significance of disseminating information to the wider society, when she talks about the online archive that she created:

> I quickly found out that most refugees and asylum seekers and even Danes, they don't understand the system at all. It is really complicated and it is made complicated on purpose actually, I think. It could be much easier to understand, and it could be used much more simply, it is very complicated, nobody understands it. Actually I found out that only a few lawyers really understand, (laughs) not even the politicians understand what they vote for or against sometimes, so I just decided to find out how things were working, understand the system. I am not a lawyer so I want to do it from the outside. I managed! (laughs). (…) I try to inform the Danish public about how complex the situation is, trying to make them understand that our laws are very cynical and not working as they should (…) and also trying to make the public understand that the refugees are not here for fun. It is not a choice they made, it is not something they do to make something out of it. They are just desperate and it is their only option. So I am trying to spread information to refugees themselves about their own situation, help them out of that and trying to make a better understanding among the public, and among the people who work with this in many ways like politicians and journalists to make them understand that it is not working as it should, and we could make it much better and things are really not fair as they are. (Christina)

As Christina sees it, the problems and issues mentioned above are not only the refugees' concern, but concern all people living in Denmark. In her view, everyone, not only refugees or asylum seekers but anyone who lives in Denmark, needs the information on asylum laws, system, and conditions of the asylum seekers. The wider society should know about the issues that the refugees face, the Danish asylum system, and its complexities, so that one can fight the anti-migrant and communitarian rhetoric and the unwelcoming attitude that one can find in the politicians' claims and in some societal responses in Denmark. Most of the organisations, as reflected in the quantitative results, disseminate information because they would like to raise awareness on the difficulties refugees and migrants face, the conditions at the asylum centres and the continuous legal restrictions from the Danish governments that make migration and asylum rules tighter and tighter.

Convivial solidarity is not only about daily activities, forming relations, and face-to-face interaction; it also has political and legal dimensions. Some of my interviewees stated that convivial practices in the form of face-to-face social interaction are not enough. They highlighted the political focus of their organisation or, as Christina quoted above, give priority to securing the asylum seekers' and refugees' legal rights. Christina further articulated that only engaging in social activities is not enough to support refugees; one must help them in legal matters:

> The main problem that asylum seekers have, also refugees to a certain degree, that is the permit to stay, the papers. That is like the core of everything else. In my view, it did not make sense to do a social visit, and maybe to bring them out of the camp, to take a walk or drink tea, listen to their story or try to help those children, to bring used toys and things like that, it was not that important compared to that huge issue, which was waiting for the decision or already having a negative decision and worrying about their future and what to do. (…) It is mainly legal assistance and guidance and practical help that we offer. (Christina)

The quote above articulates the limitations of convivial practices, by stating that doing social activities, having tea or coffee, interacting with the asylum seekers will not solve the legal issues of the asylum seekers, which are seen as crucial. Everybody needs 'the papers', a resident permit, to have access to the civic rights, to start and to be able to create a daily life in Denmark. For this reason, Christina prioritises the offering of legal advice to the asylum seekers, refugees, and migrants in general.

Within some organisations, convivial solidarity is performed as a political fight for justice, equality, and for providing legal rights to the asylum seekers. Annika is an activist and a member of a protest group formed of elderly people; her quote below points to the normative aspect of convivial solidarity. Her group challenges and opposes the government in order to change migration laws, improve the conditions at asylum centres, and inform the Danish public about what is going on there. Annika explained how and why they started their protest group:

> It (their aim to start the protest group) was to put attention to the society, to the government, of conditions of particular children in the centre, because people (Danes) did not know this, and they think that Denmark, they (Danes) are very open, human, they, when we have signed these (UN) conventions of course we keep them. Year after year, it has been proved, no. When it comes to children of refugees, we (Danes) are not keeping them (Danes do not apply the UN conventions). And even today, this summer, we could

confront some politicians in the folk meeting in Bornholm, they want to change conventions but not the child conventions, (...) and then we said 'hey, it is for all children, for Danish children, for refugees' children, asylum seekers, children coming here without their parents. How can you make law, for example, the education of the refugee children is not similar to the education of the Danish children are having?" (Annika)

In this quote, Annika stresses that 'children are children' no matter whether they are Danes or refugees or asylum seekers. She points out that asylum children should be offered the same education opportunities as the Danish children. She has a non-communitarian approach when it comes to the education of children, and she does not differentiate between the native/Danish or the refugee/asylum seeker/migrant child: children are children. She explains how the long periods of waiting and being moved from one centre to another affect the children's learning. Annika and those in her organisation/protest group regularly visit the asylum centres to learn about the conditions, and how the asylum seekers feel about them. Some of the members are guardians[7] of the children who have no parents. The convivial solidarity that they engage in has a political aim. In order to achieve political change in terms of better asylum centre conditions and migration laws, they protest on the street, write letters to newspapers and politicians, and attend the People's meeting (Folkemødet), which is a platform where politicians meet and debate with the citizens once a year in Bornholm. This political fight is an enactment of convivial solidarity; it is a fight for conviviality. It is fight for the asylum seekers, families, and children to gain an equal status and place in the Danish society, to be able to start a convivial life by being educated in Danish, by leaving the asylum centres and building social relations with people living in Denmark.

Concluding Remarks

In this chapter, I told the story of how I constructed the concept of convivial solidarity, by presenting my analytical journey from research on conviviality and diversity in Istanbul, to solidarity activities with the migrants and refugees living in Denmark. This chapter glimpsed at what goes behind the stage when we, as researchers, revise analytical concepts and see the need for constructing new ones.

In summary, convivial solidarity is oriented towards daily life and social interactions between people without putting boundaries between groups, and instead stressing what unites people, what they share as humans, their common fights and concerns. This resonates with Glick Schiller's description of cosmopolitan sociability not as tolerance of differences, but as the 'domains of commonality' that make people sociable (Glick Schiller, Darieva, and Gruner-Domic 2011). Nonetheless, convivial solidarity is not limited to social interactions but also has political and legal grounding. It sprouts from and grows with tensions at critical times, uniting and bonding the people engaged in solidarity activities. Can convivial solidarity as a concept be useful to explore a range of initiatives that support the incoming refugees to Europe? What are the limitations of this concept? Does it refer to only temporary solidarity or will it be useful for understanding the conviviality that may develop in the long-term, regarding the settlement, adaptation and inclusion of the refugees in Denmark and elsewhere? Can it be expanded to other civil society initiatives? Further research can try to explore these questions.

Notes

1. In this chapter, I leave out cosmopolitanism and super-diversity all together and focus on conviviality.
2. France, Denmark, Greece, Poland, Germany, the UK, Switzerland, and Italy.
3. This chapter presents only the data that concerns migrants and refugees.
4. The interviews were conducted in English, and to ensure clarity, grammatical mistakes were corrected.
5. Danish Migration Agency for the statistics: https://www.nyidanmark.dk/da/Tal-og-statistik/Tal-og-fakta, accessed June 17, 2019.
6. Danish civil society has a hybrid structure, where state institutions work together with civil societies (Fehsenfeld and Levinsen 2019). Especially during the peak time of the arrivals of the refugees in 2015, many municipalities relied on collaboration with refugee civil society organisations and volunteers, ranging from welcoming them, providing basic needs and helping in their registration, as well as providing Danish language classes. This was also the case in the asylum centres, where civil society organisations support the asylum seekers, such as the one mentioned in the quote.
7. To be a guardian of a child means to accept to fulfil the duties of a parent in taking care of a child.

References

Akgönül, S. 2007. *Türkiye Rumları: ulus-devlet çağından küreselleşme çağına bir azınlığın yok oluşu süreci*. Istanbul: İletişim.

Bruni, L. 2008. *Reciprocity, Altruism and the Civil Society*. London: Routledge.

Chau, A. Y. 2008. "The Sensorial Production of the Social." *Ethnos: Journal of Anthropology* 73 (4): 485–504. https://doi.org/10.1080/00141840802563931.

Cowan, J. K. 2006. "Culture and Rights After Culture and Rights." *American Anthropologist* 108 (1): 9–24.

Dayton, B. W., and L. Kriesberg. 2009. *Conflict Transformation and Peacebuilding: Moving from Violence to Sustainable Peace, Security and Conflict Management*. Abingdon and New York: Routledge.

Duru, N. D. 2013. "Coexistence and Conviviality in Multi-Faith, Multi-Ethnic Burgazadasi, the Princes' Islands of Istanbul." PhD diss., University of Sussex.

Duru, D. N. 2015. "From Mosaic to Ebru: Conviviality in Multi-Ethnic, Multi-Faith Burgazadası, Istanbul." *South European Society & Politics* 20 (2): 243–263. https://doi.org/10.1080/13608746.2015.1047080.

Duru, D. N. 2016. *Memory, Conviviality, and Coexistence: Negotiating Class Differences in Burgazadasi, Istanbul, Space and Place*. New York: Berghahn Books.

Duru, D. N., T. Spejlborg Sejersen, and H. J. Trenz. 2016. "Denmark." In *Integrated Report on Reflective Forms of Transnational Solidarity: Innovative Practices of Transnational Solidarity at Times of Crisis*, edited by Maria Kousis, Christian Lahusen, and Angelos Loukakis, 129–146.

Duru, D. N., T. Spejlborg Sejersen, and H. J. Trenz. 2018. "Solidarity in Times of Crisis: Disability, Immigration and Unemployment in Denmark." In *Solidarity as a Public Virtue?* 249–274. Baden-Baden: Nomos Verlagsgesellschaft mbH & Co. KG.

Eriksen, T. H. 2001. "Between Universalism and Relativism: A Critique of the UNESCO Concept of Culture." In *Culture and Rights: Anthropological Perspectives*, edited by J. K. Cowan, M. Dembour, and R. A. Wilson, 127–148. Cambridge: Cambridge University Press.

Federico, V., and Lahusen, C., eds. 2018. *Solidarity as a Public Virtue?: Law and Public Policies in the European Union*. Baden-Baden: Nomos Verlagsgesellschaft mbH.

Fehsenfeld, M., and K. Levinsen. 2019. "Taking Care of the Refugees: Exploring Advocacy and Cross-Sector Collaboration in Service Provision for Refugees." *Voluntas: International Journal of Voluntary and Nonprofit Organizations* 30 (2): 422–435. https://doi.org/10.1007/s11266-019-00097-5.

Gammeltoft-Hansen, T. 2017. "Refugee Policy as 'Negative Nation Branding': The Case of Denmark and the Nordics." *Danish Foreign Policy Yearbook*, 99–125.

Gidron, B., S. N. Katz, and Y. Hasenfeld. 2002. *Mobilizing for Peace: Conflict Resolution in Northern Ireland, South Africa, and Israel/Palestine*. Oxford Scholarship Online. New York: Oxford University Press.
Glick Schiller, N. 2016. "The Question of Solidarity and Society: Comment on Will Kymlicka's Article: 'Solidarity in Diverse Societies'." *Comparative Migration Studies* 4 (1): 6. https://doi.org/10.1186/s40878-016-0027-x.
Glick Schiller, N., T. Darieva, and S. Gruner-Domic. 2011. "Defining Cosmopolitan Sociability in a Transnational Age: An Introduction." *Ethnic and Racial Studies* 34 (3): 399–418.
Grillo, R. 2007. "An Excess of Alterity? Debating Difference in a Multicultural Society." *Ethnic and Racial Studies* 30 (6): 979–998. https://doi.org/10.1080/01419870701599424.
Güven, D. 2006. *Cumhuriyet Donemi Azinlik Politikalari ve Stratejileri Baglaminda 6–7 Eylul Olaylari*. Istanbul: Iletisim Publishers.
Hannerz, U. 1990. "Cosmopolitans and Locals in World Culture." *Theory, Culture & Society* 7 (2–3): 237–251. https://doi.org/10.1177/026327690007002014.
Henrik, C., M. Beyeler, R. Eichenberger, P. Nannestad, and M. Paldam. 2013. *The Good Society: A Comparative Study of Denmark and Switzerland*. Berlin: Springer.
Hirschon, R. 2003. *Crossing the Aegean: An Appraisal of the 1923 Compulsory Population Exchange Between Greece and Turkey*. Studies in Forced Migration, 12: New York and Oxford: Berghahn.
Jeffries, V. 2014. *The Palgrave Handbook of Altruism, Morality, and Social Solidarity: Formulating a Field of Study*. New York: Palgrave.
Joppke, C., and S. Lukes. 1999. *Multicultural Questions*. Oxford: Oxford University Press.
Jöhncke, S. 2011. "Integrating Denmark: The Welfare State as a National(ist) Accomplishment." In *The Question of Integration: Immigration, Exclusion and the Danish Welfare State*, edited by K. F. Olwig and K. Paerregaard, 30–53. Newcastle upon Tyne: Cambridge Scholars Publishing.
Kuyucu, A. T. 2005. "Ethno-Religious 'Unmixing' of 'Turkey': 6–7 September Riots as a Case in Turkish Nationalism." *Nations and Nationalism* 11 (3): 361–380. https://doi.org/10.1111/j.1354-5078.2005.00209.x.
Kymlicka, W. 1995. *Multicultural Citizenship*. Oxford: Clarendon Press.
Overing, J., and A. Passes. 2000. *The Anthropology of Love and Anger: The Aesthetics of Conviviality in Native Amazonia*. London: Routledge.
Phillips, D. L. 1996. "Comprehensive Peace in the Balkans: The Kosovo Question." *Human Rights Quarterly* 18 (4): 821. https://doi.org/10.1353/hrq.1996.0048.
Ring, L. A. 2006. *Zenana: Everyday Peace in a Karachi Apartment Building*. Bloomington and Indianapolis: Indiana University Press.

Taylor, C. 1992. *Multiculturalism: Examining the Politics of Recognition*. Edited by Amy Gutmann. Princeton: Princeton University Press.
Todorova, M. N. 1997. *Imagining the Balkans.* New York: Oxford University Press.
Valluvan, S. 2016. "Conviviality and Multiculture: A Post-integration Sociology of Multi-Ethnic Interaction." *Young* 24 (3): 204–221. https://doi.org/10.1177/1103308815624061.
Vertovec, S. 2007. "Super-Diversity and Its Implications." *Ethnic and Racial Studies* 30 (6): 1024–1054. https://doi.org/10.1080/01419870701599465.
Weiss, R., and P. Peres. 2014. "Beyond the Altruism-Egoism Dichotomy: A New Typology to Capture Morality as a Complex Phenomenon." In *The Palgrave Handbook of Altruism, Morality, and Social Solidarity*, edited by V. Jeffries, 71–97. New York: Palgrave.

Open Access This chapter is licensed under the terms of the Creative Commons Attribution 4.0 International License (http://creativecommons.org/licenses/by/4.0/), which permits use, sharing, adaptation, distribution and reproduction in any medium or format, as long as you give appropriate credit to the original author(s) and the source, provide a link to the Creative Commons license and indicate if changes were made.

The images or other third party material in this chapter are included in the chapter's Creative Commons license, unless indicated otherwise in a credit line to the material. If material is not included in the chapter's Creative Commons license and your intended use is not permitted by statutory regulation or exceeds the permitted use, you will need to obtain permission directly from the copyright holder.

CHAPTER 8

Bringing Conviviality into Methods in Media and Migration Studies

Erin Cory

INTRODUCTION

In this chapter, I explore the potentials of conviviality as a methodological tool for studying media, broadly conceived, in a migration context. I draw on a research project in which conviviality works as a prism to understand media practices related to migration and refugees. Based on anecdotes from the field and through consideration of the dialectic between analysis and method, I discuss how the concept is best appropriated as a methodological tool in research designs informing current and future activist-based studies in this area.

As I elucidate in this chapter, conviviality conveys a deep concern with how we understand different modes of human connection, and it possesses a renewed charge in the context of the refugee migration of 2015 and its aftermath. This notion of conviviality includes a variety of different perspectives, including living with difference, mutuality, and togetherness, valences of the term still being unpacked in current scholarship. Within the literature, however, there exists little thinking on the methodological

E. Cory (✉)
Faculty of Culture and Society, Malmö University, Malmö, Sweden
e-mail: erin.cory@mau.se

© The Author(s) 2020
O. Hemer et al. (eds.), *Conviviality at the Crossroads*,
https://doi.org/10.1007/978-3-030-28979-9_8

possibilities of conviviality. In other words, what can conviviality *do*, or rather, what can researchers *do with it* in efforts to understand the crucial connections between media, mediation, and migration? How, further, can researchers across disciplines *do conviviality* as part of an interventionist research praxis, the ethical imperatives of which are increasingly hard to ignore?

I begin with a review of the state of the field in media and migration studies before making a case for conviviality as a methodological practice. To illustrate and qualify this argument, I turn to a case study, an ethnographic research project on a social space for refugees and asylum seekers in Copenhagen, where I have been involved for nearly two years. I use this case study to lay out three features that I consider most germane to social justice-oriented media research: conviviality as an *ethical position*; conviviality as *co-production*; and the significance of *conflict* to ongoing commitments to conviviality both inside and outside the research moment.

Media, Mediation, and Migration: State of the Field

The last few years have been rife with public discussions and several strands of research related to the connections between media and migration. Studies related to news coverage have compared, for example, how local, national, and transnational accounts of immigration phenomena differ (Lawlor 2015; Varju and Plaut 2017) and the news trends that emerge in this coverage, including fear and securitisation (Lulle and Ungure 2015; Caviedes 2015), sensationalism (Musaro and Parmiggiani 2017; Greussing and Boomgaarden 2017), and humanitarian concerns (Berry et al. 2015). A review of the last decade's critical research on European media coverage and journalistic practices indicates a persistent pattern of negative representations of migrants, refugees, and asylum seekers. Results show that such groups are predominantly framed as 'security, economic and hygienic threats' to European populations (Abid et al. 2017), through binary frames as victims and intruders (Van Gorp 2005) or seen to bring about 'societal system collapse' (Matthews and Brown 2012). Others have looked at the recurring use of water metaphors (such as floods or waves) to describe refugees, depicting them as 'an unwelcome natural disaster' in de-humanising ways that leave people devoid of agency (Gabrielatos and Baker 2008; Parker 2015; see also Abid et al. 2017).

Researchers have remained interested in how migrants use media technologies and platforms to negotiate both their movements between places and issues related to immigration practicalities and, further on, their identities, upon arrival (*Mapping Refugee Media Journeys*, Gillespie et al. 2016; *Getting to Europe the Whatsapp Way*, Frouws et al. 2016).

Much of the work on media and migration privileges extant social, digital, and mass media and in so doing misses the grounded production of migrants themselves. While certainly popular and academic studies of online behaviours and digital communities in diaspora do exist (e.g. Houssein 2013; Dekker and Engbersen 2014), something falls away when human interaction and the research arena are relegated to the digital. One thing this chapter suggests, therefore, is that we think about media more broadly. By considering the city as media (e.g. Kittler and Griffin 1996) and/or studying other physical spaces as media, and by considering the researcher as a media producer, we might better account for the multiple networks (both digital and physical) that overlay and influence each other and catalogue how these networks mediate multiple identities, interactions, and societies.

For the purposes of this chapter, therefore, I deploy broad understandings of media and mediation. The first we might understand simply as the plural form of 'medium', which the *Oxford Dictionary of Media and Communication* (2016) defines in part as 'any substance or process through which reality is apprehended or constructed'. Similarly, the same volume defines 'mediation' in part as 'the role of any intervening factor in transforming a message, meaning, or experience'.

By examining the media and mediating practices of one migration-related local community, I consider how media writ large describe and produce the world, the implications of their production on peoples' lives, and the ethical consequences of research related to these issues. In so doing, I also specifically consider how researchers can both deploy and cultivate conviviality through media-centred activist research praxis.

CONVIVIALITY AND/IN THE DANISH CONTEXT

In his argument for considering the possibilities of living with alterity, Gilroy (2006) deploys the notion of conviviality to dismantle holistic notions of 'culture' and 'identity'. A more immediate iteration of 'the planetary'—a term that suggests the movement, expanse, and contingency of identity—conviviality embraces the local disruption of culture, demanding that its purveyors deny 'every notion of culture as property', opting instead for a world 'broken and dispersed by the swirling, vertiginous motion of the postcolonial world' (Gilroy 2006: 70).

Of course, Gilroy was writing about postcolonial British melancholia, theorising a redemptive way to break free from the spectres of colonialism and racism by way of a 'radical openness'. And yet these spectres of a racist past, and their persistence in the present, constitute at least an acknowledged part of British history. In the Danish context, such pasts and their legacies are only recently being exhumed from an amnesiac historical narrative (Lapiņa 2016).

The anxiety this uncovering provokes is palpable, registering as a backlash as the Danish state tries to define who belongs to the nation with administrative exactitude—through immigration 'contracts', the construction of a cultural canon, stringent immigration laws, a citizenship test, and political statements like the one issued by the Parliament in 2017, when vast segments of the population were informed that because they did not have 'Western' ancestors, they would never be Danish. The targeted group apparently included Danish-born citizens with non-Western heritage, who have lived most—if not the entirety—of their lives in Denmark.

While the belonging of these citizens hangs in the balance, they still actively contribute to the country. Refugees and asylum seekers, on the other hand, are barred from Denmark's political, social, and cultural identities, even as they are constructed as particular subjects through these very avenues. They are both discursively and visibly excluded from the cultural production about which Gilroy (2004) writes and from the cities teeming with the 'chaotic pleasures of the convivial postcolonial urban world' that he imagines (167). They reside in legal limbo, frequently for years, waiting for information on how to proceed with their hearings, or for a 'positive' decision on their cases. The spaces provided as housing by the Danish state likewise sit at the outer limits of Danish society, many situated at the outskirts of Denmark's smaller towns. Even the 'best' of these, located near Copenhagen so that inhabitants have some access to the city (and often family and friends), do not offer opportunities for cultural engagement. In recent years, the Danish state has begun to close these centres and move inhabitants to Jutland, at the westernmost reaches of the country. With this action, makeshift support systems and communities are being dismantled.

Nevertheless, in the midst of this multiply-rendered isolation, small islands of community, refuge, and *conviviality* persist. Grassroots organisations dedicated to issues pertaining to new arrivals have sprung up across

Denmark in recent years, and research interest in them has understandably increased. In the shadow of the social forces that have necessitated the presence of grassroots endeavours, it is imperative that researchers critically consider not only what they are observing in these organisations, but also what their own presence and methods might do to their production.

Conviviality: Empirical, Analytical, Methodological?

'Conviviality' continues to be debated and theorised in the literature, both as an empirical directive and as an analytical concept. While rehearsing the intricacies of its usage may be repetitive in a volume dedicated to the concept, it is important to note that much of the extant literature focuses on debates regarding conviviality's normative dimensions, often as these relate to its empirical and analytical possibilities and limitations.

As an empirical focus, conviviality calls us to observe the everyday, 'those social phenomena which are not extreme, [but] which are in-between, rather quiet' (Nowicka and Heil 2015: 12–13). Nowicka and Heil propose deploying this characteristic towards an analytical conviviality, through which social situations may be interpreted against the normative grain. The use of analytical conviviality seeks rather to gauge the continuities and changes, the solidarities and conflicts, of everyday life, and in so doing, to release the term from a pretence of togetherness as mere 'sameness' (ibid.: 12–16).

Lapiņa (2016) among others has saliently critiqued conviviality's analytical potential. Her research in Denmark challenges popular discourses of colour blindness which, she argues, attempt to silence the politics of race while simultaneously aggravating inequality (39). Indeed, she proposes that a focus on daily life might actually elide how local convivial situations still reproduce larger inequalities or stereotypes. She argues that a focus on everyday difference still may not take into account the *power dynamics* that may underpin conviviality—that is, how the idea ultimately benefits some more than others, or whose perspectives disappear in its normative conceptualisation (ibid.).

Taking these ongoing conversations as a springboard, I would like to call attention to the fact that conviviality's *methodological* possibilities have not yet been sufficiently considered in current work. This seems a source of untapped potential, particularly for action-oriented research, given the term's associations with community, difference, and social change. Conviviality's methodological possibilities stem precisely from its apparent capacity to encompass both normativity *and* conflict in its focus on the manifold interactions that comprise everyday community life.

Consideration of this productive dialectic can be found in contemporary literature on ethnographic methods. Ethnographers (e.g. Fabian 1990; Marcus 1998) have long called for researchers to move beyond work that merely informs. Approaches based on observational reporting run the risk of reproducing asymmetrical power relationships by relying heavily on interlocutors who principally serve as temporary research subjects. A countermeasure would be ethnographers' striving instead for *mutuality*, 'the promise of nontrivial understanding that is produced by researcher and researched together' (Fabian 1995: 47; qtd. in Alhourani 2017: 212). In the literature on ethnography, this mutuality is described in many ways, including 'speaking to a third' (Marcus 1998) and multivocality (Venegas and Huerta 2010), all phrases that echo conviviality's emphasis on doing everyday life together and living with difference. What might it look like to critically take conviviality to heart in research situations? What if researchers deployed it in projects focused on questioning and dismantling power structures, not only those that span a whole society, but also those located in the research moment?

In describing a research situation in which I was deeply engaged as a participant-observer, I suggest that researchers—particularly ethnographers, whose work illuminates interactions between everyday life and larger structures of influence and power—might harness conviviality towards (1) an ethical position based on aspirations for social change, which nevertheless (2) embraces conflict and (3) is based on co-production with interlocutors.

Situating Trampoline House

Founded by an artist collective in 2011, Trampoline House is an independent community space located in Copenhagen. According to its website, it offers an opportunity for refugees and asylum seekers in Denmark to find 'a place of support, community, and purpose'.[1] While the House's official materials do not specifically use the language of conviviality, its emphasis on mutual participation, integration, and social justice is clear in its mission statement, which reads in part: 'Trampoline House is a community center for asylum seekers, refugees and other citizens in Denmark. Our vision is an asylum and integration system where everyone can work, live and participate in society'. In order to work towards this vision, Trampoline House largely relies on donations and crowdfunding by its users and sympathetic members of Danish society, as its small government stipend ended when the most recent, conservative government came to power.

The House sits in the historically diverse neighbourhood of Nørrebro, which is rather centrally located in Copenhagen, but nevertheless far from many of the centres where refugees and asylum seekers live while waiting for decisions on their cases.² Nørrebro's linguistic landscape is varied, Arabic and Farsi script found at regular intervals alongside Danish and English. Independent stores and restaurants run by immigrant shopkeepers sit next to Danish-owned businesses. Several shops around Nørrebro attract a mainly immigrant clientele, which patronises them for specific goods not found in typical Danish markets. Other spaces reveal a mingling of autochthonous Danes and people who have arrived more recently. Multilingual street art marks Nørrebro as something both unique and still very much tied to the Danish capital's cityscape. In this neighbourhood where 'individual memories and the collective memory permeate each other', residents and pedestrians may experience how the city is a medium through which they negotiate their relationships to Denmark and to each other (Chikamori 2009: 153).

This is also the case at Trampoline House. The House is tucked away on a quiet street a couple of blocks from the main thoroughfare through Nørrebro. While this 'politics of place' might suggest a boundary marking (Peattie 1998) that keeps this particular space away from the literal mainstream of the neighbourhood, in many ways Trampoline House offers a microcosm of a vision for an integrated Danish society. New arrivals mingle with and work alongside young European volunteers, who are often also students researching migration. The space is colourful in every sense: banners and posters hang on the walls, plates of food from around the world are laid on the long communal tables at mealtimes, the back garden is painted in patchworks of bright colours and graffiti script, and community members converse by speaking several languages at once while playing games or chatting in the main room. This is not only solidarity, but more specifically 'solidarity with space' (Amin 2008), a conviviality predicated on civic formation in public spaces. The space of the House acts as a medium in the sense that it represents the community using it, and in how it mediates between their various identities, commitments, and experiences, a fact on which I will extrapolate in what follows.

Conviviality as an Ethical Position

In my capacity as the photography intern at Trampoline House for over half a year, I was charged with capturing the space and producing various media texts about it. In that time, I was afforded the chance to get to know many of the people who use the space, both new arrivals and Europeans. I initially came to the House for both political and research purposes, and while I considered myself fairly sensitive to issues of migration and media, the House's requirements around access and representation enforced an ethical position that I still find helpful in my current work.

While all are welcome (there is no sign-in sheet at the entrance, and access is based on trust), Trampoline House users must concretely contribute to its everyday life in order to enjoy access. This rule applies especially to volunteers, usually young Danes or other Europeans, who must commit to a certain number of hours every week. For prospective researchers, the expectations are more stringent, with three months of regular service required before one can approach the House with a proposed project. Investments of time and money (volunteers, interns, and researchers are all expected to become monthly donors to the House), as well as demonstrated commitment to the life of the House, act as safeguards against opportunistic research and as a counterbalance to the 'research fatigue' that has set in around migrant populations. The goal of this shared performance of the daily is that all members of the community, regardless of legal status, will experience and participate in an integrative space. That is, while refugees and asylum seekers might find help integrating through their interactions at the House, so too do young Danes and other Europeans get integrated into the idea of a new way of being in the world and part of a convivial milieu. These transformations are predicated in part on the fact that all members of the community move between various communities to participate in the work of Trampoline House.

New arrivals travel between asylum centres or other residential spaces to Trampoline House, a journey that requires a significant amount of time and labour: they must negotiate transportation systems in a new language, for example, and move through spaces which are not always sympathetic to migrants. Many European participants also travel to spend time at the House, moving to Copenhagen because of their interest in its projects, and using the city's public transportation to make their way deep into Nørrebro on a regular basis. Several of these volunteers noted that they had not spent much time in the neighbourhood, past its rather gentrified and hip outer blocks. Coming into Nørrebro revealed another part of the city to them, a part that is officially demarcated as a 'ghetto' by the Danish state.[3] For many new arrivals, the House represents a safe space where they do not have to perform as 'good immigrants', where they can get free legal help and counselling, and where they do not necessarily have to translate their experience to others, as the varied experiences of migration are familiar to most community members.

Capturing these everyday interactions made up much of the work I did at the House during my three-month trial period. The images of meetings, parties, classes, workshops, and other activities that I captured on film show Trampoline House as the convivial space it aspires to be. Many of these images were destined for the House's publicity campaigns. In considering such formal elements as camera angle, lighting, and subject matter, I participated in the visual production of a particular conviviality. In the moments both before and after I snapped the photographs, however, the convivial registered differently.

Because of users' often marginal positionalities, each snapshot required both preamble and epilogue. I approached participants deliberately, as dictated by the House's guidelines for photographers and videographers (which were provided to me at the start of my work), and then asked if I could photograph them in the midst of their activities. Sometimes people bowed out, leaving the frame, or requested that only non-identifying body parts be included. After taking a few shots, I reviewed them with those in the frame, as well as those who might be in the background. Once I uploaded them into the House's secure database, other staff members checked through them, a helpful secondary measure, as sometimes I neglected to account for the statuses or wishes of people who might be passing through the frame as I took the photograph. Many of these colleagues were more familiar with the community than I was and were able to identify people whose legal statuses might be compromised by posting their images on digital media.

Even in this publicity work, there was a keen sense of prioritising collaboration with new arrivals. House members had a clear role in directing photography and thus in determining how they and their space were represented. This element of co-production is central both to the workings of Trampoline House and, as we will see below, to a methodology based on conviviality.

Conviviality as Co-production

Trampoline House is meant to be a truly public, convivial space, which belongs neither to native Danes, nor to new arrivals, but is actively produced by their work in concert with each other. The House staff have developed a 'praktik' programme as one way to nurture this production and to combat the charity model of social support, which they deem patronising.[4] In the context of the asylum centres, *praktik* involves inhabitants' contribution to centre maintenance by way of menial labour like cleaning up rubbish or sweeping up cigarettes. At Trampoline House, *praktik* takes on a convivial colour, shaped as it is around such activities as cooking evening meals, caring for the community garden, and taking a language class, or using specialised skills to offer classes or services (e.g. a sewing workshop or childcare).[5] In exchange for committing to a series of these tasks each week, new arrivals have their transportation fare paid from the asylum centres to Trampoline House. After my internship ended, I volunteered for a while on the cleaning team. Twice a week, the team would do a thorough job of vacuuming, dusting, washing floors, and cleaning bathrooms. While the *praktik* system could certainly be characterised as a coercive measure to ensure participation, individuals with whom I spoke often noted that the regularity of *praktik* helped them to make new friends and to feel that they themselves were integral to the production of the space.

The House also functions as an educational opportunity for the larger public. Trampoline House's Centre for Art on Migration Politics (or CAMP, a reclamation of a key signifier of the nation-state's response to migration) is a space for art that directly deals with issues of displacement and migration.[6] It hosts work by established international artists and newer ones, especially those with refugee or migrant experiences. *De-colonizing Appearance* (2018), an exhibition curated by US media scholar Nicholas Mirzoeff, for example, drew crowds to its opening and other events and continues to be visited by school groups. Mirzoeff's involvement in the project and subsequent visits to asylum centres in Denmark prompted him to write a piece in *The Nation* which was widely shared across media platforms and drummed up solidarity for a critique of Denmark's inhumane migration policies. CAMP's contributors and curators thus envision it as a venue through which those with *and* without these experiences might connect and perhaps find inspiration for new modes of addressing the needs of refugees, asylum seekers, and migrants.

The House makes an effort to demonstrate and humanise these needs through its online media work, which includes posts on its Instagram and Facebook accounts. Most of the images of House users are taken for publicity purposes—both to encourage participation and as visual material cultivated to encourage financial support by private individuals and larger partner organisations. Along with two colleagues, both Danish MA students studying migration, I noticed that users were seldom afforded the opportunity to represent themselves. We thus began a project to produce a series of portraits for the Trampoline House website. For this project, participants (both new arrivals *and* European members) were asked to bring a single object with them to the interview. There were no guidelines other than that participants should be willing to tell the story of the object and to have it photographed, even if they did not want to be in the photographs themselves. References to migration were intentionally left out of preliminary discussions so as not to obligate participants to rehearse again the stories of their coming to Denmark and their (often ongoing) movements through the asylum system. The resulting conversations, often held with interpreters' help, focused instead on the stories evoked by the objects. The recording was transcribed and edited for clarity and conciseness, and participants were given a draft before it was to be published, to ensure narrative fidelity.

As will be explained, this project did not continue beyond the first few interviews, and the iterative process deployed in these representations continues to be reproduced, in part, on Trampoline House's Instagram account and on its website. Current interns and volunteers post profile pieces of House users on a semi-regular basis, although the focus is very much on the experience of migration from the perspective of new arrivals and volunteers, rather than on topics or stories of the respondents' choosing.

Trampoline House maintains an active online presence, its regular Instagram and Facebook posts documenting members' activities, which include hanging out at the House, participating in cultural activities hosted at the House, and also taking part in political demonstrations in various Copenhagen neighbourhoods. Members of the community 'like' and comment on these posts and respond to each other, thus continuing the co-production of conviviality in cyberspace. They share articles and add personal anecdotes to posts about demonstrations or developments in immigration legislation. These posts do the work of bridging physical spaces in which House members participate in daily life and the online world where they can revisit and add to these memories, or catch up on each other's lives. Even if they cannot visit with each other in person, members can access a mediated image of their togetherness and make it their own.

Indeed, this participatory imagining is central to Trampoline House's project: by focusing on the collaborative, everyday production of the community, the House nurtures a network that (even as the majority of community members remain in limbo) actively imagines the future. By continually reasserting the possibility of a radical democratic imaginary, community members find the revolutionary in their daily practice. Their space is, by their own description, a microcosm of what they hope to see happen in the larger culture: co-existence built through trust, collaboration, co-production, and creativity.

Conviviality and Conflict

Nevertheless, the fact remains that Trampoline House's core staff is a small team, whereas the larger group of interns and volunteers is a rotating cast, while the asylum seekers and refugees who participate in the House may do so for years while they wait for a decision on their cases. When Gilroy (2004) imagines spaces of conviviality, his sense of time is in some ways limited by his focus on the persistence of melancholia, to which conviviality is the antidote. However, different groups of people experience time—the waiting, the breakthrough, the disappointment, and the hurry—in different ways. The researchers, interns, and volunteers who cycle through the House have produced numerous MA theses, news articles, long-form essays, etc. Thus, at the same time that the House combats research fatigue by regulating who can research and when, this impermanence also brings up new questions regarding the sustainability of conviviality. Specifically: Can conviviality be something that is produced, renewed, sustained, even in unstable, changeable situations?

Although it may seem paradoxical, the conviviality found in Trampoline House is bound up not only with practices of mutuality, but also with experiences of conflict. Regular participants—refugees and asylum seekers, as well as autochthonous Danes and other Europeans—share similar quarrels with the state's handling of asylum cases and are united in their mission to combat the xenophobia that attends, and is provoked by, state policy. In fact, the conflict in which all participants find themselves provides the material for continued social justice work and campaigns and forges the

House's connections with likeminded organisations. Members of Trampoline House march through Copenhagen as part of larger demonstrations demanding things like educational access for the children of asylum seekers and better conditions in the centres, especially in the notorious deportation centre Sjælsmark. Weekly meetings serve as a place for members to air any grievances or concerns and to generate energy for upcoming demonstrations and campaigns. Likewise, the lawyers and therapists on hand at the House offer counsel as new arrivals navigate a frequently opaque and brutal immigration system.

Rarely has conflict emerged as a divisive force *within* Trampoline House, despite the fact that many members represent groups that might experience conflict in their home countries. During my time at Trampoline House, however, I found myself in the thick of one. The way in which members tried to mediate this conflict is instructive.

Trampoline House hosts a party on the first Friday of each month. Early in the evening, people gather to hear a speaker or take part in a workshop. A community meal is served, and after the plates are cleared away, the lights go down, and Goody, the House's resident DJ, slips behind his decks. The mix of dance music ranging from 1980s American tunes to Kurdish pop makes for a lively party, one in which House members of all stations take part.

I attended several of these festivities as part of my research and my personal engagement with Trampoline House. It was at one of them, in Fall 2017, that I was assaulted in an empty hallway by a member of the House, who had taken my dancing with him as an invitation to kiss me. When I tried to break free of his grip, he wrapped an arm around my neck and pulled me to him, refusing to let go and trying to turn me to face him. I was finally able to manoeuvre out of his grip and find one of the House directors. She asked me to sit down and talk with him on the spot, an injunction I refused, after which she approached him and asked him to meet her at the front of the House to talk about what had happened. He agreed but promptly disappeared from the premises. The staff member told me she would speak to him when next she saw him and encouraged me to 'take it as a compliment' in the meantime.

This initial attempt at mediation in the immediate aftermath of the assault felt obviously insufficient. At the next weekly staff meeting, I relayed this experience to the staff, volunteers, and interns. The staff member admitted her role in the incident and explained her reaction as a social justice-motivated response which forced her to consider whether I or he needed the House more. Most, though not all, members in attendance reacted negatively to this justification, and the meeting lasted an hour longer than usual as other women-identified members of the community came forward with their own stories about feeling uncomfortable or threatened at the House.

This particular conflict and the ensuing conversation provoked a series of changes at the House, beginning with a community-generated set of guidelines for social interaction, which was drawn up at a weekly House meeting. My assailant was taken aside by male staffers later that day, and he agreed to stay away from the House for a period of one month. Thus, while the conflict registered firstly as divisive, its outcome provided further material around which Trampoline House's convivial ethos could cohere.

Yet the incident also gave me pause in terms of my research and especially in terms of my methods as an ethnographer. While I felt buoyed by the community's response, and from the changes that became evident in the House, I experienced two other reactions as well. First, although I know that assault is never the victim's fault, I nevertheless harboured a sense of guilt for being part of a situation that precipitated this man's having to leave the House, even for a short while. Secondly, I wondered about my own participation in the House going forward: Would I feel the same closeness with people there and especially with this man's friends? Would they feel the same closeness with me? Would the aftermath of the incident shift the feeling in the House, and if so, would it be better to continue or to leave? How had this incident—and my narration of it—marked the fabric of this co-produced space? What effect had it had on my ethical stance, as researcher and activist? Could I still inhabit those roles in the same way? How would the memory of it mediate the feelings I and others had about the House, in terms of our safety and how this figured (or did not) in its mission?

These questions lingered, even as I dimly realised I was drifting away from Trampoline House. In subsequent months, I heard from other former members who had similar experiences, and who had decided to leave the House, and communicated with me via email and Facebook. Their decisions were difficult and painful and not made without a good deal of consideration. These members, mostly paid staff and interns who were also researchers, remain ethically and politically committed to the well-being of migrants and in their jobs and volunteer work continue to join their conflict with exclusionary and harmful state practices. However, they felt, as I did, that the ethical imperatives of engagement sometimes must be gauged against questions of personal safety and a real consideration of whether an organisation is truly committing to co-production, fair representation, and social justice, rather than merely rehearsing charitable actions that the House itself apparently understands as potentially patronising.

Our conversations, and indeed these conflicts, continue to unfold even as I write this chapter, and to be mediated both through our digital communication and by our shared experiences of Trampoline House in its best and worst moments. We have shared our writing with each other and met in person in Copenhagen to talk through what might come next, in terms of our research, activism, and participation in the House. We feel the pull of our personal commitments to our friends there and our ethical commitments to the House's mission, and at the same time, we recognise an ethical commitment to a conviviality realised through social justice aspirations, mediated conflict, and a research imperative that is truly co-productive.

Conclusion

This chapter has argued for seriously considering conviviality as an imperative and horizon of research in media and migration. In discussing the methodological potential of the term, I have suggested that it is precisely the combination of its normative properties and its embrace of conflict, as debated in previous literature, that makes it useful to social justice-oriented research. Through anecdotes from the field, I have further highlighted three emphases of conviviality that are particularly useful in ethnographic contexts: an ethical stance, co-production, and conflict.

In discussing the interplay between various convivial spaces, both physical and digital, and my role in producing representations with my interlocutors, I have tried to account for the ways in which my fieldwork at Trampoline House challenged me to take an ethical stance as both an activist and a researcher. Over time, however, it became clear to me and other activists and researchers that the House is still figuring out how best to mediate conflict

And this is part of the process.

I began this chapter on a hopeful note which perhaps seems diminished in light of the last section on the conflicts endured by Trampoline House staff members. However, these conflicts ought not to deter us from deploying conviviality, or from working towards it in our research as in our activism. Conviviality is a horizon rather than a destination, a process of frustrating but dynamic everyday growth which we would be foolish to try to force into a linear progression.

Life goes on at the House without the presence of the researchers and activists who left. Digital and physical lives still mediate the different communities at work in its daily activities. There will be more House meetings and events responding to Denmark's changing political and social landscape and the realities of new arrivals. The activists and researchers who made the decision to leave continue the dialogue of what it means to live together, to work together towards equal participation in society, and to deal deliberately and sensitively with conflict. We are still discussing the lessons—not least of all the ones that were hard to learn—with each other and will carry these questions forward in our work.

To simply look for conviviality as something to be observed or measured, conceptually debated or analysed, is not enough. Researchers and activists alike must instead work harder to engage interlocutors in the co-production of media representations, safe spaces, and convivial community. It is imperative that we do so. As the political landscape continues to shift around the world, research and activism that imagines, deploys, and works towards the convivial—in its capacity for hope as well as conflict—will be essential tools in combating the stigma and hostility that beget and are encoded in violent immigration policy.

Acknowledgment Many thanks to Tina Askanius and Tobias Linné for help with early drafts of this chapter.

Notes

1. For more, please visit: https://www.trampolinehouse.dk.
2. Danish readers will be interested in Garbi Schmidt's (2015) work on the neighbourhood's immigration history, *Nørrebros indvandringshistorie 1885–2010*.
3. For more on this topic, please see https://www.nytimes.com/2018/07/01/world/europe/denmark-immigrant-ghettos.html.
4. While it is beyond the scope of this chapter to discuss the differences between charity and activism (which are politically and social contextual and also vary between academic fields), it is worth noting that all new interns and volunteers at Trampoline House are told that the 'charity model' of social support (in which funds are distributed to those in need, or events are held to raise money for them) is not sustainable. Rather, each person—volunteer, intern, and migrant—should shoulder part of the responsibility of the House as part of their empowerment. This sentiment is displayed in

an account written for France24 (2017) by Trampoline House founder Morten Goll. https://observers.france24.com/en/20170404-copenhagen-trampoline-house-refugee-integrate.
5. It should be noted that language classes offered by the state are often given at time inconvenient to asylum-seeking and refugee families, mainly in the evening, when parents would need childcare to take these classes, but cannot find/afford it.
6. Visit https://www.trampolinehouse.dk/about-camp/ for more details.

REFERENCES

Abid, Z. R., A. S. Manan, and Z. A. A. A Rahman. 2017. "'A Flood of Syrians Has Slowed to Trickle': The Use of Metaphors in the Representation of Syrian Refugees in the Online Media News Reports of Host and Non-Host Countries." *Discourse & Communication* 11 (2): 121–140. https://doi.org/10.1177/1750481317691857.

Alhourani, A. R. 2017. "Performative Ethnography: Difference and Conviviality of Everyday Multiculturalism in Bellville (Cape Town)." *Journal of African Cultural Studies* 29 (2): 211–226. https://doi.org/10.1080/13696815.2016.1273764.

Amin, A. 2008. "Collective Culture and Urban Public Space." *City* 12 (1): 5–24. https://doi.org/10.1080/13604810801933495.

Berry, M., I. Garcia-Blanco, and K. Moore. 2015. "Press Coverage of the Refugee and Migrant Crisis in the EU: A Content Analysis of Five European Countries." Report Prepared for the United Nations High Commission for Refugees, December. Available from https://www.unhcr.org/56bb369c9.pdf. Accessed May 3, 2019.

Caviedes, A. 2015. "An Emerging 'European' News Portrayal of Immigration?" *Journal of Ethnic and Migration Studies* 41 (6): 897–917. https://doi.org/10.1080/1369183x.2014.1002199.

Chandler, D., and R. Munday. 2016. *A Dictionary of Media and Communication*. Oxford: Oxford University Press.

Chikamori, T. 2009. "Between the 'Media City' and the 'City as a Medium.'" *Theory, Culture and Society* 26 (4): 147–154. https://doi.org/10.1177/0263276409104972.

Dekker, R., and G. Engbersen. 2014. "How Social Media Transform Migrant Networks and Facilitate Migration." *Global Networks* 14: 401–418. https://doi.org/10.1111/glob.12040.

Fabian, J. 1990. *Power and Performance: Ethnographic Explorations Through Proverbial Wisdom and Theatre in Shaba, Zaire*. Madison: University of Wisconsin Press.

Fabian, J. 1995. "Ethnographic Misunderstanding and the Perils of Context." *American Anthropologist* 97 (1): 41–50. https://doi.org/10.1525/aa.1995.97.1.02a00080.

Frouws, B., M. Phillips, A. Hassan, and M. Twigt. 2016. "Getting to Europe the Whatsapp Way: The Use of ICT in Contemporary Mixed Migration Flows to Europe." Report Regional Mixed Migration Secretariat. Available from http://reliefweb.int/report/world/briefing-paper-2-getting-europe-whatsapp-way-use-ict-contemporary-mixed-migration-flows. Accessed May 3, 2019.

Gabrielatos, C., and P. Baker. 2008. "Fleeing, Sneaking, Flooding: A Corpus Analysis of Discursive Constructions of Refugees and Asylum Seekers in the UK Press, 1996–2005." *Journal of English Linguistics* 36 (1): 5–38. https://doi.org/10.1177/0075424207311247.

Gillespie, M., L. Peter Ampofo, M. Cheesman, B. Faith, E. Illiou, A. Issa, S. Osserian, and D. Skleparis. 2016. "Mapping Refugee Media Journeys Smartphones and Social Media Networks." Report The Open University/France Médias Monde. Available from http://www.open.ac.uk/ccig/sites/www.open.ac.uk.ccig/files/Mapping%20Refugee%20Media%20Journeys%2016%20May%20FIN%20MG_0.pdf. Accessed May 3, 2019.

Gilroy, P. 2004. *After Empire: Melancholia or Convivial Culture?—Multiculture or Postcolonial Melancholia*. New York: Routledge.

Gilroy, P. 2006. *Postcolonial Melancholia*. New York: Columbia University Press.

Greussing, E., and H. G. Boomgaarden. 2017. "Shifting the Refugee Narrative? An Automated Frame Analysis of Europe's 2015 Refugee Crisis." *Journal of Ethnic and Migration Studies* 43 (11): 1749–1774. https://doi.org/10.1080/1369183x.2017.1282813.

Houssein, C. 2013. "Diaspora, Memory, and Ethnic Media: Media Use by Somalis Living in Canada." *Bildhaan: An International Journal of Somali Studies* 12 (11): 87–105.

Kittler, F., and M. Griffin. 1996. "The City Is a Medium." *New Literary History* 27 (4): 717–729.

Lapiņa, L. 2016. "Besides Conviviality: Paradoxes in Being 'at Ease' with Diversity in a Copenhagen District". *Nordic Journal of Migration Research* 6 (1): 33–41. https://doi.org/10.1515/njmr-2016-0002.

Lawlor, A. 2015. "Local and National Accounts of Immigration Framing in a Cross-National Perspective." *Journal of Ethnic and Migration Studies* 41 (6): 918–941. https://doi.org/10.1080/1369183x.2014.1001625.

Lulle, A., and E. Ungure. 2015. "Asylum Seekers' Crisis in Europe 2015: Debating Spaces of Fear and Security in Latvia." *Journal of Baltic Security* 1 (2): 62–95. https://doi.org/10.1515/jobs-2016-0021.

Marcus, G. E. 1998. *Ethnography Through Thick and Thin*. Princeton, NJ: Princeton University Press.

Matthews, J., and A. R. Brown. 2012. "Negatively Shaping the Asylum Agenda? The Representational Strategy and Impact of a Tabloid News Campaign." *Journalism Criticism, Theory and Practice* 13 (6): 802–817. https://doi.org/10.1177/1464884911431386.

Musarò, P., and P. Parmiggiani. 2017. "Beyond Black and White: The Role of Media in Portraying and Policing Migration and Asylum in Italy." *International Review of Sociology* 27 (2): 241–260. https://doi.org/10.1080/03906701.2017.1329034.

Nowicka, M., and T. Heil. 2015. "On the Analytical and Normative Dimensions of Conviviality and Cosmopolitanism." Lecture held on 15 June at the Eberhard Karls University Tübingen, Germany.

Parker, S. 2015. "'Unwanted Invaders': The Representation of Refugees and Asylum Seekers in the UK and Australian Print Media." *Myth and Nation* 23: 1–21.

Peattie, L. 1998. "Convivial Cities." In *Cities for Citizens: Planning and the Rise of Civil Society in a Global Age*, edited by M. Douglass and J. Friedmann, 247–252. Chichester: Wiley.

Schmidt, G. 2015. *Nørrebros indvandringshistorie 1885–2010*. Copenhagen: Museum Tusculanum.

The Observers/France24. 2017. "Copenhagen's 'Trampoline House' Helps Refugees Integrate." Available from https://observers.france24.com/en/20170404-copenhagen-trampoline-house-refugee-integrate. Accessed June 7, 2019.

Van Gorp, B. 2005. "Where is the Frame?" *European Journal of Communication* 20 (4): 484–507.

Varjú, V., and S. Plaut. 2017. "Media Mirrors? Framing Hungarian Romani Migration to Canada in Hungarian and Canadian Press." *Ethnic and Racial Studies* 40 (7): 1096–1113. https://doi.org/10.1080/01419870.2017.1266007.

Venegas, K., and A. Huerta. 2010. "Urban Ethnography: Approaches, Perspectives and Challenges." In *New Approaches to Qualitative Research: Wisdom and Uncertainty*, edited by M. Savin-Baden and C. Howell Major, 154–161. New York: Routledge.

Open Access This chapter is licensed under the terms of the Creative Commons Attribution 4.0 International License (http://creativecommons.org/licenses/by/4.0/), which permits use, sharing, adaptation, distribution and reproduction in any medium or format, as long as you give appropriate credit to the original author(s) and the source, provide a link to the Creative Commons license and indicate if changes were made.

The images or other third party material in this chapter are included in the chapter's Creative Commons license, unless indicated otherwise in a credit line to the material. If material is not included in the chapter's Creative Commons license and your intended use is not permitted by statutory regulation or exceeds the permitted use, you will need to obtain permission directly from the copyright holder.

CHAPTER 9

Post-2015 *Refugees Welcome* Initiatives in Sweden: Cosmopolitan Underpinnings

Maja Povrzanović Frykman and Fanny Mäkelä

Introduction: Moral and Political Dimensions of Cosmopolitanism

Researchers have shown that seemingly "apolitical" volunteering for refugees framed within humanitarian parameters is actually highly political. Fleischmann and Steinhilper's (2017) review of research on the upsurge in German citizens' commitment to refugees in 2015 suggests that, by avoiding politically contextualising their own work, volunteers became complicit in an increasingly repressive migration regime that reproduces hegemonic inequalities and hierarchies. On the other hand, these authors point out the potential of current volunteering for initiating political transformations, in line with Rancière's (1999, 2010) understanding of the political as a "rupture" in the dominant order. They see unique points of access for refugees

---

M. Povrzanović Frykman (✉)
Faculty of Culture and Society, Department of Global Political Studies, Malmö University, Malmö, Sweden
e-mail: maja.frykman@mau.se

F. Mäkelä
Malmö, Sweden

© The Author(s) 2020
O. Hemer et al. (eds.), *Conviviality at the Crossroads*,
https://doi.org/10.1007/978-3-030-28979-9_9

to German society, but also political possibilities that foster change towards more egalitarian relations, in spaces of encounters similar to those described in this volume by Duru (Chapter 7) and Cory (Chapter 8). While these and several other chapters in this volume make a strong case for conviviality as a notion that is opening new analytical venues, the following chapter takes a step back and deals with the cosmopolitan values and visions in which potential modes of conviviality may be grounded. Relating to a specific historical conjuncture of refugee migration and altered mobility regimes, this chapter focuses on *Refugees Welcome* initiatives in Sweden, notably in the post-2015 context. We thus respond to Braidotti et al. (2013: 3) call for an understanding of cosmopolitanism that is "more attentive to the material reality of our social and political situation … with specificity rather than generality, groundedness rather than abstractness". In line with Skrbiš and Woodward's (2013: ix) statement in the preface to their book on the uses of the idea of cosmopolitanism, we do not see it as "a hallelujah moment for social scientists trying to conceptualise a better society", but as a process which allows for moving closer to the possible cosmopolitan ideal—a process that requires engaging by doing.

Recognising the shortcomings of applying cosmopolitanism as a normative concept to empirical realities of "living-with-difference" (see Nowicka, Chapter 2 in this volume), we do not discuss the newly created spaces of encounters between refugees and residents but analyse *Refugees Welcome* initiatives' cosmopolitan underpinnings. We employ it as a concept that may help us understand how particular and universal concerns and aspirations for social justice are conjoined in a specific setting of volunteering and activism in Sweden after 2015.

Reviewing the literature dealing with the moral, political (or legal) and cultural cosmopolitan doctrine, and how each represents the impact of the idea of universal membership (or world citizenship) on morality, political institutions and cultural identity (Etinson 2011), is beyond the scope of this chapter. For the attempted analysis, we find useful the differentiation between the moral and the political/institutional dimension of cosmopolitanism (Held 2013).[1] It helps us discern the view of all human beings requiring equal moral respect and concern from an institutional focus that is occupied with questions about how cosmopolitan principles can be embedded in practice.

As stated by Held (2013), the principles of equal respect, equal concern and the priority of the vital needs of all human beings are not principles for some remote utopia (see Lettevall, Chapter 5 in this volume); existent forms of political regulation and law-making create powers, rights and constraints that go beyond the claims of nation states. However, as will be displayed below, the realities of unequal political treatment of those whose chances and choices are distorted by the luck (Brock 2019) of having been born in/belonging to a war-ridden country are a source of great frustration for pro-refugee volunteers and activists. While trying to act upon their values that we frame as cosmopolitan, they face the limitations imposed by Swedish legal and political context that are part of how "current global systems are failing the ethical concerns of moral cosmopolitanism" (Held 2013: 30).

In the following sections, we briefly provide background information about the emergence of *Refugees Welcome* initiatives in 2015, review relevant former research and present our interview material. We then analyse our interviewees' reflections on their volunteering and activism through the lens of cosmopolitanism. In the concluding section, we relate our results to the theoretical work on cosmopolitanism that specifically sets it in the context of recent refugee migration (Caraus and Parvu 2019).

Background

The official refugee reception services in Sweden, and in the city of Malmö in particular, faced an unprecedented challenge when more than two-thirds of the 163,000 asylum seekers entering Sweden in 2015 arrived in the last four months of the year.[2] It took six weeks for the authorities to respond and in their absence civil society (Spurk 2010) stepped in. Volunteers under the banners of different formal and informal civil society organisations, Christian, Islamic and Jewish congregations and individuals, managed the overwhelming situation in Malmö where up to 2000 refugees were being received on a daily basis. They welcomed them and provided donated clothes and refreshments, sanitary products and toys, information and practical guidance, money for their continued journey or shelter for the night (Povrzanović Frykman and Mäkelä 2019).

The volunteers managed the situation widely perceived as "crisis" that was overwhelming in both practical and emotional terms. *Kontrapunkt*—a cultural and social centre promoting activism, volunteering and personal engagement that proclaimed support for refugees long before the events of 2015 (Povrzanović Frykman 2016) —became one of the most prominent places where refugees were assisted by over 1100 volunteers. Between September and November, 1000 portions of food were cooked and served there daily (Rescala 2016).

This reinforced the existing image of Malmö[3] as "the capital of solidarity" characterised by the presence of a strong and prominently leftist civil society (Hansen 2019),[4] but also brought to the fore internal differentiation already present prior to the 2015 "crisis", between formal and informal organisations and between "ordinary" volunteers and "activists", where "activism" denotes leftist political engagement. Moreover, it actualised the dilemma of whether civil society groups should compete with or attempt to substitute state activities (Pries 2019), while the unprecedented civil society engagement actually replaced the authorities that were unprepared for taking full control of their mandate.

As the level of emotions and devotion to the task was high, the people participating in the civil society response were utterly frustrated when they were eventually replaced by officials and professionals, dismissed as "only volunteers" and forbidden to offer any donated food to the incoming refugees. The disbelief and shock—described by many as a truly traumatic moment—came on 21 November 2015 when the Swedish government introduced checkpoints at the Swedish border with Denmark, at which the incoming people could be prevented from entering the country (Povrzanović Frykman and Mäkelä 2019).

While *Kontrapunkt* recognised the urgency of volunteering but retained high profile in left-wing extra-parliamentary political activism, *Refugees Welcome to Malmö* made it clear that they were politically and religiously unattached, making it easier for them to cooperate with state officials. They had 800 volunteers and most of our interviewees (see ibid.) stated that they joined *Refugees Welcome to Malmö* because it did not take sides: there was no conflict between their humanitarian ambition and personal political and religious beliefs. In 2015, the impetus for immediate humanitarian effort stemmed from the image of "crisis" (Fassin 2016), and it ceased once the refugees stopped entering Sweden in large numbers. During the autumn of 2015 a lot of *Refugees Welcome* initiatives popped up in cities all over Sweden, but only a few of the spontaneous volunteers' initiatives evolved into NGOs. However, a number of new civil initiatives and organisations have emerged in the aftermath of the events of 2015. *Refugees Welcome Sweden* died out, but was resurrected and is today an umbrella association that focuses on providing a structure and aid to local initiatives with the refugees, as well as working to strengthen support in Sweden for what they call "a long-lasting and humane asylum system in Sweden".[5]

Former Research

Civil society in Sweden has been studied previously (Svedberg and Trägårdh 2006), but little attention has been paid to the grass-roots initiatives of 2015 discussed in this chapter. Initial research was done mostly by students who addressed the questions of motivation (Mäkelä 2016; Rescala 2016), internal competition (Ghita 2016), compassion and perceptions of volunteers' own privilege (Mårs 2016). Our research explored the volunteers' motivations, but also conflicts and political ambiguities within the *Refugees Welcome to Malmö* civil initiative (Povrzanović Frykman and Mäkelä 2019). A study comparing the situation in Sweden and Germany focuses on emotional aspects of pro-refugee mobilisations (see Kleres 2018), while a recent volume presenting the state of the art of research on *Refugees Welcome* initiatives in Europe (Feischmidt et al. 2019) provides insights into manifold tensions between motives, idea(l)s and outcomes in the field of volunteering (see e.g. Karakayali 2019; Turinsky and Nowicka 2019; Vandevoordt and Verschraegen 2019) that are highly pertinent to the discussion this volume invites on perceptions of difference, practices of inclusion and feelings of obligation, and the ways of theorising them. This chapter contributes to the literature that seeks to understand the social and political developments of *Refugees Welcome* initiatives beyond the immediacy of "crisis" (e.g. Fleischmann and Steinhilper 2017; Funk 2016; Jäckle and König 2017). In addition, contributions are made to the understanding of motivations and experiences of volunteering and the "new" forms of volunteering that are autonomous and unaffiliated.

The Material

Our ongoing research is based on in-depth interviews conducted by Fanny Mäkelä in Malmö in 2016 and 2018 with the volunteers engaged in different *Refugees Welcome* initiatives in Sweden.[6] The interviews conducted in 2016 focused on the experiences of people who were practically involved in *Refugees Welcome to Malmö* in the autumn of 2015, while the interviews from 2018 focused on post-2015 context and the volunteers' reflections on the dynamics of value-based visions guiding their work and the practical outcomes of that work.[7]

The body of material includes 18 interviews with men and women ranging from 22 to 68 years of age (at the time of interviewing), in various professions, and with different levels of education. Political party sympathies cover a wide spectrum; however, most of the interviewees voted for the Left Party (Vänsterpartiet). About half of the interviewees have a Swedish origin, while others come from a number of different countries and continents.[8]

In this chapter, we focus on the perceptions and self-reflections of four persons who have had a prominent role in the post-2015 *Refugees Welcome* initiatives in Sweden.

Tobias is 47, has a university education and works as a coordinator for families hosting young homeless people. He is of Danish background but has lived in Sweden for 30 years. Prior to 2015, Tobias engaged in voluntary work with asylum seeking Palestinians and human rights work with the Roma people in Malmö, who are mostly from Romania. Besides being engaged in *Refugees Welcome Sweden* in 2015, he is the initiator and chairman of a post-2015 national umbrella version of this organisation.

Gemila is 33, holds a university degree and works as head of the unit for accommodations for unaccompanied minors. Gemila's mother is Polish, her father is Iraqi and she has lived in Sweden for 29 years. Before 2015, she volunteered in a Red Cross women's shelter. Besides being engaged in the board of *Refugees Welcome Sweden*, she is the initiator and chairperson of post-2015 *Refugees Welcome Malmö*.

Kamal is 30 years old and came to Sweden from Lebanon with his family in the 1990s. He is a teacher, but for the moment he works with coordinating the official refugee reception and inclusion in the municipality where he lives. On the 7 September 2015, he started *Konvoj för medmänsklighet* (Convoy for humanity) with cars driving through Europe and back to Sweden picking up refugees, creating a safe way to seek asylum. He simultaneously founded a local *Refugees Welcome* initiative which today has a regional scope with himself as chairman; he is also a member of the board in *Refugees Welcome Sweden*. Before the autumn of 2015, Kamal had some experience of volunteering with the collection and distribution of clothes to homeless in the local foundation *Glöm aldrig William Petzäll*.

Kajsa, our fourth interviewee quoted, is a Swedish born 27-year-old, holds a university degree and works professionally as a project leader. Prior to 2015, she was volunteering in *The Swedish Network of Refugee Support* (FARR),[9] *No One is Illegal*[10] and the *Asylum Group*.[11] Kajsa was involved in the refugee reception from the start and is the national coordinator of *Refugees Welcome Housing*[12]—one of the organisations that are part of the *Refugees Welcome Sweden* network. They recognise a need for alternative accommodations and hence match landlords with asylum seeking refugees,

refugees with a temporary residence permit, and refugees that have been denied asylum and therefore live in Sweden "illegally". They do this in order to fight isolation and create a culture of mutual integration.

Specificities of the Swedish Context—And Its Changes

In the Swedish cultural context, the Social Democratic idea of *folkhemmet*—"the people's home"—is crucial for understanding the background of our interviewees' views and values. Every citizen is protected "from the cradle to the grave" by a number of social rights (Lewin 2013: 30). In 1928, Per Albin Hansson used the family as a metaphor and stated that in a family no one looks down on the other, no one tries to get an advantage on another's expense and the strong don't prey on the weak. In the good home, there is equality, care, cooperation and helpfulness (ibid.). *Folkhemmet* has thus created fundamental values of equality and social justice that permeated Swedish society for over 90 years—the values that our interviewees repeatedly referred to. Sweden, widely viewed both domestically and internationally to be "a champion of high global morals" (Tanner 2016), has been historically refugee-friendly, receiving resettled refugees through the United Nations since 1950. Moreover, Tobias sees the civil engagement for asylum seekers as embedded in a particular tradition of civic movements in the country:

> We had a luxury situation here in Sweden, that people could organise – and we should use this! I like the notion of *folkrörelse* – civic movement. We have a unique history of *folkrörelse* here in Sweden. The workers' movement, women's movement, peace movement, environmental movement. We have a history as a people rich in movements.

As the quote suggests, Tobias is optimistic about the potential of the *Refugees Welcome* movement in Sweden. However, the other interviewees quoted here do not share his optimism. Kajsa observed that many of the people who volunteered at Malmö Central station in 2015 now, years later, do not consider that those who arrived are still in Sweden waiting for residence permits.[13] Gemila also talked about issues of disinterest and a lack of commitment. In 2017, she tried to start up a local *Refugees Welcome* initiative in the county where she worked at that time. She called meetings and "people came, but there was no one who wanted to get involved, the engagement had died out". In the winter of 2017 back in Malmö, she tried reviving the old *Refugees Welcome to Malmö*, "but it also died pretty quickly actually, the name bore it, but it died".

Kamal's story starts with the opportunity to practice solidarity, but leads to failing engagement as a result of the political context:

> In Autumn 2015, … it was all we learnt about Sweden that we grew up in … about what my [with emphasis] Sweden is. [pause] It was now we could practice it. It was now that we could show what we were raised like and we had the country with us. So, we started to do things, together we built these groups, and people just said "yes, of course", … "sure, what can I do", no question about it, "we do it". [pause] "we do it". [pause] And I thought, this is what activism is about, we can change the world! But it is not like that. The moment Sweden changed its official standpoint, it took the air out of the entire movement. Then instead it was "yes, we do what we can even if our state does not succeed with it – so we do what we can", but then it was "we do what we can but the state is also against us". So it was like it, it pulled the air out of everything [with emphasis] and it was like all of those [volunteers] who have spent a lot of time but were really not familiar with this, they disappeared, it was the outermost circle that usually never participates, they disappeared. The core remained, and the core got smaller and smaller with fewer people who were the most active, and many burnt themselves out and many quit.

From having had one of the most generous refugee and asylum policies in Europe, the Swedish government began adopting stricter legislation and policy reforms to narrow benefits for refugees (Tanner 2016) and, as presented at the Asylum Group's webpage,[14] implementing "a systematic rejective refugee politics". Kamal stated: "We are betraying all our ideals, we… we are abandoning everything we have learnt is right". Kajsa gets very frustrated by the politicians' picture of refugee reception and the way this picture is accepted by the general public without any questions being asked. Since late 2015 with the closing of the borders all she hears is,

> the discussion that 'we cannot manage any more' – that one can believe that Sweden as a privileged country can exist in a global world without taking part in the consequences of the wars and catastrophes that take place in the world!

Kamal puts a lot of blame on the government consisting of the Social Democrats and the Green party for the change in values among the population. By endorsing the right-wing position concerning refugees as a burden, they made volunteers "feel ashamed for being humane", as if it was "wrong to work for a better world". Tobias instead sees the changes in treatment of refugees by the Swedish state in a broader context of "the Western world" closing its ranks to protect its privileges:

> This what happens in the Western world – that we would not be able to help people, that is exaggerated, that is sick, to be a part of the problem and not take responsibility! It is defect.

This strong stance points to the "defect"—even "sick", morally unattainable—character of this non-recognition of shared responsibilities. Similarly to Gemila's remark that "we have lost the core values of what it means to be human", it resonates with the cosmopolitan ideal of the global civil society discussed by Hensby and O'Byrne (2019), who see it as both a normative project and a space for ethical debate. Indeed, the fundamentally ethical dimension of civic engagement for refugees—in direct relation to Held's (2013) moral cosmopolitanism—comes forward in our interviewees' reflections on the values guiding their volunteering and advocacy work, discussed in the following section.

Cosmopolitan Values, Moral Obligation

"The reason I engage is not because engaging gives me, like, a warm and cosy feeling", said Gemila. Similarly, Kajsa stated: "One doesn't engage because it is fun. One can just continue living one's own life. It is about solidarity, it feels important". When describing the situation with refugee arrivals to Malmö Central station in 2015, Tobias presented it as a moment of "enormous solidarity", where asylum seekers "were welcomed by fellow humans". He further explained that he lived for longer periods "in other cultures", learned other languages, and therefore, "cares very much for globalisation issues that are incredibly important today":

> I think that borders have a lesser importance in a globalised society we live in today. That is why migration issues are so incredibly important. Because people, for different reasons, must move in this world. And we have one world and I think that one has to be able to move freely in the entire world.

Since we ourselves cause many of the reasons that force people to move. All from environmental catastrophes to war, persecution and so on. So, to lock people out from settling and living in freedom is fully incomprehensible. These are, approximately, the basic values I have in my work.

This quote clearly positions Tobias as a person who does not see the refugees just as "needy others", but who understands global connections and disparities of privilege in the "one world we have" and thus claims shared responsibilities. He also said that "if one stretches it really far politically, it is often the Westerners themselves who caused many of those problems in parts of the world that are in crisis".

Without presenting himself as cosmopolitan, Tobias adheres to the cosmopolitan principle that "highlights the responsibilities we have to those whom we do not know, but whose lives should be of concern to us" (Brock 2019: 315). Furthermore, he appears as cosmopolitan as he communicates "a reflexive and critical engagement with globalization" (Hensby and O'Byrne 2019: 336):

I want us to work for a globalized world, where we can use each other positively, help each other, and share. We otherwise counteract our own existence, for, like, no man is an island, as they say [he laughs], so it is. So, this what we detect now, I feel it is a favour of a kind, to participate in what is happening. It feels a bit like, it is now that the vital decisions are made and how we want to have it: is it a more closed world or do we go towards a more open world – that is where we stand and try to weigh now. (…) *Refugees Welcome*-movement can hopefully be a seed of a more open world.

Recognising Difference, Recognising Agency

Cosmopolitanism engages ideas around identity and difference (Moore 2013) and the critique of cosmopolitanism points out that it reinforces fixed categories of human difference originating from the colonial past. As Nowicka (forthcoming) argues, "reduced to moral obligation to humanity, cosmopolitanism inadequately addresses the challenges of relationship with the other, for even if we are all humans, we are all different, and this difference matters" (see also Nowicka, Chapter 2 in this volume). Importantly, in our material the recognition of difference does not imply othering, but is rather in line with the rejection of a stance that—as succinctly phrased by Erikson (Chapter 3 in this volume)—difference is a threat and sameness is a prerequisite for sharing. Or, as in Gemila's elliptic formulation concerning the refugees: "They are no fucking Aliens! They aren't; they are people as any other people".

When saying "I have heard such histories, it cannot be described, I don't know what it is that makes people want to continue living!", Tobias appears shaken by the encounters that made him acutely aware of his own privileges. At the same time, he is aware of the oppressive character of the categories, based on legal status or recognition of neediness, that reduce refugees to victims and deny their agency:

> These people have been through so much, there is nothing to say. And then, to come to a society that is oppressing you or taking away your rights, to live as a part of some kind of statistics, that is for me totally beyond understanding – it is people, and each and every one has a personal story that is their reason for coming here. One should listen to them, not lump them together as 'refugees' or one or another 'group'. No, one should not do that. I understand the need, but no. That is what is motivating me in this work, to actually lift people who are incredibly vulnerable, who absolutely don't have any reason to 'be victims'. They are victims, but they did not put themselves in such position.

This resonates with Fine's (2019) warning placed in the context of discussion of cosmopolitan solidarity: "If we turn victimhood into a master status, we are faced with the paradox that compassion for the victims can also strip them of their humanity" (Fine 2019: 368).

Tobias means that refugees should not only feel welcome, but that they should also treat their experience as refugees as part of their life, rather than as a discrete event, and build on that experience as they continue living in Sweden. He further maintains that it is important to work *with* the asylum seekers and not *for* them. However, including the asylum seekers in *Refugees Welcome* initiatives is a major problem. Even if there are instances of (former undocumented) asylum seekers becoming prominent activists (see Hansen 2019), the volunteers cannot work in an inclusive way to the extent that they wish. Tobias explained that "the asylum seekers are afraid of engaging, they believe it is not good for their 'case'", i.e. the possibility of getting residence permit. When they eventually receive a residence permit, possibly after seven years, their life starts, but the "bubble" of waiting in uncertainty has torn a person "to no worth at all". An entire life starts again, and their first priority is not to get engaged in volunteering or in political activism. However, ideally, Tobias claims, the pro-humane asylum politics movement should be led by people with personal experience of asylum seeking.

Tobias also worked with stateless Palestinians who "had a very difficult asylum process in Sweden". He recounted problems where Palestinians who had lived in Sweden for seven or eight years without receiving residence permits behaved negatively towards the Syrians who obtained permits far more quickly. Finding himself "involved in a Middle Eastern thing" as a mediator between two camps "felt fully bizarre", but enabled learning and understanding:

> Sitting between two groups of very frustrated men and trying to reach some kind of Swedish consensus – that was just impossible! But one learned incredibly much. I have such a great respect for different cultures, how one mediates, and how one acts – it is a very big lesson learned that I wish I had gotten more of. … It was an interesting and important experience that helps in working with refugees.
>
> I have worked so much with the anti-Semitic part that there is – it is so deeply rooted and, in a way, it is very difficult to deal with. You must have an understanding for it in order to try to process it. One will never be able to understand fully, but it is very important to have an insight, to understand the frustration, and anger. We have had a luxury of living here!

What Tobias recounted was a lesson in how cosmopolitanism needs to be situated in the social situations here and now as well as in the concreteness of historical contingencies elsewhere in the world (Pendenza 2017). As noted by Trujillo (2015), cosmopolitanism that seeks to overcome existing differences presupposes their existence and the possible tension between them. The political dimension of cosmopolitanism thus regards "a dynamic effort for increasing inclusion in a single community, whilst maintaining differences" (Trujillo 2015: 13).[15]

RELATION TO INSTITUTIONS: INTEGRATIVE VS. TRANSFORMATIVE ROLE?

The interviewees quoted in this chapter hold prominent positions in the post-2015 pro-refugee and pro-humane asylum politics movement in Sweden and have a strong voice in formulating its principles and goals. The way they frame their engagement confirms Hensby and O'Byrne's (2019: 339) observation about a fundamentally ethical dimension of civil society. However, the felt necessity of doing something about the perceived injustices here and now—in this case concerning asylum seekers in Sweden—brings to the fore the tension between integrative and transformative aspects of civil engagement that these authors see as an undercurrent of civil society today in general. By working with (or even instead of) existent institutions of state and municipalities, the volunteers risk the trap of working with "passion for compassion devoid of politics" (Wilkinson 2019: 379), ignoring the institutional side of the refugees' problems. This is obvious and frustrating to our highly politically conscious interviewees. Gemila, for example, made a cynical comment:

> What volunteers do is that they are scraping what society like, stepped on […] volunteers 'feed the cats in the backyard', [pause] those summer cats that no one wanted, so. Like that which society failed to take care of, the things they dropped, there the volunteers and the civil society step in.

Kajsa holds that civil society "takes much more responsibility than it should" and that "the state should take more responsibility instead". However, she sees civil society as an important "catalyst" for positive change. This change refers to, for example, how people who live with refugees due to the *Refugees Welcome Housing* initiative, "can understand how twisted the entire Swedish asylum system really works". Kajsa sees this as very important, since Swedish citizens who are voting with regard to migration issues should know the legal and institutional realities of those issues.

While engaging in work to shift public and state opinion in Sweden towards support for a society where everyone's equal worth is mirrored in politics, these volunteers also engage in direct contact with asylum seekers to facilitate the fulfilment of those asylum seekers' urgent needs. They express a kind of pragmatic realism about their own potential influence, as seen in Kamal's reflections on the start of his volunteering in 2015: "I started at the wrong end, I wanted to have big changes, I should have started with the small ones". Gemila says that it has been good for her to professionally work for a municipality, since "one learns a lot".

At the *Refugees Welcome Sweden* webpage, a collaborative approach is promoted: "We believe that cooperation between governments, agencies, non-profits, and citizens is critical to create a long-lasting and humane asylum system in Sweden" (http://www.rwsverige.se/about/). Tobias said he considered collaboration with the municipalities and the Swedish

Church as the best way of addressing specific local needs concerning refugees, since "no one has all solutions and answers". Similarly, Kajsa stated:

> Migration is a challenge for the entire society. The authorities cannot resolve it on their own; private persons should not resolve in on their own. There is a need for organising and strategic thinking engaging several different actors, to find good solutions for the individuals.

Gemila dismisses the current Swedish asylum regime as "offensive" and "inhumane":

> I never believed that Sweden would end up where we are today, no one is doing anything, everyone just stands there and looks and thinks "this is a necessary evil". We are letting people drown in the Mediterranean Sea because it is a 'necessary evil'; [pretends to be upset] "God forbid that I should pay 20 kronor more in taxation, oh my God! Think if I cannot buy a new iPhone as Christmas present for my children since a damned refugee should come here!".

For Gemila, the current politics is the greatest obstacle, together with the society in which civic engagement is fading away—"on the way to die out", and at the same time the activists are "hitting the wall, all of them". When asked about her motivation for volunteering and activism after 2015, Gemila said she feels that what she does working with refugees professionally is not enough. Moreover, she presented an instance of historical reflexivity (see Glick Schiller 2016) in proposing a very dark possible future:

> I feel that [long pause] I want to have done something, I don't want to have stood there and not have, or at least not have tried to influence. [long pause] Because when I sit in a camp, with [long laughter] with a number on my arm, I don't want to say "I didn't know, I didn't see it coming", to be completely honest.

Both Tobias and Kamal wish that *Refugees Welcome* should not (need to) exist. Kamal dreams of "a world without refugees based on problems with human cause, social problems, problems with war":

I believe in, [pause] I am such a naive person who still believes in world peace. I think the only way to stop the refugee, if I may dream – that is what we should work with, to stop the war, to be a peace movement, a new peace movement.

While Kamal goes to the core of the problem by emphasising that stopping the war is "the only honorable way" of dealing with refugees, Tobias focused on Sweden where he sees civil society as the only humane alternative to the authorities and their *paragrafrytteri*, a Swedish expression for a kind of cynical and numerical legalism and machinelike administration. He hopes to be able to contribute to political change in Sweden and to create "a more compassionate system, humane in the process, a more humane system":

Compassion should be the guiding star of political decisions, but I think that we [*Refugees Welcome* movement in Sweden] first and foremost must act politically; we must, as the questions of migration are political. So, if we should influence, we must do it politically, influence for compassion, turn compassion into politics. ... I want to be a good person, not a good politician.

These words, again, resonate with theoretical discussion of cosmopolitanism, namely with Fine's (2019) understanding of cosmopolitan solidarity that is fundamentally built upon compassion. However, unlike compassion's nature as a matter of emotion and subjective consideration, solidarity is "a legal and political concept, denoting a shared responsibility for seeing through a particular project" (ibid., 368).

While Gemila hinted at the moral controversies of humanitarian practice (Wilkinson 2019) when stating that the *Refugees Welcome* movement will always be a humanitarian movement since they are working with a humanitarian vulnerable group, Kamal outlined the dilemma more clearly. A rhetorical question he posed about *Refugees Welcome*'s actual purpose made clear the dilemma between the integrative, system-supportive and the transformative, system-changing roles of civil society:

To work with the refugees and their rights, yes, it sounds good, but what does it mean in practice – is it about language cafés? There are other groups [to engage with that] I believe, I think we should engage in opinion building.

Conclusion

This chapter exemplified how the moral and political dimensions of cosmopolitanism (Held 2013) are intertwined in pro-refugee volunteering and activism. Our analysis displayed how cosmopolitanism can point to the universal aim of equality and at the same time demand that it is realised locally (Trujillo 2015). None of our interviewees employed the notion of cosmopolitanism when reflecting on their engagement with and for refugees. However, they outlined a normative order that emerges as a political project towards a reconstruction of society along lines of equality and justice (Siapera 2019), in line with the statement found at their organisation's webpage: "Refugees Welcome Sweden envisions a world where people are free from war, persecution and institutional discrimination. It is our mission to make Sweden a welcoming place for all refugees" (http://www.rwsverige.se/). The analysed narratives communicate the position of moral cosmopolitanism that, as pointed out by Held (2013: 30) translates into duties of global justice, to the protection of universal human rights, and to reforming unjust systems so that they are in line with cosmopolitan moral principles. It does not appear as a desired but chimeric "fantasy" (see Nowicka, Chapter 2 in this volume), but rather as "a concrete objective, a foreseeable situation, capable of being achieved in our world. ... a goal that needs to be formulated, cultivated and promoted" (Cebolla and Ghia 2015: 4). Indeed, our interviewees do not only talk about principles but put them into action: they initiated and lead a solidarity organisation with a number of sub-organisations specialised in practical work with refugees as well as in opinion building; they work to incite others to engage; and they are involved in day-to-day activities with refugees. We delved into the individual level of processes that require engaging by doing (Skrbiš and Woodward 2013), and we hope this chapter makes a convincing case for the analytical benefits of such an approach. At the same time, we analysed aspirations as situated in the social dynamics of volunteers' groups and organisations and as anchored in the historical context of specific societal values (Pendenza 2017).

The interview excerpts we presented do not reproduce universalising narratives, but resonate with a critical cosmopolitan stance (see Delanty 2006) described by Glick Schiller and Irving (2015: 5) as "aspirational, self-problematizing and aware of incomplete and contested nature of any cosmopolitan claim". Opposite to seemingly "apolitical" volunteering for refugees framed within humanitarian parameters, our interviewees' engagement clearly attempts political change. They understand that the institutionalisation of what we see as cosmopolitan principles guiding their work requires the entrenchment of these principles in law and public fora at diverse levels (Held 2013). Their ultimate aim is that their volunteering should become superfluous—when a "lasting and humane" asylum system is established in Sweden and the responsible institutions truly take over the task of helping asylum seekers, while granting them room for defining their needs and exercising their agency.

Scholars have observed that "the extent to which civil society movements have been able to induce political reforms to prevent the reproduction of social inequalities has historically been one of its key shortcomings" (Hensby and O'Byrne 2019: 339). A thorough understanding of the role of post-2015 *Refugees Welcome* initiatives in political transformations in Sweden remains a matter of further research. However, this chapter made clear the need to situate the analysis in a broader political context. In the case of post-2015 *Refugees Welcome* initiatives, this proved to be overwhelmingly important for understanding why the unprecedented civil society engagement for refugees met its abrupt end, but also why the principles it is based on present a sound ground upon which it may be resurrected as a political project.

In conclusion, we would like to relate our results to Caraus and Parvu's (2019) inspiring attempt to theorise cosmopolitanism by setting it in the context of refugee migration (see also Caraus and Paris 2019). They see migration and cosmopolitanism as consubstantial, since migration, without impediments, is a given starting point for a cosmopolitan "citizen of the world". Focusing on undocumented migrants' protests that are opposing anti-cosmopolitan stances generated by the increasing numbers of refugees and economic migrants, these authors develop a novel notion of radical cosmopolitanism. It refers to a bottom-up politicisation through anti-deportation protests of undocumented persons, organised by the movements such as *Sans Papiers, No Borders* and *No One Is Illegal*, that "contain in nuce new demands and new visions of the world" (Caraus and Parvu 2019: 426). Caraus and Parvu (ibid., 420) see these protests as acts of cosmopolitan citizenship that contest existent terms of political community and identity; they point at the "radical cosmopolitan potential" of such acts. They claim that such "migrant activism is inherently cosmopolitan" and "has a direct cosmopolitanizing effect" (ibid., 425), as the very act of protesting contests border regimes of nation states and thereby projects the world without borders or with porous borders. These authors point to "the quiet, invisible transformation of the world" that takes place when migrants "clandestinely defy the borders and expose the contingencies of citizenship without ever intending it" (ibid.).

In consent with this view, we propose to enlarge its scope to the activists and volunteers such as the ones involved in post-2015 *Refugees Welcome* initiatives in Sweden. Their intended political goals grounded in the claim of rights for human beings and not for citizens of a particular state, their rejection of the category of "illegal" people and any categorical units of difference, their work with refugees, including the demonstrations they co-organise with undocumented migrants (see Hansen 2019), the lectures they organise, the texts they publish on their organisations' digital platforms, as well as their proneness to historical reflexivity and critical self-reflection, all contribute to a bottom-up cosmopolitanisation of present-day Sweden, hopefully with transformative effects that will allow for future modalities of convivial life to develop.

Acknowledgements We wish to express our profound thanks to the interviewees for their willingness to participate in our research.

Notes

1. "Moral cosmopolitanism often translates into corresponding duties of global justice, to the protection of universal human rights, and to reforming unjust international systems so that they are in line with cosmopolitan moral principles. This moral dimension can be related to, but can also be distinct from, institutional cosmopolitanism, which focuses primarily on examining what institutional designs might best implement the normative considerations of its moral counterpart" (Held 2013: 30).
2. In 2015, Sweden had the highest number of asylum seekers per capita in the European Union, second only to Germany in absolute numbers, although first in terms of the number of people arriving from Syria. For more details, see Tanner (2016).
3. With a population of more than 330,000, Malmö is Sweden's third largest city. The inhabitants' average age is 38.5 years and 48% of those between 25 and 64 years of age have tertiary education. They originate from 178 countries (32% were born abroad and 12% have parents who were born in other countries) (Malmö stad 2016).
4. Focusing on the effects of the acts of prefigurative politics, Hansen's (2019) only touches upon *Refugees Welcome* in 2015. However, her ethnographic research on left-wing extra-parliamentary activism in Malmö is an important backdrop for the analysis attempted in this chapter.

5. "*Refugees Welcome Sverige* is a Swedish non-profit organization that works to include refugees in the Swedish society. We believe that cooperation between governments, agencies, non-profits, and citizens is critical to create a long-lasting and humane asylum system in Sweden. We believe that this is crucial in order for Sweden to continue being an open and compassionate country that promote and protect people's civil rights", http://www.rwsverige.se/, accessed July 1, 2019.
6. The interviews were conducted and transcribed by Mäkelä in Swedish. The quotes in the text are translated into English by both authors.
7. The notion of volunteer is used in this chapter as an umbrella term for anyone who engaged in volunteer work. However, while some people interviewed by Mäkelä stressed that they see themselves as volunteers but not as activists, the interviewees quoted in this chapter used both terms when reflecting on their own engagement and on *Refugees Welcome* initiatives in general. For discussion of ambiguity of the notion of activist in the context of left-wing activism in Malmö, see Hansen (2019).
8. For details on all research participants, see Povrzanović Frykman and Mäkelä (2019). A highly pertinent discussion of the implications of migrant origin in activism (see Glick Schiller 2015; Hansen 2019) is beyond the scope of this chapter. Let it suffice to note here that, when critically assessing current Swedish asylum politics, they used "we" to refer to "Sweden" and "the Swedes".
9. FARR (Flyktinggrupperna och Asylkommitteérnas Riksråd) is an umbrella organisation that supports on national scale individuals and groups that promote the right to seek asylum. For more details, see https://www.farr.se/sv/in-english.
10. For details, see https://www.ingenillegal.org/english/.
11. *The Asylum Group in Malmö* is a non-profit organisation that works with and for asylum seekers and refugees on hiding since 1991. For more details, see http://asylgruppenimalmo.se/english/.
12. For details, see https://refugees-welcome.se/?lang=en. See also *Welcome Housing* Facebook page https://www.facebook.com/refugeeswelcomesverige/posts/667049040169305/, where the following text is available in English and Swedish: "Let's share everyday life, society and the world. ... Refugees Welcome is Global-Global Solidarity".
13. In 2013, Swedish migration authorities decreed that all Syrians granted any form of protection would receive permanent residence, but two years later "Sweden rolled back its permanent residence policy for all newly arriving Syrians, and has proposed granting only temporary status to successful asylum seekers of all nationalities, including Syrians" (Tanner 2016).
14. "International conventions that Sweden has ratified are not being adhered to and gross violations of right to asylum occur. ... UN has given Sweden most

attention for having sent people to countries where they are susceptible to torture," http://asylgruppenimalmo.se/english/, accessed June 1, 2019.
15. "In the inclusive versions of cosmopolitanism, a positive cosmopolitan claim is prevalent: the point is not to deny the relevance of necessary differences, but to build a balance between differences in a community of destiny. Cosmopolitanism is an aim to be achieved, presumably with continuous new challenges" (Trujillo 2015: 14).

References

Braidotti, R., B. Blaagaard, and P. Hanafin. 2013. "Introduction." In *After Cosmopolitanism*, edited by R. Braidotti, P. Hanafin, and B. Blaagaard, 1–7. Abingdon: Routledge.

Brock, G. 2019. "Seeking Global Justice: What Kind of Equality Should Guide Cosmopolitans?" In *Routledge International Handbook of Cosmopolitanism Studies*, 2nd ed., edited by G. Delanty, 315–325. Abingdon: Routledge/Taylor & Francis.

Caraus, T., and E. Paris, eds. 2019. *Migration, Protest Movements and the Politics of Resistance: A Radical Political Philosophy of Cosmopolitanism*. New York: Routledge.

Caraus, T., and C-A. Parvu. 2019. "Cosmopolitanism and Migrant Protests." In *Routledge International Handbook of Cosmopolitanism Studies*, 2nd ed., edited by G. Delanty, 419–429. Abingdon: Routledge.

Cebolla, L., and F. Ghia. 2015. "Introduction." In *Cosmopolitanism: Between Ideals and Reality*, edited by L. Cebolla Sanahuja and F. Ghia, 1–10. Newcastle upon Tyne, UK: Cambridge Scholars Publishing.

Delanty, G. 2006. "The Cosmopolitan Imagination: Critical Cosmopolitanism and Social Theory." *The British Journal of Sociology* 57 (1): 25–47.

Etinson, A. 2011. "Cosmopolitanism: Cultural, Moral, and Political." In *Sovereign Justice: Global Justice in a World of Nations*, edited by D. P. Aurelio, G. De Angelis, and R. Queiroz, 25–46. Berlin and New York: Walter de Gruyter. https://doi.org/10.1515/9783110245745.1.25.

Fassin, D. 2016. "From Right to Favour: The Refugee Crisis as a Moral Question." *The Nation*, April 5. Available from: https://www.ias.edu/news/fassin-refugees-thenation. Accessed June 20, 2019.

Feischmidt, M., L. Pries, and C. Cantat, eds. 2019. *Refugee Protection and Civil Society in Europe*. Houndmills and Basingstoke: Palgrave Macmillan.

Fine, R. 2019. "The Idea of Cosmopolitan Solidarity." In *Routledge International Handbook of Cosmopolitanism Studies*, 2nd ed., edited by G. Delanty, 362–371. Abingdon: Routledge.

Fleischmann, L., and E. Steinhilper. 2017. "The Myth of Apolitical Volunteering for Refugees: German Welcome Culture and a New Dispositif of Helping." *Social Inclusion* 5 (3): 17–27. https://doi.org/10.17645/si.v5i3.945.

Funk, N. 2016. "A Spectre in Germany: Refugees, a 'Welcome Culture' and an 'Integration Politics'." *Journal of Global Ethics* 12 (3): 289–299. https://doi.org/10.1080/17449626.2016.1252785.

Ghita, C. 2016. Competitive Activism. An Investigation of the Activists and Volunteers in the 2015 Refugee Crisis. MA thesis, Lund University. Available from: https://lup.lub.lu.se/student-papers/search/publication/8894736.

Glick Schiller, N. 2015. "Diasporic Cosmopolitanism: Migrants, Sociabilities and City Making." In *Whose Cosmopolitanism?: Critical Perspectives, Relationalities and Discontents*, edited by N. Glick Schiller and A. Irving, 103–120. New York, NY: Berghahn Books.

Glick Schiller, N. 2016. "The Question of Solidarity and Society: Comment on Will Kymlicka's Article 'Solidarity in Diverse Societies'." *Comparative Migration Studies* 4 (6). https://doi.org/10.1186/s40878-016-0027-x.

Glick Schiller, N., and A. Irving. 2015. "Introduction, What's in a Word? What's in a Question?" In *Whose Cosmopolitanism?: Critical Perspectives, Relationalities and Discontents*, edited by N. Glick Schiller and A. Irving, 1–22. New York, NY: Berghahn Books.

Hansen, C. 2019. *Solidarity in Diversity: Activism as a Pathway of Migrant Emplacement in Malmö*. Doctoral dissertation in International Migration and Ethnic Relations, Malmö University. Dissertation series in Migration, Urbanisation, and Societal Change, 7. Malmö: Holmbergs. http://muep.mau.se/handle/2043/29782.

Held, D. 2013. "Cosmopolitanism in a Multipolar World". In *After Cosmopolitanism*, edited by R. Braidotti, P. Hanafin, and B. B. Blaagaard, 28–39. London: Routledge.

Hansby, A., and D. J. O'Byrne. 2019. "Global Civil Society and the Cosmopolitan Ideal." In *Routledge International Handbook of Cosmopolitanism Studies*, 2nd ed., edited by G. Delanty, 336–350. Abingdon: Routledge.

Jäckle, S., and P. D. König. 2017. "The Dark Side of the German 'Welcome Culture': Investigating the Causes Behind Attacks on Refugees in 2015." *West European Politics* 40 (2), 223–251. https://doi.org/10.1080/01402382.2016.1215614.

Karakayali, S. 2019. "The Welcomers: How Volunteers Frame Their Commitment for Refugees." In *Refugee Protection and Civil Society in Europe*, edited by M. Feischmidt, L. Pries, and C. Cantat, 221–241. Houndmills and Basingstoke: Palgrave Macmillan. https://doi.org/10.1007/978-3-319-92741-1_8.

Kleres, J. 2018. "Emotions in the Crisis: Mobilising for Refugees in Germany and Sweden." In *Solidarity Mobilizations in the "Refugee Crisis": Contentious Moves*, edited by D. della Porta, 209–241. Basingstoke: Palgrave Macmillan.

Lewin, L. 2013. "Samling kring folkhemmet [Coming Together Around *folkhem*]." In *Mellan folkhem och Europa* [Between *folkhem* and Europe], edited by L. Bennich-Björkman and P. Blomqvist, 20–39. Stockholm: Liber.

Malmö stad. 2016. "Fakta och statistik [Fact and Statistics]." Available from: http://malmo.se/Kommun--politik/Fakta-och-statistik.html. Accessed January 7, 2018.

Mäkelä, F. 2016. 'Jag var tvungen att göra någonting'. *Refugees Welcome to Malmö* och volontärernas berättelser om flyktingkrisen hösten 2015 ['I Had to do Something'. *Refugees Welcome to Malmö* and the Stories of the Volunteers Regarding the Refugee Crisis During the Fall of 2015]. BA thesis, Malmö University. Available from: http://hdl.handle.net/2043/20897.

Mårs, D. 2016. Between Compassion and Privilege: Identity, Responsibility and Power Among Volunteers Engaged in Refugee Reception. MA thesis, Lund University. Available from: https://lup.lub.lu.se/student-papers/search/publication/8887216.

Moore, H. 2013. "The Fantasies of Cosmopolitanism." In *After Cosmopolitanism*, edited by R. Braidotti, P. Hanafin, and B. Blaagaard, 97–110. Abingdon: Routledge.

Nowicka, M. forthcoming. "Hospitality, Cosmopolitanism and Conviviality: On Relations with Others in Hostile Times." In *On Cosmopolitanism in a Global Age*, edited by V. Cicchelli and S. Mesure. Leiden: Brill.

Pendenza, M. 2017. "Societal Cosmopolitanism: The Drift from Universalism Towards Particularism." *Distinktion: Journal of Social Theory* 18 (1): 3–17. https://doi.org/10.1080/1600910x.2017.1290668.

Povrzanović Frykman, M. 2016. "Cosmopolitanism in Situ: Conjoining Local and Universal Concerns in a Malmö Neighbourhood." *Identities: Global Studies in Culture and Power* 23 (1): 35–50 (special issue "Seeing Place and Power", edited by N. Glick Schiller and G. Schmidt). https://doi.org/10.1080/1070289x.2015.1016525.

Povrzanović Frykman, M., and F. Mäkelä. 2019. "'Only Volunteers'? Personal Motivations and Political Ambiguities within *Refugees Welcome to Malmö* civil Initiative." In *Refugee Protection and Civil Society in Europe*, edited by M. Feischmidt, L. Pries, and C. Cantat, 291–318. Houndmills and Basingstoke: Palgrave Macmillan. https://doi.org/10.1007/978-3-319-92741-1_11.

Pries, L. 2019. "Introduction: Civil Society and Volunteering in the So-Called Refugee Crisis of 2015—Ambiguities and Structural Tensions." In *Refugee Protection and Civil Society in Europe*, edited by M. Feischmidt, L. Pries, and C. Cantat, 1–23. Houndmills and Basingstoke: Palgrave Macmillan. https://doi.org/10.1007/978-3-319-92741-1_1.

Rancière, J. 1999. *Disagreement: Politics and Philosophy*. Minneapolis: University of Minnesota Press.

Rancière, J. 2010. *Dissensus: On Politics and Aesthetics*. London: Continuum Publishing Group.
Rescala, I. 2016. Why Do Volunteers Help: A Qualitative Study of Volunteer's Reasons to Help in the Reception of Refugees in Malmö 2015. MA thesis, Master of Applied Cultural Analysis (MACA), Lund University. Available from: https://lup.lub.lu.se/student-papers/search/publication/8906097.
Siapera, E. 2019. "Refugee Solidarity in Europe: Shifting the Discourse." *European Journal of Cultural Studies*. Online first. https://doi.org/10.1177/1367549418823068.
Skrbiš, Z., and I. Woodward, eds. 2013. *Cosmopolitanism: Uses of the Idea*. Los Angeles, London, and New Delhi: Sage.
Spurk, C. 2010. 'Understanding Civil Society'. In *Civil Society & Peacebuilding: A Critical Assessment*, edited by T. Paffenholz, 3–27. Boulder and New York: Lynne Rienner.
Svedberg, L., and L. Trägårdh, eds. 2006. *Det civila samhället som forskningsfält. Nya avhandlingar i ett nytt sekel* [Civil Society as a Research Field. New Dissertations in a New Century]. Stockholm: Riksbankens jubileumsfond & Gidlunds förlag.
Tanner, A. 2016. "Overwhelmed by Refugee Flows, Scandinavia Tempers Its Warm Welcome." *Migration Information Source*, February 10. Available from: https://www.migrationpolicy.org/article/overwhelmed-refugeeflows-scandinavia-tempers-its-warm-welcome. Accessed June 11, 2019.
Trujillo, I. 2015. "Cosmopolitanism and Human Rights." In *Cosmopolitanism: Between Ideals and Reality*, edited by L. Cebolla Sanahuja and F. Ghia, 10–34. Newcastle upon Tyne: Cambridge Scholars Publishing.
Turinsky, T., and M. Nowicka. 2019. "Volunteer, Citizen, Human: Volunteer Work Between Cosmopolitan Ideal and Institutional Routine." In *Refugee Protection and Civil Society in Europe*, edited by M. Feischmidt, L. Pries, and C. Cantat, 243–268. Houndmills and Basingstoke: Palgrave Macmillan. https://doi.org/10.1007/978-3-319-92741-1_9.
Vandevoordt, R., and G. Verschraegen. 2019. "Subversive Humanitarianism and Its Challenges: Notes on the Political Ambiguities of Civil Refugee Support." *Refugee Protection and Civil Society in Europe*, edited by M. Feischmidt, L. Pries, and C. Cantat, 101–128. Houndmills and Basingstoke: Palgrave Macmillan. https://doi.org/10.1007/978-3-319-92741-1_4.
Wilkinson, I. 2019. "Humanitarianism and Cosmopolitanism." In *Routledge International Handbook of Cosmopolitanism Studies*, 2nd ed., edited by G. Delanty, 372–382. Abingdon: Routledge.

Open Access This chapter is licensed under the terms of the Creative Commons Attribution 4.0 International License (http://creativecommons.org/licenses/by/4.0/), which permits use, sharing, adaptation, distribution and reproduction in any medium or format, as long as you give appropriate credit to the original author(s) and the source, provide a link to the Creative Commons license and indicate if changes were made.

The images or other third party material in this chapter are included in the chapter's Creative Commons license, unless indicated otherwise in a credit line to the material. If material is not included in the chapter's Creative Commons license and your intended use is not permitted by statutory regulation or exceeds the permitted use, you will need to obtain permission directly from the copyright holder.

CHAPTER 10

The Bridge: Redux—The Breakdown of Normative Conviviality

Per-Markku Ristilammi

On 12 November 2015 the Swedish government decided to impose austere measures in order to stem the influx of refugees over the Öresund Bridge.[1] Implemented from 21 November onwards, border controls were applied where the police entered trains at the first stop on the Swedish side of the border. Some weeks later, on 4 January, shipping and train companies were required to conduct ID controls prior to allowing people to pass into Sweden—later obligatory passport controls were imposed for all who crossed the border. For the citizens of Sweden and Denmark this was something that they had not experienced for generations. Even before the Schengen Agreement, the Nordic passport union had meant that Nordic citizens could travel freely between countries. Now this was no longer the case.

An unprecedented number of refugees had sought asylum in Sweden because of the civil war in Syria and the instability in Afghanistan and Iraq. Families and individuals that had survived perilous journeys across

---

P.-M. Ristilammi (✉)
Faculty of Culture and Society, Department of Urban Studies, Malmö University, Malmö, Sweden
e-mail: per-markku.ristilammi@mau.se

© The Author(s) 2020
O. Hemer et al. (eds.), *Conviviality at the Crossroads*,
https://doi.org/10.1007/978-3-030-28979-9_10

the Mediterranean and the so-called Balkan route, had turned up at the Swedish borders. In the weeks before the decision to close these borders, Swedish media had been overrun by representations of people arriving at the central railway station in the city of Malmö—the endpoint of the bridge connection. The bridge thus had become a symbol for Sweden's open borders with a large number of volunteers from different non-governmental organisations (NGOs) waiting to help and guide incoming refugees (see Chapter 9). The city archive in Malmö took the initiative to document the convivial activities pertaining to interactions between asylum seekers, the authorities and the NGOs.[2] However, with the introduction of border controls, this aura of openness was suddenly breached. From representing connectivity, the Öresund Bridge suddenly transformed to representing a point of defence against those in need of asylum.

In this chapter the concept of conviviality will be used as an analytic concept around which recent developments concerning the changing role of state borders in Europe will be discussed. Recent discussions around conviviality have highlighted tensions in the various ways the concept has been used. Originally used by Paul Gilroy (2004) as a concept that concentrates on modes of togetherness against the backdrop of social, racial and religious conflicts and tensions, conviviality now has more recently proliferated several different, somewhat contradictory, discussions (Valluvan 2016). Normative and prescriptive uses of the concept have been critiqued as hiding underlying social and racial inequalities and thus avoiding the political dimension (Nowicka and Heil 2015).

One important line of discussion has largely been conducted on the basis of empirical research that has concentrated around the social problems within "multi-cultural" parts of European cities. The notion of conviviality has therefore not been utilised in a more general sense. This chapter aims to highlight a specific kind of normative state-driven conviviality through the example of the Öresund Bridge, in order to show how the concept of conviviality can be used in an analysis of changing roles, or what I propose to call *states of the state*. The bridge and the surrounding region was part of a bi-national project of conviviality at its inauguration in 2000 (Ristilammi 2000), but 15 years later border controls signalled a breakdown of this specific form of conviviality. This chapter seeks to show, with ethnographic examples from border-crossing experiences at the bridge in 2000, 2015 and the present-day, how this breakdown of conviviality opens up for a new form of biopolitical regime at the border, turning the bridge into a *zone of the abject* (Foster 2015).

Before: The Convivial Border Region[3]

When inaugurated on 1 June 2000, the bridge was hailed as a commemoration of a new Europe, a Europe of regions, with a diminished role to be played by nation-states. Processes of economic and cultural globalisation meant that the old Europe and its borders belonged to the past, surpassed by inevitable historical forces. The Schengen Agreement, with its focus on the free movement of labour and capital, was a political symbol of this new order. Old differences and strifes were to be forgotten with the heads of states of Sweden and Denmark evoking a shared history of conviviality between them at the bridge's inauguration—conveniently omitting the fact that the greatest number of wars between any two European countries had actually been fought between Denmark and Sweden. However, in the year 2000, all such conflicts were forgotten and the two countries joined in what was newly coined as the Øresund/Öresund Region.

A string of public events was launched in order to celebrate this newly pronounced regional conviviality.[4] Citizens on both sides of the border were invited to partake in events at the bridge, providing spaces where collective feelings could become linked to the new region. One such events opened the bridge up to pedestrians letting them meet and mingle under the impressive 204-meter-high pylons at the centre of the bridge. Another event was a half-marathon where runners traversed the bridge and became part of a kinaesthetic experience—an event where runners blended impending exhaustion with the visual impact of being 60 meters above the water below (Ristilammi 2002b).

The biggest event—the inauguration of the bridge—was televised live. Audiences waved Danish and Swedish flags, symbolically underscoring the orchestration of border conviviality. Two trains coming from opposite directions met at the middle of the bridge, royalty descended from both trains and greeted one another at the border. Event organisers wanted to provide a 5-minute broadcast for CNN—they actually were given 15 minutes of air time. At the same time, the bridge became entangled in a collective kinesthetic, emotional and medialised experience of state-induced conviviality leading to collective memories being formed for those who had taken part in events (Ristilammi 2002a).

These memory processes connected to collective events start with an overflow of meaning that transcends lexical discourse. The statement, "You should have been there", marks the importance of the event. Some events become so important that words are "not enough" to describe them.

They enter into an affective realm which is still simultaneously connected to a discourse of conviviality (Wetherell 2015). This excess of meaning solidifies into objects and places channelling collective forms of meaning and creating a sense of shared history (cf. Ristilammi 2000).

One way in which history was evoked in the event management process was through a notion of *modernity revisited*. It was not a return to an economy built on an industrial mode of production. Malmö had been a city with a strong industrial heritage, with ship-building industries located on its waterfront. The symbolic dismantling of this heritage took place in 2002 when a large gantry crane, the Kockums Crane, was dismantled and shipped to South Korea.[5] At this time, the new and symbolic landmark of the bridge had been in place for 2 years. The Öresund project had an officially branded book with the following text on its cover:

> In July 2000 the opening of a fixed link between Copenhagen, Denmark and Malmö, Sweden will herald the beginning of a new era for northern Europe. It will be the opening of a new region. The opening of countless possibilities and opportunities for inhabitants, travellers and businesses. The start of a new future.

By evoking a new future, the spectral apparition of an old future was conjured in the form of the failure of the old industrial modernity to meet the economic realities of the present. The city of Malmö was to rise as a phoenix from its industrial past, aided by this new region.

As an impressive piece of infrastructure, the bridge itself was a triumph of up-to-date industrial techniques, but the future management of the bridge was caught in the trappings of a new neoliberal, seemingly post-industrial, economy. Exhaustive media attention on the number of vehicles crossing the bridge was akin to the kind of monitoring usually reserved for companies on the stock market. So, on the one hand the building of the bridge was a return to large-scale investments in infrastructure, something that was characteristic of industrial modernity. On the other hand, this very return created a framing for the different branding techniques so prevalent in a neoliberal economy. The industrial monumentality of the bridge thus formed a very ambiguous backdrop to the different inaugural events associated with its opening.

The insistence of the new neoliberal economy for constant change, connected to the need for brand stability, was perfectly merged within the images of the stable bridge and the constant stream of people moving across it. The infinity symbol (∞) was superimposed on maps of the Öresund Region in order to conjure up the notion of the region as a *growth machine* with perpetual mobility.[6] The notion of conviviality between nations built on historical ties, evoked in the opening ceremonies of the bridge, slowly gave way to a togetherness built on commerce and trade.

Liquid Modernity and the Formless State

In this frame of mind, national identity belonged to an older era where the state embodied stability and security, both inwards and outwards, but now a specific formlessness of the state resulted from what could, in Bauman's terms, be called a *liquid modernity* (Bauman 2000). Mobility across the bridge was to forge new hybrid identities, with the states assumed to be pliable enough to accommodate such a change. With an international airport at one of the ends of the bridge, the thought was to attract international capital and investment, while attending to the needs of those that Nigel Thrift called the *fast subjects*, the embodiments of international investment capital (Thrift 1996). The emphasis on speed, mobility and *liquidity*, seemed to demand states with loose contours, that could adapt to flows of capital. From the viewpoint of conviviality, the togetherness in the region could not be *too* strong so as to hinder the adaptability of the work force. A specific balance had to be struck when organising projects, linked to the opening of the bridge, that were associated with identity. Care would have to be taken not to bolster overly nationalistic sentiments when the symbolic forces of the nation states, such as royal houses, were evoked.

From a political perspective, the event-making process, the process of co-organising events on the bridge, was clearly a case of *normative conviviality* promoted on the state–state level with projections into the future about a specific Öresund identity, not only in terms of branding, but also as a real possibility for resident identity in Sweden and Denmark, aimed at a reformulation of the modernity project into a new liquid form. One event, a collaboration between art institutions on both sides of the border, called "The Culture Bridge", was meant to celebrate the role of art and history in the region. The "Culture Bridge" was supposed to be a coming together in the name of Nordic modernities—while being steeped in history the event was a very future-oriented enterprise. One of this event's highlights was a celebration, in the form of a theatre performance, of the 100-year anniversary of Arne Jacobsen, a futurist Danish architect and the designer of iconic design classics, such as the The Swan and The Ant chairs. Öresund's identity was clearly to be a modernist one with weak ties to nationalities. The aim of the normative conviviality of state-driven events was to balance the opposing forces of nationalism and seamless liquid modernity, but risked entering into another state of state, one that I would call a *plasmatic* one. The plasmatic state could be seen as a short lived, volatile state of state, one which eventually must return to solidity or liquidity, or otherwise threaten the state itself.[7]

A few years after the opening of the bridge, the situation was bleaker for the consortium that had built it. The number of cars crossing the bridge, which was used to measure its economic success, failed to reach the expected 11,000 per day, with the number of people travelling to work from one side of the bridge to the other also falling well below expectation. The growth machine seemed to be coming to a halt. In many ways, the notion of a new future had given way to a feeling of returning to the struggling present-day—the only difference was that now there was an expensive bridge to manage. Events were no longer used in order to manage popular support for the bridge. Closing the Öresund connection during high winds and vehicle breakdowns in the alternative tunnel proved that the bridge's construction was vulnerable, both practically and symbolically.

Also visible, this time on the political plane, was an increasing emphasis placed on the differences between states. The ever-increasing restrictions associated with Danish migration policy created concerns at the Swedish national political level, something that led politicians to use Denmark as a negative example. Likewise, Danish politicians and intellectuals used Sweden as an example of a country where political correctness prevailed at the expense of freedom of speech. Differences, not conviviality, seemed to be symbolised by both the bridge and region. Commuters and other travellers still continued to use the bridge, as did the "fast subjects" that populated executive lounges at Copenhagen Airport, but the rhetorical power of the bridge and its associated region started to disappear from 2010 onwards.

At this stage the bleak afterglow from the bridge's opening was considered a metaphor for the internationally successful TV crime series "The Bridge", where differences between neighbouring nations were used for dramatic effect (Askanius 2017). The characters in the series conveyed an underlying feeling of cultural differences between neighbours, highlighting national character traits not so easily overcome. The series pictured a challenged conviviality, whether state-driven or not. The different police bureaucracies of the two states was an illustration of the prevailing importance of national difference with the bridge depicted as a dangerous opening, a liability in the armour of the state, hovering between the liquid and the plasmatic—a threat.

Now

For refugees in the winter of 2015, crossing the bridge was another kind of event, entering an affective realm where the excess of meaning was not something designed to foster regional feelings, but instead where excruciating experiences of traumatic passages were invoked. Voices heard over tannoys in train carriages pulling in to Hyllie station on the Swedish side of the border made it clear to everyone, commuters, tourists and refugees alike, that the power of the state was to be imposed on them in the form of very specific border crossing rituals[8]—guards standing at wire fences ready to check identity papers; police, some with dogs, entering the train, scanning faces, comparing them with pictures and focussing the gaze of the state on some faces more than others (Peterson 2017). Commuters became tired of presenting their documents and tourists were perplexed—tension began to rise. The *biopolitical state machinery* performed its task, to regulate the nature of the bodies entering the jurisdiction of the state, by pushing those that were unwanted into the *zone of the abject* (Foucault 1978; Foster 2015) and by neutralizing any notion of normative conviviality. Embodied in the form of border guards and police, the mythical body of the state, materialized in its spectral form (Gil 1998: 143f.). For some of those that passed the border the scrutinizing eye of the state morphed into the realm of electromagnetic imagery surpassing the boundaries of one´s body (x-rays of knee joints), creating truth effects about biological age.[9]

States of the State in the Öresund Region

One problem, evident in the construction of the region even before events of 2015, was the difference between the notion of the diminishing importance of the nation-state, inspired by globalisation theories, and the everyday experiences of actors trying to facilitate cross-border initiatives, such as cooperation between universities or local tax authorities. It became obvious to these actors that the rules and regulations of the nation-state were still present in the minuscule workings of different bureaucracies.

"Ways of doing things" had a profound impact on those who wished to have an everyday life that entailed crossing the border.

However, events in 2015 pushed the "stateliness" of the border to a new level. States entered into a plasmatic state that could not be sustained, a perceived "death zone" for the political structure of the state. Despite signals of hospitality radiating from the Swedish state, the sheer number of asylum seekers released something that could be called the "deep state".[10]

Using Agamben's ideas one could argue that commuters found themselves in a double camp where the jurisdiction of both states created a grey area that was virtually impossible to navigate with any logic (Agamben 1998). What was left were the interests of "bare" states in "deep" mode.

One might see the enforcement of austere migration policies in the autumn of 2015 as a core activation of the Weberian iron cage (or more correctly the iron shell) *"stahlhartes Gehäuse"*, a bureaucracy that, in its last instance, is able to contain and shape the form of the state. The formless, or plasmatic (or even phantasmagoric), iteration of the neoliberal, neomodern state, shape shifted under pressure. Formlessness turned into the penal state (Barker 2017, 2018), a state not in flow, not liquid, but in regulatory mode, making distinctions, diagnosing, politicizing biology—acting out the machinations of the old modernity.[11] This became even more evident with the treatment of refugees and their legal status. The region was an attempt to evoke the future, as a form of modernity revisited, where past ghosts of a monocultural society were re-evoked (cf. Hellström and Petersson 2002: 13). Derrida sees the return of past ghosts as a form of phenomenological conjuring trick (Derrida 1994: 125ff.), with the ghosts being conjured by personification and a suspension of time. And herein lie the possibilities associated with creating timeless spaces, perhaps not initially anticipated when creating a region.

The refugees, stripped of their legal rights, became trapped in a position both inside and outside the law, where their "spectral past"[12] survived and haunted both their dreams and the fears of the host-country (Diken and Bagge-Laustsen 2003). The authorities way of dealing with this "spectrality" was, and still is, spatial and temporal incarceration shielding the state from those both outside and inside of the national jurisdiction. In one sense we could view these spectralities as a form of phantom pain, of attachments lost and convivialities shattered.

The train pulling into the station takes the form of a phantom vehicle, never reaching its final destination, forever transporting refugees destined to remain in limbo. At least this was how the refugees were perceived in the autumn of 2015, that is, forever on the run, never reaching their goal, always heading further north, abjected by the state. Thus, it is the state that decides the limits of the reach of conviviality. Embodiments of the state scan faces on the train looking for signs of ethnic alterity mixed in with the anxiety of the unwanted. The coach becomes a distributive vehicle for the "deep" state's core reflexes, the nervous system that works beyond politics (Taussig 1993).

In the weeks before these austere migration laws were enforced by the state, an exceptional mobilisation of civic hospitality took place on both sides of the border. Instead of the gaze of the "bare state", the notion of unconditional face-to-face meetings, in Levinas' sense, had been the guiding rule for the many volunteers who met migrants when they stepped off the trains (Levinas 1990). The central train station, a non-place, in Marc Augée's sense,[13] had become a space of sanctuary where conviviality prevailed (Augée 1995). However, this was not the case for long. When the bridge was effectively closed to asylum seekers not carrying the proper documentation (the majority of them), this specific form of civil conviviality waned.[14]

It was obvious at this stage that the newcomers were not the "fast subjects" of liquid modernity but were something else. The "slow subjects" seemingly dragging their "spectral pasts" into secure/securitising camps within the neo-modern body of the state—not even forming part of the old modernity that was once created by the Nordic welfare states. When the face-to-face hospitality of common people was challenged by the closing of the border, asylum seekers became meaningless subjects to the state. When the refugee asks: What is the jurisdiction? The state answers: It depends on who you are! When the refugee asks: Who am I? The state answers: You tell me!

The "eye" of the state turned from a convivial disinterest, to a watchful scanning for unwanted bodies. The time/space-specific vantage point of Gilroy's iteration of conviviality was born in the convulsions of Western states entering into the formless, unsustainable death zone of the plasmatic state. The question is "How are the people without common pasts going to live together?" Now the pasts: cultural, ethnical, biological enter into the biopolitical sphere again.

The Bridge as an Abjective Infrastructure

What was meant to be an infrastructure designed to foster economic growth, a virtual growth machine, turned into another form of regulatory machinery. The bridge became part of a biopolitical mechanism driven by state regulation and group interests.

Now the bridge embodies the return of sovereign territoriality, not in the form of the power of a sovereign, but in form of a state configured as a regulatory mechanism of power beyond politics. On an everyday scale the shapeshifting of the state has manifested itself in the regulatory bodies moving through trains, scanning faces and scrutinising documentation, with fleeting or permanent affect. Artefacts such as fences, yellow vests, digital cameras, passports and infrared cameras in the tunnel became part of a new form of power that reflected, not only the diminishing role of the region, but also a new form of state.

The bridge became part of an infrastructure where the "subordinate parts of an undertaking", namely the state, morphed into an iteration slowly shapeshifting all over Europe, rendering meaningless the "slow subjects" of the world. The normative conviviality from the age of transnational region building disintegrating into "bare mode" states with traces of conviviality being confined to the "normality" of the everyday life of commuters bearing the correct documents.

Notes

1. From Swedish government official website: http://www.regeringen. se/artiklar/2015/11/regeringen-beslutar-att-tillfalligt-aterinfora-granskontroll-vid-inre-grans/ and http://www.regeringen.se/4ae76f/ contentassets/23c37b142cd54d658d660dc5ca27afe5/sarskilda-atgarder-vid-allvarlig-fara-for-den-allmanna-ordningen-eller-den-inre-sakerheten-i-landet-prop.-20151667.
2. From the City of Malmö official website: https://malmo.se/Kultur--fritid/Kultur-och-fritid-nyheter/2018-03-16-ANKOMST-MALMO.-Roster-om-flyktingmottagandet-hosten-2015.html.
3. The account and analysis of the events surrounding the bridge's opening in 2000 stems from my participation in the project "Frambesvärjandet av en transnationell region. En flervetenskaplig studie av Öresundsområdet", led by Orvar Löfgren and Per-Olof Berg (see Berg 2000; Ristilammi 2002b, 2005a, b, 2006, 2007, 2010).

4. At the time of the bridge's opening, at the beginning of the 2000s, the notion of events and *event-making* was en vogue among economical analyses connected to the so-called *New Economy*. Such events were new kinds of marketing and governance strategies connected to the volatility of the neoliberal economy precisely because they catered to emotions instead of calculative intellect (Ristilammi 2002b).
5. From Wikipedia: https://en.wikipedia.org/wiki/Kockums_Crane.
6. The concept of *growth machine* was initially coined by Harvey Molotch in the 1970s as way of critically describing the specific economic and social processes regarding land use leading to the growth of cities (Molotch 1976).
7. One apparition of the plasmatic state could be the "spectrality" that haunts the state in specific historical moments (Gil 1998: 143f.).
8. As Nancy Wonders has shown, all kinds of border crossings contain a performative dimension where bodies are being staged in very specific rituals (Wonders 2006).
9. MRI scanning of knee joints: http://www.bbc.com/news/world-europe-42234585.
10. The notion of the "deep state" was initially coined as a concept that described the power of the Turkish military.
11. This tendency of shapeshifting belongs to the realm of stasiology, where *stasis* contains the necessary tension between movement (*kinesis*) and firmness within the field of the political (Feldman 2015: 9ff.).
12. The baggage of experiences, memories, mourning and longing of refugees.
13. Although influential when published, describing places like airports as beacons of super-modernity, it also became criticized for omitting the fact that non-places also produce non-people.
14. This started before the demand for documentation. Pure exhaustion had taken its toll among the volunteers (see elsewhere in this volume).

References

Agamben, G. 1998. *Homo Sacer: Sovereign Power and Bare Life*. Stanford: Stanford University Press.

Askanius, T. 2017. "Engaging with *The Bridge*: Cultural Citizenship, Cross-Border Identities and Audiences as 'Regionauts'." *European Journal of Cultural Studies* 22 (3): 1–20. https://doi.org/10.1177/1367549417722093.

Augee, M. 1995. *Non-Places: Introduction to an Anthropology of Supermodernity*. London and New York: Verso.

Barker, V. 2017. "Penal Power at the Border: Realigning State and Nation." *Theoretical Criminology* 21 (4): 441–457. https://doi.org/10.1177/1362480617724827.

Barker, V. 2018. *Nordic Nationalism and Penal Order: Walling the Welfare State.* London and New York: Routledge.
Bauman, Z. 2000. *Liquid Modernity.* London: Polity Press.
Berg, P.-O., ed. 2000. *Invoking a Transnational Metropolis: The Making of the Øresund Region.* Lund: Studentlitteratur.
Derrida, J. 1994. *Spectres of Marx, The State of the Debt, the Work of Mourning & the New International.* London: Routledge.
Diken, B., and C. Bagge Laustsen. 2003. "Zones of Indistinction—Security, Terror and Bare Life." In *Territories—Islands, Camps and Other States of Utopia*, edited by A. Franke. Köln: Verlag der Buchhandlung Walther König.
Feldman, A. 2015. *Archives of the Insensible: Of War, Photopolitics and Dead Memory.* Chicago and London: The University of Chicago Press.
Foster, H. 2015. *Bad New Days: Art, Criticism, Emergency.* London and New York: Verso.
Foucault, M. 1978. *The History of Sexuality. Volume 1, An Introduction/Michel Foucault; Translated from the French by Robert Hurley.* New York: Pantheon Books.
Gil, J. 1998. *Metamorphoses of the Body.* Minneapolis and London: University of Minnesota Press.
Gilroy, P. 2004. *After Empire: Melancholia or Convivial Culture?* Abingdon: Routledge.
Hellström, A., and B. Petersson. 2002. *Temporality in the Construction of EU Identity.* Lund: CFE Working Papers.
Levinas, E. 1990: *Time and the Other.* Pittsburg, PA: Duquesne University Press.
Molotch, H. 1976. "The City as a Growth Machine: Toward a Political Economy of Place." *The American Journal of Sociology* 82 (2): 309–322.
Nowicka, M., and T. Heil. 2015. *On the Analytical and Normative Dimensions of Conviviality and Cosmopolitanism.* Tübingen: Eberhard Karls Universität.
Peterson, A. 2017. "Humanitarian Border Workers in Confrontation with the Swedish State's Border Making Practices: 'The Death of the Most Generous Country on Earth'." *Journal of Borderlands Studies.* https://doi.org/10.1080/08865655.2017.1402199. Published online November 17, 2017.
Ristilammi, P.-M. 2000. "Cultural Bridges, Events and the New Region." In *Invoking a Transnational Metropolis: The Making of the Øresund Region*, edited by P.-O. Berg, 95–108. Lund: Studentlitteratur.
Ristilammi, P.-M. 2002a. "Vitt ljus – Vitt brus: Om regionala födelsesmärtor." *Come In—Go Out. Det 10. billede.* Copenhagen: Kunstakademiets Arkitektskole, Fonden Kulturbro, Informations Forlag.
Ristilammi, P.-M. 2002b. "Ballonger och fantomkänslor." In *Öresundsbron på uppmärksamhetens marknad. Regionbyggare i evenemangsbranschen*, edited by P.-O. Berg and A. Linde-Laursen. Lund: Studentlitteratur.

Ristilammi, P.-M. 2005a. "Afterthoughts on Modernist Necropoles." *Ethnologia Europaea*, 35 (1): 107–112.
Ristilammi, P.-M. 2005b. "Spectral Events: Attempts at Pattern Recognition." In *Magic, Culture and The New Economy*, edited by O. Löfgren and R. Willim, 87–95. Oxford and New York: Berg.
Ristilammi, P.-M. 2006. "Stealth." *Ethnologia Europaea*, 35 (2): 88–90.
Ristilammi, P.-M. 2007. "Urban globalisering i Öresundsregionen. Mångkulturalitetens varierande grader av synlighet." In *Öresundsgränser: Rörelser, möten och visioner i tid och rum*, edited by F. Nilsson, H. Sanders, and Y. Stubbergaard, 352–368. Göteborg and Stockholm: Makadam Förlag.
Ristilammi, P.-M. 2010. "I brons skugga." In *Regionauterna – Öresundsregionen från vision till vardag*, edited by O. Löfgren and F. Nilsson, 157–164. Göteborg and Stockholm: Makadam Förlag.
Taussig, M. 1993. *The Nervous System*. London and New York: Routledge.
Thrift, N. 1996. *Spatial Formations*. London: Sage.
Valluvan, S. 2016. "Conviviality and Multiculture: A Post-integration Sociology of Multi-ethnic Interaction." *Young* 24 (3): 204–221. https://doi.org/10.1177/1103308815624061.
Wetherell, M. 2015. "Trends in the Turn to Affect: A Social Psychological Critique." *Body & Society* 21 (2). https://doi.org/10.1177/1357034X14539020.
Wonders, N. 2006. "Global Flows, Semi-Permeable Borders, and New Channels of Inequality: Border Crossers and Border Performativity." In *Border, Mobility and Technologies of Control*, edited by S. Pickering and L. Weber. Dordrecht: Springer.

Open Access This chapter is licensed under the terms of the Creative Commons Attribution 4.0 International License (http://creativecommons.org/licenses/by/4.0/), which permits use, sharing, adaptation, distribution and reproduction in any medium or format, as long as you give appropriate credit to the original author(s) and the source, provide a link to the Creative Commons license and indicate if changes were made.

The images or other third party material in this chapter are included in the chapter's Creative Commons license, unless indicated otherwise in a credit line to the material. If material is not included in the chapter's Creative Commons license and your intended use is not permitted by statutory regulation or exceeds the permitted use, you will need to obtain permission directly from the copyright holder.

CHAPTER 11

Charting a Convivial Continuum in British Post-war Popular Music 1948–2018

Hugo Boothby

On June 22, 1948, the Empire Windrush arrived at Tilbury Docks on the River Thames carrying one of the first large groups of post-war Caribbean migrants. Under the 1948 Nationality Act, commonwealth citizens were recognised as British citizens, an agreement revoked in subsequent iterations of this Act. Many of the commonwealth citizens that migrated from the West Indies to Great Britain during this early post-war period never claimed the British passports that were rightfully theirs and remain undocumented. Under the UK government's 2010 policy of a 'hostile environment'[1] for illegal immigrants, this group of now elderly undocumented migrants of the 'Windrush generation' has been denied public services and threatened with deportation. In 2018, the unfair treatment of these British citizens created a scandal that engulfed the government, forcing the then Home Secretary Amber Rudd to resign. This manifestation of institutional racism in the year of the seventieth anniversary of the arrival of the Windrush appears to be in direct opposition to the convivial formations Paul

H. Boothby (✉)
Malmö University, Malmö, Sweden
e-mail: hugo.boothby@mau.se

© The Author(s) 2020
O. Hemer et al. (eds.), *Conviviality at the Crossroads*,
https://doi.org/10.1007/978-3-030-28979-9_11

Gilroy detected in the early 2000s, what he described as the emergence of 'Britain's spontaneous, convivial culture' (Gilroy 2004: xi).

CONVIVIALITY

In this chapter, conviviality is understood as the social formations and cultural practices that emerge through an experience of living with difference, what Magdalena Nowicka and Steven Vertovec describe as 'the ways, and under what conditions, people constructively create modes of togetherness' (2014: 342). For Gilroy, conviviality as a concept is specifically useful when exploring British racial identity politics because it addresses formations where

> racial, linguistic and religious particularities do not – as the logic of ethnic absolutism suggests they must – add up to discontinuities of experience or insuperable problems of communication. (2006: 27)

For Magdalena Nowicka and Tilmann Heil, the possibility of convivial formations departs from the question 'How is minimal sociality possible?' (2015: 12); this understanding of a minimal sociality is useful here because it indicates formations that suggest 'consensus, consideration and respect' but can equally accommodate 'tension, conflict and frustration' (Nowicka and Heil 2015: 13). The duality of conviviality and hostility evident in experiences of post-war Caribbean migration and how they find expression within popular music is a recurring theme in this chapter.

Popular music is an important site at which to trace convivial formation and its relationship with migration within the UK because it offers a productive site at which vibrant intermixture, combination and cross-fertilisation have taken place. Within Caribbean influenced post-war British popular music, it is possible to trace a clear convivial continuum[2] in which the combination and radical intermixture of musical forms from Africa, the Caribbean, Britain and the United States is a defining characteristic and thread of continuity. As such, the music of the convivial continuum exists firmly within what Paul Gilroy terms the Black Atlantic (1993). Although the music of the convivial continuum is defined by the heterogeneous elements from which it borrows, it is at the same time the product of the traditions and histories of the localities in which it is produced and experienced making it possible to identify a tradition of British popular music that is creole but that remains distinctively British in character (Gilroy 2003; Gilbert 2014; Reynolds 2013; Hancox 2018).

Convivial Continuum Playlist

A convivial continuum of British creole popular music can be traced through calypso, reggae, post-punk, jungle, two-step garage, dubstep and grime. In an attempt to capture key points along this convivial continuum, I structure this chapter around a playlist of selected tracks. The earliest recording included here is Lord Kitcheners' calypso *London Is the Place for Me* (1948), the most contemporary is Novelist's grime track *Stop Killing the Mandem* (2018), and these tracks bookend a selection of music spanning 70 years, beginning with the arrival of the Windrush and ending in 2018 with the Windrush scandal and the consequences of the British government's hostile environment for illegal immigrants. I hope that readers of this chapter will also be listeners and use the selection of music referenced throughout the text as a soundtrack complimentary to their reading.

Playlist Track 1: 'Has It Come to This' The Streets (2002)

Popular music is one important site where Paul Gilroy observes emerging convivial formation in the UK during the 2000s, and it is in *Has It Come to This* (2002) that Gilroy hears articulation of a convivial British identity in which 'racial difference is not feared. Exposure to it is not ethnic jeopardy, but rather an unremarkable principle of metropolitan life' (2004: 105).

The influence of Jamaican reggae, British two-tone ska, European electronic dance music, British jungle and American hip hop are all evident in the music of The Streets, making them an excellent example of British artists that borrow from and exist along the convivial continuum that I map in this chapter.[3] In combining distinct and disparate elements into harmonic coordination, the music of The Streets and other music along the convivial continuum is able to provide a 'grass roots' or 'bottom-up' articulation of social formations that disrupt essentialised racial categories. I argue here that these processes of combination and intermixture are best understood in terms of creolisation and that it is in the composition and performance of creolised music, and in the listening practices that surround it, that potential is afforded for the enacting of convivial formation. Creolised music is considered here as both signifying-practice (Hebdige 1999 [1979]) and for its potential to enact corporeal affect (Gilbert 2009).

CREOLISATION

Caribbean influenced British popular music that demonstrates radical intermixture and combination is often described as hybrid (Gilroy 2004; Gilbert 2009; Hancox 2018), but in this chapter, I choose instead to define these processes in terms of creolisation. I use creolisation as a compliment to conviviality, in-part because theories of creolisation are better suited to capturing the hostility that remains intertwined with conviviality. Here, I take Stuart Hall's definition of creolisation as a point of departure:

> Creolization in this context refers to the processes of 'cultural and linguistic mixing' which arise from the entanglement of different cultures in the same indigenous space or location, primarily in the context of slavery, colonization and the plantation societies characteristic of the Caribbean and parts of Spanish America and Southeast Asia. (Hall 2015: 15)

Hall suggests that as a concept, creolisation can be expanded from its 'meanings and conditions of existence in the French Antilles to other parts of the Anglophone Caribbean' and that it can also be relevant in application to black British cultural forms (ibid.: 25). In this broader definition, creolisation within cultural production thus becomes

> a potential new basis from which popular creativity which is distinctive, original to the area itself, and better adapted to capture the realities of life in the postcolony, can be and is being, produced. (Hall 2015: 19)

Creolisation as a concept is also useful here because it avoids the biological connotations that the term hybridity carries and the implication of evolutionary processes in which there is linear progress advancing towards a desired, stable and normative social formation. Creolisation also aligns closely with conviviality with Encarnación Gutiérrez Rodríguez detecting in creolisation an analogue to the fluidity, and breakdown of dichotomies and hierarchies captured within conviviality. For Gutiérrez Rodríguez (2015: 97), 'creolization stands at the heart of a political and ethical project of conviviality'.

Playlist Track 2: 'London Is the Place for Me'
Lord Kitchener (2002 [1948])

The arrival of the Empire Windrush in 1948 has become a defining moment in the narrative of post-war British Caribbean migration as well as an important event for British popular music (Boakye 2017: 343; Hall 2003: 419; Hancox 2018: 33; Stratton and Zuberi 2014). One of the passengers on the Empire Windrush was Trinidadian calypsonian Aldwyn Roberts, who used the stage name Lord Kitchener. Legend has it that Lord Kitchener composed the first two verses of his song *London Is the Place for Me* during the voyage itself, and there is Pathe News Reel footage of him singing the song as he disembarks at Tilbury Docks. *London Is the Place for Me* gained a new contemporary audience when re-released in 2002 on a critically acclaimed compilation of British calypso.

London Is the Place for Me has the distinctive rolling two-beat of a Trinidadian calypso, but on this recording, the percussive elements are low in the mix with the voice and lyrics prominent, the melody is carried by the voice but also brass and woodwind instruments. This track is significant as a document of the beginning of a convivial continuum within post-war British popular music because it marks the emergence of the first distinctively creole musical form popular with a mass audience in the UK (Hall 2003: 423). Calypso carries with it a history of creolisation not only in the speech patterns in which it is sung but also in the influence it carries from Trinidadian carnival. It is here that Christian celebrations and pagan ritual were appropriated, combined and translated within plantation society, becoming what Stuart Hall describes as a 'ritualized popular resistance' (Hall 2003: 423). This ritualised popular resistance finds expression in lyrics that document both positive and negative experiences of migration. In the second verse of *London Is the Place for Me*, Lord Kitchener poignantly asserts his rights to belonging, singing that he is 'glad to know my mother country'. Although the lyrics on *London Is the Place for Me* are upbeat and positive, the lyrics on other Lord Kitchener tracks of this era like *Sweet Jamaica* (1952a) and *If You're Not White You're Black* (1952b) are more cynical capturing experiences of racism and the trials of migrant life. The vivid storytelling tradition within British calypso leads Hall to claim that it is the form of expression that offered the 'most telling insights into the early days of [Caribbean] migrant experience' (2003: 424).

The contradictions of a local British creole vernacular are also audible in the incongruous musical juxtapositions evident on the track *London Is the*

Place for Me. Particularly, striking is a simple solo piano motif that opens and closes the track. On first listen, it seems out-of-place, disconnected from the rest of the music. On re-listening, it is clear that the sparse piano chords pick out the melody of Big Ben's chimes, an aural symbol of Britishness. The chimes of Big Ben are of course evocative of London, a central character in the song, but the sedate lullaby cadences of this opening and closing motif are at odds with the upbeat dance rhythms of the rest of the song, this contrast making the piano sound slightly sinister, perhaps even melancholy in comparison with the positivity of the rest of the track. This drawing together of disparate elements, the re-imagining of Big Ben a symbol of British Parliamentary democracy and authority as a lullaby, is consistent with processes of mimicry and recombination evident in Trinidadian carnival culture from which calypso emerged. This incongruity is consistent with a creole aesthetic in that it captures processes of what Hall terms translation. For Hall, concepts of translation or transformation are useful in capturing the contradictory nature of creole culture. While Creole culture may be creative and vibrant, it also remains troubled and unfinished. For Hall,

> Translation always bears the traces of the original, but in such a way that the original is impossible to restore. Indeed, 'translation' is suspicious of the language of the return to origins and originary roots as a narrative of culture (Hall 2015: 16).

It is this refusal of return that 'troubles' (ibid.) creole culture, opening it up as a site that can accommodate both expressions of conviviality and hostility.

Reggae

Although calypso was the first post-Windrush Caribbean music to find mass popularity among British audiences (Hall 2003: 423), the musical genre that remains pivotal, and continually referenced and re-versioned, along the convivial continuum is reggae. In their writing about reggae, both Stuart Hall and Denis-Constant Martin recognise it as a creolised form. Stuart Hall describes how reggae appears as if it were

> grounded in an authentic African source and the return to origins, [but it] turns out, when examined more closely, to be another variant in the long and complex creolization repertoire. (Hall 2015: 24)

Similarly, Denis-Constant Martin places reggae as a creolised form, supporting his claim through musicology:

> Reggae took shape when drums and rhythms preserved in maroon communities – therefore construed as coming from Africa – were used to fertilise borrowed North American rhythm and blues, and soul music. (Martin 2013: 26).

Jamaican reggae's mixing of African rhythms with American blues, soul and R&B was then mixed again with British influences as reggae records were shipped from Jamaica to Caribbean communities in London, Birmingham and Bristol to be played out by local sound systems[4] where these records could be 're-versioned'[5] in the process of performance for local audiences. Diverse expressions of local British reggae emerged from these processes of re-versioning producing popular styles that permeated deep into mainstream British pop culture.

Playlist Track 3: 'Silly Games' Janet Kay (1979)

One of the most distinctively British variations of reggae that emerged during the 1970s was lovers rock. A defining record within this genre was *Silly Games* (1979), sung by Janet Kay, but written and produced by Dennis Bovell.[6] Bovell describes how lovers rock and *Silly Games* were designed to show Britain was an innovator and agenda-setter within international reggae. *Silly Games* was recorded with both Caribbean and British born musicians and Bovell maintains that this style of music could never have been produced anywhere else but Britain (Bradley 2000: 370).

The track's principle innovation within reggae was its distinctive drum beat, played mainly on the hi-hat near the bell of the cymbal with an occasional off-beat played on the snare drum. Bovell describes this new British 'riddim'[7] as 'sort of remotely African and a bit calypso' (Bradley 2000: 370), placing *Silly Games* firmly as part of a British creole repertoire. *Silly Games* was hugely popular reaching number 2 in the UK singles chart. Bovell describes how during the summer of '79 it dominated the airwaves and public space:

For about a month it's like all you can hear on the radio or in shops or at discos [and] because this was the height of summer so everybody's got their windows open. (Bovell in Bradley 2000: 372)

The mainstream success of reggae tracks like *Silly Games* demonstrates how creolised musical forms seep into the soundscapes of everyday British life creating a shared musical space, affording convivial formation in both the mundane practices of radio listening and shopping and the communal experiences of dancing in clubs.

Playlist Track 4: 'Newtown' The Slits (1979)

Reggae is also an important ingredient in other variants of British creolised music. Intermixture and combination between punk and reggae are for example well documented in Dick Hebdige's seminal analysis of punk subculture and its articulation of resistance through music and fashion (1991 [1979]). Hebdige recounts how reggae was one element taken up in the processes of bricolage that were integral to the distinctiveness of punk (1991 [1979]: 27). Gilroy also emphasises the significance of Caribbean culture to this subculture arguing that the history of punk cannot be properly understood without recognising the influence of reggae on its 'white ethnicity' (Gilroy 2003: 387). Processes of intermixture between punk and reggae in the UK can be seen for example in the converging of their audiences into movements of social mobilisation such as Rock Against Racism (RAR) and the huge outdoor concerts and festivals in which punk and reggae musicians performed together in solidarity against the rise of the far right.

The Slits were one of those groups active within RAR and within who's music the influence of reggae can be clearly heard. On The Slits' track *Newtown* (1979), we hear a deep reggae bassline combined with spiky punky guitars and lyrics that deliver a biting critique of the cultural conformity of Britain's 1970s town planning. *Newtown*, like *Silly Games*, is produced by Dennis Bovell, a central figure within both the British reggae and post-punk[8] scenes. In her autobiography, The Slits' guitarist Viv Albertine describes how the band chose Bovell as producer because he understood reggae and its influence on their music (2014: 212). It was Bovell himself that 'played' matches, cigarettes, a glass and spoon to create the dub reggae like percussion that builds *Newtown's* quirky dance rhythms (Albertine 2014: 219–220).

Creolisation and the Work of Conviviality

Dick Hebdige understood punk and reggae, and its intermixture, as a site of representation and that it was through this signifying-practice that musicians and audiences, producers and consumers, could work to encode and decode meaning. It is through this process of both production and active consumption that the music of The Slits and Janet Kaye's *Silly Games* might be understood as what musicologist Denis-Constant Martin would call a site of identity construction (2013: 3), where music becomes a repository of collective memory, tangled and untangled through playing and listening and through this process offering identification with subjectivities that move beyond fixed and essentialised racial identities. For Martin, it is creolised music's potential to preserve and then reanimate long and hidden histories that make it an important site within processes of identity construction and even for the construction of narratives of reconciliation (2013: 49). Paul Gilroy follows a similar thread to Martin describing how the production and consumption of Caribbean influenced British music could have progressive potential as a site of 'cultural work that incorporated defensive and affirmative elements: working over and working through the memories of slavery and colonialism, past sufferings and contemporary resistances' (Gilroy 2003: 388).

Although acknowledging creolised music's progressive potential, we should remain attuned to its contradictory tendencies and be wary of simply singling out the 'creative vibrancy' and fluidity of identification within its processes of intermixture and combination. Hall's notion of translation, and the impossibility of complete translation, provides a useful way to acknowledge the disjuncture or hostility that can also be accommodated within creole cultural production. Hall argues that

> Translation is an important way of thinking about creolization because it always retains traces of those elements that resist translation, which remain left over, so to speak, in lack or excess, and which constantly then return to trouble any effort to achieve total cultural closure. (2015: 16)

Dub reggae, the genre that Dennis Bovell so skilfully references in his production for The Slits song *Newtown*, is a good example of creole music in which this 'troubling' or lack of closure finds clear expression. Jamaican dub reggae producers and recording engineers were pioneers in establishing a tradition of music production where the recording studio itself is the primary instrument of composition. Dub's key innovation was the stripping away of elements from an existing multi-track recording, removing the vocal, guitar or other key melodic elements, to leave only the bass and drums. Dub production is quite literally a process of translation or re-interpretation in which existing recordings become re-versioned and remixed. What is significant here is that it is dub's process of remixing or translation that is accepted as the primary site of creation. In dub reggae, the remixer or engineer is acknowledged as the primary author of the work, not the musicians or the composer of the song. In dub reggae, it is the incompleteness of the translation, the engineer's skill in balancing 'lack' and 'excess' that carries authorship and aesthetic value.

Playlist Track 5: 'Steadie' by Blackbeard (1980)

A good example of this genre in its British context is a track called *Steadie* (1980), from the album *I Wah Dub* (1980) another Dennis Bovell production recorded under the name Blackbeard. On *Steadie*, we hear how Bovell the dub mixer strips back the track to its bassline, dropping out and then reintroducing melodic elements like the guitar and piano; these melodic elements come often only in short bursts and with heavy reverb or echo added. The dynamics and progression of the track come from this re-versioning of a repetitive rhythm rather than harmonic progression or melodic variation. Another of dub reggae's defining characteristics that is evident on this track is the emphasis on deep bass frequencies and the potential they have when played loud on a reggae sound system to act on the body, to physically move or bind together a community of listeners.

The processes of subtraction or deconstruction that we hear on *Steadie*, the absence that defines this track against the original recording, together with the excessive use of reverb and echo, provide explicit expression of both the 'lack' and 'excess' that work as Hall describes to trouble total cultural closure. A lack of closure is also emphasised in an aesthetic that prioritises the continual re-working of a recording into numerous different versions. Hall uses Jacques Derrida's notion of 'différence', to capture the significance of the lack of closure or 'inbetweenness' that he finds evident within creolised culture:

> No translation achieves total equivalence, without trace or reminder. This is the logic of 'différence' in the Derridean sense: of a kind of difference which refuses to fall back into its binary elements'. (Hall 2015: 16)

The fluidity of identification suggested in différence is important in that it connects creolisation to conviviality's potential to disrupt binary oppositions and articulate identity positions that transcend absolute racial categorisation. This fluidity opens up the progressive potential of creolisation and conviviality, but it also allows us to be attentive to the disjuncture, incompleteness or hostility that also finds expression within calypso, reggae, post-punk and other music of the convivial continuum.

Jungle

The processes of combination and intermixture that are evident in reggae and post-punk recur and develop through subsequent iterations of Caribbean influenced British popular music finding clear expression again in electronic dance music of the 1990s, 2000s, and 2010s. Reggae, particularly the production techniques of dub reggae, is an important influence on British electronic dance music and can be heard in dance music's emphasis on bass frequencies, its preference for repetition over harmonic progression and the centrality of re-versioning and remixing in its production aesthetic.

Jungle is an African diasporic dance music that like lovers rock before it combines together disparate musical elements to produce innovative music that is distinctively British. Jungle's primary innovation was to combine radically speeded-up breakbeats[9] with deep reggae like basslines. In jungle, the bassline runs at half-speed to the drums, dancing to jungle is like dancing to reggae, and one locks into the slower groove of the bassline not the hyperkinetic drums. Jungle producers developed sophisticated techniques for 'chopping-up', manipulating and reordering sampled breakbeats,[10] either emphasising syncopation to maximise the affective potential as a dance music, or creating computer programmed drum patterns that mimicked the virtuosity of a jazz drummer. Jungle is characterised by the 'cut and paste' aesthetic that music technologies like the digital sampler afford, enabling producers to bring together seemingly disparate elements into improbable harmonic coordination.

Playlist Track 6: 'Original Nuttah' Shy FX Featuring UK Apache (1994)

Original Nuttah (1994) produced by Shy FX with vocals by UK Apache is a good example of the bricolage and radical combination of disparate source material that is evident within jungle and that remains a feature of sample-based dance music along the convivial continuum. Shy FX the producer of *Original Nuttah* uses short sections from a variety of existing recordings to build a complex musical collage. The track starts with siren-like horns taken from the Cypress Hill track *I Wanna Get High* (1993), and the breakbeat is sampled from *Amen, Brother* (1969) a funk track by The Winstons.[11] The vocal from UK Apache mirrors the diverse source material used to create the music. In the opening bars of the track, UK Apache switches between Jamaican and British accents, giving call outs to both Kingston and London, using lyrical phrasing common to Jamaican ragga[12] and also South Asian Bhangra.[13] Jeffery Boakye describes the first part of this vocal as a 'chaotic introduction of self in which you can actually hear competing identities jostling for position' (2017: 46).

UK Apache was born in London, the son of an Indian South African mother and an Iraqi father, his imitations of the Jamaican sound system MCs that he grew up listening to remain slightly incongruous, but nonetheless made him a cult figure within the jungle scene. In an interview for a BBC documentary in the year this track was released, UK Apache describes how jungle became an important site of identification and expression for him

> Jungle, because it's from England. I can really relate to it, it's important to me because I'm born here. I'm from England and London, and nobody can tell me I'm not from here. Once I was ashamed of being British, but it's like jungle draw me back into my roots, where I'm from. (UK Apache, BBC Jungle Documentary 1994 in Hancox 2018: 42)

Boakye describes how *Original Nuttah* and UK Apache's vocal delivery resonated strongly with his own experiences of the fluidity of racial identification within the diverse communities of inner-city London:

> He [UK Apache] legitimised non-black blackness. He made me realise that identity was a shifting idiosyncratic reality that had more to do with biography than geography. He represented a perfect storm of conflicting identities, an identity crisis made virtuous, the exact same construction of self that typifies second and third generation [British] people of colour. (Boakye 2017: 47)

Like lovers rock and post-punk, it is possible to see how jungle with its processes of combination and intermixture can be a site at which fixed or essential racial identities are contested at the level of representation making it a space where Martin's 'identity construction' (2013) and Gilroy's 'cultural work' (2003) can find expression, a space where identity positions that are fluid and complex can be explored through the processes of both producing and consuming music.

CONVIVIALITY WITHIN CORPOREAL AFFECT

Although theories of representation offer one tool with which to decode the potential for conviviality within jungle's radical bricolage, to understand the significance of creolised music along a convivial continuum, it is also important to examine how music and sound generate experience that moves beyond construction of meaning at the level of representation. Jeremy Gilbert applies theories of affect[14] to explore music's potential to act on the physical body; 'music's specificity lies in the fact it is registered not just cognitively but at the level of the physical body, in ways which visual and linguistic media are not' (2004: 3). Paul Gilroy is also attentive to the affective potential of the music of the Black Atlantic stating we should be wary of the 'limited idea that we encounter sound only, or even mainly through our capacity to hear and make interpretive sense of it' (Gilroy 2003: 391).

Theories of affect and how they apply to music listening are particularly appropriate here because of the emphasis that reggae and electronic dance music place on bass frequencies and how they act on the body (Henriques and Ferrara 2014). Julian Henriques (2003: 451) describes the affective force of reggae sound systems as 'sonic dominance',[15] for Henriques, sonic dominance occurs 'when and where the sonic medium displaces the usual or normal dominance of the visual medium' (2003: 452). Steve Goodman (2010) describes this same affective potential of reggae and electronic dance music as 'bass materialism'.[16] All these writers address in different ways the potential for loud music, particularly music that emphasises bass frequencies and affective rhythms, to transverse boundaries and transform the body. It is in this way that reggae and its sound system culture, and the electronic dance music which has borrowed from reggae, can be heard to enact a 'community of listeners' (Farinati and Firth 2017: 18; Gilroy 2003: 385), a group of people joined together through sound. In his study of bass frequencies in music and their potential to affect, Paul C. Jasen observes that 'when bass permeates and modulates, it binds bodies together (putting them literally on the same wavelength)' (2016: 22).

It is jungle's 'cosmopolitan and hybrid' nature (Gilbert 2014: 183) and in its potential to enact corporeal affect that Jeremy Gilbert finds the music's progressive potential, arguing that jungle explores 'new ways of feeling and being which can have wider social and political consequences' (Gilbert 2014: 183). The political potential of creolised music and its potential to transfigure essentialised identity positions leads Gilbert to make the claim that during the 1990s and 2000s jungle

> has clearly played a positive role in helping to inoculate London and the wider UK against the fascist virus, by creating shared modes of corporeal intensity which transfigure elements previously felt to be "black" and "white" into music and dance forms which move beyond these categories altogether. (2009: 4)

In this way, music's potential for corporeal affect becomes another site at which the minimal sociality of convivial formation can be enacted.

Playlist Track 7: 'Distant Lights' by Burial (2006)

During the 2000s, British dance music continues to evolve, refine and develop the processes of re-versioning, combination and intermixture that are evident in dub reggae and jungle. One of these subsequent iterations of Caribbean influenced electronic dance music is dubstep, which in the 2000s emerged from the same London clubs, raves and pirate radio networks that had incubated jungle in the 1990s. Dubstep is primarily an instrumental music that like jungle before it uses breakbeats as its main rhythmic element, but in contrast to jungle's hectic tempo in dubstep, the music is slowed to a sedate crawl. On the track *Distant Lights* (2006), we hear dubstep producer Burial, directly referencing dub reggae in his use of reverb and echo effects. We also hear the removal of melodic instrumentation in the mid-range frequencies between 3 kHz and 6 kHz that like dub gives this recording an eerie hollowed-out feel. The hollowness of the music is further emphasised because Burial uses only sampled vocals which he re-edits, processes and manipulates degrading the audio by removing frequencies important for intelligibility. Mark Fisher links Burial's production techniques specifically to reggae and what he describes as dub's 'privileged role of voice under erasure' (Fisher 2014: 99). A signature of Burial's music is also its shrouding in a hiss of static reminiscent of vinyl crackle or analogue tape noise. For Fisher, these processes of sampling and collage, subtraction and erasure, and the referencing of older analogue technologies have a disorienting effect, evocative of a haunting.

Hauntology

To articulate the haunted nature of Burial's music, Mark Fisher and Simon Reynolds follow Stuart Hall to Jacques Derrida, but this time applying Derrida's concept of hauntology (1994), this develops further Derrida's earlier theory of differénce in conceptualising the incompleteness of translation that Hall detects within creolised culture. In his writing on hauntology, Derrida evokes the figure of the spectre as a metaphor. A spectre is neither dead nor alive, present nor absent, it is a being that is simultaneously of the past and from the future (Derrida 1994: 12). The instability and fluidity of the spectre follow differénce in allowing for a disruption of binary oppositions that is ontologically consistent with both creolisation and conviviality. Fisher places Burial and hauntological music firmly within a postcolonial context, arguing that 'hauntology begins in the Black Atlantic, with dub [reggae]' (Fisher: 2006).[17] I equate here the haunting that Fisher perceives within dub reggae and dubstep with what Hall describes as the 'troubling' (2015: 16) of creolised cultural production. Hauntology is useful in developing this thread further because as Fisher notes hauntology acknowledges a diachronic perspective in a way that différance does not (2014: 18).

An evocation of 'a time that is out of joint'[18] is a recurring theme in Derrida's writing on hauntology leading scholars to place hauntology and cultural production that permits a hauntological reading as a form of 'memory work' (Demos 2013; Fisher 2014; Reynolds 2006, 2011). Memory work here becomes a useful compliment to the 'cultural work' and processes of identity construction that Paul Gilroy and Dennis-Constant Martin hear afforded within the production and consumption of creolised popular music. Fisher draws on Freud to describe the haunting of Burial's music, its 'troubled' nature, in terms of an unresolved mourning (2014: 103). For Fisher, this mourning[19] is a progressive mode of memory work in direct opposition to the 'postimperial melancholia' presented by Gilroy as conviviality's countervailing force.

For Fisher, the power of a hauntological mourning lies not only in its potential to work through the past traumas of slavery and colonialism but also in its potential to evoke alternative futures. In this way, Fisher argues that the music of Burial allows us to be

> haunted by events that had not actually happened, futures that failed to materialise and remained spectral. (2014: 107)

The translated, incomplete or troubled nature of calypso, reggae, post-punk, jungle and dubstep here all become creolised sites at which to articulate or experience identity positions that are non-binary and anti-essential. At the level of signifying-practice but also at the level of corporeal affect. In this way, there is an enacting of modes of togetherness that exist in a continual state of flux and transformation, both re-working past traumas but also conjuring better, but often transient, futures.

Playlist Track 8: 'Stop Killing the Mandem' by Novelist (2018)

Grime is one of the contemporary Caribbean influenced British musical genres that follows from calypso, reggae, post-punk, jungle, two-step garage and dubstep along the convivial continuum. The grime track I include here is *Stop Killing the Mandem* (2018) by Novelist released in the year of the 70th anniversary of the arrival of the Empire Windrush. In his exhaustive history of grime, Dan Hancox traces its origins directly to post-war Caribbean migration and the musical traditions of reggae and jungle, arguing that 'grime is a direct product of Caribbean sound-system culture' (2018: 37) and that its innovative sound and distinctive vocal delivery results from the fact that the artists and producers are

> mostly second- or third-generation black Britons who were just estranged enough from their cultural roots in the Caribbean or Africa, or both, and far enough along the lineage of unique - British dance styles – acid house, jungle, drum 'n' bass, UK garage – that they could draw from them all, while never being too in thrall to any of them. (Hancox 2018: 38)

Novelist is a good example of a second generation of grime artists whose lyrics demonstrate a clearer political engagement than one finds in jungle, dubstep or even the earlier iterations of grime (Hancox 2018: 282–284). *Stop Killing the Mandem* takes inspiration directly from a Black Lives Matter march that Novelist attended in 2016, with his lyrics critiquing both institutional racism and the narrative of black on black violence within British inner-cities. In the music, we hear synthesised sounds that Novelist uses to evoke, police sirens, car alarms or hospital heart monitors, all combined together with a furious sub-bass designed to physically move bodies on the dance floor (Novelist, August 2018). Novelist describes how the music mirrors the lyrics and is written to sound like a 'warning', to be 'alarming' and 'abrasive'. In an interview with a music production magazine, Novelist explains that

> People should be alarmed when they hear *Stop Killing the Mandem*, because it's an alarming message, it's an alarming topic. […] when you hear the song […] It's NOT supposed to make you right. It's supposed to make you [aware that] people are getting killed […] it is supposed to make you feel that this is important, so that's why its abrasive. (Novelist, August 2018)

Although grime is often abrasive with lyrics articulating experiences of marginalised British African diasporic youth, it is a musical form that remains inclusive and representative of the broader convivial cultures evident within the 'super-diverse' East and South London districts from which it emerged (Wessendorf 2014: 392; Hancox 2018: 41). Hancox connects grime's expression of conviviality to what he describes as a 'neighbourhood nationalism' (Back 1996). What Hancox sees in grime is a

> positive identification with the local area and the people in it, one that often transcends racial divisions […] even while racism and hostility remain commonplace in the city and the nation at large. (2018: 151)

Both Dan Hancox and Jeffery Boakye argue that grime's neighbourhood nationalism can also accommodate broader imagined communities that stretch beyond the inner-city postcodes within which grime originated. One example of grime's ability to connect with diverse audiences is its increasing popularity at the summer music festivals that attract huge audiences in the UK. Boakye notes that

> For all its antagonism, paranoia, anger and aggression, grime is actually hugely inclusive […] the fact that grime is becoming a festival staple is no accident, offering a unifying soundtrack for Millennials of all colours. (Boakye 2017: 339)

This celebration of creolised British music by audiences of tens of thousands at contemporary summer music festivals has strong parallels with the convivial formations enacted at RAR music festivals in the late 1970s, in both cases capturing the 'minimal sociality' within which Magdalena Nowicka and Tilman Heil see conviviality emerging (2015: 12). Although imperfect and transitory, this is one site where we see creolised music of the convivial continuum offering articulations of identity and belonging that challenge the racism of the British government's hostile environment for illegal immigrants and its treatment of the Windrush generation.

Conclusion

In this chapter, I have charted a convivial continuum within Caribbean influenced British post-war popular music. Beginning with the arrival of the Empire Windrush in 1948, I trace a continuum through calypso, reggae, post-punk, jungle, two-step garage, dubstep and grime. The convivial continuum describes a tradition of British popular music that is characterised by its processes of combination and intermixture. Creolisation is the preferred term to capture these processes of combination and intermixture because it captures the fluidity, the incomplete translation, that 'troubles' (Hall 2015: 16) this music. The music of the convivial continuum is significant within the British postcolonial context because it offers a site of 'cultural work' (Gilroy 2003). As a process of cultural work, this music can be a site of identity construction (Martin 2013) through signifying-practice, but also importantly within the music's potential for 'corporeal affect' (Gilbert 2009), when sound acts on physical bodies transforming them and affecting an interconnected community of listeners. In this way, calypso, reggae, post-punk, jungle, two-step garage, dubstep and grime can all become creolised sites at which to articulate or experience identity positions that are anti-essential and that disrupt racial hierarchies. Gilroy argues that it is within these convivial formations that racial difference becomes an 'unremarkable principle of metropolitan life' (2004: 105). This reading however leaves conviviality open to the criticism that it is inattentive to racism, prejudice and hostility within everyday lived experience. In acknowledging the spectres of the transatlantic slave trade and colonisation that haunt British creolised music, hauntology (Derrida 1994) becomes a useful corrective. It is the haunted, troubled or unfinished nature of British creolised music that opens it up as a site at which to mourn past traumas but also within which it is possible to imagine better but spectral futures.

Notes

1. The Home Office policy of a hostile environment for illegal immigrants came into effect in October 2010 under Theresa May as Home Secretary. In 2012, while serving as Home Secretary Theresa May stated, 'The aim is to create, here in Britain, a really hostile environment for illegal immigrants' (Hill

2017). Theresa May became British Prime Minister in 2016 and presided over the Windrush scandal.
2. The theory of a convivial continuum is inspired by the theory of the 'hardcore continuum' first posited by Simon Reynolds (1999, 2013) describing a lineage of British electronic dance music that exhibits radical combination and intermixture between Caribbean, United States and British popular music.
3. On this track, Mike Skinner emphasises his position in a continuing tradition of British creolised music calling out to 'all jungle and garage heads', fans of genres earlier along the continuum. Jeffery Boakye (2017) also places Skinner and The Streets as a precursor to grime, a contemporary British creolised music.
4. Sound system describes the powerful amplifiers and loudspeaker arrays that enable operators to play music at high volume. The speakers and amplifiers are designed to emphasise the affective potential of bass frequencies.
5. Reggae sound system culture prioritises recorded music, with exclusive vinyl pressings of instrumental tracks called 'dubs' or 'version sides' used as the backing tracks for local vocalists to perform over.
6. Denis Bovell was born in Barbados, moving to London aged 12. Bovell has been prolific as a musician, producer and reggae sound system operator, playing and recording music in genres as diverse as reggae, pop, rock and post-punk.
7. Riddim is the Jamaican patois pronunciation of rhythm and denotes the instrumental accompaniment to a reggae song, specifically the drum pattern and bass line.
8. The Slits are one of those groups defined as post-punk. A progression from punk in which artists retained punk's DIY aesthetic and confrontational attitude but in which the influence of rock became less audible and influences from other music such as reggae, jazz, funk and the avant-garde became more important.
9. The 'breakbeat' is a section of a funk or soul record where the other instruments drop away to leave only the drummer playing solo for a two or four bar measure.
10. Sampling describes the process in which a producer uses digital recording technology to take part of an existing recording so that it can be used to create a new piece of music.
11. *Original Nuttah* also contains samples from two reggae tracks by Anthony Red Rose *Fat Thing* (1985) and *Tempo* (1985) and samples of dialogue from the film *Goodfellas* (1990).
12. Ragga is a subgenre of reggae in which the instrumentation is primarily electronic and the vocal delivery is often aggressive.
13. Bhangra is popular music associated with the Punjabi diaspora in Europe.

14. For Jeremy Gilbert, '"affect" is a term which denotes a more or less organised experience, an experience probably with empowering or disempowering consequences, registered at the level of the physical body, and not necessarily to be understood in linguistic terms' (Gilbert 2004: 2).
15. Sonic dominance refers to the super-liminal whole-body experience of audition, immersed in the materiality of bass and the force of its physical presence in the bowl between the speaker stacks of a sound system (Henriques 2003).
16. 'Bass Materialism is the collective construction of vibrational ecologies concentrated on low frequencies where sound overlaps tactility' (Goodman 2010: 196).
17. Simon Reynolds also makes a convincing argument for dub reggae's haunting observing that the word 'dub' may derive from 'duppy' Jamaican patois for ghost (2006: 26).
18. Simon Reynolds connects the time-out-of-joint nature of hauntology specifically to the processes of collage and combination that is made possible by sampling and the séance like process of bringing together music from different times and spaces to create new objects (2011: 314).
19. Paul Ricoeur interprets Freud's concept of mourning as a process of reconciliation, in contrast melancholia is a mode of remembering where the object is lost without hope of reconciliation (1999: 7).

References

Albertine, V. 2014. *Clothes, Clothes, Clothes, Music, Music, Music, Boys, Boys, Boys.* London: Faber and Faber.
Back, L. 1996. *New Ethnicities and Urban Culture.* London: Routledge.
Boakye, J. 2017. *Hold Tight: Black Masculinity, Millennials and the Meaning of Grime.* London: Influx Press.
Bradley, L. 2000. *Bass Culture: When Reggae Was King.* London: Penguin.
Demos, T. J. 2013. *Return to the Postcolony: Specters of Colonialism in Contemporary Art.* Berlin: Sternberg Press.
Derrida, J. 1994. *Spectres of Marx: The State of Debt, the Work of Mourning and the New International.* London: Routledge.
Farinati, L., and C. Firth. 2017. *The Force of Listening.* Berlin: Errant Bodies Press.
Fisher, M. 2006. "Phonograph Blues." *K-Punk*, October 19. Available from http://k-punk.abstractdynamics.org/archives/008535.html. Accessed September 17, 2019.
Fisher, M. 2014. *Ghost of My Life: Writings on Depression, Hauntology and Lost Futures.* Winchester: Zero Books.
Hall, S. 2003. "Calypso Kings." In *The Auditory Culture Reader*, edited by M. Bull and L. Back, 419–425. Oxford: Berg.

Hall, S. 2015. "Creolité and the Process of Creolization." In *Creolizing Europe: Legacies and Transformations*, edited by E. Gutiérrez Rodríguez and S. A. Tate, 12–25. Liverpool: Liverpool University Press.
Hancox, D. 2018. *Inner City Pressure: The Story of Grime*. London: William Collins.
Hebdige, D. 1991 [1979]. *Subculture: The Meaning of Style*. London: Routledge.
Henriques, J. 2003. "Sonic Dominance and the Reggae Sound System Session." In *The Auditory Culture Reader*, edited by M. Bull and L. Back, 451–480. Oxford: Berg.
Henriques, J., and B. Ferrara. 2014. "The Sounding of the Notting Hill Carnival: Music as Space, Place and Territory." In *Black Popular Music in Post-World War 2 Britain*, edited by J. Stratton and N. Zuberi, 131–152. London: Ashgate.
Hill, A. 2017. "'Hostile Environment': The Hardline Home Office Policy Tearing Families Apart." *Guardian Online*, November 28. Available from https://www.theguardian.com/uk-news/2017/nov/28/hostile-environment-the-hardline-home-office-policy-tearing-families-apart. Accessed October 17, 2018.
Gilbert, J. 2004. "Signifying Nothing: 'Culture,' 'Discourse' and the Sociality of Affect." *Culture Machine* 6. Available from https://culturemachine.net/deconstruction-is-in-cultural-studies/signifying-nothing/. Accessed June 12, 2019.
Gilbert, J. 2009. "The Hardcore Continuum?" *DanceCult Journal of Electronic Dance Music Culture* 1 (1). Available from https://dj.dancecult.net/index.php/dancecult/article/view/274. Accessed June 12, 2019.
Gilbert, J. 2014. "Break/Flow/Escape/Capture: The Energy and Importance of the Hardcore Continuum." In *Black Popular Music in Post-World War 2 Britain*, edited by J. Stratton and N. Zuberi, 169–184. London: Ashgate.
Gilroy, P. 1993. *The Black Atlantic: Modernity and Double Consciousness*. London: Verso.
Gilroy, P. 2003. "Between the Blues and the Blues Dance: Some Soundscapes of the Black Atlantic." In *The Auditory Culture Reader*, edited by M. Bull and L. Back, 381–396. Oxford: Berg.
Gilroy, P. 2004. *After Empire: Melancholia or Convivial Culture?* Oxon: Routledge.
Gilroy, P. 2006. "Multiculture in Times of War (an Inaugural Lecture Given at the London School of Economics)." *Critical Quarterly* 18 (4): 27–45.
Goodman, S. 2010. *Sonic Warfare: Sound, Affect, and the Ecology of Fear*. Cambridge: MIT Press.
Gutiérrez Rodríguez, E. 2015. "Archipelago Europe: On Creolizing Conviviality." In *Creolizing Europe: Legacies and Transformations*, edited by E. Gutiérrez Rodríguez and S. A. Tate, 80–99. Liverpool: Liverpool University Press.
Jasen, P. C. 2016. *Low End Theory*. London: Bloomsbury.
Martin, D. C. 2013. *Sounding the Cape: Music, Identity and Politics in South Africa*. Cape Town: African Minds.

Novelist. 2018. "Video Interview with Future Music Magazine." August. Available from https://www.youtube.com/watch?v=wVYG61JxZeQ. Accessed May 1, 2019.
Nowicka, M., and T. Heil 2015. "On the Analytical and Normative Dimensions of Conviviality and Cosmopolitanism." Available from https://www.euroethno.hu-berlin.de/de/forschung/labore/migration/nowicka-heil_on-the-analytical-and-normative-dimensions-of-conviviality.pdf. Accessed June 12, 2019.
Nowicka, M., and S. Vertovec. 2014. "Comparing Convivialities: Dreams and Realities of Living with Difference." *European Journal of Cultural Studies* 17 (4): 341–356.
Reynolds, S. 1999. "Adult Hardcore." *The Wire Magazine* 182: 54–58.
Reynolds, S. 2006. "Haunted Audio." *The Wire Magazine* 273: 26–33.
Reynolds, S. 2011. *Retromania: Pop Culture's Addiction to Its Own Past*. London: Faber and Faber.
Reynolds, S. 2013. "The Wire 300: Simon Reynolds on the Hardcore Continuum: Introduction." *The Wire Magazine*. Available from https://www.thewire.co.uk/in-writing/essays/the-wire-300_simon-reynolds-on-the-hardcore-continuum_introduction. Accessed August 23, 2017.
Ricoeur, P. 1999. "Memory and Forgetting." In *Questioning Ethics: Contemporary Debates in Philosophy*, edited by R. Kearney and M. Dooley, 5–17. London: Routledge.
Stratton, J., and N. Zuberi. 2014. "Black Popular Music in Britain Since 1945: An Introduction." In *Black Popular Music in Post-World War 2 Britain*, edited by J. Stratton and N. Zuberi, 1–10. London: Ashgate.
Wessendorf, S. 2014. "'Being Open, But Sometimes Closed'. Conviviality in a Super-Diverse London Neighbourhood." *European Journal of Cultural Studies* 17 (4): 392–405.

Discography and Listening

Albertine, V., A. Forster, T. Pollitt, and P. Romero. 1979. "Newtown" [recorded by The Slits, produced Dennis Bovell] on *Cut*. London: Island Records.
Bevan, W. 2006. "Distant Lights" [recorded by Burial] on *Burial*. London: Hyperdub.
Bovell, D. 1979. "Silly Games" [recorded by Janet Kay] 7″ single. London: Scope.
Bovell, D. 1980. "Steadie" [recorded by Blackbeard] on *I Wah Dub*. London: More Cut Records.
Kankam, K. 2018. "Stop Killing the Mandem" [recorded by Novelist] on *The Novelist Guy*. London: MMMYEH Records.

Roberts, A. 2002 [1948]. "London Is the Place for Me" [recorded by Lord Kitchener] on *London Is the Place for Me: Trinidadian Calypso in London 1950–1956*. London: Honest John's Records.

Roberts, A. 2002 [1952a]. "Sweet Jamaica" [recorded by Lord Kitchener] on *London Is the Place for Me: Trinidadian Calypso in London 1950–1956*. London: Honest John's Records.

Roberts, A. 2002 [1952b]. "If You're Not White You're Black" [recorded by Lord Kitchener] on *London Is the Place for Me: Trinidadian Calypso in London 1950–1956*. London: Honest John's Records.

Skinner, M. 2002. "Has It Come to This" [recorded by The Streets] on *Original Pirate Material*. London: Locked On/679.

Williams, A., and A. W. Lafta. 1994. "Original Nuttah" [recorded by Shy FX featuring UK Apache] 12″ single. London: Sour.

Open Access This chapter is licensed under the terms of the Creative Commons Attribution 4.0 International License (http://creativecommons.org/licenses/by/4.0/), which permits use, sharing, adaptation, distribution and reproduction in any medium or format, as long as you give appropriate credit to the original author(s) and the source, provide a link to the Creative Commons license and indicate if changes were made.

The images or other third party material in this chapter are included in the chapter's Creative Commons license, unless indicated otherwise in a credit line to the material. If material is not included in the chapter's Creative Commons license and your intended use is not permitted by statutory regulation or exceeds the permitted use, you will need to obtain permission directly from the copyright holder.

CHAPTER 12

Footballers and Conductors: Between Reclusiveness and Conviviality

Anders Høg Hansen

INTRODUCTION: HISTORIC OCCASIONS—A FOOTBALL
MATCH AND A HUMAN EXHIBITION

In a personal correspondence in April 2018, British cultural theorist Paul Gilroy comments on a particular event concerning one of the cases of this chapter.

> It was clear that this was a historic occasion and I was delighted to have had the chance to witness it / Laurie had lit up that season and we all knew he was leaving so there was a mood of farewell about that. He and I are the same age and grew up in the same area of London so I always had a particular identification with him / The game wasn't much though it was nice to see so many black spectators in the ground. Laurie took one of those artistic corner kicks.

The historic occasion which Gilroy commented upon was 'just' a testimonial football match for a player named Len Cantello that took place

A. H. Hansen (✉)
Faculty of Culture and Society, Malmö University, Malmö, Sweden
e-mail: anders.hog-hansen@mau.sc

© The Author(s) 2020
O. Hemer et al. (eds.), *Conviviality at the Crossroads*,
https://doi.org/10.1007/978-3-030-28979-9_12

40 years ago, on May 1979 at the UK football club West Bromwich, just outside Birmingham. However, it had a particular formation of players that made it novel, at a particular time in British history—and in football history. Gilroy mentions a Laurie. That was Laurie Cunningham (from now on just Laurie), characterised as a soul boy, music-lover and dancer by his biographer Dermot Kavanagh (2017: 44)—often gliding elegantly over the muddy pitches until envious tackles began to damage his promising career. Laurie was on that day in May 1979 in a team of black players—of African-Caribbean heritage—only, gathering most of the few black players that played in the British football league at the time. They were up against a more common sight: a team of white players only, including Len Cantello. All the black players dressed in white, and the opponents black and white stripes and black shorts. Testimonials were commonly ritualised and celebratory affairs—and this one was too, yet with an added edge or surprise in its way of addressing colour, multiculture and competition in contemporary football in Britain. BBC TV journalist Adrian Chiles in 2016 made an hour-long TV documentary *Whites vs. Blacks: How Football Changed a Nation* that included new interviews with many of the former players, now in their late 50s. In 2017, the first and only biography on Laurie Cunningham came out (by Dermot Kavanagh). One iconic image depicts Laurie with his West Bromwich teammates, the muscular forward Cyrille Regis, captain of the black team at the match and defender Brendon Batson. The three players were that year to be nicknamed *The Three Degrees* (after an American female soul trio)—and in a recent book called 'The Men who changed British football forever' (Rees 2014).[1]

West Bromwich is next to Handsworth in Birmingham, documented some years later (1986) in filmmaker John Akomfrah's[2] debut documentary *Handsworth Songs*. Close by too was the home of *Centre for Contemporary Cultural Studies*, at Birmingham University. At the time of The Three Degrees and the testimonial, the Jamaican-British media and cultural studies scholar Stuart Hall was leading the centre in his last year in office.[3] A postgrad research student of the centre at the time, around 1979, was Paul Gilroy. In his footnotes in one of its working paper collections (1980), he notes his joy of watching West Bromwich on Saturdays. In the late 1970s and early 1980s, I followed them intensely, the English league being televised every week—and I was most often in the armchair in the front of the then black and white TV (Fig. 12.1).[4]

The black v white testimonial event—alongside other popular signs of integration as well as disintegration and tension in late-1970s Britain—can

Fig. 12.1 Laurie Cunningham in action for West Bromwich, 1979 Alan Williams/Alamy Stock Photo. This image is not included in the Creative Commons Attribution 4.0 International License

be seen as a significant echo of a heritage of colonialism. The tension which characterised the cities in the midst of economic crisis was turned into a more cheerful spectacle.

The TV documentary, the Cunningham biography and recent writings and events (a memorial sculpture on *The Three Degrees* was launched in West Bromwich in May 2019) mark a renewed focus on particular black players and tensions in British football. Laurie is my first case of two. The second case[5] is also concerned with Caribbean migration and a form of living memorial of colonialism. It is about the St. Croix-born Victor Cornelius (from now on just Victor), who in 1905 was shipped to Denmark as a 7-year old, alongside his 4-year-old half-sister, Alberta Roberts. They were going to be extras in a human exhibition at a colonial festival at the amusement park Tivoli, Copenhagen (Freiesleben 1998; Frank Larsen 2008). The Danes, it seems, needed black subjects from their colonies to amuse them with. Victor and Alberta were picked from poor widowed mothers at the then Danish-owned colony of St. Croix in the Caribbean Virgin

Islands and sailed to Denmark. Victor ended up staying in Denmark all his life, while his half-sister Alberta died in Copenhagen of tuberculosis aged only 15, in 1917, just weeks before the Danish Virgin Islands were sold to the USA (that had developed a strategic interest in the islands during World War I).

A few years later Victor was a successful student at a teacher's college outside Copenhagen. Image 2 turns the human exhibit positioning of Victor around completely. Here we see a free-spirited Victor, confidently posing and 'conducting' his life, literally, with fellow musicians at the teacher's college.

During 2017–2018, the 100th anniversary year of the sale of the islands, this historical legacy of Denmark's colonial past is re-opened through art pieces, historical debates, and exhibitions and monuments. The Danish colonial history had by no means had a proliferate public coverage or clearly visible place in the school curricula, yet 2017 marks some kind of turning point. In the midst of a variety of initiatives and public debate, an exhibition about Victor appeared in small-town Nakskov—assisting the sculpture of him at the train station square, in the town where he worked all his life after graduating teacher's college at Jonstrup college near Copenhagen. Victor had written his own autobiography back in 1977 and since then he has been documented by several writers and a filmmaker, notably Birgit Freiesleben in 1998 and the journalist Alex Frank Larsen, in 2005, in a TV documentary and book about Danish descendants of the country's former colonies (Fig. 12.2).

Living Beyond and Within Race—Reclusive Openness, Opacity, Conviviality

The quite different journeys of Laurie and Victor developing their talent in two Western postcolonial societies mark particular strategies of playing and living with different allegiances which I will begin to develop. Nowicka and Heil, in their work on cosmopolitanism and conviviality (2015), argue that there are plenty of peaceful situations in which people live or/and work 'beyond their identities', and 'despite their differential positions in social structures' (2015: 12). The mainly British footballers of the testimonial match (the black team of Caribbean or African heritage), in most cases from a working-class background, mirrored a particular positive dynamic or integration. A thrown-togetherness for fun and play, but also a clear

Fig. 12.2 Victor conducting. CC BY-SA License/https://commons.wikimedia.org/wiki/File:Cornelins_1.jpg

expression of antagonism and destructive tensions characterised the country. A wave of so-called muggings had filled the media most of the decade (see, e.g., Hall et al., *Policing the Crisis*, 1978), since Powell's infamous speech 10 years earlier,[6] tensions had risen and a new crisis had captured the former empire, with Thatcher taking over. On the football pitches, in dance halls/clubs and as well in band formations, as in the second wave of ska/blue beat, some other signs of peaceful play were prominent, but so was the general fragility.

In addition to articulation of postcolonial forms of predicament and expression in both cases, the UK case draws from allegiances and connections between football, music and a crisis of industry, while the Danish case also marks a turn-around or redemptive figure, which also could be used as a perfect early example of integration? Victor turned his life around from a colonial exhibit to a carrier of Nordic/European choir music values and teaching. From his youth and onwards, Victor began to establish musical meetings and festivity that encouraged new forms of interactions and carriers of the convivial, or something sacred for those with interest and skills (not necessarily in a *religious sense* although he also turned strongly to religion, as documented in his biography, 1977). Importantly, his teaching and notably his work on music and his choir became vessels for those he sang or worked with to express themselves.

Both Laurie and Victor, I argue, need a specific theorisation to make sense of their ambiguous roles, as wilful tricksters, I would put it, yet also enigmatic and self-protective. Drawing upon the notions of *reclusive openness* and *conviviality*, in particular, I will open the discussion. The notion of *reclusive openness* (self-coined) could be an oxymoron. It may convey the tense ambiguities of diasporic and displaced identities (Cohen 2017). The word *reclusive* may be traced to the French *reclus*, an adjective describing a person who hides. Often with the purpose of meditation. A person or a group may become *reclusive*—in particular when faced by a majority culture. One may as a way of coping try to find track(s) for survival—and maybe in that process develop or create one's own openness. *Openness* is in philosophy a state of transparency and also in our era a cherished state of free and open access to information and data. However, we may try to rethink *reclus* and *open* together as a form of *conviviality* where more protected communicative spheres and 'caves' lead to another kind of openness, identity development and cohabitation. This leads me to the next point, trying to elaborate on a third notion carrying a stronger note on the postcolonial predicament. I am referring to a situation as well as process of living reclusive openness; An opaque and changing state, where identity is never clear or singular. Glissant's notion of *opacity* may be able to capture this ambiguity and lack of transparency—and furthermore help to nuance the notion of the reclusive, but also to add a creolity or complexity of openness of identity. Difference is here in a space that is neither elitist, ethnic, nor subcultural, but diverse within, as a habitual ideal.

Reclusivity or what we could also call a form of *with-drawnness*—whether pushed back or willingly seeking such a protected state—can lead to another state of being. Such as, an openness within a community or in spaces where one feels that he/she can perform and be what she wants—like e.g. Laurie's dancefloor, football pitch or Victor's music classrooms or white choir practices which may be seen as such spaces 'beyond identity' in Nowicka and Heil's sense.

Let me explore some general understandings of the *reclusive* and its implications for thinking around gaze and race. As Meghan Tinsley noted (in a response to an earlier version of the chapter), the involuntary reclusiveness of the racialised subject may be liberating? (Tinsley 2018). A black person is in Western contexts largely subjected to a white gaze and surrounded by a white majority that does not live sensing its own colour/race. Tinsley connects her point to Glissant's notion of *opacity*. Glissant's *opacity* or a right to opacity (Glissant 1997) operates with a 'stubborn shadow' (Simek 2015), a fuzziness or a creative repertoire of surprise which performs in parts as attempts to escape a framing gaze. A performance or modes of deflection that does not quite make the white/powerful able to understand or read you. The *opacity* is here in parts a tricky veiling or a disguise of tricks (apropos creolity), which the subject uses tactically to escape the gaze and reinvent herself or make him not readable/transparent. This creates a situation where the white cannot read the black, while this 'you', the black, were fully able to read the white/the coloniser—the latter reasoning inspired by Bhabha's discussion of mimicry (1994: 85–92).[7]

Both Laurie and Victor had such repertoires. Laurie was an enigma in the dressing room, kept to himself. Yet, he was also quite expressive and flamboyant—in clothing and on the football pitch—and also on the dance floor, where he spent just as much time as on football (Kavanagh 2017: 49). Kavanagh writes that a person that dressed so lavishly might be assumed to be extrovert, but on the contrary he was not. Cautious with strangers, he was—and; 'the clothes he loved to wear sent out a message so powerful that they succeeded in deflecting attention away from the person wearing them' (2017: 75)—a sign of a tactical or habitual opacity? The singular Laurie easily splitting himself up in several stage personas or 'multiplicities' (Rodwick in Demos, debating Glissant 2009: 123)? *Opacities* can coexist and converge, as Glissant writes (1997: 191).

The artistic kicks Gilroy mentioned (quote at beginning) was performed by doing corner kicks with the outside of his foot, with the left foot from left side of the pitch, and right foot at the other side. Laurie was not alone in his desire not to conform, but he had something else, his silky skills and dressing, his floating on the pitch. His athleticism produced an offer of a tour with a Harlem ballet ensemble. Furthermore, as many of his fellow black footballers, he chose not to respond to banana throwing and stick during games. Several black players of the time said that they heard every utterance of racism but tried to channel it into an urgent focus on the game instead (e.g. Regis 2010; Hazell in Chiles 2016; Kavanagh on Laurie 2017). This can be seen as one way of trying to stay opaque or non-confrontational, not by submitting to the humiliation, but by 'avoiding the tackle' and frustrating the racist roarers.

The White Choir—Victor in Nakskov

My introduction to Victor Cornelius was assisted by an image of the man in convivial control. Pausing for a pose during a musical situation, with Victor at the centre, conducting. I now return to him with another group of music folks: singers from his choir of nurses formed around 60 years later set up to sing for patients in hospitals. The choir came about when Victor is in bed in the hospital of Nakskov in Southern Denmark some years earlier. Treatment is going well and when he is fresh enough to sit up, his doctor, Jokum his name was, tells him to play a song on his Hohner harmonica. He chooses a Swedish waltz. Soon nurses and other patients join in dancing. When he is fresh enough to stand he plays regularly for his hospital ward. He survives the cancer and sets up the *White Choir* in Nakskov singing at local events, in churches and in the hospital. Similar choirs are established in the region (Fig. 12.3).

Fig. 12.3 The White Choir 1981. CC BY-SA License/https://commons.wikimedia.org/wiki/File:Cornelins_3.jpg

In his autobiography (1977), Victor recalls a particular moment after arrival in Denmark when he became an extra in the colonial festival in Tivoli. Victor is eventually caved to stay put—since he constantly ran over to the Greenland-sections, not wanting to stick around in the arranged Caribbean space. When put into a cave, he spits on a notable getting too close (Cornelins 1977; Frank Larsen 2008). The two met many years later and reconcile on warm terms, a mark of Victor's conviviality. So humiliatingly abused to begin with, but able to turn it around and to meet anew and embrace the person that came to look at him as an animal.

After the spitting event in Tivoli, 13 years later, St. Croix and 2 other Danish-owned Virgin Islands, where Denmark earned a massive income on slavery at sugar plantations for over 150 years, were sold to the USA. Victor was allowed to stay in Denmark although authorities had tried to persuade him to continue schooling in the USA. He did not want to leave. He was doing well at Jonstrup teacher college in Denmark where he often takes up the role as conductor, as noted earlier in the chapter. He became a school teacher and then deputy inspector at a Nakskov school, where he also taught music.

In 2017, I met one of his former music students, Timme Ørvad, who says that he does not know how Victor got around to do teaching and administration too, it was music, which was his passion. He says the following about a school friend (later to be his wife) and his own introduction to music: 'My wife played violin with him and she sang in a girl choir he set up at the school, while for me the guitar fell down in my hands', Timme explained (Ørvad 2017). Timme and his future wife were both influenced by Victor. They proceeded to the music conservatory in Copenhagen and became music teachers and composers.

BLACK AND WHITE

Today, a third of the top English football league's players are of African-Caribbean origin—much in disproportion of the few per cent of the population they number (in addition to the many non-UK players brought to the premier league). The multi-ethnic outlook of the English premier league is if not unremarkable, then at least a reality where its important turning point was back around 1979 when there was only a handful of black players in the top league, including those three mentioned at West Bromwich in Birmingham. At the testimonial are also three other top-level black players, Hazell and Berry from Wolves (also a midlands club, a rival) and Crooks from Stoke. Crooks, today a football commenter, was missing from Adrian Chiles 'Black and White' TV documentary from 2016, mentioned in the introduction.

In the documentary, Chiles not only tracks down many of the players of the time and interviews them about the event. He also follows up interviewing more recent generations of players, to get a sense of changes in the game. Nobody wants to take the credit or the blame for the original idea for this white and black game, Chiles says—although a recent The Guardian article by Simon Burnton (2016) claims the idea coming from Cantello and Regis discussing the event. They thought this set-up would cause attention—and produce some additional quid's in retirement bonus for Cantello via more people on the terraces. The game was well visited for a testimonial. The Guardian, back in 1979, called it 'tasteless' and noted it could ignite violence among the crowds. It went by peacefully. Chiles peculiarly keeps the whites and black separate also in the interviews, apart from a final convivial get-together of players from both teams. A bunch of well-known white players says they hardly remember the event—but had noted that there were more Asian and black people on the terraces than ever before. These groups were following football on TV—but many were scared to enter the stadiums where they risked rubbing shoulders with the National Front.

The black players, on the contrary, remembered it as something special. They noted that they were making history and this was a fantastic event for them. 'A novelty thing, which was fun', Brendon Batson said, who since has worked in the Football Association advocating for more black players to become involved in managing roles. The testimonial was a sign that a problem was recognised and performed and not ignored anymore. They now spoke of the emerging collective using a broad category of ethnicity or African-Caribbean heritage. All the black players had heard about each other, but they were spread out as a minority that on their own had to conform to the white game and the shouting. With the testimonial they were granted an opportunity to come together and built and extend their community, uniting with other black players who had been through the same trials. In the dressing rooms, racialisation was played out on another level of embodied conviviality. One thing is the tackles. Then there is the banter, the stripping naked, and the sharing of creams. 'what's going on there?' 'Daren't put it on', older white players would respond (Back et al. 2000: 152).

Outside on the stadium terraces, large parts of the mainly white spectators in those days regularly threw racist jargon and bananas at black footballers. They may have become approved in the rites of the fans, as long as they were one of our boys (Mercer in Back et al. 2000: 76), but as Cyrille Regis, one of the black West Bromwich players, said it. 'At the time we were going to Millwall, Chelsea and Tottenham and 10.000 were singing nigger, nigger, lick my boots'. Regis dies suddenly of a heart attack, aged 59, in early 2018 (while the previously mentioned memorial statue for *The Three Degrees*, depicting Laurie and teammates Regis and Batson, was in the planning phase[8]). Regis cortege passed by the stadium in West Bromwich and a special service was held there. Back in 2008, he was made MBE, member of the order of the British Empire, for services to the voluntary sector and to football (Regis 2010: 237–238) 2010. Queen Elisabeth pinning the medal on his chest is also included in the picture section of his autobiography (2010).

The players of African-Caribbean heritage who lived with the problem and just had to continue playing had for that fleeting event thrown themselves together as a force. One of the young talented teenage players, Vernon Hodgson, had to put his career on hold after the 1979-game due to a bad knee he had had for a year. He went to drink heavily for some years, but was saved by the bins, as he says to Chiles, when Chiles found him at work as bin man.

Black youngsters, many second-generation Caribbean or arrived in the UK as children, were at the time around 1979 in different ways exploring belonging to Britain—and through sports and music carving out new routes of identity. Laurie often invited fellow white players with him to black music clubs in Birmingham. It was a time where *Ska* revival and post-punk merged audiences and playing spaces and bands among black and white people. However, also particular racist fractions of skinheads created tense friction. Conviviality and conflict lie close (Nowicka and Vertovec 2014: 346, using Karner and Parker research from a contemporary study of Birmingham, UK). Dancing to the new music and shouting white supremacy. *Suggs* from one of the white bands, Madness, that built themselves on Jamaican Prince Buster with their initial ska-sound, once explained that they were performing to fractions of the more radical skinheads doing racist chants and *sieg heil*. The music, on the other hand, an embrace of the new Black Britain, was as far from that salute as it could be. The *Skinheads* had initially removed themselves from the middle-class hippies and embraced the Jamaican dance moves and music which they thought were cool. Yet, the racism lived. It was ambivalent times.

The Birmingham area, including Coventry, where some black and white Ska-bands emerged from, was a stronghold for promoting integration, maybe even colour-blindness. However, the National Front fans and the racist fractions of skinheads were also on the terraces shouting and throwing bananas at black players. The gloom and doom of the post-industrial city and the era, though sparkled with new popular music fusions, are captured in The Specials (black) swan song and video *Ghost Town* (before a split and a reformation as AKA Special).

Almost 40 years later, Chiles' documentary can be interpreted as a rather pleasing pad to social progress since the roars on the terraces, muddy pitches and ghost towns, yet with a definite sting in the tail, as Jasper Rees notes (2016). Racism has now moved from the terraces into social media, according to several contemporary and recent players. Director Chiles also met Les Ferdinand, a former black footballer, presently Director at QPR, and one of the few former footballers of African-Caribbean heritage to reach a management position.[9] 'We can make as many of these documentaries as you like', he warned, 'but you won't change what's in people's heads right now'. The documentary came at a time when winds against immigration to Britain blow colder now again.

Deflection and Break-Away Individuals

The material of the chapter shares a focus on 'break-away' paths or remarkable, *key episode* incidents (Thomsen using McAdams 2013) that brings to light particular social field's *convivial* forms of cohabitation and conflict. Victor exhibited in Tivoli, but later a conductor at college and then initiating a choir. His story is the tale of the self-made and adaptive newcomer which postcolonial Denmark so conveniently cherishes—and his achievements were certainly remarkable. However, such celebratory discourses, as Lapina notes, might allow inequalities to slip out of the debate (Lapina 2016: 39). We may be aware of the pros and cons of the healing-seeking or *reconciliatory* nature—and ask why they are shaped as they are and for whom are they portrayed? Furthermore, such narratives may perform a particular *working-through* of difficult lives (Ricoeur using Freud 1999: 5–11) towards an end point of 'success after all'. Kavanagh captures well lows and highs of Laurie's life, while the exhibition in Nakskov, taking us through

Victors life as a visual memoir (with a strong focus on his public life), is somehow less multi-faceted.

Laurie was tightrope-dancing between ballet and football, before the vicious tackles of Spain. After 2 good years at West Bromwich, he was sold to Real Madrid at the age of 23, and from then on, with glimpses of genius, notably in the beginning, injuries make his trouble begin. He returned to England several times and in the course of his career plays for many clubs after his early days with first Leyton Orient, then West Bromwich—before the big sale to Real Madrid in the Summer of 1979. Ironically, one year before his death, he in 1988 joined Wimbledon FC. He was then in his early 30s, a more muscular figure, who had had to turn his previous habitual grace into something more solid after a plague of injuries. Wimbledon FC was a surprise. The club was a crazy gang of rough and tough—as un-Laurie as it could get (as John Barnes put it, in Kavanagh 2017: 89). Wimbledon FCs first team, apart from playing tough, had a tactic of just looping the ball into the opponent's defence and get people forward. Statistically it would higher the chances of scoring, to have the ball close to goal often, they believed. Somehow it worked; they reached the FA cup final in 1988 and win it. Laurie comes on the pitch as substitute. He had deflected again, joined another crowd, and despite all signs of break down, he was in the midst of another kind of conviviality.

PLAY THE GAME WILFULLY—AND PLAYFULLY

Valluvan writes about how ethnic differences should cease to require scrutiny (Valluvan 2016: 207). He refers to Amin's work, where conviviality is defined as 'indifference to difference' (207). Research into conviviality, as for example Gilroy's work from 2004, discusses modes of interaction and cohabitation replacing or reworking older notions of multiculturalism or cosmopolitanism. The cases of Laurie and Victor can be grasped as stories of agency rather than stuckness, carrying *redemptive* plotting and *generative* life practices (after McAdams 2005), or stories to live by as markers of hope and encouragement—and thereby also as memories for the future; memory work to continue to play the 'game' 'wilfully' but also playfully.

Research, such as the material introduced in this chapter, that draws upon the use of biography, interviews, letters and diaries as a sort of historical records, can lead to questions around representation of past events. These genres carry their degree of 'noise', one could say. They may not be viewed as 'high fidelity' when it comes to information or facts about the actual past events, but rather as rich sources in the way they reveal how subject's did see themselves and their worlds, as Caine points out (2010: 75)—or rich in their ways of thinking *in and about time*, I would add. They are not just historical sources ('History' deals with collective time versus the arbitrary time of the individual life in autobiography, as Popkin notes, 2005: 11). Instead they are mediations of spaces of anxieties about failed projects and future imaginings (King using Stoller 2012: 19). Kavanagh, Laurie's biographer, maps a rich life but also a series of misgivings and a failed project. Laurie however kept returning. Victor may more easily fit into the redemptive life story tale, cosy material for a more pleasurable or convivial and postcolonial tale. The guy who made it through, and who taught us (he was a teacher) and who even whipped us (it may be stretching it, but here we have a man whose ancestors experienced 150 years of brutal slavery). At the exhibition in Nakskov in August 2017, a film of video letters of his former students reminiscing Victor is shown. A guy remembers he was given 25 beats for some sort of unruly behaviour. At beat number 10, he is hurt and he pulls his hand aside. Then Victor starts from the beginning, whip 1, and so forth. It is however all told in a light-hearted, good-humoured way. The exhibition, and the video letters, celebrates Victor after all.

Some research says (Frank Larsen 2008) that he was also given the task of beating unruly boys. At this time, beatings were legal and common. The question is if the male teacher Victor was different from any other? Would he risk out or do differently than other teachers?

Victor was respected. He was often taking the role of yard guard during breaks. Often standing at the fence chatting with other students, being very social. Passers-by would look, his colour was different, but he also fitted in.

The school was a space of interdependence we could say. So is the football team. Nowicka and Heil note this importance of interdependence alongside the unremarkable, when trying to understand conviviality (2015: 14). Victor was possibly slapping, and definitely singing and giving music student Timme, the earlier mentioned music student of Victor (and his wife) had some of the most precious moments of their youth. Timme emphasised Victor's strong humanitarian values and his musical inspiration (interview, 2017), which later brought him and his wife to the music conservatory.

High Exposure and 'The Stopping Down' of Aperture

Laurie and Victor both became highly exposed in their communities. Victor recalls how he and his half-sister Alberta were taken for a walk to the exhibition in Tivoli, after just arriving, and how all the whites wanted to pinch them or check them out. Laurie too, in other ways in the more multi-ethnic cities of London and Birmingham 70 years later. Laurie's white girlfriend Nikki recalls a stroll with Laurie after a night out. Some blokes approach them, threateningly, spitting at Nikki. Nikki tells Adrian Chiles how Laurie avoided one of the men's attack on him and in defence tipped him to the ground. Later, the guy, a fan of West Brom it appeared, slowly got up and realised '… you are Laurie, I love you…'. So, this was Laurie, the skilled footballer he was a fan of, not an ordinary black guy having a walk with his white girlfriend (Nikki Brown in Chiles 2016).

The exposed, framed and highly visible person can only respond with deflection, to keep a sense of self, we may argue. If one is put in one frame one day, and the next day or year seen as something else, this may force the framed to seek spaces of refuge or reinvention. From the cave to the choir, from the muddy pitches to offerings of a ballet career. Then later on to the crazy gang of Wimbledon. There were also roads not taken and myths followed. Interestingly, Victor continued to believe that he was on a mission to Denmark to teach and not to be sent back to St. Croix (Cornelins 1977; Frank Larsen 2008). Laurie never wrote his memoirs. Using Glissant's notes or call for *opacity* (1997: 193), we do not necessarily have to fully grasp either Laurie or Victor, or their 'stopping down' (reducing light coming in to the camera while gaining a depth of field/focus). Their deflections, or ways towards refuge, may be unclear for us, and still we can act in solidarity with them.

Glissant makes an interesting attempt at thick description of opaque or reclusive communication between him and a silent walker who kept passing by on a beach route near his garden and the ocean. Glissant had watched him many times passing, and they had noted each other, but the walker clearly wanted privacy. Glissant tried to call him politely with a hand gesture. The walker returned it with recognition, but also (in Glissant's interpretation, pp. 121–127) as a 'wink' or a 'hi' meaning: 'I have seen you, hi to you, but let us not go further in conversation'.

So, let us just be pleased with what we know about Laurie and Victor, what they gave, open, yet reclusive or opaque—and act in solidarity.

Laurie and Victor were two different characters in various ways resurging or unleashing different aspects of their given, often racialised identities. They had their games against reduction or public attempts to 'corner them in any essence' (Glissant 1997: 192). Laurie's ballet-football, 'a black Nureyev' (famed Russian ballet dancer, Kavanagh 2017: 79), was just one mode or sign of his displacing of labelling. The same could be said of Victor's embrace of Danish songs, enlightenment and values of civilisation—the values he praised in his autobiography (1977), and which he thought he was taken to the West to teach.

Ending Notes

Victor, brought to Denmark solely as a colonial 'artefact' for exhibiting purposes, was 30 years later becoming the star and the talk of small-town Nakskov with his love for music and his teaching skills and sociality. Later in life, he toured the country and then initiated a choir. Victor had married a Swedish white woman, had three kids and lived in that small town all his life. He was eventually buried next to his wife, as he wished, near the small town of Nakskov.

Laurie brought his English girlfriend, Nikki, with him to Madrid (the one interviewed by Chiles in the TV documentary and who experienced the assault when she and Laurie were out strolling). Nikki and Laurie separated some years later, but on friendly terms. Laurie had a child with Spanish Silvia a few years before his early death in a car crash in Madrid in 1989. Nikki, whom Laurie had met at a London dance floor just before he joined West Bromwich, was closing the casket. Laurie is buried in North London.

Notes

1. Laurie and the handful of other very talented black players that came into the best English league in the 1970s paved way for a rising generation of black footballers. The history of black footballers in Britain is eloquently documented in Onura's *Pitch Black* (2015).
2. John Akomfrah is a UK filmmaker of Ghanaian descent, a founder of the Black Audio Film Collective in 1982.
3. A recent film by Johan Akomfrah is his intimate portrait of Stuart Hall in *The Stuart Hall Project* (2014) compiling archival clips and interviews with Hall himself and with music by one of Hall's favourite artists, Miles Davis. The movie is at the same time a history of Britain and British cultural studies. Lola Young, Faye Ginsburg and I debated this movie at a screening and

seminar event at Malmö University in September 2014, the debate later edited for publication in Høg Hansen, Young and Ginsburg, 2015 (see, e.g., Høg Hansen et al. 2016).
4. West Brom's football these days is a different affair. When the writing of this article was begun, the team were rock-bottom in premier league. When completed, they are in the second tier, just missing promotion to premier league.
5. The material of this chapter, alongside a range of other cases, is planned to be expanded and included in a monograph of 12 thematically related cases and life stories that reconstructs the journeys of enigmatic lives, tracing their private journeys and public exposures. The intended collection may include material from Britain and Denmark, Sweden, USA, Israel-Palestine, Tanzania and Mozambique. The discussions, notably the work on *reclusive openness* in this chapter, draw from e.g. Høg Hansen (2016).
6. Conservative MP Enoch Powell's strong anti-immigration speech in Birmingham, UK, in April 1968, which led to his sacking, but made Powell famous and it is commonly assumed that it triggered popular sentiment against immigration.
7. I am indebted to several commenter's for inspiring me to link *reclusive openness* to *opacity* and more closely discuss race under this theoretical framework; first of all, Meghan Tinsley (correspondence 22 January 2018, after a conference presentation in December 2017), but also the use or mentioning of Glissant by Kerry Byström, Oscar Hemer, Per-Markku Ristilammi and Temi Odumosu on various occasions.
8. Search for funding delayed the realisation of a memorial sculpture. A model is shown in Chiles documentary where Chiles and Cunningham's family visits an atelier with the work in progress. It is to be launched at the town centre of West Bromwich on 22 May 2019, see e.g., Guttridge (2019).
9. A formerly famed black defender at West Brom, Darren Moore, though in April 2018 took over managing at the club when they bottom of the premier league. He became the first Jamaican manager in a premier league club ever. A change of style to more attacking football and also more wins established him as a cherished character, also as manager. However, a series of bad results next spring (the club now were among the best in the second tier) led to an early sacking of Moore in March 2019.

References

Back, L., T. Crabbe, and J. Solomos. 2000. *The Changing Face of Football*. Oxford: Berg.
Bhabha, H. 1994. *The Location of Culture*. London: Routledge.
Burnton, S. 2016. "The West Brom Testimonial." *The Guardian*, November 24.

Cohen, P. 2017. Personal Email Correspondence, May 30. Feedback on Book Proposal.
Cornelins, V. 1977. *Fra St. Croix til Nakskov*. Copenhagen: Frimodts.
Caine, B. 2010. *Biography and History*. London: Palgrave.
Centre for Contemporary Cultural Studies, Gilroy, P. et al. 1982. *The Empire Strikes Back*. Birmingham: CCCS, University of Birmingham/Routledge.
Chiles, A. 2016. *Whites vs Blacks: How Football Changed a Nation*. Documentary, BBC.
Demos, T. J. 2009. "The Right to Opacity". *October* 129: 113–128. https://doi.org/10.1162/octo.2009.129.1.113.
Frank Larsen, A. 2008. *Slavernes slægt*. Copenhagen: DR Forlag.
Freiesleben, Birgit. 1998. *Fra St. Croix til Tivoli. En historisk betretning om to vestindiske børns lange rejse* (This book is also available in English, with substantial parts of the autobiography included). Forlaget ACER.
Gilroy, P. 2004. *After Empire: Melancholia or Convivial Culture*. Abingdon: Routledge.
Gilroy, P. 2018. Personal Email Correspondence, April 3.
Glissant, É. 1997. *Poetics of Relation*. Ann Arbor: University of Michigan Press.
Guttridge, R. 2019. West Brom Three Degrees Statue to Be Unveiled in May. *Express and Star*, March 25, https://www.expressandstar.com/sport/football/west-bromwich-albion/2019/03/25/west-brom-three-degrees-statue-to-be-unveiled-in-may/.
Høg Hansen, A., L. Young, and F. Ginsburg. 2016. "Mediating Stuart Hall". In *Voice & Matter*, edited by O. Hemer and T. Tufte. Gothenburg: Nordicom.
Høg Hansen, A. 2016. "Reclusive Openness in the Life of Eugene Haynes." medium.com.
Kavanagh, D. 2017. *Different Class: The Story of Laurie Cunningham*. London: Unbound.
King, M. T. 2012. "Working with/in the Archives." In *Research Methods for History*, edited by L. Faire and S. Gunn, 13–29. Edinburgh: Edinburgh University Press.
Lapina, L. 2016. "Besides Conviviality." *Nordic Journal of Migration Research* 6(1): 33–41. https://doi.org/10.1515/njmr-2016-0002.
McAdams, Don. 2005. *The Redemptive Self: Stories Americans Live By*. Oxford: Oxford University Press.
Nowicka, Magdalena, and Tilmann Heil. 2015. "On the Analytical and Normative Dimensions of Conviviality and Cosmopolitanism." Eberhard Karls University Lecture.
Nowicka, M., and S. Vertovec. 2014. "Comparing Convivialities: Dreams and Realities of Living-with-Difference." *European Journal of Cultural Studies* 17 (4): 341–354. https://doi.org/10.1177/1367549413510414.
Onunua, E. 2015. *Pitch Black*. London: Biteback Publishing.

Ørvad, T. 2017. Interview by Anders Høg Hansen, October 17 (T Ørvad is a Former Student of Victor Cornelius).
Popkin, J. 2005. *History, Histories & Autobiography*. Chicago: University of Chicago Press.
Rees, J. 2016. "Whites vs Blacks: How Football Changed a Nation." *The Telegraph*, November 27.
Rees, P. 2014. *The Three Degrees: The Men Who Changed British Football Forever*. London: Constable.
Regis, C. 2010. *My Story (As Told to Chris Green)*. London: André Deutsch.
Ricoeur, P. 1999. "Memory and Forgetting." In *Questioning Ethics*, edited by R. Kearney and M. Dooley, 5–11. London: Routledge.
Simek, Nicole. 2015. "Stubborn Shadows." *Symploke* 23 (1–2): 363–373. https://muse.jhu.edu/article/605678.
Thomsen, Dorthe. 2013. *Livshistorien*. Århus Universitetsforlag.
Tinsley, M. 2018. Personal Email Correspondence, January 23.
Valluvan, S. 2016. "Conviviality and Multiculture: A Post-integration Sociology of Multi-ethnic Interaction." *Young* 24 (3): 204–221. https://doi.org/10.1177/1103308815624061.

Open Access This chapter is licensed under the terms of the Creative Commons Attribution 4.0 International License (http://creativecommons.org/licenses/by/4.0/), which permits use, sharing, adaptation, distribution and reproduction in any medium or format, as long as you give appropriate credit to the original author(s) and the source, provide a link to the Creative Commons license and indicate if changes were made.

The images or other third party material in this chapter are included in the chapter's Creative Commons license, unless indicated otherwise in a credit line to the material. If material is not included in the chapter's Creative Commons license and your intended use is not permitted by statutory regulation or exceeds the permitted use, you will need to obtain permission directly from the copyright holder.

CHAPTER 13

Impurity and Danger: Excerpt from *Cape Calypso*

Oscar Hemer

You *can* get lost in Stellenbosch. The first day at the Institute, ze walks out in the wrong direction, following Marais street instead of van Riebeck, and when ze realises the mistake and tries to correct it, without either a map or the direction of hir residence, ze soon gets disoriented in the lofty labyrinth of shaded pave walks and white rectangular buildings, departments, dormitories, all belonging to the University; like a city plan by Le Corbusier, sanitary, modern, conspicuously white, buzzing with students who have just returned from the summer break, Afrikaans-speaking, conspicuously white with scattered exceptions in pairs or small groups, their faces shades of brown, not black, *bruin-mense*, as they were benevolently branded by their white superiors. Ze is going to walk these streets every day in the coming months, but this first impression of disorientation will persist in a latent feeling of estrangement. Where is ze? It could be a campus town anywhere in the affluent West, California, Australia, a subtropical Holland—*Hottentot Holland*—a garden city with vineyards climbing the

---

O. Hemer (✉)
Faculty of Culture and Society, School of Arts and Communication, Malmö University, Malmö, Sweden
e-mail: oscar.hemer@mau.se

backdrop of the majestic mountains. This is the cradle of apartheid. It's hard to believe, unless you think of it as benevolent evil. D. F. Malan, the first prime minister of the apartheid state was chancellor of Stellenbosch University when his National Party ascended to power in 1948. His hat and pipe, a rock-hanger and a few bookshelves are left as curious props in a corner of the University museum, between the ethnographic display of tribal cultures and the dull mimicry of modern art. Dr. Hendrik Verwoerd, the engineer rather than the architect, the brutal implementer of the master plan, had been Professor of Sociology at this same university in the formative 1930s, but his imprint is somehow retouched from the records. His as staunch successor, John Vorster, was a former Law student at Stellenbosch, and Verwoerd's closest collaborator in the Ministry for Native Affairs, Werner Eiselen, had held the chair as Professor in *Volkekunde*, the science of physical and cultural anthropology that formed the academic basis for the ideology of apartness and separate development. Eiselen, the benevolent racist, loyal bureaucrat and perverse visionary, proposing total separation as the only way in which African cultures could be protected from the pernicious effects of urbanisation (Kross 2002: 60). Ze looks for vestiges of oppression, of surveillance, the fencing off of the barbarians at the gate, but dividing lines are invisible or internalised, not blurred; the campus security policing the streets is so discrete that one could take them for road workers in their orange vests. While xenophobia rampages the country, Stellenbosch remains a bubble, even when load shedding blacks out the streets, the whites confidently torch their way back to their moderately armoured residencies.

A discretely grey hardcover copy of the third impression (from 1970) is delivered with the eminent library service that brings whatever ze orders from the anonymous librarian all the way to hir desk within a day or two. The yellowed pages are full of pencil underlining and notes, and ze finds these reader's comments, made during the dark times, as intriguing as the text itself; the first library stamp is from 1975, the book has been frequently borrowed in the late '70s and early '80s, but only sporadically thereafter. How was it read, ze wonders, during the State of Emergency; as subversive critique or as ideological support of the politics of purity outlined and implemented by Afrikaner academics, all affiliated with Stellenbosch University. This was arguably the ideological cradle of apartheid (although two of the Afrikaner fellows protest vehemently against hir allegation, made in passing over lunch, and stress that the racial segregation was long established as an integral part of the British colonial indirect rule; group area laws were implemented already in 1913, after the formation of the union, long before the Nationalist Party's takeover in '48).

Ze imagines the author of these notes as one and the same Afrikaner student, who has struggled with the English, dictionary in hand, and had to look up and translate consecrated (*heilige*) and profane (*goddelose/heidense*). Written in 1966, in High Modernity, in the heyday of Western rationality and Technology-Optimism, *Purity and Danger* is a radical cultural self-examination—"...*[W]e shall not expect to understand other people's ideas of contagion, sacred or secular, until we have confronted our own*" (Douglas 1966: 28)—which portends the civilisation critique and the postmodern breakup of the '70s and '80s. High Modernity coincides with High Apartheid—a yearly growth rate of six to seven per cent, dislocations, evictions, expulsions, obscene exploitation, the negation of modernity, reversing the influx from country to city, returning unwanted labour units to the miserable reservoirs called homelands (later *Bantustans*), while the white citizens prosper in unprecedented wealth (Dubow 2014: 99–101).

Dirt is essentially disorder. Separating, purifying, demarcating and punishing transgressions have as their main function to impose system on an inherently untidy experience. Only by exaggerating differences (within-without, male-female, black-white) is a semblance of order created (Douglas 1966: 4).

A semblance of difference? False diversity—as the apartheid regime's encouraging of the con festivals in the Cape, letting the coloured show their colours; even the queers come out of the closets to parade at the white masters' back. The queer coloured, that is, subject to the indifferent white gaze in the non-existent public sphere, the non-public non-space of absent contagion.

Why? Simon, one of hir fellows at the Institute, gave hir the book with this intriguing title, by the late sociologist Charles Tilly (2006). Written under the verdict of a terminal cancer, which most certainly added a special clarity to the thought, it is, as the subtitle reads, about "what happens when people give reasons ... and why". Simon was one of the first to analyse the outbursts of deadly violence against "foreigners and strangers" in May and June 2008, a carnage reminiscent of and as abhorrent as the "black-on-black" butchery of the interregnum years. As ze is reading, new vile xenophobic attacks are being carried out, in Soweto and other black holes of the persisting apartheid cityscape, targeting Somali vendors, often in the presence of the police, who in some instances even participate in the looting. A month later Durban will explode in murderous rage, instigated by the Zulu king in leopard-skin garment, spreading inwards from the dismal townships to the city centre; ze will watch the footage in awe, the familiar street signs, the city mall, the burning tyres, threatening thugs with *pangas* and *iwisas* and kicked-around strangers running for shelter. Yesterday's breaking news of the bullying and harassment of black secondary school children by their white peers and self-appointed superiors will be forgotten. The concerned expert panels assembled on prime time in all the news channels to discuss why race is re-emerging as top obsession of the South African mind twenty years after the demise of apartheid will reconvene to explain the xenophobic logic of inclusion and exclusion.

Why is indeed the most pertinent question. Why do victims become perpetrators? Have the former guest workers in their own country simply internalised the *Bantustan* mentality?[1] Ze sees Heribert Adam and Kogila Moodley for a coffee at the Institute, after just having finished reading their comparative study on "xenophobia, citizenship and identity in South Africa, Canada and Germany". The chillingly premonitory analysis could not have been timelier. Why? Apartheid is only part of the answer, and Neo-liberalism but another partial reason. Xenophobic attitudes are equally strong among elites, black as white, and increasing in all groups, with Indians being slightly more tolerant than others. On the other hand, ecumenical tolerance still prevails; neither Islamism nor Islamophobia are as yet featuring in the public debate. The South African divided society has long learned to co-exist with diversity. That, says Heribert, is the main hope to overcome xenophobia. And yet now, in contrast to 2008, ANC leaders are coming out with coded xenophobic statements, Zuma's own son even breaking the code, in allegiance with the Leopard-skin pillbox king.

Sin is fundamentally conceived as a material impurity. Blood, a holy substance endowed with miraculous power, is expected to remove the stain of sin (Eichrodt 1933). But since the common verb for making atonement can be translated as both "wipe away" and "cover", the meaning may just as well be interpreted as "covering up one's guilt from the eyes of the offended party by means of reparation" (ibid.).

Covering up one's complicity... *Responsibility-in-complicity*. Ze orders Mark Sanders' analysis of the intellectual and apartheid; ze was aware of its existence, but never read it before, although ze read Sanders' later book on the TRC. Now *Complicities* appears as one of the really important analyses of the complexities at the core of the South African transition (*a good verdict for a book, to mature with age*).

"When opposition takes the form of a demarcation from something, it cannot, it follows, be untouched by that to which it opposes itself. *Opposition takes its first steps from a footing of complicity"* (Sanders 2002: 9). Therefore, the negotiation of complicity should be an essential moment in intellectual responsibility.

A year later, on hir return to the Western Cape, ze will disclose another correspondence; Jacob Dlamini's Askari, *the beautifully disturbing "story of collaboration and betrayal in the anti-apartheid struggle".*

How different would the history of apartheid sound, asks Dlamini rhetorically, if told not as the story of racial war but of what we might call a fatal intimacy between black and white South Africans (2014: 2)[2]? It is an intriguing assumption, given that the subject of the interrogation is Glory Sedibe, the defector, traitor, sell-out, turn-coat, collaborator, Comrade September *turned apartheid agent* Mr X1, abhorred by both his former fellow freedom fighters in the ANC and his later white trash superiors at Vlakplaas. Complicity is mutual, collaboration always marked by ambiguity ... The ruthless Askari, perpetrator and victim, fell outside the frame of the TRC. Nobody wants to acknowledge that in the apartheid dusk most cats were grey.

The most captivating part of Adam and Moodley's book is the couple's concluding autobiographies; she, an Indian from Durban, granddaughter of indentured labourers, he a German war child, a catholic conservative turned radical rebel of the Frankfurt Institute for Social Research, their fates unite in Durban during high apartheid, transgressors of the Immorality act forced in exile for loving across the race barrier; now Canadians, world citizens, intercontinental commuters...

Hir own biography has none of the cosmopolitan ingredients. Ze was privileged middle-class, though growing up in one of Malmö's "Million programme" inner suburbs, and naturally assumed an attitude of superiority and alienation. Only after moving to Stockholm, to become a journalist, did ze start to identify with Malmö, and precisely for the "cosmopolitanism" ze had hardly experienced hirself. The Yugoslav immigrants, ze remembers, were commonly patronised. Southern Europeans in general were looked down upon. In retrospect it is hard to understand where this inherent prejudice came from. Hir family was liberal, open-minded. Culturally homogeneous Sweden of the 1960s was programmatically modern and affirmatively anti-racist (*avant la lettre*), with its prominent jazz scene and mixed marriages. The Swedish Sin was transgressive, the most defiant degree of Immorality. Ze received Stokely Carmichael's *Black Power* as a guerdon in 7th grade, while never even reflecting on hir own assumed sense of privilege and superiority. Ze recalls with shame the bullying of the few Jews, not for being Jews, but because they were strange, non-conformant, yet trying hard to appease, bearing the humiliation with resignation, and how ze never interfered in their defence but rather added to the insults. This is as shameful as hir blatantly racist declarations after the first (tough) encounters with the US reality on hir adolescent great tour of the Americas. In the course of the journey's first three days, ze was robbed twice, at the YMCA in New York and the Greyhound bus station in San Francisco, and then next to raped by a Vietnam veteran who helped hir report the second robbery and offered hir his place to stay, only to demand that ze give him a handjob, and barely letting hir get away with that.

At lunch the next day, Ulrike from Austria, who was surprised that Swedes would go to Turkey—and even Iran!—for transplantations, and who, when confronted, admitted her prejudice, says that the interesting thing about studying apartheid at its roots is that it forces you to confront the racist in yourself.

When ze comes upon the central passage on *Dirt as matter out of place*, ze finds to hir surprise that there are neither notes nor underlining in four pages. Has the reader jumped them, or skimmed them so extensively that the reading literally has left no marks? Ze thinks of the scribbled notes as reflections of the words' imprint on the reader's mind; reading as a physical, bodily, sensual practice, the tangible text tattooed over yellowish pages of living skin.

Where there is dirt there is system. Dirt is the by-product of a systematic ordering and classification of matter, in so far as ordering involves *rejecting inappropriate elements*. Hence, "our pollution behaviour is the reaction which condemns any object or idea likely to confuse or contradict cherished classifications" (Douglas 1966: 35).

In South Africa, by contrast to India, it's not the clash between dogmatic conflicting identities, but the very opposite: insecure, fragile identities searching to assert themselves, develop self-esteem, escape humiliation and reverse denigration (Adam and Moodley 2013: 193). Hence, it's rather a lack of identity that instigates murder. Xenophobic violence as identity assertion reverses daily humiliation. Reverses and relieves. Perpetration is apparently joyful, as noted by Simon (*funny that ze come across his quote just after eating lunch with him*); the emotional dimension of xenophobia symbolically frees the perpetrators from the real deprivation (Bekker 2010: 137).

The re-appearance of *necklacing*; the powerless community assuming power by deciding over life and death in a gruesome ritual. *Punishment by burning tyre*. The stabbing of Emmanuel Sithole in Alexandra in front of the camera captures the moment of murderous impulse, whereas the necklacing of Angolan shebeen owner Joseph Hipandulwa in Kayelitsha is unbearable to even imagine (Adam and Moodley, 195). Like the beheading by knife of IS prisoners. Is the gruesomeness the perversion of this humiliation in reverse? Cleansing by fire, by fear, by fury—targeting the vulnerable, powerless *makwerekwere*, while the real culprits for the misery of the murderers are immune from their rage, since they have the power to retaliate. Julius Malema's young supporters put tire necklaces on statues commemorating World War I ... (*Hans-Dieter, the new German fellow warns that the removal of Cecil Rhodes from the UCT campus will be the beginning of a Culture War:* Soon they'll start burning books that remind of colonial times).

The Institute is a refuge. Nobody disturbs hir; the only requirement is to be there, in situ, to participate in the lavish lunches, Monday to Friday, and the afternoon seminar every week, when the researchers present their findings to each other. After seminars there is always wine and snacks, generous yet moderate; what remains in the bottles is left to self-service when tables are cleaned, but nobody would dream of overdoing the welcome, let alone go somewhere else to continue the party. Some even go back to their offices after the seminars. Michael, the composer, artist in residence since more than half a year, virtually lives in his room on the ground floor, with an electric piano and a mattress, on which he naps after lunch, and the note blades of his work in progress papering the walls. But he is receding to

Cape Town over the weekends, where his wife is soon going to meet up from their second home in London.

Elmi, a surgeon from Cape Town, commutes from home and is sometimes late or not appearing at all, because she has been summoned to her clinic. "I had to do a kidney", she excuses herself with a smile, and looks as if she had just come from an invigorating session of Pilates at the nearby gym. She works on a project on the global organ trade and transplantation industry and speaks, in her seminar, about the difficulties in matching organ donors and recipients when the genetic variation is as vast as it is in South Africa (*ze pricked up hir ears: did ze get that right? Is genetic variation a euphemism for racial differences? Does mixing augment or diminish the genetic variation? Are there strictly medical arguments to support creolisation and contamination?*) Ze knocked on Elmi's door for an answer, but she couldn't give hir a straight one. In the long run, yes, but in a short perspective there is vulnerability. In the long run we are all coloured. But in the short run we are all dead. *Vanitas vanitatum omnia vanitas.*

The fear of blood mixing haunts not only the Boer, but all white settlers;

> in an abyssal historical irony, given the origins of the tongue in which Afrikaner nationalists ground their identity, it shuns hybridity and measures purity. (Sanders 2002: 82)

Not only the hybrid is abominated, but everything that breaks the classifications, stated by the merciless God. An English-speaking black is the most frightening abomination. Even the opponents of apartheid (*avant la lettre*) opt for racist solutions. Olive Schreiner, writer and feminist pioneer, and explicit opponent to Cecil Rhodes' colonial savagery, talks of South Africa as "a mixture of races", but only in a social sense, since she, like everyone else, opposes miscegenation; her vision of a federation of South African states, as opposed to the Union of 1910, is a vision of a racially separated society that clearly resembles the radical apartheid visions of ethnic nations in separate development (ibid.).

The crux is of course simply that the whites are a minority, and in a state where all citizens were given equal opportunities, they would be a powerless minority. In a state of unchecked miscegenation, they would be "ploughed under" by the black masses, tarnished, vanished … *tainted by the tar brush.*

God's stepchildren ... Coetzee points to the direct parallel to the Christian ideas of 'falling from grace' and 'original sin' (1988: 141). Shame is not strong enough to denote the original mixing of fluids because black blood is a form of defilement; a formless horror evading description – much like the HIV virus, which can be kept at bay, at best, but never cured. The only way the polluted community can cleanse itself is by expelling the polluter. And the only way that the responsible polluter can put an end to the suffering is by sexual abstinence, thereby killing the taint (virus) and extinguishing the bloodline that carries it – the ever-damned tradition of hybrid impurity.

For the architects of apartheid, apart-ness means the self-determination of every nation, and the principle that no nation be dominant over another. Those who take this notion seriously propose *Total Separation*. Werner Eiselen, the founder of *Volkekunde*, never described African cultures as explicitly inferior to "white" culture, but regarded them as being in a state of decline, due to the corrupting contact with "white" society. Subsequently, they ought to be protected from foreign (white, modern) influence and given the chance to develop in line with their own particular cultural imperatives. The favoured metaphor to illustrate that each culture contained its own dynamic for development was Hans Christian Andersen's fairy tale about the ugly duckling that is able to flourish only when it finds itself among its own kind (Eiselen 1948).

Eiselen (1920) conjures the image of Bantu barbarians at the gate, ironically alluding to the white paranoia provoked by "black-peril" propaganda. But, instead of enhancing the advancement of black intellectuals, his conclusion is that they should be saved from the inevitable disappointment of realising that, however hard they tried, they would never be accepted members of the white society, due to racial prejudice. The mission-educated blacks (*the abominable English-speaking blacks, mimicking English gentlemen*) were doomed to be an "intellectual proletariat" (ibid.).[3]

The only proponent of mixing is Breyten Breytenbach, who launches the idea of *Zuid-Afrikanerdom* as opposed to the nationalist purism of Afrikanerdom, and defines it as a culture of hybridity (*basterskap*).

> We are a bastard people with a bastard language. Our nature is one of bastardy. It is good and beautiful thus. We should be compost, decomposing to be able to combine again in other forms. Only, we have walked into the trap of the bastard who has acquired power. [...] And like all bastards – uncertain of their identity – we began to adhere to the concept of purity. That is apartheid. Apartheid is the law of the bastard. (Breytenbach 1982: 156)

Note the ambiguous value in the word bastard... *Bastervolk, bastertaal, basterskap* are positive notions, on which a new inclusive identity can be built—but the baster is a *bastard* in the conventional sense that the word has attained. And when Breytenbach returns to Paradise a decade later, at the beginning of the transition, it's only the latter meaning that remains:

> The Afrikaners aren't such reprehensible bastards after all. If you leave them to their own devices, they don't really bother other people. The problem is that their minds were warped by European exclusivism. At least they have a modicum of respect for nature and for animals. (Breytenbach 1993: 80)

Elmi's husband, Stephanus, is a musicologist, and also a friend of Michael and Aryan. Ze meets the three of them at the screening of Aryan's latest film, *Threnody for the Victims of Marikana*, at the University of the Western Cape. The threnody for the striking mineworkers of Marikana in the Gauteng, who were massacred by the police on 16 August 2012, is a shortened version of the film *Night Is Coming*, Aryan's contribution, as one of three invited artists, to an academic collaboration between the universities of Stellenbosch, Oxford and Harvard on *Music and Landscape*. The film was supposed to be screened at Harvard, at the third seminar/workshop, but it wasn't because it was thought to have misrepresented what happened in Stellenbosch. (*Not what the prominent participants had expected, after flying in, having a good time at the restaurants and wineries and club floors, and flying back to the USK with the contention that the New South Africa has come a long way*, as Aryan put it, or as ze reads his scorn.) The threnody leaves nobody unmoved. What does it mean to look at the footage of the massacre through the eyes of the killers? Not the bragging perpetrators, as in Joshua Oppenheim's *The Act of Killing*, but yet the ones who pull the trigger, the police, the state of decision, life or death, the police state; we are looking over the shoulder of the executioners of a ritual murder, in a state of police, we are witnessing and partaking, complicit in the decomposition, seeing through listening, hearing through watching, the percussive reality of South Africa. Marikana is disturbingly absent in the public memory, a void in the story of the post-apartheid, post-transition nation in the making, the dissonance of an unimaginable Sharpeville in democracy, a Soweto uprising, a state of emergency, a red alert, again, rewinded memories erased; the violent democracy, the virulent police state. And the presence of this absence, the melancholy of the threnody ... Aryan, urged to comment, sits down among the audience and lets the images speak, that's how he works as an artist, the provocateur, *l'enfant terrible*, but never as an empty gesture, always with a purpose, a bit like Jean Rouch and Edgar Morin in *Chronique d'un été* (1960), turning the tables, calling the viewer ... The productivity of inadequacy (*ze can't quite remember the meaning of that note; oh yes, it had to do with Harvard's refusal to screen Aryan's film, with the consequence that it travelled far beyond usual academic circles*). His inadequate report of an academic encounter, a conference proceeding contaminated with the brutal footage of the police state. Yes, a perfect example of contamination in the sense that ze is striving at in hir yet to outline project.

How can we live with the presence of the absence? What do we do with the knowledge? "Who is the main actor?" asks one in the audience, a student in his late twenties, scared, as he puts it, by the suggested continuity from the apartheid state. "Who is the responsible?" "You are", says Aryan. "What are you going to do now?"

The troubling thing about Marikana is that it doesn't go away. It is not an event with a beginning and an end, it is still there, in its present absence or absent presence... we are watching it as it unfolds over the shoulder of the police, complicit in the act, in our own inaction, unable to think rationally, adequately.

Somebody asks what Musicology and Stellenbosch are getting out of it, and Stephanus rightly comments that Aryan would not have been able to do the film about Marikana without them. He needs that kind of structure. Aryan does not object. It's a brilliant example of miscegenation of art and academia, an exemplary illustration of what art and academia can accomplish—in disjuncture.

Pollution is like an inverted form of humour, it does not amuse, but the structure of its symbolism uses comparison and double meaning like the structure of a joke (Douglas 1966: 122). The symbolism of the body's boundaries is used in this kind of unfunny wit to express danger to community boundaries. The Coorgs in Karnataka were so obsessed by fear of dangerous impurities entering their system that they treated the body as if it were a beleaguered town, every ingress and exit guarded for spies and traitors. Anything issuing from the body is never to be re-admitted, but strictly avoided (123). *The sociological counterpart of this anxiety is a care to protect the political and cultural unity of a minority group* (124).

> Again, it's hir own underlining – or, rather, hir exact transcription, supplemented with "Appadurai" and an expression mark. Ze makes the note to check whether A. refers to D. He must! But you can never be sure. The forking paths often run in parallel, without crossing. In their analysis of xenophobia, Adam and Moodely referred to Freud's narcissism of small differences (1961), but not to Appadurai's *Fear of Small Numbers* (2006), let alone *Purity and Danger*, which latter they of course most probably were aware of, as cultivated intellectuals, but not regarded as a relevant reference. Discipline borders are just as carefully policed as genre borders; no, not even necessarily policed, there is simply no cross-going traffic.

Anne Phillips, with whom ze invites Antjie Krog for lunch at the Institute, says she admires hir courage to write about South Africa. She has herself decided not to, after realising the complexities. Antjie also questions hir project in an indirect way. Writing across borders, she says, presupposes that you are confident within your borders, inferring that the vast majority of South Africans aren't; all those who are not writing in English for a white audience (and a white publisher). Ze objects and argues against the seemingly essentialist position; the same that ze criticised in hir reading of *Begging to Be Black* (2009), the somehow discouraging conclusion of the Transition trilogy, that it is impossible to imagine the other as yourself. For a moment the lunch talk is turning uncomfortable and ze wonders why ze envisioned collaborating with Antjie in hir research proposal. But then afterwards, in hir office, she gives some valuable suggestions, as if their collaboration were already a fact and the farewell is on a friendly collegial note. (*The day after ze receives a mail from her, saying: i think why we do not see eye to eye is because both of us are trying to address the intolerance we see in our respective societies, but your intolerance is a first world one and mine a third world one and behove different strategies.*)

> Envy and narcissism. Envy turned on outsiders. The former victims turned perpetrators single out target groups for their apparently superior abilities. Violence becomes a desperate but decisive method of last resort with which perpetrators compensate for their own shortcomings (Du Toit and Kotze 2011). The real

culprits—the indigenous elite in cahoots with the old ruling-class—cannot be targeted, since they still wallow in the glory of liberation and effectively silence dissent. The government's lip-service condemnation of xenophobia conceals the fact "that ours is a neo-apartheid state managed by yesterday's anti-apartheid revolutionaries" (Mngxitama 2009).

The threat of the "nearly-we" who imperil our self-concept. "The ugliest manifestations of racism are reserved for immigrants who look, act and talk like us. The more they try to emulate and imitate us, the harder they attempt to belong, the more ferocious our rejection of them" (Vaknin 2011). Germany's extermination of the Jews is the historical proof of this logic (and a forceful argument against assimilation, as proposed by anti-migrant nationalists). But why does minimal difference trigger hostility? Adam and Moodley quote Indian psychoanalyst Sudhir Kakar (1996: 189):

> The community in which we are socialised is part of our personal identity. And the clash between internalisation of social rules, i.e. *culture*, and a person's natural drives is solved through the projection of "bad" representations onto others; first inanimate objects and animals and later people and other groups.

The disavowed bad representations need such "reservoirs"—Muslims for Hindus, Arabs for Jews and vice versa—which also serve as convenient repositories for rages for which no clear-cut addressee is available (Volkan 2006).

> Is it really reversible? Some groups are obviously more prone to become reservoirs of bad representations; currently Muslims and Gypsies, previously Jews, Kaffirs, Coolies, Boers... Aryans vs. Jews is not reversible, nor Americans vs. Mexicans. Not even Hindus vs. Muslims, even if that would be closest to an equal and reversible demonization. (There is an interesting passage in David Malouf's novel *The Great World* (1990), centred on the Australian World War II experience, when the Australian POWs realize that they, in the eyes of the Japanese, are no better than coolies; that the Japanese in fact wish to turn them into coolies – a fate that they, in their self-assured confidence of white superiority, regard as unfathomable, as the horror of horrors.)

Pollution rules, in contrast to moral rules, are unequivocal. They do not depend on intention or a nice balancing of rights and duties. The only material question is whether a forbidden act has taken place or not (Douglas 1966: 130). Physical crossing of the social barrier is treated as a dangerous pollution. The polluter becomes a doubly wicked object of reprobation, first because he crossed the line and second because he endangered others (139).

When attacked from the outside, solidarity within is fostered. When attacked from within by wanton individuals, these can be punished, and the structure publicly reaffirmed. But the structure can also be self-defeating. *Perhaps all social systems are built on contradiction, in some sense at war with themselves* (140).

Again, a lucid, revolutionary thought, against the grain of her time, defying both socialist and liberal utopianism; not the end of history, nor the realisation of classless communism, but the perpetual paradox of dual impossibilities: neither growth nor degrowth, neither black nor white.

Ze tries to imagine the mental regimentation and self-deception of an entire community, the complacency of complicity, maybe as banal as the evil of indifference. Or ignorance. The benevolent police state. The very building for the Arts and Social Sciences, where Volkekunde was taught until 2002, disturbs the harmonious picture with its blatant brutality. The concrete colossus, previously named after Verwoerd's successor, B. J. Vorster, was constructed on the rubble of the evicted "coloured area", Die Vlake, overlooking the new white neighbourhood on the other side of Merriman Avenue, anonymous one-storey buildings, chain-houses, villas, a huge gas station, parking lots; no traces, not even a plaque of remembrance of this Stellenbosch's own District Six. The former Lückhoff Skool, which was also given or traded to the expanding university, is now a centre for community interaction, dutifully telling its story in non-committal half-truths, like the grand display of the university's history, decade by decade, in the University Museum. It would take hir many weeks to find out, but that was where ze ended up in hir first disorientation, a lively square in what had once been Die Vlake, now, again, a fringe area, where the white city ends, a Somali coffee shop and a coloured hairdresser, where ze drops in for a haircut and asks for the direction to Dorp Street, the only street name ze recalls; two months later ze will accidentally rediscover the hairdresser, who will smilingly recall hir and repeat the haircut, and suddenly the pieces of the inner and outer map fall together, and the contours of this other parallel city appear in a flash of illumination, like the stroboscopic lights of the Springbok Pub, less than a stone throw away in the corner of Andringa and Merriman. It all makes sense.

Dirt is (only) dangerous as long as some identity clings to it. When identity is lost (pulverised, rotted, dissolved) it enters the mass of common rubbish. It is unpleasant to poke about in the refuse to try to recover anything, for this revives identity (160). *So long as identity is absent, rubbish is harmless and does not even create ambiguous perceptions. Even the bones of buried kings rouse little awe and the thought that the air is full of the dust of corpses of bygone races has no power to move. Where there is no differentiation there is no defilement.*

The quest for purity is pursued by rejection. It follows that when purity is not a symbol but something lived, it must be poor and barren. It is part of our condition that the purity for which we strive and sacrifice so much turns out to be hard and dead as a stone when we get it. [*"Purity" and "rejection" are here not only underlined but encircled by the anonymous Afrikaner student, as is the following entire sentence:*]

Purity is the enemy of change, of ambiguity and compromise.

What is, then, the attraction of the barren, of that which is hard and dead as stone? Sartre (1948) portrays the anti-semite as someone who wants to adopt a mode of life in which reasoning and the quest for truth plays only a subordinate part, in which nothing is sought except what has already been found, in which one never becomes anything but what one already was.

But is it a choice to reason falsely? Purity cannot be consciously conceived as un-true. Yet anything that questions the assumed truthfulness and threatens the order will be condemned as pollution – or contamination.

Douglas, more radical in thought than Sartre, critiques the implicit division between "our thinking" and the rigid black and white reasoning of the anti-semite. Because, she writes [*and this is doubly underlined and encircled*] the yearning for rigidity is in us all (162). *The little perpetrator.* Sanders expounds on a self-critical remark in the TRC report, on its failure to focus sufficiently on the dimension of "moral responsibility", stating that the attention on *the deeds of the exceptional perpetrator led to "fail[ure] to recognise the 'little perpetrator' in each of us"* (Sanders 2002: 3); whereas Breytenbach adds the insight that, as an intellectual, it is not enough to resist the system in its overt manifestations, but *it is necessary to find the roots of the conversion of foldedness with the other into forms of complicity in its denial* (ibid.: 157). This is what makes apartheid exemplary for the intellectual as a figure of responsibility-in-complicity. It is necessary to have not only an ideal of freedom or autonomy but an account of sufficient power to capture how that ideal is, at a fundamental level, susceptible to perversion as something like apartheid (ibid.: 190).

The lasting insight of Black Consciousness was that apartheid was not, in any essential sense, an achievement of separateness at all, but it was a system of enforced separation that, paradoxically, generated an unwanted intimacy with an oppressive other [*unwanted, or ambiguously desired?*]. In a narrow sense, it decreed apartness; in a general sense, it disavowed relation (foldedness in human being with the other). "If such a disavowal of relation is what tends toward support for apartheid, it is an acknowledgement of this complicity and its disavowal at the heart of apartheid that is the essential starting point of any opposition to apartheid".

Already on hir first Saturday night in Stellenbosch, Aryan suggested that ze go to "try hir moves" at the Springbok Pub. Ze was tired and hesitant; if it weren't for the expectation to see Aryan there, ze would not have gone, thinking that it would be a posh or hip show-off venue for the beautiful people (*why did ze expect that?*). It was the opposite. Ze had a couple of Black Label (*Black Labour, White Guilt*) in the sports bar, to dare approach the dance floor in the other room, irresistibly drawn by the drums and base and the videos projected on the wall, assuming to be viewed as a sexagenarian voyeur, a freak, the only white among coloureds, certainly the eldest on the floor. But the atmosphere is one of familiarity, the women in their thirties or forties, with their friends or their husbands, curiously observing hir and inviting hir to dance with them, embedding hir in unpretentious hospitality, and ze is overwhelmed by their welcoming warmth. The sound of the Cape, the progenies of this crossroads, the breed of three hundred years of intimacy, wanted or unwanted, defying the boundaries of slave and master, white and black; the *bruin-mense* as the Afrikaners called them, in affection and contempt, less than white but better than black, privileged among the unprivileged, yet despised for being half-caste, for being neither-nor, without tribe—the left-overs of humankind, as Madame De Klerk so lovingly called them. Bastards, like the Afrikaners, but of a darker shade; the fine divisive line could cut a family in two, siblings ending on each side of the insurmountable border. Humble bastards, inconsolably compromised by their not-quite-white-ness. On hir second visit to the Springbok Pub, ze arrives at the end of a birthday party; now ze's recognised, prompted to eat and drink, and one of the pitiful husbands teaches hir to dance properly ... Syncopating surprisingly to—ze searches in vain for the proper metaphor—Saturday night insouciance.

After finishing reading ze still has problems to grapple the ambiguity. Dame Douglas to-be outlines a possible dichotomy between dirt-affirming and dirt-rejecting philosophies. Whereas the latter are typically incomplete but optimistic, the former tend to be more complete (complex) and also pessimistic. Yet, although fascinated by transgressions, she remains herself essentially a conservative friend of order.

Notes

1. D. Everatt in special issue of the journal *Politikon*, 2011, in Adam and Moodley (2013: 37).
2. The notion of "fatal intimacy" is borrowed from Njabulo Ndebele.
3. The term "intellectual proletariat" was borrowed from historian Arnold Toynbee.

References

Adam, H. and K. Moodley. 2013. *Imagined Liberation: Xenophobia, Citizenship and Identity in South Africa, Germany and Canada*. Stellenbosch: SUN Press.
Appadurai, A. 2006. *Fear of Small Numbers: An Essay on the Geography of Anger*. Durham: Duke University Press.
Bekker, S. 2010. "Explaining Violence Against Foreigners and Strangers in Urban South Africa: Outbursts During May and June 2008." *The African Yearbook of International Law* 16, 125–149.
Breytenbach, B. 1982. *A Season in Paradise*. New York: Persea Books.
Breytenbach, B. 1993. *Return to Paradise*. London: Faber and Faber.
Coetzee, J. M. 1988. *White Writing: On the Culture of Letters in South Africa*. New Haven and London: Yale University Press.
Dlamini, J. 2014. *Askari: A Story of Collaboration and Betrayal in the Anti-Apartheid Struggle*. Johannesburg: Jacana.
Douglas, M. 1966. *Purity and Danger: An Analysis of Concepts of Pollution and Taboo*. London: Routledge & Kegan Paul.
Dubow, S. 2014. *Apartheid 1948–1994*. Oxford: Oxford University Press.

Du Toit, P. and H. Kotze. 2011. *Liberal Democracy and Peace in South Africa*. Johannesburg: Palgrave Macmillan.
Eichrodt, W. 1933. *Theologie des Alten Testaments*. Leipzig: Hinrich.
Eiselen, W. W. M. 1920. "Die Naturellevraagstuk: 'n Lesing gchou op 7 Mei 1920 voor die Filosofiese Vereniging van die Universiteit van Stellenbosch".
Eiselen, W. W. M. 1948. "Die Bevolkingsvraagstuk van Suid-Afrika, Sosiologies Beskou met Besondere Aandag aan die Arbeidsgemeenskap van Blankes en Naturelle en die Implikasies van Apartheid," 'n referaat gelewer op die Simposium van i Julie, 1948, van die Jaarvergadering van die Akademie vir Wetenskap en Kuns te Orange Free State.
Freud, S. 1961. *Civilization and Its Discontents*. 1st American ed. New York: W. W. Norton.
Kaganof, A. 2014. *Night Is Coming: Threnody for the Victims of Marikana*. Cape Town.
Kakar, S. 1996. *The Colors of Violence*. Chicago: The University of Chicago Press.
Krog, A. 2009. *Begging to Be Black*. Cape Town: Random House Struik.
Kross, C. 2002. "W. W. M. Eiselen: Architect of Apartheid Education." In *The History of Education Under Apartheid, 1948–1994: The Doors of Learning and Culture Shall Be Opened*, edited by P. Kallaway. New York: Peter Lang.
Malouf, D. 1990. *The Great World*. London: Chatto & Windus.
Mngxitama, A. 2009. "We Are Not All Like That: Race, Class and Nation After Apartheid." In *Go Home or Die Here: Xenophobia and the Reinvention of Difference in South Africa*, edited by S. Hassim, T. Kupe, and E. Worby, 189–208. Johannesburg: Wits University Press.
Sanders, M. 2002. *Complicities: The Intellectual and Apartheid*. Durham, NC: Duke University Press.
Sartre, J.-P. 1948. *Anti-Semite and Jew [Réflexions sur la question juive]*. New York: Schocken Books.
South Africa, Truth and Reconciliation Commission. 1999. *TRC Report*. Vols. 1–5. London: Macmillan.
Tilly, C. 2006. *Why? [What Happens When People Give Reasons… and Why]*. Princeton, NJ: Princeton University Press.
Vaknin, S. 2011. *Malignant Self-Love: Narcissism Revisited*. Prague: Narcissism Publishers.
Volkan, V. 2006. *Killing in the Name of Identity*. New York: Ingram.

Open Access This chapter is licensed under the terms of the Creative Commons Attribution 4.0 International License (http://creativecommons.org/licenses/by/4.0/), which permits use, sharing, adaptation, distribution and reproduction in any medium or format, as long as you give appropriate credit to the original author(s) and the source, provide a link to the Creative Commons license and indicate if changes were made.

The images or other third party material in this chapter are included in the chapter's Creative Commons license, unless indicated otherwise in a credit line to the material. If material is not included in the chapter's Creative Commons license and your intended use is not permitted by statutory regulation or exceeds the permitted use, you will need to obtain permission directly from the copyright holder.

CHAPTER 14

Seeing Johannesburg Anew: Conviviality and Opacity in Khalo Matabane's *Conversations on a Sunday Afternoon*

Kerry Bystrom

In the early months of 2017, the South African cities of Johannesburg and Pretoria saw over 30 immigrant shops looted, homes burnt down, and a mass anti-immigrant march. This violence was sparked, according to some commentators, by Johannesburg mayor Herman Mashaba's proclamation that '[migrants] are holding our country to ransom and I am going to be the last South African to allow it'.[1] Its targets: foreign nationals from other parts of Africa, including Somalis, Nigerians and Zimbabweans, who were drawn to South Africa since the end of apartheid in 1994 for the physical safety and economic prosperity it seemed to promise. These events seem an uncanny replay of similar attacks in 2015, when King Goodwill Zwelinthini's remarks brought about mass violence in KwaZulu-Natal (Desai 2015: 247–248). They further echo the riots of 2008 which began in the Johannesburg township of Alexandra but spread out across the country. In total over 100,000 people were displaced and 62 so-called foreigners

K. Bystrom (✉)
Bard College Berlin, Berlin, Germany
e-mail: k.bystrom@berlin.bard.edu

© The Author(s) 2020
O. Hemer et al. (eds.), *Conviviality at the Crossroads*,
https://doi.org/10.1007/978-3-030-28979-9_14

(including black South Africans of smaller ethnic groups) were killed (see, *inter alia*, Landau 2010: 213–214; Strauss 2011: 104; Desai 2015).

The 2008 riots themselves did not come out of nowhere but, as we will see, reflected hostility building since apartheid ended and democracy as well as a 'new' South African nationalism was inaugurated in 1994. As Achille Mbembe argues, to understand and effectively counter the logic of 'nationalism', 'national interest' and 'national security' driving this consistent hostility and violence against immigrants—habits of thought and action themselves imposed on the African continent through the process of colonisation and lodged ever more securely in place through the racialised intensification of global neo-liberal capitalism—requires rethinking basic understandings of identity, sovereignty, social ties and political membership, in a way that allows us to deprioritise borders and emphasise 'flows, networks and circulation' (2017a, b). Mbembe writes: 'To come up with an entirely different paradigm consonant with the deep spirit of our own [African] history, we explicitly need to embrace our long-held traditions of flexible, networked sovereignty, mutual security, integration through incorporation and of universal right to temporary sojourn (hospitality)' (2017b).

This is a massive task, to be sure. Yet some years previously, in their collection *Johannesburg: The Elusive Metropolis* (2008), Mbembe and Sarah Nuttall pointed to part of the way forward when they highlighted modes of reading the city based on the encounters and interdependencies that make up quotidian urban life. By examining the city as something composed of 'actual bodies, images, forms, footprints, and memories' as well as 'infrastructures, technologies and legal entities', they suggest, Johannesburg can be productively redefined as an 'Afropolitan' zone (Mbembe and Nuttall 2008: 8, 24). Turning the focus on the individual as he or she makes the city, materially and imaginatively, and in relation with others—rather than reiterating a gaze that clumps people together into groups with differential claims to a city that pre-exists them—decentres the mass prospect created through nationalist logics of interest, security and exclusion and the borders this prospect necessitates.

In this chapter, I pose Khalo Matabane's experimental film *Conversations on a Sunday Afternoon* (2005) as a visionary text that helps us imagine such an approach, as it conjures Johannesburg anew by examining the desires and lived experiences of citizens, refugees and immigrants as they intersect in the city and ultimately revives at least the dream of this city as a site of hospitality. I use two main theoretical lenses to parse this film: *conviviality* and *opacity*. The first speaks to everyday encounters across race, gender, ethnicity, and other relevant social distinctions which form the weave of postcolonial urban life and which can, at least in Paul Gilroy's famous formulation, generate a creolised, vibrant and welcoming counterculture to the sharpening ethnic definitions and divisions of modern society (2005: xv; see also Nowicka and Vertovec 2014: 344). As Magdalena Nowicka and Steven Vertovec put it, conviviality is fundamentally concerned with 'how to make spaces more positively interactive, or conversely how spaces might become more convivial through everyday practices and routines of people inhabiting them' (2014: 350). While it has many resonances with cosmopolitanism, it seeks to take more fully into account the unequal power relations lurking in cosmopolitical theory and grapples with the limits of multiculturalism as a model for society (Gilroy 2005: 59; Nowicka and Vertovec 2014: 346). It is also fundamentally bound up with feeling and affect (Gutiérrez Rodríguez 2011). As I will show, Matabane's film is centrally about how ordinary interactions (or what Gilroy calls 'ordinary virtues and ironies [of] listening, looking, discretion, friendship' [2005: 67]) in the parks and streets of Johannesburg—with all of their affective intensities—may bridge the deep rifts between people of different races, genders and nationalities who inhabit this specific urban space.

While highlighting how tracing and feeling solidarity is key to combatting old and new forms of segregation, however, Matabane is careful not to romanticise everyday encounters. Indeed, his film shows just how tenuous the ties created through them can be as it underscores the need to unsettle assumptions regarding easy translation across difference underlying many understandings of conviviality.[2] For this reason, I turn to Édouard Glissant's (1990) concept of opacity. Glissant suggests how European (or in the case of Matabane's film otherwise privileged by virtue of citizenship) subjects tend to demand 'transparency' from others in order to classify them as fully human, as people deserving of respect and hospitality (1990: 189–190). Yet, 'to feel in solidarity with [an Other] or to build with him or to like what he does, it is not necessary for me to grasp him. It is not necessary to try to become the other (to become other) nor to "make" him in my image' (Glissant 1990: 193). Rather, what is called for is 'respect for mutual forms of opacity' both of the individual of specific communities (Glissant 1990: 194). How to come to this respect for opacity is a key dilemma represented in *Conversations on a Sunday Afternoon*. The close reading of the film below suggests that developing habits of vision or attentiveness that encompass conviviality and opacity together may be crucial for bringing into being a critically 'Afropolitan' space—one that acknowledges difference and conflict while being open to the other and in fact made in common with him or her, and one based in local models of flow and circulation to which Mbembe (2017b) points.

Matabane, who came of age more or less with the start of the country's democracy, has been hailed as a key member of a new generation of young black filmmakers (Moyer-Duncan 2011: 72). He spent much of his early career making activist documentary films. As he notes in an interview with Audrey McCluskey, he sees the 'essence of filmmaking' as 'a response to injustice':

> What do I feel about a world that has so much inequality in it, so much injustice, and [such] lack of compassion, even from black people. My films are like a little guerilla warfare. That's how I like to think about filmmaking – war against [oppressive] systems. (2009: 122; see also Moyer-Duncan 2011: 73)

Such an orientation is clear in works leading up to *Conversations*, including *The Young Lions* (1999), which traces how militant revolutionaries from the MK (the armed wing of the ANC) experience 'freedom' and *Love in the Time of Sickness* (2001), focused on the impact of HIV and AIDS. Work following *Conversations* (2005), itself generically hybrid, has turned towards feature films but continue a politically focused and issue-based approach, as evident from titles like *State of Violence* (2010) and *Nelson Mandela: The Myth & Me* (2013).[3]

The issue he tackles in *Conversations* is the influx of migrants to Johannesburg from war-torn regions that occurred after the end of apartheid and the relationship that South Africans have to these immigrants. If the film precedes the xenophobic riots of 2008 and their more recent iterations mentioned in this chapter's opening, Matabane draws attention to gathering rainclouds announcing a storm (Moyer-Duncan 2011: 73). As many scholars have pointed out, South African democracy was marked by a paradox regarding foreign immigrants and asylum seekers from its very start (see, *inter alia*, Peberdy 2001; Landau 2010; Strauss 2011: 104).[4] Sally Peberdy, for example, details how, on the one hand, the ANC promulgated a progressive, human rights-based constitutional order that values diversity and offers certain protections to all individuals living in South Africa regardless of citizenship. It also reached out towards the rest of the continent through African Renaissance discourse. On the other hand, officials and organs of the state discursively and operationally excluded non-nationals and black African non-nationals in particular (Peberdy 2001: 16). She shows convincingly how the ANC's national project, which had the positive aim of providing a sense of belonging to all South Africans after the exclusions of apartheid, was built on a xenophobic logic that stressed the difference between citizens and non-citizens and their entitlements (2001: 24, 28–29). Black Africans from outside of South Africa were the main foils in this process and were depicted as endangering the moral health of the nation, increasing criminality and draining scarce resources (Peberdy 2001: 21, 24–25). To counter such perceived threats, legal regulations originating under apartheid were ratcheted up, with reductions in permits for temporary workers, more border policing, 'increasingly draconian measures to raise the rates of identification, arrest, detention and repatriation of undocumented migrants' and orders for the denial of 'access to services like healthcare, education and utilities to undocumented (and other) migrants' (Peberdy 2001: 16–17, 21–23).

Reflecting such policies, by the late 1990s, South Africans of all races viewed African immigrants with suspicion (37% seeing them as a threat to jobs and 48% as a 'criminal threat') and in 1998 'fully 25% of the nation call[ed] for a complete ban on migration' (Danso and McDonald 2001: 115–116). There were also scattered but consistent reports of violence against immigrants. Loren Landau argues that the history of apartheid rule combined with ANC statecraft of the kind indicated by Peberdy both encouraged poor black citizens to see foreigners as 'demons' stopping the success of transformation and created a 'demon' of violence where these poor black citizens were willing to take matters into their own hands when they saw the government unable or unwilling to deliver its promises (2010: 216–217). This second demon grew in strength as time passed from 1994 with 'the evident failures of the national rebirth' in the form of economic transformation and future prospects (Landau 2010: 226–227). Landau quotes one South African speaking approvingly in the wake of the 2008 riots: 'We are not trying to kill anyone but rather solving the problems of our own country. The government is not doing anything about this, so I support what the mob is doing the get rid of foreigners in our country' (2010: 229).

Immigrants thus found themselves in a precarious situation. Ethnographic studies of Johannesburg in the late 1990s point to a set of common experiences. Of his interviews with Congolese and Nigerian immigrants, Alan Morris reports: 'The overwhelming view among the informants was that South Africans have little or no empathy for their plight' (1998: 1124). They faced an exclusionary racism and violence including police brutality, they suffered financially because of employer discrimination, and they lacked the safety of legal protections that come with legal papers or citizenship (Morris 1998: 1122, 1129–1133). Longer narrative accounts echo these hardships, stressing how they result in a long-term alienation from South African society. I have written elsewhere about Simão Kikamba's semi-autobiographical novel *Going Home* (2005), which recounts an Angolan refugee's painful experience of trying to make a life for himself in Johannesburg but getting constantly locked out of his home, the city, and any sense of future (Bystrom 2016: 140–144). Jonny Steinberg captures a similar experience in *A Man of Good Hope* (2015), which tracks Somalian refugee Asad Abdullahi from Somalia through Africa to South Africa. Shortly after arriving in the Johannesburg district of Mayfair in early 2004, Abdullahi is reunited with an uncle and looks forward to a new life. Yet, as Steinberg chronicles, Abdullahi's uncle's murder in his shop in Port Elizabeth only a few months later makes a mockery of this dream, becoming the first in a long line of violent instances (including his own attack as part of the 2008 riots) that force Abdullahi ultimately out of South Africa. Steinberg describes Abdullahi's existence in South Africa in the following manner: 'On his shoulders rests the incessant burden of dodging his own murder' (2015: xiv).

This then is the setting of Matabane's filmic intervention. *Conversations* was sparked by a conversation that Matabane had with an Eritrean refugee woman while travelling in Germany (McCluskey 2009: 121; Moyer-Duncan 2011: 73), an encounter which had strong resonance both on the local/personal and the global levels. In one interview, Matabane describes the film as a 'love letter' to the Eritrean woman (McCluskey 2009: 121). In another, he describes it as a 'love letter' to his country itself, stating: 'In making this film, I wanted to understand the people who left their countries because of these wars and were shaping and being shaped by my country. The film is...a love letter to my country, a provocative one that will force us to debate our attitudes towards our refugees' (Writing Studio n.d.).[5] The 'love letter' is a perhaps unusual genre through which to call out prejudice and to ask for change, but it speaks to emotion invested in the dream of transformation, of a hospitable and just South Africa made possible in 1994 and cherished by South Africans and immigrants alike.[6] It also lends a sense of urgency as this dream runs out of time, and what Matabane sees as greed and apathy threaten to turn the country into something else, driving him away from it (Moyer-Duncan 2011: 73).[7]

The plot of Matabane's 'love letter' is straightforward. A South African poet named Keniloe, who 'can't make sense of the world', happens to encounter a Somalian refugee named Fatima in the park in Hillbrow one Sunday afternoon. He is reading Nuruddin Farah's *Links* (2003), a novel about the Somalian civil war. When Fatima sees him reading this novel, she stops to find out if he is Somalian. The next Sunday, Keniloe encounters Fatima again. This pattern is repeated for a third time, when the poet convinces her to tell him her story of the war. Moved by her testimony, he decides that he wants to write about her. However, when he goes to the park to look for her the following Sunday afternoon, she has vanished. The film then chronicles Keniloe's attempt to find Fatima, asking strangers in the park and on the street if they know her. In the process, he records their endlessly multiplying stories of war and displacement.

What is not straightforward is the film's formal construction—and I will focus on just two elements, its principle of contingency and its insistent blurring of the line between 'reality' and 'fiction'—which allows Matabane skilfully to both trace and enter into flows of what Kathleen Stewart (2007) calls 'ordinary affects' in ways that may help to suture together Johannesburg's divided population. 'Ordinary affects', Stewart argues, are 'the varied, surging capacities to affect and to be affected that give everyday life the quality of a continual motion of relations, scenes, contingences and emergences' (2007: 1–2). 'They work not through "meanings" per se, but rather in the way they pick up density and texture as they move through bodies, dreams, dramas, and social worldings of all kinds. Their significance lies in the intensities they build and in what thoughts and feelings they make possible' (Stewart 2007: 3). Phrased slightly differently, they are 'a tangle of potential connections… They surge or become submerged. They point to the jump of something coming together for a minute and to the spreading lines of resonance and connection that become possible and might snap into sense in some sharp or vague way' (Stewart 2007: 4).

What I am calling the principle of contingency underlies the structure of the film and characterises much of its style. Matabane notes in an interview: 'There were no rehearsals… I wanted to make a film that was like life itself, to go into the unknown' (Machen 2017). Using this framework, with no script, in 19 days and on a shoestring budget (Sosibo 2006; Moyer-Duncan 2011: 73), Matabane is able to trace the emotional intensities that arise from accidental encounters as they 'surge and become submerged', and sometimes 'snap into sense', to echo Stewart's (2007: 4) language. The first of these exists between Keniloe and Fatima. Keniloe, as I have noted, begins the film immersed in *Links*. Farah's novel documents the struggle of Jeebleh, an expatriate Somali, to come to terms with the chaos in Mogadishu. The city Jeebleh finds seems bereft of human connection, as he discovers on arrival by witnessing an airport 'game' in which armed youths take potshots at disembarking passengers and kill a woman and a child before his eyes (Farah 2003: 15–16).[8] As Keniloe reads out the description of this airport 'game', he, like Jeebleh, confronts the question of war. What does it mean to live through such conditions? What happens when the bonds that tie people in a certain place together come undone? When even the most basic human solidarity is stripped away? These questions are transported to Johannesburg as Keniloe acts out the part of the airport youths, pretending to shoot random passers-by using his finger as a gun, and then turning the trigger on himself.

It is while Keniloe is swept up in these questions that Fatima appears, a shimmering apparition. In her brief testimony to him, she shares the experience of watching her father and brother being shot next to her, of being shot herself, of being evacuated from the hospital in Somalia to Kenya and eventually sent alone to South Africa. The visual frame is so close up to Fatima's face that you can almost feel her sorrow leaking from her eyes and nose, and with a series of cuts to black as she herself falters or begins to cry, suggests an absolute immersion in her experience. Keniloe is, in a way, able to momentarily live in her skin, and this exchange binds him to her. I think here of Sara Ahmed's definition of emotion as a point of conjuncture between a person and an 'object' or 'other', when something or someone presses into us and we respond to him or her; emotion becomes a kind of glue sticking us to others in particular configurations (2004: 6).

Keniloe's refusal to become unglued, his quest to maintain the surge of affect binding him to Fatima, is what inspires him to search for her after she disappears, and sparks a series of further contingent encounters that resonate with each other and turn the city *otherwise*. In his journeys up and down the streets of Hillbrow and eventually beyond it to Yeoville, Berea and Mayfair, looking for someone who might direct him to Fatima, he meets two women who remind him: 'most of us are refugees'. 'What', they ask, 'do you want in particular about Somalia?' These specific women left Kenya to avoid female genital circumcision. Keniloe also meets people fleeing from chaos in the DRC, a former child soldier from Uganda, a woman who escaped the military dictatorship in South Korea, a family who had moved from Gaza so that the children would not grow up surrounded by missile attacks, and a shopkeeper from Afghanistan. While none of these stories has the same sticky power for Keniloe as Fatima's, they each have their own 'punctum' (Barthes 1980).

Keniloe's interviews with these refugees are interspersed with meetings with others immigrants who came to Johannesburg for 'greener pastures'. These could be financial, as in the case of the male undocumented workers from Malawi he interviews at the Lindela Deportation Centre who followed an old road to South Africa to escape poverty. 'We are all Africans', they state again and again to Keniloe; in a pan-Africanist updating of the abolitionist mantra 'Am I not a man and a brother?', they argue for better treatment because 'we are all blacks and brothers'. Migration can also be an intellectual pilgrimage. The desire to be part of a global experiment in multi-racial democracy is articulated by Trinidadian intellectual Ronald Suresh Roberts. Describing South Africa as his home, Roberts claims: 'home is a notion that has to do with where you feel that what you are doing matters. To be part of what South Africa is doing now is something that matters to everyone in the world'. While Roberts' statement gets laden with irony by his own stories of experiencing xenophobia and the stories of mistreatment told by many refugees and migrants, it also offers a dreamscape of what South African society could be.

The picture that comes together from these interviews, each seemingly as accidental as his first meeting with Fatima in the park, is of Johannesburg as a place of refuge for thousands of souls who have lost their homes and have not quite been able to forge new ones. They register the kinds of discrimination and indignity meted out regularly to immigrants at this time. However, despite such experiences, they also show affection for the city and value the relative safety of Johannesburg's streets.[9] Lirija, a Serbian woman who came to South Africa six months after the NATO bombing in Belgrade in 1999, recalls for Keniloe watching bombs fall around her in the street, seeing burnt people hanging in whole or part from windows of damaged buildings, and eventually having her own house burnt down. While she stands on a street in Hillbrow in front of a building that looks, one might think, bombed out, she draws attention to the marked difference between Johannesburg and Yugoslavia. 'I go out on the street at 2am and people ask

"Why are you going out so late?" But this is safe, there is no bombs, nobody is bombing us'. Such a feeling is reiterated in testimonies from Gaza and Afghanistan. The idea that South Africa provides, or *could* provide, a space of peace is echoed again and again.

Keniloe's search for Fatima thus turns into a project that both places him in an affective network with others and reconfigures the imaginative social geography of the city. The memories of violence that these migrants share with Keniloe help to redefine Hillbrow as something *other*. Rather than a site of strife and disintegration, inhabited by groups suspicious of each other, the city becomes Stewart's (2007: 4) 'tangle of connections'. The ordinary encounter in the park highlights and conjures into being a convivial urban space shaped by citizens and non-citizens alike. Or, to use the language of affect, which as I already noted is central to the operations of conviviality, it is a 'bloom-space' of narrative, full of stories waiting to find expression, and to be linked to others in a chain of voices—which, I might also add, is the kind of solution to social disintegration that Farah (2003) proposes in *Links*.

The spectator is not exempted from this expanding chain of voices, since Matabane seems to want to inspire in his audience the kind of response that Keniloe has to Fatima—to create a contingent prick that instils a desire to know more, to connect further. This is underscored by the documentary style of the film, and here I come to the unstable relation between its 'real' and 'fictional' worlds (see McCluskey 2009: 120; Moyer-Duncan 2011: 73; Machen 2017). Keniloe is a fictional figure, as are certain characters such as Keniloe's wife and a mysterious preacher who visits him in the park. However, the majority of the characters seem to be real inhabitants of Hillbrow, Berea, Yeoville and Mayfair.[10] Fatima, for instance, plays herself in the film, and there is Ronald Suresh Roberts. Matabane thus calls for a mode of reading or viewing which, as Hedley Twidle describes in another context, 'plays across different genres and addresses rather than remaining trapped within these protocols of exchange that thrive in an endless series of tired oppositions' (2012: 24); though he does so, and as Stephen Clingman responds to Twidle, not to mark 'the boundary between fiction and non-fiction' but to explore it as a 'space of contiguity and crossing, the space of navigation' (2012: 52). Such generic instability allows Matabane to explore the importance of fiction in shaping what Stewart (2007: 3) terms our 'social worldings' without sacrificing the immediacy of the connection created by authentic testimony.

Conversations on a Sunday Afternoon, however, is not a simple celebration of the power of storytelling to create emotional ties between people or to turn the city into a space of refuge. It is also a warning about the failure of connection, the way positive affect can become 'submerged' or lost, or flip into anxiety, discomfort, or disavowal. In other words, it shuttles between the production of conviviality and the insistence on opacity. This becomes crystal clear at the conclusion of the film. Here Keniloe finally finds Fatima's house and asks to record her story, as he has recorded so many others. She refuses. 'I really don't interest that story', she says and shuts the curtain.

There are of course many possible explanations for Fatima's reaction: she might find Keniloe strange and his persistence a burden; she may not be interested in making connections with (male) South Africans given other places she looks to for home and community; she may fear repercussions for speaking with him; the events he asks her about may be too traumatic to return to. These are just a few of the options, and each of them could likely be expanded and supported by recent research.[11] But rather than trying to pin down explanations, I prefer to follow Thomas Keenan's example and interpret Fatima's refusal 'as an act and not simply as a message' (2004: 447). This is first and foremost an act of refusal. Reminding us of affect's undecidability, of the power any party in the circuit has to arrest its flow or deflect it in a new direction, Fatima refuses to participate in the emotional economy her prior testimony set in motion and severs the relation between her and Keniloe. In the process, she highlights the distances that remain even once paths and stories have crossed. Anders Høg Hansen importantly speaks of reclusiveness in another contribution to this volume (Chapter 12). Similar in spirit, I code this refusal as a demand for opacity in Glissant's (1990) sense, as a claim to keep oneself unknown, to fail to be transparent and available for the purposes of another. Positively stated, it is a claim for agency and integrity of the self, the ability to chart one's own course, and to keep the secrets one desires.

This insistence on opacity leaves Keniloe, in Cara Moyer-Duncan's felicitous term, 'flummoxed' (2011: 74). Yet the break or caesura of a foreseen narrative also opens the possibility of him coming to a different relation with Fatima and refugees and immigrants more generally. One reaction might be to recognise misrecognition, for Keniloe to face that what he thought about Fatima, his sense of understanding her, was a projection, and to ask what factors allowed this misrecognition to occur. As he looks for Fatima that fourth Sunday in the park, just before he realises she's gone missing, he records the beginning of a poem: 'I see rivers running to the sea/ I see storylines unfolding in front of me/ I see you, Fatima'. The unfolding of the film prompts us to ask: Did he really 'see' her at all? A related line of questions opened by this encounter addresses Keniloe's position vis-a-vis Fatima as a writer in particular, and the ethics of his quest to tell her story. James Dawes, meditating on journalists and storytellers who write stories of atrocity, raises the following concerns:

> Who nominates you to publicize pain and suffering you can walk away from? How does one avoid the trap of commodifying intense suffering to elicit maximum effect (or career advantage)? How do you resolve the paradox that your audiences hunger for these images and stories of calamity both because they want to understand the world and their moral responsibilities to it, and because they are narrowly voyeuristic? (2007: 166)

Further: how do you deal with the hope of victims who think something will change for the better because they tell you their stories, when it is very likely the case that nothing will change? What about the risks of re-traumatisation (Dawes 2007: 174–177, 181)? Such queries call into doubt some of Keniloe's under-examined ambition regarding Fatima's experiences and require a reckoning if his project is to go forward.

These questions, of course, pertain not only to Fatima but also to all the others whose stories Keniloe has captured—suggesting a need to return to and reassess these earlier interviews. Indeed, Fatima is not the only one who resists Keniloe's questioning. One young woman from Ethiopia critiques him from inside her testimony, saying that she wishes to return 'home' to Addis Ababa so she won't have to explain herself to everyone all the time. Even more reclusive are the women that Keniloe tries to interview in the Lindela Deportation Centre, who hide their heads in their hands when he approaches them on a picnic bench. Unwilling to give up, Keniloe searches for women to interview inside the female hall, and the women lay down on the floor and cover their faces, clearly wary of being captured on camera. Keniloe's actions vis-à-vis these women are actually disturbing in his blindness to their desire for opacity.

The importance of such a reflexive turn to (re)examine Keniloe's interactions with the refugees and immigrants is reiterated in the film's closing sequence. This is a flashback to an earlier scene of the men at the Lindela Deportation Centre as they are herded behind bars and readied for transit to their home countries. In some ways, their is the most troubling story uncovered by Keniloe, because their self-representations touch a raw nerve—sparking uncomfortable affective relays. Their calls for solidarity based on a shared blackness, noted above, are mixed in this particular scene with an impish resistance; they refuse to be contained by the role of the victim that many other interviewees feel comfortable with and they themselves take on at times and instead make up a song that highlights their agency and willingness to flout whatever South African barriers might be thrown at them. The lyrics—which insist that deportation is 'useless, useless, You're wasting your time. I will come back'—seem designed to stoke the fears of nativists even as their call for open borders, the ability to migrate like the birds, and to seek hospitality in other parts of the continent tries to undercut them. These men are enigmatic figures both available and unavailable for co-option into the story Keniloe wants to write, or rather temporarily available, until the window onto their jail cell closes or a moment and a mood shifts into another.

Like Keniloe, indeed with him, spectators are offered the chance to engage in such reflection, and with it the opportunity to build a more complex understanding of both those pushed towards Johannesburg by war or poverty and their own position in relation to them. Beyond the emotional glue, whether understood as pity, empathy or something else entirely, that comes from stories of victimhood is an opaque subject that may or may not conform to either hostile desires for eviction or beneficent desires for inclusion. They have their own agendas, logics and dreams. Working to undercut the logics of exclusion thus involves not only the need to figure out how to engage with and feel for the traumas and experiences of immigrants and refugees, but also that of respecting their desires and the limits they put up; to find ways of living with mismatches, disappointments, parts and paths that may not fit into pre-imagined plotlines. This is not easy. There is no instruction manual.

The image of the closing curtain or shutting window sits uneasily with the image of the city as a 'bloom-space' of narrative and its production of convivial culture. Yet Matabane's provocation is precisely to ask how these fit together, to raise questions about what exactly his love letter means and what to do from there, which themselves extend well beyond the boundaries of the film and are ultimately up to the spectator to answer. As Moyer-Duncan puts it, 'Matabane refuses to offer his audience a tidy ending, ultimately raising more questions than answers' (2011: 74).

Asking such questions is, I would argue, the heart of the film as a political and aesthetic intervention. Just before explaining that *Conversations* was meant to both help him understand refugees and to serve as a 'love letter' to provoke fellow South Africans to debate their views on immigration in a quotation cited above, Matabane notes: 'This film…is my form of protest but also a symbol of my faith in cinema that it can contribute to socio-political change' (Writing Studio n.p.). *Conversations*, however, is not exactly typical of consciousness-raising genres. Its experimental hybrid form and weird soundtrack are too alienating for a mass audience.[12] It engages partially but not wholly in a project that Helene Strauss (2011) identifies as 'cinema as social recuperation'—where, she argues, more widely available anti-xenophobic films like Adze Ugah's *The Burning Man* (2008) give needed depth to South African visions of immigrants, beyond reduction to suffering or bare life, by creating affective, bodily centred stories.[13] Rather, I would argue that the film's profoundest political edge comes by calling into question the boundaries between the 'imagined' and the 'real' in the hopes that this might trouble other entrenched boundaries—like that between 'citizens' and 'foreigners'.

Resisting any singular categorisation as 'fact or fiction, imagined or real', the filmmaker points out how 'in our daily lives we all move between the real and the unreal, the conscious and unconscious' and suggests that his film aims to capture this 'bizarre' aspect of life (Machen 2017). Matabane's interest in exploring the way fiction, the felt and the imagined, moves into and shapes our lives and 'social worldings' (Stewart 2007: 3) is reflected in the important role Farah's novel *Links* plays in setting Keniloe on his path. It is also modelled by the way fictional scenes between characters tend to flow into documentary encounters. Moving from these examples, the film can be seen to offer itself out as a puzzle for spectators to inhabit. Here, fiction is a cognitive and emotional training ground for spectators to enter into; structured around actual conditions and modes of oppression, but inaugurating a process of imagination that stretches the self, connects it to others, opens options and builds habits of perception, identification and questioning. I return to the suggestion made above that the film asks spectators to join the chain of stories that Keniloe constructs as he tries to 'make sense of the world'—looking again at a city that contains real possibility, examples of endurance, determination and creativity, and also many kinds of anger, despair and confusion—but with both open hearts and a respect for distance, an understanding of what one fails to see or know, a readiness to cope with unexpected turns. These are all needed to allow all the inhabitants of Johannesburg to flourish together.

From one angle, the events of 2008 suggest that Matabane's faith in the power of cinema is misplaced. From another, this xenophobic violence then and its echoes in 2015 and 2017 only underscore the need to sharpen imaginative capacities in the way *Conversations* offers. Doing so may allow us to begin to see anew and properly the people who share and co-produce our city spaces—in Johannesburg, from around the world but especially from the African continent—and from there work with them to solidify affective ties and create the actual groundwork for the politics of movements, flows and links of which both filmmakers and social scientists dream.

Notes

1. See, for instance, 'Ground Up', https://www.dailymaverick.co.za/article/2017-02-24-groundup-mashaba-has-incited-xenophobia-says-immigrants-spokesperson/; 'South Africa Xenophobic attacks', https://www.npr.org/2017/02/25/517262398/south-africa-xenophobic-attacks; 'In South Africa', https://www.washingtonpost.com/world/in-south-africa-a-surge-in-xenophobia-leads-to-violence/2017/02/24/dbf8d864-fecf-4d14-b6f5-3a25d8c46b61_story.html?noredirect=on&utm_term=.6fc56358be25 and 'Xenophobic violence', https://www.aljazeera.com/indepth/opinion/2017/03/xenophobic-violence-rainbow-nation-170301075103169.html.
2. While as Nowicka and Vertovec have pointed out, 'Conviviality and conflict lie close to each other' (2014: 346), there seems to me not enough attention to conflict in conviviality studies.
3. For a filmography, see McCluskey (2009: 129), Moyer-Duncan (2011: 72), and the entry 'Khalo Matabane: Filmography' on Indymedia: https://www.imdb.com/name/nm1988834/?ref_=tt_ov_dr.
4. See Bystrom (2016: 121, 138–139), for a previous overview of these paradoxes and attitudes to immigration in this and the following paragraph, drawing on Perbedy, Danso and McDonald and others.
5. See Matabane's interview 'Proudly South African Filmmaking: Conversations on a Sunday Afternoon', with *The Writing Studio*, available online at http://www.writingstudio.co.za/page1340.html. Last accessed May 2012.
6. Peter Machen (2017), referring to Matabane's description of the film as a 'love letter to South Africa', notes that: 'It is a love letter that acknowledges a bittersweet South African reality that borders on schizophrenia…while the country offers a global embrace, it is also a nation full of ingrained prejudices, institutional discrimination and xenophobia'. Moyer-Duncan also refers to this quotation (2011: 74).
7. Moyer-Duncan points to a piece by Sosibo which underscores these conditions and Matabane's sense of disorientation: 'I feel displaced', Matabane

notes, 'the country feels foreign to me and I just don't recognize it' (Sosibo 2006; Moyer-Duncan 2011: 73). Similarly, Matabane states to McCluskey that 'I feel a real sense of displacement. I completely feel like a refugee. I feel I don't belong' (2009: 127).
8. For a more detailed reading of *Links*, see Bystrom (2014).
9. Helene Strauss's brief summary of the film is apposite here: 'The documentary-style conversations he [the "fictionalized poet"] has with the people [migrants he encounters while searching for Fatima] function as a meditation on the memories, stories, experiences and vulnerabilities that bind human lives together. As such, the film presents a colourful picture of the richness and complexity of migrant experience, thus indicating that social existence for these people operates along a differentiated scale of significance that cannot be defined solely in terms of absence of legal or civil rights' (105).
10. Matabane discusses the origin of the characters in his *Writing Studio* interview (np). See also Moyer-Duncan (2011: 73).
11. Speaking to a potential lack of interest in being fully tied into the South African community, for instance, an article of note by Landau (2014) shows how migrants in South Africa and elsewhere in Africa are not always focused on remaining in their 'host' countries, but use bottom-up modes of 'tactical cosmopolitanism' to achieve partial forms of inclusion in 'estuaries' or landing zones seen as temporary environments, while remaining oriented in multiple directions, towards other places and communities.
12. While the film garnered international critical reception and local and international prizes, it had a very poor showing in South African box offices (Moyer-Duncan 2011: 74–75).
13. As Strauss notes, 'cultural production on the topic of intra-African interactions within South Africa [can be] an important resource for resisting the epistemic distortions that inform hostility directed at those perceived as outsiders' (2011: 104). It does so, at least in Ugah's film, by 'expand[ing] the terms through which migrant subjectivity is commonly conceived' and highlighting the 'lived, affective body'—as well as social connections spun around this body—at the heart of discussions of migration that often reduce migrants to stereotypes of pain and suffering (Strauss 2011: 104). Such 'social recuperation' can 'reweave[e] the complex affective and interpersonal threads that constitute the experiential fabric of migrant subjectivity' (Strauss 2011: 107). *Conversations*, as we have seen, takes a slightly different approach, focusing less on detailed individual narratives than on how the accumulation of stories create a collective weave, and pressing more forcefully on the ethical questions of how to know and engage others (though Strauss also sees this question in Ugah's film [2011: 112–113]).

References

Ahmed, S. 2004. *Cultural Politics of Emotion*. London: Routledge.
Barthes, R. 1980. *Camera Lucida*. New York: Hill and Wang.
Bystrom, K. 2014. "Humanitarianism, Responsibility, Links, Knots." *Interventions* 16 (3): 405–423.
Bystrom, K. 2016. *Democracy at Home in South Africa: Family Fictions and Transitional Culture*. New York: Palgrave Macmillan.
Clingman, S. 2012. "Writing Spaces: Fiction and Non-Fiction in South Africa." *Safundi* 13 (1–2): 51–58.
Danso, R. and D. A. MacDonald. 2001. "Writing Xenophobia: Immigration and the Print Media in Post-apartheid South Africa." *Africa Today* 48 (3): 115–137.
Dawes, J. 2007. *That the World May Know: Bearing Witness to Atrocity*. Cambridge, MA: Harvard University Press.
Desai, A. 2015. "Migrants and Violence in South Africa: The April 2015 Xenophobic Attacks in Durban." *The Oriental Anthropologist* 15 (2): 247–259.
Farah, N. 2003. *Links*. New York: Penguin.
Gilroy, P. 2005. *Postcolonial Melancholia*. New York: Columbia University Press.
Glissant, E. 1990. "For Opacity." In *The Poetics of Relation*, translated by Betsy Wing. Ann Arbor: University of Michigan Press.
Gutiérrez Rodríguez, E. 2011. "Politics of Affects. Transversal Conviviality." *Transversal* 1. http://eipcp.net/transversal/0811/gutierrezrodriguez/en.
Keenan, T. 2004. "Mobilizing Shame." *South Atlantic Quarterly* 103 (2–3): 435–449.
Landau, L. 2010. "Loving the Alien? Citizenship, Law and the Future in South Africa's Demonic Society." *African Affairs* 106 (435): 213–230.
Landau, L. 2014. "Conviviality, Rights and Conflict in Africa's Urban Estuaries." *Politics and Society* 43 (3): 359–380.
Machen, P. 2017. "Conversations with Us All." Peter Machen. http://www.petermachen.com/khalo-matabane.html.
Matabane, K. 2005. *Conversations on a Sunday Afternoon*. Johannesburg: Matabane Filmworks.
Mbembe, A. 2017a. "Scrap the Borders That Divide Africans." *Mail & Guardian*, March 17. https://mg.co.za/article/2017-03-17-00-scrap-the-borders-that-divide-africans.
Mbembe, A. 2017b. "Africa Needs Free Movement." *Mail & Guardian*, March 24. https://mg.co.za/article/2017-03-24-00-africa-needs-free-movement.
Mbembe, A. and S. Nuttall. 2008. "Introduction." In *Johannesburg: The Elusive Metropolis*, edited by Achille Mbembe and Sarah Nuttall. Durham, NC: Duke University Press.
McCluskey, A. 2009. "Khalo Matabane." In *The Devil You Dance With: South African Film Culture*, 120–209. Chicago: University of Illinois Press.

Morris, A. 1998. "Our Fellow Africans Make Our Lives Hell: The Lives of Congolese and Nigerians Living in Johannesburg." *Ethnic and Racial Studies* 21 (6): 1116–1136.

Moyer-Duncan, C. 2011. "New Directions, No Audiences." *Critical Interventions* 5 (1): 64–80.

Nowicka, M. and S. Vertovec. 2014. "Comparing Convivialities: Dreams and Realities of Living-with-Difference." *European Journal of Cultural Studies* 17 (4): 331–346.

Peberdy, S. 2001. "Imagining Immigration: Inclusive and Exclusive Politics in Post-1994 South Africa." *Africa Today* 48 (3): 15–32.

Sosibo, K. 2006. "Conflicting Conversations." *Mail & Guardian*, October 20. https://mg.co.za/article/2006-10-20-conflicting-conversations#.WsdXWk_44iQ.email.

Steinberg, J. 2015. *A Man of Good Hope*. New York: Random House.

Stewart, K. 2007. *Ordinary Affects*. Durham, NC: Duke University Press.

Strauss, H. 2011. "The Cinema of Social Recuperation: Xenophobic Violence and Migrant Subjectivity in Contemporary South Africa." *Subjectivities* 4 (2): 103–120.

Twidle, H. 2012. "In a Country Where You Couldn't Make This Shit Up: Literary Non-fiction in South Africa," *Safundi* 13 (1–2): 5–28.

Writing Studio. n.d. "Proudly South African Filmmaking: Conversations on a Sunday Afternoon." http://www.writingstudio.co.za/page1340.html.

Open Access This chapter is licensed under the terms of the Creative Commons Attribution 4.0 International License (http://creativecommons.org/licenses/by/4.0/), which permits use, sharing, adaptation, distribution and reproduction in any medium or format, as long as you give appropriate credit to the original author(s) and the source, provide a link to the Creative Commons license and indicate if changes were made.

The images or other third party material in this chapter are included in the chapter's Creative Commons license, unless indicated otherwise in a credit line to the material. If material is not included in the chapter's Creative Commons license and your intended use is not permitted by statutory regulation or exceeds the permitted use, you will need to obtain permission directly from the copyright holder.

Index

A

Activism, 138, 158–160, 166–168, 172, 175, 178, 180–183, 270
Activist research, 147
Affect, 5, 29, 32, 72, 106, 116, 118, 130, 131, 139, 198, 205, 215, 216, 218, 220, 222, 269, 273, 274, 276, 277
Afrikanerdom, 255
Akomfrah, John, 228, 242
Altruism, altruistic, 133
Apartheid, 10, 45, 57, 248–252, 254, 255, 257, 261, 262, 267, 268, 270, 271
Appadurai, Arjun, 3, 5, 15, 44, 258
Arendt, Hannah, 92, 99
Arizpe, Lourdes, 24, 25, 30
Askari, 251
Asylum Group, 170, 172
Asylum politics, 176
Asylum seekers, 9, 115, 129, 131, 132, 134–140, 146, 150–152, 154, 156, 157, 167, 171, 173, 175, 177, 181–183, 190, 196, 197, 270

B

Bantustan, 249, 250
Bauman, Zygmunt, 193
Beck, Ulrich, 3, 5, 6, 30
Bildung, 77
Biopolitical regime, 9, 191
Black Consciousness, 262
Border controls, 9, 132, 190, 191
Bovell, Dennis, 209–212, 221
Breytenbach, Breyten, 255, 256, 261
Burial, 216, 217

C

Caillé, Alain, 6, 24, 25
Cape Town, 11, 254
Castro, Américo, 107–110
Chiles, Adrian, 228, 236–238, 241–243
Civility, 17, 23, 25, 30

Civil society, 24, 25, 30, 31, 54, 112, 125, 126, 129–134, 140, 167–169, 173, 177, 179, 181
Coexistence, 20, 22, 57, 97, 125–128
Collaboration, 17, 25–27, 32, 129, 153, 156, 177, 194, 251, 256, 258
Colonial, 7, 105, 107, 108, 114, 115, 174, 229–231, 235, 242, 249, 253, 254
Coloured, 249, 254, 260, 262
Common good, 18, 26, 59, 105, 106, 110–112
Compassion, 25, 27, 169, 175, 177, 179, 270
Complicity, 251, 260–262
Conflict, 6, 23, 24, 27, 29, 30, 57, 73, 97, 126–128, 146, 149, 150, 156–160, 168, 169, 190, 191, 204, 238, 270, 281
Convivencia, 2, 106, 107, 109, 110, 128
Convivialist Manifesto, 6, 24
Conviviality, 2–4, 6–10, 15–17, 20–24, 26–32, 51, 54, 58, 65–67, 69–74, 78, 79, 81, 83, 90, 91, 105–107, 110–113, 115–120, 125, 126, 128, 129, 134, 139, 140, 145–151, 153, 155, 156, 159, 160, 166, 190–195, 197, 198, 204, 206, 208, 213, 215, 217, 219, 220, 230, 232, 235, 236, 239, 240, 268, 269, 276, 277
Conviviality as method, 6, 7, 9, 21, 70, 72, 78, 106, 110, 112, 136, 159, 191, 232
Convivial tools, 105, 106
Co-production, 146, 150, 153–156, 159, 160
Cornelins, Victor, 229, 234, 235, 241

Cosmopolitanism, 2–5, 7–9, 15, 16, 27, 31, 54, 65, 66, 72, 79, 83, 89–93, 95–101, 126, 127, 140, 165–167, 174, 176, 179–182, 184, 230, 239, 252, 269, 282
Cosmopolitanism from below, 3, 5
Cosmopolitics, 92, 100
Courtesy, 17, 20–23, 30, 31, 129
Creolisation, 2, 4, 6–10, 44–47, 49, 50, 52, 54, 58–60, 105, 106, 113–115, 118, 119, 205–207, 209, 211, 213, 217, 220, 254
Creolisation vs. Hybridisation, 4, 11
Cunningham, Laurie, 228, 229, 243

D
Dansk Folkeparti, 131, 132
Decolonisation, 7, 115
Denmark, 2, 9, 52, 125, 129, 131–133, 135, 137–140, 148–151, 154, 155, 160, 168, 190–192, 194, 229, 230, 234, 235, 238, 241–243
Derrida, Jacques, 196, 212, 217, 220
Die Vlake, 260
Diversity, 2, 3, 6, 8, 15–17, 20, 21, 23, 25, 30, 51–57, 65, 91, 125–128, 130, 139, 249, 250, 270
Documentary film, 10, 270
Double consciousness, 51
DuBois, W.E.B., 51
Durban, 250, 251

E
Effective history, 92, 99
Eiselen, Werner, 248, 255
Environment, 10, 24, 25, 30, 32, 71, 117, 120, 203, 205, 220, 282
Ethnography, 9, 52, 53, 112, 125, 127, 146, 150, 159, 182, 191, 248, 272

F

Farah, Nuruddin, 273, 274, 276, 280
Fisher, Mark, 216, 217
Folkhemmet, 171
Foster, Hal, 191, 195
Foucault, Michel, 195
Frank Larsen, Alex, 230, 235, 240, 241
Freud, Siegmund, 217, 222, 238, 258

G

Geselligkeit, 69–71, 80, 81
Gilbert, Jeremy, 205, 206, 215, 216, 220, 222
Gilroy, Paul, 2, 3, 5, 16, 20, 22, 23, 28, 45, 48, 51, 54, 73, 79, 83, 90, 106, 112, 113, 147, 148, 156, 190, 198, 204–206, 210, 211, 214, 215, 217, 220, 227, 228, 233, 239, 269
Glick Schiller, Nina, 3, 8, 112, 113, 129, 134, 140, 178, 180, 183
Glissant, Édouard, 4, 6, 9, 10, 50, 105, 106, 113–115, 118–120, 232, 233, 241–243, 269, 277

H

Hall, Stuart, 23, 44, 206–209, 211, 212, 217, 220, 228, 231, 242
Hannerz, Ulf, 4, 44, 46, 47, 127
Hansson, Per Albin, 171
Haskalah, 66–68, 80
Hauntology, 217, 220, 222
Held, David, 3, 166, 167, 173, 180–182
Hernando, Almudena, 17–20, 28–31, 33
Herz, Henriette, 8, 65–69, 71, 72, 81–85
  Jugenderinnerungen, 73, 74, 83, 84
Herz, Marcus, 68, 69, 74, 76, 84

Hospitality, 89, 93, 97, 98, 100, 196, 197, 262, 268, 269, 279
von Humboldt, Wilhelm, 76, 78, 84

I

Identity, 8, 10, 16–20, 23, 27–29, 31, 32, 43, 46, 48–56, 58, 59, 73, 91, 92, 108, 112, 119, 126, 128, 129, 131, 147, 148, 151, 166, 174, 181, 194, 195, 204, 205, 211, 213–220, 230, 232, 237, 242, 250, 253–256, 259, 261, 268
Illich, Ivan, 2, 7, 9, 26, 30, 105–107, 110, 111, 115, 117, 119
Imperial, 7, 107, 109, 113
Individuality, 8, 17–20, 27, 29, 33
Islamism, 46, 58, 250
Islamophobia, 250

J

Jewish salon, 68
Johannesburg, 10, 267–270, 272–275, 279–281

K

Kaganof, Aryan, 256, 257, 259, 262
Kant, Immanuel, 8, 68, 76, 89, 90, 93, 95–100
Kavanagh, Dermot, 228, 233, 238–240, 242
Kay, Janet, 209, 211
Kitchener, Lord, 205, 207
Kontrapunkt, 167, 168
Krog, Antjie, 258

L

Levitas, Ruth, 8, 93–95, 100
Links, 273, 274, 276, 280, 282

M

Malan, D.F., 248
Malmö, 2, 167–170, 172, 173, 182, 183, 190, 192, 193, 243, 251, 252
Manifesto, 6, 24–26, 33
Marikana, 256, 257
Matabane, Khalo, 10, 268–270, 272–274, 276, 279–282
Material, 19, 21, 22, 26, 56, 72, 110, 113, 114, 118, 119, 126, 127, 129, 131, 150, 155, 156, 158, 166, 167, 169, 174, 213, 214, 238–240, 243, 250, 259, 268
Mauritius, 8, 46, 49, 50, 55–58
Mbembe, Achille, 268, 270
Media, 9, 52, 56, 109, 115, 130–132, 145–147, 152–155, 159, 160, 190, 193, 215, 228, 231, 238
Men, 19, 20, 25, 55, 67, 76, 77, 130, 169, 176, 228, 241, 278, 279
Metamorphosis (*Verwandlung*), 6
Methods, 6, 8, 26, 90, 93–95, 100, 129, 145, 149, 150, 158, 258
Migrants, 29, 49, 52, 54, 113, 115–118, 125, 129–132, 134, 135, 137–140, 146, 147, 152, 154, 158, 160, 181–183, 197, 203, 207, 267, 270, 271, 275, 276, 282
Migration, 2, 5, 7–10, 16, 17, 23, 52, 65, 66, 91, 93, 106, 109, 110, 112, 113, 115–119, 129, 130, 132, 134, 137–139, 145–147, 151–155, 159, 165–167, 173, 177–179, 181, 183, 194, 196, 197, 204, 207, 218, 229, 271, 275, 282
Mintz, Sidney, 45
Miscegenation, 45, 254, 257
Modernity, 7, 18, 21–23, 30, 45, 49, 114, 119, 192–194, 196, 197, 249
Morada vital, 108, 109
Moral cosmopolitanism, 91, 167, 173, 180, 182
Multiculturalism, 2, 8, 53, 55–57, 65, 79, 91, 115, 125–128, 239, 269
Muslim, 49, 53, 55, 56, 58, 108, 109, 120, 132, 133, 259

N

Nakskov, 230, 234, 235, 238, 240, 242
Necklacing, 253
Négritude, 50
No One is Illegal, 170, 181
Novelist, 205, 218, 219
Nowicka, Magdalena, 2–4, 6–8, 15, 16, 66, 72–75, 78, 79, 83, 91, 112, 129, 149, 166, 169, 174, 180, 190, 204, 219, 230, 232, 240, 269, 281

O

Ontology, 44, 46, 51, 55, 106, 113
Opacity, 6, 10, 232, 233, 241, 243, 269, 277, 278
Öresund bridge, the, 9, 190, 191

P

Political cosmopolitanism, 91
Pollution, 252, 257, 259, 261
Princes' Islands, Istanbul, 126
Public space, 18, 24, 26, 27, 29, 30, 151, 209
Purity, impurity, 10, 46, 51, 55, 57, 59, 248–250, 254, 255, 258, 261

R

Race, racialism, racist, 21, 22, 27, 108, 114, 115, 148, 149, 232, 233, 237, 238, 243, 248, 250–252, 254, 269
Radical cosmopolitanism, 181
Refugees, 2, 5, 7, 9, 10, 30, 52, 89, 91, 93, 98, 100, 112, 113, 115, 125, 129–134, 137–140, 145, 146, 148, 150–152, 154, 156, 161, 165–168, 170–183, 190, 195–197, 268, 272–275, 277–280, 282
Refugees, the plasmatic state, 194, 196
Refugees Welcome, 7, 9, 166–171, 174, 175, 178, 179, 181–183
Refugees Welcome Housing Sweden, 170, 177
Refugees Welcome Sweden, 168, 170, 177, 180
Regis, Cyrille, 228, 233, 236, 237
Relation, 4, 6, 16, 17, 21, 22, 26, 29, 31, 32, 48, 56, 66, 71, 74, 78, 80, 92, 100, 105, 106, 109, 120, 126, 127, 133, 136, 137, 139, 166, 173, 262, 268, 269, 273, 276, 277, 279
Relationality, 112, 119
Responsibility, 111, 160, 173, 177, 179, 251, 261
Rhodes, Cecil, 253, 254
Risk Society, 5

S

Sartre, Jean-Paul, 261
Scandinavia, 192
Schleiermacher, Friedrich Daniel, 67, 70–75, 78
  Toward a Theory of Sociable Conduct, 8, 66, 69
Schreiner, Olive, 254
Separate development, total separation, 248, 254
Shack/Slumdwellers International, 5
Shy FX and UK Apache, 213
Ska/blue beat, 231
Slavery, 7, 46, 48, 206, 211, 217, 235, 240
Slits, The, 210, 211, 221
Sociability, 67, 69–73, 96, 97, 140
Solidarity
  altruistic solidarity, 125, 126, 133
  convivial solidarity, 9, 125, 126, 129, 133–140
  mutual solidarity, 44, 125, 126, 133
Spain, 2, 107–109, 239
State conviviality, 8, 9, 16, 24, 31, 146, 156, 191, 194, 195, 197
Stellenbosch, 247, 248, 256, 257, 260, 262
Stewart, Kathleen, 273, 274, 276, 280
Streets, The, 205, 221
Superdiversity, 5, 44, 55
Sweden, 2, 7, 9, 91, 132, 166–172, 175–183, 190–192, 194, 195, 243, 252
Sweden autumn 2015, 168–170, 172
The Swedish Network of Refugee Support (FARR), 170, 183

T

Taylor, Charles, 17, 18, 20–22, 27, 33, 128
Tension, 2, 3, 10, 20, 23, 25, 27, 73, 78, 126, 128, 129, 134, 136, 140, 169, 176, 177, 190, 195, 204, 228, 229, 231
Thrift, Nigel, 193
Togetherness, 2, 8, 17, 24, 28, 65, 73, 91, 145, 149, 156, 190, 193, 204, 218, 230
Tolerance, 21, 27, 53, 55, 66, 134, 136, 140, 250, 258

Transatlantic Slave Trade, 49, 109, 220
Transnational solidarity organisations (TSOs), 130, 135
Transversal conviviality, 6, 106, 116
Truth and Reconciliation Commission (TRC), 251, 261
Turkey, 126, 129, 132, 252

U
Universalism, 90, 92
Utopia, 90, 92–101, 166
Utopian history, 90, 93–95, 99, 100

V
Valluvan, Sivamohan, 1, 128, 190, 239
Varnhagen, Rahel, 67, 68
Veit, Dorothea, 67, 75
Verwoerd, Hendrik, 248, 260
Volkekunde, 248, 255, 260

Volunteering, 9, 131, 133, 165–170, 173, 175, 177, 178, 180, 181
Vorster, B.J. (John), 248, 260

W
Weber, Max, 43
West Bromwich Albion, 228, 229, 235, 237, 239, 242, 243
Western Cape, 251, 256
Wirkungsgeschichte, 92
Women, 20, 21, 24, 25, 29, 66–69, 71, 75–78, 80, 100, 117, 118, 130, 132, 169–171, 262, 274, 275, 278

X
Xenophobic violence in South Africa, 10, 253, 281

The manufacturer's authorised representative in the EU is Springer Nature Customer Service Centre GmbH, Europaplatz 3, 69115 Heidelberg, Germany. If you have any concerns regarding our products, please contact ProductSafety@springernature.com

Printed and bound by CPI Group (UK) Ltd, Croydon, CR0 4YY

23/03/2026

02076677-0002